Babur

This biography illumines the life and times o. ___ ___under of the Timurid-Mughal Empire, Zahir al-Din Muhammad Babur. Despite his remarkable achievements in founding a great empire and writing an extraordinary autobiography, his achievements as a ruler, writer and human being are unsung. He has been reduced to a little more than a footnote in most histories of the Timurid-Mughal Empire.

The book is based on the study of Babur's Chaghatai Turkish autobiography and poetry, Persian historical texts and research undertaken in the Ferghanah Valley and Samarqand, his Central Asian homeland. It analyses the three different phases of Babur's tumultuous reign – his time in Central Asia, Afghanistan and India. It studies the Turco-Mongol environment of his homeland, his administration in Afghanistan, and the Timurid ideology and personal motivation which led him to invade India.

It discusses the evolution of his military tactics and analyses the role of firearms in his victories over Afghans and Rajputs. This work also foregrounds Babur's personality – his exceptional intelligence and knowledge, skills as a ruler, and his sensibility as an individual. It presents Babur not only as a successful conqueror but also as an equally charismatic individual at par with his celebrated grandson, Akbar.

Stephen Frederic Dale is Professor Emeritus of South Asian and Islamic History at Ohio State University. He is the author of *Islamic Society on the South Asian Frontier: The Mappilas of Malabar, 1498–1922, Indian Merchants and Eurasian Trade, 1600–1750, The Garden of the Eight Paradises: Babur and the Culture of Empire in Central Asia, Afghanistan and India (1483–1530), The Muslim Empires of the Ottomans, Safavids and Mughals* and *The Orange Trees of Marrakesh: Ibn Khaldun and the Science of Man*.

BABUR
Timurid Prince and Mughal Emperor,
1483-1530

Stephen Frederic Dale

CAMBRIDGE
UNIVERSITY PRESS

University Printing House, Cambridge CB2 8BS, United Kingdom

One Liberty Plaza, 20th Floor, New York, NY 10006, USA

477 Williamstown Road, Port Melbourne, vic 3207, Australia

314 to 321, 3rd Floor, Plot No.3, Splendor Forum, Jasola District Centre, New Delhi 110025, India

79 Anson Road, #06–04/06, Singapore 079906

Cambridge University Press is part of the University of Cambridge.

It furthers the University's mission by disseminating knowledge in the pursuit of education, learning and research at the highest international levels of excellence.

www.cambridge.org
Information on this title: www.cambridge.org/9781108470070

First published 2018

Printed in India by Rajkamal Electric Press, Kundli, Haryana.

A catalogue record for this publication is available from the British Library

ISBN 978-1-108-47007-0 Hardback
ISBN 978-1-107-10726-7 Paperback

For Lillian

Table of Contents

List of Illustrations and Maps   ix

Preface   xi

Abbreviations   xv

Introduction   1

1. Qazaq: A Timurid Vagabond   23

2. Padshahliq, Governance, in Kabul   59

3. Mulkgirliq: The Act of Kingdom-Seizing   95

4. Padshahliq, Governance, in Hindustan   137

5. Gurbatlıq: An Indian Exile   175

Conclusion   209

Glossary   221

Bibliography   225

Index   235

List of Illustrations

1. Babur feasts with Baiqara Mirzas in Herat, December 1506

2. Babur describes construction of Bagh-i vafa *charbagh* in Adinapur in 1508/1509

3. Babur celebrates the Timurid-Mughal Empire with Timurids and Safavid and Uzbek envoys, December 1528

4. The Ludi tomb, Shish Gumbad, in Delhi

5. The tomb of Babur in Kabul

List of Maps

1. A map of Ferghanah Valley (Chapter 1)

2. A map of Mawarannahr, Afghanistan and Hindustan (Chapter 2)

3. A map of Afghanistan and Hindustan (Chapter 5)

Preface

In 2004, I published a biography of Babur titled *The Garden of the Eight Paradises: Bâbur and the Culture of Empire in Central Asia, Afghanistan and India (1483–1530)*. The size of the book reflected years of research on the history and culture of Babur's homeland in the Ferghanah Valley of modern Uzbekistan, including Chaghatai Turkish language study and multiple trips to Central Asia. The result was a massive, complex, and for most readers, bewilderingly-detailed work that included elaborate meditations on autobiography, the multiple meanings of the word Turk, classical Persian and Turki verse and Greco-Islamic thought among other subjects. I realized soon after its publication that by pouring nearly everything I had learned about Babur, his culture and the bewilderingly chaotic politics of the time, I left most readers gasping for air. Perhaps, even more to the point of readership, the book of its size, with maps and coloured plates was far too expensive for most potential readers in South Asia – the natural audience for a study of the founder of the Mughal Empire, designated here as the Timurid-Mughal Empire.

It is not often one has a chance to correct a problem such as this, but many years after the biography's publication, I had conversations with my good friends and academic colleagues – Gyan Pandey and Ruby Lal – when I lamented the fact that most of the millions of literate South Asians had never read the book, which, for all its many faults, still addressed many important issues about Babur's personality and Central Asian culture that are little understood outside the offices of a few scholarly specialists in the region. Gyan Pandey suggested that I write another, shorter and more accessible biography, utilising the knowledge I had acquired while working on the original work, but framed in an entirely different way. He also helpfully put me in touch with the editors of Cambridge University Press in New Delhi, who agreed to consider the idea and eventually commissioned a new work. I was delighted to have the opportunity to publish a book with this eminent press in India, having previously worked with its Cambridge offices on other projects in the past and with its marvellous editor Marigold Acland. I am grateful to Qudsiya Ahmed of Cambridge University Press, in Delhi, for welcoming me to produce this completely new version of Babur's biography in India, where I have spent so many wonderful years as a student and scholar. I am also deeply indebted to members of the editorial board at Cambridge Press in Delhi for their careful copyediting, which substantially improved the quality of the final draft of the manuscript.

Biographies of Zahir al-Din Muhammad Babur are inevitably based upon his autobiography, usually titled the *Babur Nama(h)*, the *Book of Babur*, but known to many of his contemporaries simply by the title *Vaqayi'* or 'Events'. Readers of this biography and scholars interested in the subject should know that the three editions of the *Vaqayi'* are essential sources for a study of Babur's life. The fundamental and absolutely essential edition is by Eiji Mano of Kyoto University, who made it his life's work to produce a scholarly edited version of Babur's original Turki text. His impeccably edited and beautifully printed *Bâbur-Nâma (Vaqayi')* (Kyoto: Syokado, 1995) was supplemented a year later by a second volume of the 'Concordance and Classified Indexes' (Kyoto: Syokado, 1996). This latter volume lists every word and phrase in which that word appears, as well as contains special sections devoted to individuals, tribes and clans, geography and poetry. A second essential edition is by Annette Susannah Beveridge, *The Bâbur-nâma in English* (London: Luzac, 1922), which is based on the Turki text of Babur's *Vaqayi'* discovered by her husband, the British Indian official and Persian scholar, Henry Beveridge. It is superbly edited with many insightful footnotes and indices. Annette Beveridge also edited this lithograph copy of the original manuscript with a preface and indexes in both English and the original script titled *The Bâbur-nâma* (London: Luzac, repr. 1971). The third of these essential editions is Reşit Rahmeti Arat's modern Turkish translation of Babur's Turki text, which contains a unique set of notes by Y. Hikmet Bayur to Turco-Mongol terminology. It is titled *Gazi Zahirûddin Muhammad Babur: Vekayi Babur'un Hâtıratı* (Ankara: Türk Tarih Kurumu Basimevi, 1943). Arat's translation clarifies many difficult passages of Babur's original text and Bayur's notes explain many critical customs and institutions of Turco-Mongol society, such as *yasal* or 'battle-order' – the order Babur used to organise his forces on several critical occasions.

Supplementing these editions of the *Vaqayi'* are the only two contemporary texts, which offer additional insight into Babur's personal and political life, and that of his son and heir Humayun. These are the memoirs of Babur's Mongol cousin Mirza Haidar Dughlat, who lived with Babur in Kabul for three years. He later served Humayun and eventually became governor of Kashmir, and the memoir of Babur's daughter, Gulbadan Begim, who knew her father briefly as a very young girl in Agra just before his death. W. M. Thackston has edited Mirza Haidar's Persian text in one volume and produced an edited translation of the text in a second volume. These two volumes are the Persian text: *Tarikh-i Rashidi, A History of the Khans of Mughulistan* (Cambridge: Harvard University, 1996) and the English translation: *Tarikh-i Rashidi, A History of the Khans of*

Mughulistan (Cambridge: Harvard University, 1996). Gulbadan Begim's memoir has been translated and edited by the remarkable Annette Susannah Beveridge. It contains Beveridge's substantive introduction to Gulbadan Begim's life, as well as the printed text of the original and only surviving manuscript of the Persian text and an English translation. Beveridge has also included an unusual appendix with biographical details of women connected to Babur and Humayun. This volume is Beveridge's *The History of Humâyûn* (*Humâyûn-Nâma*) (London: Royal Asiatic Society Oriental Translation Fund, 1902).

In this current version of Babur's biography, I have eliminated long explanatory footnotes devoted to complex linguistic questions, such as readers will find on pages 15–17 in the 2004 edition. I have also eliminated the macrons that indicate long vowels in Arabic and Persian, retaining only the signs for *hamza*, as in the poet's name Nava'i and *'ain*; in the common name 'Abd. I have given full transliterations to many critical terms in the glossary. Babur wrote his *Vaqayi'* in the language he identified as Turki, nineteenth-century European scholars referred to as Chaghatai Turkish and present-day scholars in Uzbekistan term 'Old Uzbek'. Turkish language does not distinguish between long and short vowels, but it has two distinctive features, vowel harmony and a soft g or ğ. I have largely retained the use of vowel harmony, will be most noticeable when umlauts appear and at the end of words, when an undotted i or ı is used, as in the word *arıq*, or irrigation channel, and pronounced something like the syllable 'uh' in American English, and when the plural form of words shifts from –'ler' to –'lar', depending on the previous vowel. The soft g or ğ has been omitted except in the case of the word *yiğit*, or youth. Thus, Babur's senior commanders are referred to as *beg*, which would be properly written as *beğ* and pronounced bey, as in Ottoman and modern Turkish.

Babur's Turki only rarely consists entirely of Turkish vocabulary. It is highly Persianised, as was his culture. His sentences also contain many Arabic words, especially religious vocabulary, long since absorbed into Persian and Turkish usage in Iran and Central Asia. Sometimes he writes sentences, which contain all Persian and/or Arabic words distinguished only by a Turki verb. This is particularly true of his verse, which is modelled on the dominant Persian literary *lingua franca* of Central Asia. His prose style is usually simple and direct, but more complex and elusive when he is discussing personal relations or psychology. In those particularly difficult passages, I have often studied Arat's modern Turkish translation to clarify my understanding of Babur's intent.

In these many years of fascinating engagement with Babur's works and his Central Asian milieu, I have incurred immense scholarly debts as I sought the help of other scholars. I have been fortunate to know Thomas Allsen and Peter Golden, benefitting from conversations with them and learning from their work on Mongol and Turkish history and linguistics. I have derived similar benefits from discussions with Beatrice Forbes Manz and Maria Eva Subtelny, who have written important books and articles on Temür and his descendants – the Timurids. I am profoundly indebted to the Japanese scholar Eiji Mano. His text and Concordance of Babur's Turki *Vaqâyi'* and his many scholarly articles made this work possible. His impeccable scholarship constitutes the essential basis for anyone who wishes to study Babur's remarkable autobiography. He also graciously welcomed my wife and me when we visited him in Kyoto. I am also indebted to Chris Andrew for allowing me to use one of his many photographs of Babur's tomb in Kabul in this volume and to Ardeth Anderson who has prepared the maps. Most of all, I am grateful to my wife Lillian Ming-tse Li, herself a historian of China, who has listened patiently to anecdotes about Babur's life over many years, encouraged me to write this revised version and suggested important changes as I wrote. The precise title of this volume is also hers. I have dedicated this book to her as a small acknowledgement of her influence on my life and work.

Abbreviations

BN-B-Beveridge,	The Bâbur Nâma in English
BN-M-Mano,	Bâbur-Nâma (Vaqâyi')
HN-Gulbadan Begim,	The History of Humâyûn (Humâyûn-Nâma)
TR-Haidar Mirza,	Tarikh-i Rashidi`

Illustration 1: Babur feasts with Baiqara Mirzas in Herat, December 1506.
Photo courtesy: British Library: Or. 3714 v. 2 f260.

Illustration 2: Babur describes construction of Bagh-i vafa *charbagh* in Adinapur in 1508/1509.
Photo courtesy: British Library: Or. 3714 v. 2 f173v.

Illustration 3: Babur celebrates the Timurid-Mughal Empire with Timurids and Safavid and Uzbek envoys, December 1528.
Photo courtesy: British Library: Or. 3714 v. 4 f491v.

Illustration 4: The Ludi tomb, Shish Gumbad, in Delhi.
Photo courtesy: Author's photo.

Illustration 5: The tomb of Babur in Kabul.
Photo courtesy: With kind permission of Christopher Andrew.

Introduction

Zahir al-Din Muhammad Babur (1483–1530) was an individual of major political and literary importance in the early modern era and beyond. Politically, he was a pivotal figure in the history of both Central Asia and India. Thus, by successfully conquering the north Indian heartland between 1526 and 1530, he initiated a Timurid Renaissance, revitalising the dynastic history of Temür's descendants by founding what has come to be known erroneously as the Mughal or Mongol Empire. In literature, he wrote the world's single most vital, revealing and engaging dynastic autobiography, an incomparable work of humanistic interest that also contains unique information about Central Asian life and politics and Indian society in the late fifteenth and early sixteenth centuries. Babur once wrote to a kinsman, upbraiding him for failing to join the coalition fighting the Uzbeks – the Timurids' implacable enemies, by reminding him: 'a person's acts outlive him… Wise men have called an illustrious name a second life'.[1] Doubly illustrious as a conqueror and writer, he has enjoyed a considerable second life, although not as fully or meaningfully as he deserves considering his achievements. This biography represents an effort to ensure that his first life is better understood in order that his second might be more widely and sympathetically acknowledged.

Babur, as he is simply and usually known, was a fifth-generation patrilineal descendant of the Central Asian conqueror Temür, also known as Tîmur-i lang, 'Timur the Lame' or Tamerlane (1336–1405). He traced his descent through Temür's son Miran Shah (1366–1408), once a governor of parts of Afghanistan and Iran. On his mother's side, he was a fifteenth-generation matrilineal descendant of Chinggis Khan (1162–1227) through Chinggis Khan's son Chaghatai Khan (1226–42), who had ruled Mongol territories in Central Asia. In dynastic terms, Babur referred to himself either as a Turk, or a Timurid, and like other patrilineal descendants of Temür, he inherited the title *mirza* – an Arabic-Persian contraction of the phrase *amir zadeh*, son of an *amir*, a prince or noble. His Chaghatai Mongol male kins were known as *khans*, after their patrilineal descent from Chinggis Khan.[2] Babur never thought of himself as a Mongol, but his dual descent justifies calling his Indian conquests the Timurid-Mughal Empire.

Babur Mirza was born at Akhsı, then a major urban settlement located on the northern bank of the Syr Darya River, east-southeast of Tashkent, in the bucolic Ferghanah Valley of modern Uzbekistan. Ferghanah was part of a larger region historically known in Arabic as Mawarannahr, the 'land beyond the river' Amu Darya, which divides the modern states of Uzbekistan and Afghanistan. In classical Western sources, Mawarannahr was known as Transoxiana, the land beyond the Oxus, the Greek name for the Amu Darya. Sometime before his 12th year, his father appointed him to preside over the modest fortified settlement of Andijan, located in the eastern part of the valley. His father 'Umar Shaikh Mirza held Ferghanah as his Timurid appanage or territorial appointment, while 'Umar Shaikh's brothers – Babur's paternal uncles, Sultan Ahmad Mirza and Sultan Mahmud Mirza – ruled Samarqand and Badakhshan, respectively. Babur's Chaghatai Mongol uncle, Mahmud Khan, the Khaqan or Great Khan of the Chaghatais, controlled Tashkent.

Babur was born into a dystopian political world. More particularly for the Timurids, it was a fragmented and ever-shrinking world, characterised by internecine conflicts among their Timurid and Mongol kin and the increasingly aggressive incursions which the Uzbek Turkic tribal confederation had been making into their homelands in Mawarannahr. He inherited his father's Ferghanah appanage after 'Umar Shaikh died when his Akhsı riverside dovecote collapsed into a ravine in 1494. At that exact moment in his 12th year, Babur was thrust into a political maelstrom as both his Timurid and Chaghatai Mongol relatives descended on his Andijan base, hoping to seize part or all of the rich Ferghanah Valley for themselves. After repulsing their onslaught, Babur, now an adult according to the custom then, quickly adapted to the atomistic, unforgiving political environment of this late Turco-Mongol Central-Asian world by organising the first of several subsequent attempts to seize Samarqand – Temür's capital and the goal of every ambitious Timurid *mirza*.

Babur spent the next decade alternating between his efforts to occupy and hold Samarqand and trying to survive the military disasters that followed each one of his attempts. Not only did individual Timurids lack any sense of dynastic unity, but the more cohesively organised Uzbeks took advantage of the late Timurid malaise to drive Babur from the Ferghanah Valley in 1504. Under their leader Shaibani Khan, Uzbeks executed his Timurid kin and later his Chaghatai Mongol relatives, who in 1502 had belatedly come to his aid from their homeland in Mughulistan, the territory now included within the Chinese province of Xinjiang. Fleeing Ferghanah and pursued by Shaibani Khan, Babur was able to seize Kabul in December 1504. Long a Timurid outpost, and last held by his other paternal uncle Ulugh Beg Kabuli until his death in 1502, Kabul provided Babur with a relatively secure base, which for many years he held while hoping to be able to return north to occupy and rule from Samarqand.

He was able to seize Samarqand once again in 1511 with the help of troops from Safavid Iran, but after another devastating defeat by Uzbek troops, he was forced to abandon the city for the third time in his young life. Fleeing south to Badakhshan in northern Afghanistan, he gradually abandoned hope of resurrecting a Timurid state in Samarqand. By 1514 or 1515, he turned his attention to a politically-fragmented North India as the last viable territory where he could resuscitate

Timurid fortunes. After launching a series of probing expeditions from Kabul into the Punjab in the 1520's, conflicts among the perennially feuding tribesmen within the Afghan Ludi state, led by Sultan Ibrahim Ludi, offered him the chance to invade India. After ferrying the Indus River on 16 December 1525 with some 7,000 to 8,000 troops, Babur defeated Ibrahim Ludi and a vastly superior Afghan force on 20 April 1526 at the Battle of Panipat, about 50 miles north of Delhi. Seizing the Ludi treasuries in Delhi and at their capital Agra, Babur spent the next 4 years in an increasingly exhausting attempt to pacify Hindustan, while inviting Timurid and Chinggisid kin to join him and share the wealth of his imperfectly subjugated Timurid-Mughal Indian Empire.

The Autobiography

A biography of Babur has to be written in the most part as a commentary and analysis of his autobiography the *Vaqayi*, or 'Events', which he wrote in his native language Turki, later known in Europe as Chaghatai Turkish.[3] He attracted very little scholarly attention in the Eurasian World before he defeated Ibrahim Ludi at Panipat and began carving out a new Timurid Empire on the plains of Hindustan. No contemporary, or near-contemporary writer, produced a biography of Babur. That includes the important Herat historian Khwandamir, who joined Babur in Agra in September 1528.[4] Perhaps Khwandamir, like later scholars, felt none was needed given the depth and richness of the *Vaqayi*. Babur's cousin and younger contemporary, the Mongol Haidar Mirza Dughlat Kurkan, wrote a history of the Mongols that contains valuable passages relating to Babur, and his daughter Gulbadan Begim wrote a memoir recalling what she remembered of her father as a young child.[5] Both works contain deeply appreciative recollections of their relative and father, but they touch on only brief portions of his life. The *Vaqayi*, a work of more than 600 pages in the Japanese scholar Eiji Mano's impeccably edited Turki text, remains the principal source of information about Babur. And it is a wonderful source, so engaging that readers, the very few who actually read the complex text, are usually so dazzled by its unique qualities that they speak about it in rapt admiration, only very rarely stopping to consider its significance in whole or in part.

William Erskine, one of the early translators into English of the late sixteenth-century Persian translation of Babur's work, exemplifies this reaction in his careful and readable 1854 biography of Babur. He writes, first commenting on the character traits he perceives in the *Vaqayi*.

> Bâber was certainly one of the most illustrious sovereigns that ever filled an eastern throne. His character was happily compounded of most of the

qualities that go to form a great prince and a good man. He was bold, enterprising, full of ardour, and possessed of the commanding talents that sway and lead the minds of men. His temper was frank, confiding and gay, and maintained through the life the freshness of youth. He had strong affections, the warmest domestic feelings, and was devotedly attached to his relations and friends, and ready to sympathize with the pleasures and the sufferings of human beings of every class. Keenly alive to whatever was grand and beautiful, he cultivated knowledge of every kind with unwearied assiduity and with proportional success. Glory in every shape inflames his imagination, and he attained to a rare eminence of power and renown.

Then turning to the text itself, Erskine continues:

But of all his literary works, his Commentaries are by much the most remarkable. The first part contains a continuous narrative of his early life and troubles; the later portions consist of fragments of a journal, written from time to time and often from day to day; some comprising accounts of his most celebrated exploits, others being merely short entries or jottings, as if to assist his future recollection, and frequently referring to the incidents of his private life. 'His Memoirs,' says the historian of India, 'are almost singular in their own nature, and perfectly so if we consider the circumstances of the writer. They contain a minute account of the life of a great Tartar monarch, along with a natural effusion of his opinions and feelings, free from disguise and reserve, and no less free from all affectation of extreme frankness and candour. The style is plain and manly, as well as lively and picturesque; and, being the work of a man of genius and observation, it presents his countrymen and contemporaries in their appearance, manners, pursuits, and actions as clearly as in a mirror. In this respect, it is almost the only specimen of real history in Asia; for the ordinary writers, though they give pompous accounts of the deeds and ceremonies of the great, are apt to omit the lives and manners even of that class; while everything beneath their level is left entirely out of sight. In Bâber, the figures, dress, tastes and habits, of each individual introduced are described with such minuteness and reality, that we seem to live among them, and to know their persons as well as we do their characters. His description of the countries he visited, their scenery, climate, productions, and works of art and industry are more full and accurate than will, perhaps, be found, in equal space, in any modern traveler; and considering the circumstances in which they were compiled, are equally surprising.'[6]

Most readers of the *Vaqayi'* would probably agree with the substance of Erskine's enthusiastic account and they would be right to do so. Babur draws readers into his life as partisans to ensure that he will have a widely admired second life, and that was unquestionably one of his fundamental reasons for writing. One of his most effective techniques is to describe his emotional state at critical points in his tumultuous career, for instance, recounting how he cried as a young man after military setbacks in Ferghanah, or suffered exhaustion and depression following campaigns and serious illnesses in India. How often have readers ever encountered in the literature of the pre-modern world an admittedly desperate, weeping young warrior, or a depressed but reflective conqueror? His is a genuinely moving autobiography, and its many unique qualities explain why Erskine suggests that it represents the only specimen of a real history in Asia.

Babur also writes with a strikingly modern sensitivity to possible charges of bias or misrepresentation. His apologia is never more effective than when he describes how he reacted to an attempted coup against him in Kabul in 1507, when several maternal or Chaghatai Mongol relatives joined with some formerly close companions to replace him as the ruler of the city. In the passage, he first alludes to this event and then broadens out his claim of objectivity.

> By writing this I do not mean to complain. It is the truth that is written, *rast hikayat tur kim bitib tur.* I do not intend to praise myself in what I have written; what has been written is exactly what occurred. In this History I pledge that everything shall be truthfully written, and that every act will be chronicled accurately. It follows that I have divulged everything good and bad that is known, concerning father and elder brother; of them all I have set down carefully the known virtues and defects. And I have revealed all the known faults and virtues of kinsmen and strangers. Let the reader excuse; let the listener not censure.[7]

Does Babur always tell the truth? It is impossible to tell when he discusses human motivation because his account of events nearly always constitutes the only surviving record. He is remarkably candid about his own military failures in Ferghanah and Samarqand, which he frankly admits were due to his own inexperience. Whether he fairly appraises others is far more difficult to say. As he indicates in this passage, he praises but also openly criticises relatives or others he knew personally or by report. As will be seen, he has drawn a surprisingly candid portrait of Sultan Husain Baiqara of Herat, the ruler of the Timurid capital city, who oversaw the florescence of the Perso-Islamic and Turki culture there in the late fifteenth century. In his mini biography of the Sultan and members of his court, he does usually balance praise with blame or outright condemnation, something no court historian, dependent on patronage, would ever consider doing. This is refreshing, but readers must always keep in mind, however difficult it is to resist the temptation of accepting Babur's engaging account as absolutely truthful, however original his style, however compellingly dramatic his narrative, however precise in his descriptions of architecture, geography, flora and fauna, however all of the virtues William Erskine accurately ascribes to his work, Babur wrote as an autobiographer. He always interpreted events and people based on whether they served his interest. He never considered another person's interest or point of view.

Reminding readers of the danger of uncritically accepting a single version of complex historical events is not meant to diminish the exceptional nature of Babur's *Vaqayi'*. Its value far exceeds even its appeal as an engaging, personally revealing autobiography, for it illumines so many different aspects of the politics, society and culture and even the environment of the late fifteenth- and early sixteenth-century Central Asia, Afghanistan and India. First and foremost, the *Vaqayi'* is significant as a text that was written to inform and educate his descendants. It serves both as a source of carefully compiled geographical, administrative and social information for the Ferghanah Valley, eastern Afghanistan and Hindustan and as a type of *nasihat namah*, a treatise of practical advice, for readers trying to navigate the treacherous political shoals of this era in all three regions.

Babur, who throughout the text demonstrates a probing analytical intelligence and belief in the value of precise data, prefaces the narrative parts of each of his book's three sections – Ferghanah, Kabul and Hindustan – with surveys of these regions, topography, economy, society, flora and fauna. His accounts represent a kind of pre-modern gazetteer, easily comparable in value in many respects to nineteenth-century British-Indian district gazetteers. Babur describes the Ferghanah Valley and Samarqand, but he writes most extensively of Kabul city and its surrounding *tumans* or districts, providing critical information on topics that would have been useful for later rulers. His Hindustan gazetteer is far less complete, as he spent only 4 years in the country. He tells readers that he planned to include more information when he was able to, not knowing he would fall deathly ill a short time later.

Apart from its importance as a gazetteer, Babur's *Vaqayi'* serves another function – as a source of advice for future monarchs, a *nasihat namah*, or a book of advice or a mirror for Timurid princes. It is, however, a special, deeply personal kind of mirror rather than the standard, largely impersonal or generalised examples of this genre, such as the well-known *Qabus-namah*.[8] Abu'l Fazl, Akbar's minister and court historian, characterises the work in this way as: 'The Memoirs of Bâbur, the Conqueror of the World…may be called a code of practical wisdom. It is an

Institute for all earthly sovereigns and a manual for teaching right thoughts and ideas.'[9] Whether Babur's literate great-grandson Jahangir (r. 1605–27) viewed the text this way when he read it is impossible to say. He did not in any case respond to its 'right thought and ideas' during his many years spent in an alcoholic and drug-induced haze.

Nonetheless, Babur sometimes explicitly relates lessons he has learned during his tumultuous life. Many date to his Ferghanah days, such as his pointed admission when he lost two crucial battles by failing to post sentries or the formal lesson he relates about events that occurred after he had dealt harshly with a band of recalcitrant Mongol troops. These troops rebelled against him after he allowed them to be stripped and plundered in revenge for doing the same to Babur's men. Following his narrative of the rebellion, Babur pauses to conclude two things about his dealings with Mongol troops. First, treachery was an innate part of Mongol nature. Second, military actions cannot be made rashly without considering their possible consequences many times over.[10]

Such lessons abound in the text, and Babur also frequently punctuates important observations with aphorisms, more often than not quotations from one of the many great Persian-language poets. Sa'adi's *Bustan* and *Gulistan* and Firdausi's *Shah-Namah* often serves his purpose, as they did when he hectors his frustratingly imperfect son and heir Humayun for having written from Kabul that he preferred solitude. Replying to him from Agra, Babur remarks, 'Solitude is a vice in kingship.' Then to drive home the point he quotes a verse from Sa'adi.

> If your feet are fettered, learn to be content,
> But if you are lone horseman, follow your own way.[11]

Babur dispenses more advice throughout the *Vaqayi'*, but not always targeting his beleaguered son. He sometimes draws lessons from wonderfully mundane events, such as the danger of having parties in which men drink wine and eat the intoxicating sweet *ma'jun*. He warns his readers off this practice following a particularly dissolute party on a small boat in 1519 writing: 'A *majun suhbati* [a social gathering with *ma'jun*] never goes well with an *'araq and chaghir suhbati* [a liquor and wine gathering]!'[12] Perhaps, Babur intended this advice for his sons, Humayun and Kamran, who sometimes attended these parties, or more often staged their own, and needed to be reminded of these dangers.

Apart from its value as a gazetteer and mirror for princes, the *Vaqayi'* offers vital insights into many aspects of Babur's career. Not the least of these is what it demonstrates about the influence of dynastic legitimacy, both as a profoundly powerful motivating ideology for someone like Babur, who inherited an assumption of sovereign right, and also as a force of almost gravitational attraction in drawing in thousands of disparate individuals to support an otherwise impecunious political and military failure. This was Babur's situation in 1504, when as a hunted refugee at age 23 he fled from the Uzbek conquerors of his homeland south to Afghanistan with fewer than 300 men, mainly on foot, his mother, two small tents and hardly any weapons, and yet, attracted thousands of Mongol troops, who joined him in a dramatic tableau that he rejoices to describe, solely because he was a Timurid.[13] Babur sought Samarqand as a Timurid, was hunted by his Uzbek enemies as a Timurid, survived a series of disasters because he was a Timurid and conquered Hindustan as a Timurid.

Yet, even more significant than what the *Vaqayi'* illustrates about the power of legitimacy is that Babur implicitly reveals to modern readers about the social and political ethos of late fifteenth-century Timurids, enabling them to understand the type of state Babur imagined for what he describes as the dusty, wind-swept and altogether charmless plains of Hindustan. Even so, long after his death in 1530, many scholars and a far broader literate public, continue to think of Babur as another marauding, nomadic barbarian from the Central Asian steppes. They are right to recognise his aggressive *mentalité*, for he celebrates his *mulkgirliq*, his Timurid 'kingdom seizing' or imperial ambition. Yet Babur, like his father 'Umar Shaikh Mirza and most contemporary Timurids, lived between campaigns as a sedentary that is urban, Hanafi Sunni Muslim, literate in both his native Turki and Persian, with a considerable knowledge and memory of poems from Persian verse classics such as the *Shah-Namah* – Firdausi's semi-mythological Iranian epic.[14]

The Ferghanah Valley was a geographically constricted and bucolic environment, with relatively modest towns, but Babur reveals his delight in splendid urban spaces when he waxes lyrically about beautiful structures in Samarqand and later speaks with unfeigned admiration of the monuments and sophisticated urban culture of Sultan Husain Baiqara's Herat. His preferred social venue was the *suhbat*, the congenial gatherings of comrades, poets and musicians held in a *chahar bagh* or *charbagh*, the quadrilateral Persianate garden. When he began pacifying Hindustan, he often alternated descriptions of his military campaigns with accounts of time spent re-creating his idealised formal garden environment in and around Agra. He saw himself in cultural terms as a representative of a civilised Perso-Islamic society, and criticised isolating Hindu life of separate castes as lacking the civilised traits of congenial social intercourse, *ikhtilat u amizish,* and what he describes as the *amad u raft*, the 'coming and going' or visiting back and forth by all manner of Timurids, high born or not.

The *Vaqayi'* is therefore, and for many different reasons, an extraordinary source. It contains idiosyncratic information on a remarkable range of different subjects.

These range from Babur's personality, interests and motivations to precisely observed descriptions of flora and fauna to Babur's uniquely detailed accounts of four battles he fought in Afghanistan and India, whose information and insights into military tactics cannot be matched by any other source for this period of Islamic or Central Asian history. Even then his narrative of events introduces readers to the unpredictable, ad hoc nature of empire building, offering a realistic picture of what traditional sources may describe as a seamless process managed by a great conqueror. As an autobiography the *Vaqâyi'* is, though, inevitably focussed on the person and the moment, whether that moment is in Ferghanah or Kabul or Hindustan. As a conqueror immediately concerned with the next campaign, the fate of his family and relatives and the political situation within and outside India, Babur says little about Indo-Muslim history and almost nothing about Indo-Muslim society. Looking beyond the individual to his legacy, thoughtful readers will be frustrated if they tried to evaluate the significance of Babur's conquest by relying solely on the evidence of the *Vaqayi'* and failed to learn something of what had come before as well as what followed after.

Indo-Muslim History

Babur wrote that shortly after taking Kabul, he began to covet North India, which Muslim writers knew as Hindustan. As a literate individual, who spent two decades on India's Afghan doorstep, he was familiar with the history of Muslim rule of the region. He compared himself favourably to the two Muslims from Afghanistan, who had previously plundered and/or conquered Hindustan. The first was Mahmud of Ghazna (d. 1030), the descendant of a Turkic *ghulam* or slave-soldier, who plundered northwest India in order to finance conquests in Iran, but who, by occupying Lahore and patronising Perso-Islamic writers and scientists, laid the base for Muslim rule and Perso-Islamic culture in the north. Mahmud was followed by Sultan Shihab al-Din Ghuri (Mu'izz al-Din) (d. 1206), the representative of a primitive, impoverished Afghan lineage, who overthrew the remnants of Mahmud of Ghazni's state in Afghanistan, while learning how much an enterprising conqueror could steal from populous and, from the Afghan perspective, fabulously wealthy India. There is a certain pleasure in having the original nature of the early Ghurid state confirmed by learning that some of its coinage featured the Hindu goddess of wealth – Lakshmi – but no religious motto.[15] Unlike Mahmud, Ghurid Sultans not only plundered India, but began to govern it as well, establishing what has come to be known as the Delhi Sultanate.

Between 1206, when Shihab al-Din Ghuri died to be succeeded by his own *ghulam*, and 1398, when Babur's ancestor Temür invaded India and plundered Delhi of its treasury, elephants and artisans, Hindustan was governed by a series of four Muslim dynasties. They shared several traits, the first and most obvious of which was that they governed as sultans and not as caliphs. The Sultans exemplified the politically fragmented phase of Muslim history that evolved because the 'Abbasid Caliphate of Baghdad (750–1258) had declined, allowing the rise of independent rulers of various ethnicities, who acquired power unrelated to the original religious mission of Muhammad's successors. The fourteenth-century Arab-Muslim philosophical historian Ibn Khaldun (1332–1406) discussed the traits of this class of pragmatic Muslim rulers in his late fourteenth-century text – the *Muqaddimah*.[16]

Ibn Khaldun cited the work of the Muslim jurist and political theorist al-Mawardi (972–1058), who theorised about the relations between the Caliphate and sultanates at a time when Buyid Shi'i *amir*s from Mazandaran in northern Iran controlled the nearly impotent 'Abbasid Caliphs.[17] Just as al-Mawardi distinguished between governments based on Islamic law, the *shari'ah*, and those founded on power, in Arabic *sultan* Ibn Khaldun contrasted the status of the first four Pious Caliphs, who succeeded Muhammad, with sultans of his day. These later rulers, he argued, lacked the spiritual authority and moral purpose of the Caliphs, but founded states based solely upon power and money.[18] Ibn Khaldun said these rulers might patronise Islamic institutions and members of the clerical class or *'ulama'*, but he insisted they did not govern according to religious precepts, relying instead on 'rational' or Machiavellian considerations to ensure their survival.

Scholars have generally seen the Ghaznavids as the original prototypical sultans – men without distinguished lineages or religious prestige, whose identity as military slaves highlighted the reality of the power state of Muslim rulers in the late 'Abbasid era. Nonetheless, the Ghaznavids originated as *ghulam*s of the cultured Iranian Samanid dynasty of Bukhara (r. 818–999) and were knowledgeable about and associated with the flourishing Perso-Islamic culture of Khurasan – one of the historic centres of Iranian civilisation. The Ghurids, who destroyed Ghaznavid power in Afghanistan, represented a far more primitive variant of Ibn Khaldun's model, and they were followed as rulers of North India by a series of military slaves and military adventurers, whose two centuries of sultanates represented the worst aspects of the power state in the Islamic world, perhaps even more crude, unstable, unenlightened and brutal than the ephemeral sultanate regimes that Ibn Khaldun knew from North Africa. These were states far removed from the great centres of Islamic culture in Iran, Iraq, Syria and Egypt. Their principal legacy was the expansion and consolidation of Muslim rule in northern and central India.

Babur was a sultan in Ibn Khaldun's sense of the term, but as a Timurid, he was enriched with two legacies that his Delhi Sultanate predecessors lacked: legitimacy and a sophisticated Perso-Islamic cultural identity. The lack of dynastic legitimacy in the Delhi Sultanate is highlighted by the fact that after Shihab al-Din Ghuri's death, he was succeeded by his *ghulam* Iltutmish (r. 1210–36) and then by a series of ten sultans, who 'reigned' in Delhi amidst often devastating factional violence. It is symptomatic of this problem that in the thirteenth century, succession in Delhi was confirmed by the *bay'at* oath of Turkic commanders and other notables rather than being guaranteed by the prestige of name or lineage.[19] In 1296, this situation was partly altered by the rise of the two ephemeral family dynasties the Khaljis (r. 1290–1320) and the Tughluqs (r. 1320–98). However, it was not until Muhammad b. Tughluq became ruler that a Delhi Sultan came to power by succeeding his father. Political insecurity was a defining characteristic of the Delhi Sultanate throughout its history.

What is particularly relevant for an appreciation of Babur's reign is the attention that these insecure Delhi Sultans gave to legitimise themselves as Muslim monarchs by patronising and subsidising the growth of a to Muslim clerical and institutional infrastructure. The Ghurid's successor and really the first sultan of Delhi, their *ghulam* Iltutmish (r. 1210–36), exemplified Sultanate rulers' concern with their legitimacy in the effort he made to present himself as the guardian of Muslim law – the *shari'ah*, in the Muslims' newly conquered territories. 'An integral part of the Iltutmish's effort to ensure political control was to project a self-image, where the Sultan appeared in the dual role of conqueror and protector of the Holy Law.'[20] Iltutmish sought and received recognition from the 'Abbasid Caliph, systematically encouraged the development of an indigenous *'ulama'*, and lavishly patronised the construction of religious architecture of all kinds, including a massive Friday or 'cathedral mosque, a *masjid–i jami* in Delhi. Iltutmish's concern for his Islamic reputation and the growth of a state-sponsored clerical class was exceptionally important for him and later Sultanate rulers, who otherwise lacked dynastic legitimacy and prestige'.

Muhammad bin Tughluq (1324–51), a century later, persisted in this concern by demonstrating reverence for the post-Mongol Egyptian Caliphs Abu'l Rabi' Sulaiman (d. 1340) and Abu'l 'Abbas (1341–52); distributing lavish presents to various clerics and demanding that members of his court observe the public formalities of Islamic piety.[21] As the Moroccan traveller, Ibn Battuta testified when he visited India, the Sultan was also famous for welcoming Muslim clerics and a wide variety of foreigners to the country, including Ibn Battuta himself, who was appointed as *qadi or qazi* after he reached Delhi in 1333. 'The king of India', he remarks, 'makes a practice of honouring strangers… The majority of his courtiers, palace officials, ministers of state, judges and relatives by marriage are foreigners'.[22] As he crossed into India from Afghanistan, Ibn Battuta met both Sufis and *'ulamâ'*, who had arrived from important towns and cities in both Iran and Central Asia. In Sind, for example, he met a former *qadi* of Herat, the capital of Iranian Khurasan and also the late fifteenth-century cultural and political capital of the Timurids, then ruled by Babur's relation, Sultan Husain Baiqara. This man 'Ala al-Mulk, known as Fasih al-Din, 'The Eloquent of the Faith', had come, Ibn Khaldun learned, 'to join the service of the kings of India'. Later in Multan, he met another *qadi* from Tirmidh or Tirmiz – a city on the Amu Darya River. He had arrived in India with his family, brothers and relatives, who had been notables in Samarqand and Bukhara – the foremost urban centres in Mawarannahr. With such men seeking employment, Indo-Muslim culture became enriched with a sophisticated class of clerics, even as Sultanate regimes stagnated in other respects.

Muhammad bin Tughluq, who was so eager to welcome foreigners to his kingdom, exemplified the Delhi Sultanate institution at its most nakedly powerful, brutal and cynical. He combined capricious authoritarian power, ceremonial ostentation with conspicuously formal Islamic piety. Ibn Battuta introduced his character sketch of the man by writing [T]he king is of all men the most addicted to the making of gifts and the shedding of blood'. Following this introduction, he describes the Sultan's lavish gifts to different individuals and a series of grisly executions – of a prominent cleric Shihab al-din and a number of *qadi*s, *shaikh*s and notables, as well as alluding to the forcible exile of some elite members of the Delhi population between 1327 and 1329. Two of his victims – Tughan al-Farghani and his brother – were 'notables' from Babur's Ferghanah Valley homeland, and they may even have been natives of Babur's Andijan. Muhammad Tughluq's patronage of Islamic institutions and insistence on public piety, combined with his alternating support and execution of clerics, exemplifies the Muslim sultanate at its most capricious. It is tempting, if psychologically questionable, to attribute some measure of Muhammad Tughluq's brutality to his dynastic insecurity, an ever-present sense of danger that all Delhi Sultans must have felt in varying degrees.

More than a century and a half later, Babur's Timurid-Mughal Empire represented the climactic case of an Indo-Muslim sultanate. Babur conquered India to preserve a Timurid dynasty and to ennoble himself. He was no less intent than Sultanate rulers on extracting wealth for his supporters, and clerics were conspicuously absent from his entourage and later advisors. At the end of his life, he also referred to his rule as a sultanate. Yet, the Timurid-Mughal Empire Babur founded represented the Muslim power state at its most polished and sophisticated; a dramatic contrast in nearly every respect from Muhammad Tughluq's regime. It was leavened by the lineage and culture of its founder and it evolved under Akbar into an exceptional form of the sultanate as an enlightened, intellectually vibrant, early modern empire.

There are formidable contrasts between men such as Iltutmish, Muhammad Tughluq and Babur and the times in which they lived. First and foremost, Babur came to power in both Afghanistan and Hindustan supremely confident of his legitimacy. His descendants continued to publicise their Timurid lineage in miniature paintings. However, it may have meant little to the larger Indian Muslim population. Babur scarcely even alludes to Indo-Muslim clerics or religious institutions. That is not to say he would have ignored a Muslim caliph had one still ruled in Baghdad, only that his legitimacy and that of his descendants derived first and always foremost from his prestigious Timurid lineage. Inspired by his Timurid descent to conquer, Babur was saved by it in Afghanistan in 1504. The prestige of the dynasty was demonstrated by the political reality of Timurid-Mughal succession struggles in India, which until the early eighteenth century involved only members of the Timurid lineage.

Then, there is Babur's cultural inheritance as one of the later Timurids. His cultural personality as a literate Sunni Muslim urbanite reflected the evolution of Timurid society from the cruelty of Temür's devastating campaigns to his descendants' embrace of high Perso-Islamic culture. This evolution reached its heights and decadent political depths in the late fifteenth-century Herat, where Sultan Husain Baiqara (1469–1506) and his close friend Mir 'Ali Shir Nava'i presided over the florescence of Persianate urban literary and artistic culture, as well as contributing to the rise of Turki as a literary language on the Persian model.[23]

> The Timurids immersed themselves in the pursuits and luxurious trappings of their new life, assimilating the symbols of Perso-Islamic monarchical traditions with the celebration of their own Turco-Mongo past... The history of the Timurid dynasty is also a history of its arts; artistic production was so closely intertwined with political, social and economic events that they must be discussed together. The changed circumstances and orientation of the dynasty after Timur's death served as a direct impetus for an accelerated cultural program... The interests of the new aristocracy were pursued primarily within the context of urban Islam in Iran and Central Asia.[24]

As a product of late Timurid culture and confident of his dynastic claims, Babur campaigned and governed as a far more secure, confident and cultured individual, a more civilised monarch than any of the Delhi Sultans. While benefiting from his very own successful publicity, it is nonetheless easy to see how greatly Babur's sultanate differed from that of his Delhi sultanate predecessors. Babur's own level of religious and cultural sophistication was impressive. Initially in Ferghanah, he heard Persian classics and was tutored by a well-educated cleric, also a Naqshbandi Sufi. Subsequently, during his time in Samarqand, he acquired some basic understanding of the innovative Greco-Islamic astronomical research of Temür's grandson Ulugh Beg (1394–1449). He also exhibited his aesthetic appreciation for the city's imposing urban architecture and Persianate gardens and his knowledge of the geometric principles of Timurid architectural design.[25] Later in Kabul, he took time to further his religious education and translate a major work of Hanafi Sunni law into his native Turki. Then in Hindustan, in a sustained effort of cultural imperialism, he worked constantly to Persianise, in his view to civilise, its flat arid landscape with *charbagh*s, where he could enjoy *suhbatlar*, his favoured social and cultural gatherings. From what little is known of Sultanate era rulers' personalities, none of the men who came to power during the Sultanate era possessed Babur's multifaceted and sophisticated cultural instincts.

While contrasting Babur's embryonic sultanate with that of his predecessors, it is nonetheless important to add that as a conqueror of Hindustan, he was a legatee of the Delhi Sultanate past in three important respects. He inherited a long-established, complex and sophisticated Indo-Muslim clerical class, a thriving Indo-Persian literary culture and a contentious population of Afghan tribes. Given the security of his lineage and the presence of a substantial *'ulama'*, it is not so surprising that he does not describe the work of a single prominent *'alim* during his 4 years in India. He mentions Muslim rulers and frequently alludes to 'Hindustani *amir*s' during his campaigns, but otherwise he is completely silent about and perhaps simply comfortable with the Indo-Muslim religious culture he encountered in Agra and elsewhere. His lack of expressed interest in religious affairs was also understandable because as a Muslim sultan he did not have to act like Iltutmish and create Muslim religious institutions in India *ex nihilo*, 'from nothing'.

Babur also found and knew he would find in India comfortably recognizable Sufi lineages, which had been founded during the Sultanate era. He shows he was familiar with the Chishti Sufi order and knew of its importance, for just after his victory at Panipat he made it a point to take the time to circumambulate two Chishti tombs in Delhi and to mention his visit. One belonged to the famous *shaikh* Nizam al-Din Auliya. The other commemorated a formerly prominent member of the order – Qutb al-Din Bakhtiyar Kaki Ushi (d. 1235), a native of the town of Ush as his *nisba* indicates in eastern Ferghanah, who migrated to India around 1228.[26] Babur had visited Ush a number of times as a young man, which he praised for its gardens and orchards, so it is possible he learned about Qutb al-Din's Chishti identity during his tumultuous days in Ferghanah. His well-known attachment to the Naqshbandi Sufi order obviously did not preclude him from demonstrating his reverence for other devotional figures. It only reminds readers how much Sufi spiritualism meant to him, as it did to later Timurid-Mughal rulers.

Babur also conquered a Hindustan where his second language, Persian, had long been used as an administrative language and where many Iranian migrants had created a thriving Persianate historical and literary culture. New Persian – Persian written in the Arabic script – had begun to thrive under the patronage of the Samanids of Bukhara – owners of the *ghulam*, who later established the Ghaznavid state. The Samanid dynasty had been founded in 892 by an ethnically Iranian land-owning family, whose members had served as governors for the ʿAbbasid Caliphs. An early example of the sultanate phenomenon analysed by Ibn Khaldun is that the Samanids helped to foster the reappearance of Persian language and literature at a time before Oghuz Turks and Mongols overran Mawarannahr and Iran. A period memorably labelled the 'Persian Intermezzo' by the Russian émigré scholar Vladimir Minorsky, its great monument and credit to Samanid patronage was the epic Persian poem of Firdausi (940–1020), the *Shah-Namah*.[27]

From this period forward, Persian gradually became established as the administrative language and high cultural lingua franca of the eastern Islamic world. In Afghanistan and India, first Ghazna and then Lahore attracted Persian-language poets and writers. These included Sanaʾi Ghaznavî (1045–1131), Masʿud Saʿd Salman (1048–c. 1131) and the important Iranian philosophically influenced historian Bayhaqi (c. 995–1077). Salman, whose family emigrated from Hamadan in Iran to Lahore, helped to introduce Persian, which also became the prestigious lingua franca of South Asian Muslims. It was also in Lahore that the scholar of Sufi orders Hujwiri (c. 990–1072) wrote the first extant of Persian-language treatise on Sufism – the *Kashf al-Mahjub*.

The emigration of Iranian literati that began with the Ghaznavids, continued with the later Ghaznavids in Lahore and through the reign of the Delhi Sultans, as both émigrés and native-born Indian Muslims generated a formidable Persianate literature well before Babur arrived.[28] Indeed, the Sultanate years featured the most famous Indo-Persian poet in South Asian Muslim literary history. This was Amir Khusrau Dihlavi (1253–1325), the single Indo-Persian writer who was and still is well known in the wider Persianate world beyond India and a poet whose work Babur's father, ʿUmar Shaikh Mirza, knew well.[29] Babur was familiar with Amir Khusrau, since he had heard his father recite some of the poet's verses in Ferghanah. No Persian-language poet of the Timurid-Mughal era ever achieved comparable fame.

Amir Khusrau is a memorable figure, important in Indo-Muslim cultural history for a number of reasons, not the least for his vast corpus of works in various modes, including the *Nuh sipihr*, or 'Nine Spheres', in which he wrote implicitly challenging Babur's later negative reaction to India – *kishvar-i Hind ast bihishti bizamin*, 'The country of India is paradise on earth'.[30] He is also well known for his *masnavi, Qiran al-sa'dain*, 'The Conjunction of Jupiter and Venus' – the 'celebration' of an astrological moment usually associated with Temür or with his descendant, the Timurid-Mughal ruler Shah Jahan, who claimed to be the 'Second Lord of the Auspicious Conjunction'.[31]

Amir Khusrau is significant for two other reasons. He was the first prominent Indo-Persian writer who also wrote in Hindavi or Hindi, which other Sufi authors of the Sultanate period used to create an entire body of what might be termed devotional romances.[32] He is also associated with two major Sultanate cultural figures: the Indo-Persian historian Zia al-Din Barani (1285–1357), one of the three outstanding historians of the era, and Nizam al-Din Auliya (d. 1325), the Chishti Sufi whose shrine Babur circumambulated at Delhi and which continues to be the focus of moving devotional performance known as *Qawwali*.[33] Khusrau, Barani and Nizam al-Din, the poet, historian and Persian-speaking Sufi, collectively personify the vitality of Indo-Persian culture in the late thirteenth and fourteenth centuries.[34]

If the Sultanate bequeathed to Babur a sophisticated clerical class and thriving Indo-Persian literary culture, it also left him and his descendants with a large population of Afghans who had been moving into Hindustan since the mid-thirteenth century if not well before. Regarded as useful auxiliary forces by Sultanate rulers, Afghans were perceived as frightening barbarians by some Indo-Persian intellectuals, 'the lowest and basest of the low and base born'.[35] The sophisticated Amir Khusrau characterised Afghans living in and around Delhi as 'Man-slaying demons… Their heads are like big sacks of straw, their beards like combs of the wearer, long-legged as the stork but more ferocious than the eagle… Their voices horse and shrill like that of a jack-daw, their mouths open like a shark…'[36] Nonetheless, whatever their appearance, the late thirteenth-century Sultanate ruler Balaban (r. 1266–87) settled large numbers of Afghans on lands in the Sind and northwestern India. 'Alal al-Din Khalji (1296–1361) enrolled many to help defend the northwest during the Mongol invasions, and he also began appointing some Afghans to high military ranks.[37] These tribesmen continued to enter India in large numbers during Muhammad Tughluq's reign, and two clans of Ludi Afghans were among the Afghans who secured important positions in the later Tughluq era and again following Temür's invasion and sacking of Delhi in 1398. Indeed, one Ludi chieftain held Sambhal in the post-Temür era and another, Daulat Khan Ludi, exercised considerable power in the Punjab at this time.[38]

The Political Context in 1526

When Babur entered Hindustan in December 1526, he arrived in a country with a turbulent Muslim political history, a substantial Indo-Muslim population with a highly developed clerical class and Sufi tradition, a vibrant Indo-Persian cultural tradition and a large, contentious population of Afghans. What naturally concerned him the most at that precise moment was the political situation, and he briefly summarised what he knew or later learned about the topography of rule in India. He identified seven 'respected and independent rulers' of Hindustan at the time of his invasion, while just alluding to the existence of 'many rajas' throughout Hindustan, some submissive to Muslim rule, the others independent. Of the seven major states, he lists five Muslim and two Hindu dynasties and links several of the Muslim rulers with the Tughluqs – the last pre-Timurid dynasty of the Delhi Sultanate. [39]

These five Muslim rulers are as follows: First was Ibrahim Ludi (1517–26) of the Ludi Afghan tribal confederation (1451–1526), whose ancestors, Babur reports, had been 'water-carriers', *saghgha*, of the Tughluqs (c. 1320–98). They were successors to the ephemeral Sayyid dynasty (1414–51) that came to power in the Punjab and Delhi after Temür's invasion. Second was Sultan Muhammad Muzaffar of Gujrat (Gujerat) (d. 1526) of the Muzaffarid dynasty (1391–1583), a descendant of Rajput converts to Islam, whose forbearers had been 'wine servers', *sharabdar*, to the Tughluqs. Third were the Bahmanis of the Deccan (1347–1527), whose founder had been a governor who revolted against the Tughluqs, but whose rulers in Babur's day had been reduced to figureheads. Fourth was Sultan Mahmud of Malwa or Mandu, its capital city, the ruler of a dynasty (1392–1562) Babur identifies as Khilji (Khalji), whose founder had been a governor of the Tughluqs. [40] At that time, Babur wrote that this dynasty had lost most of its territory to the Rajput, Rana Sanga'. Fifth was Nusrat Shah of Bengal, a member of the brief Husain Shahi dynasty (1494–1538), whose father, Babur reports, was a *saiyid*, a descendant of the Prophet Muhammad, and therefore, of Arab descent. The two Hindu rulers Babur mentions are: the Raja of Vijayanagar of the Tuluva dynasty (1503–1614) in the Deccan and Rana Sanga' of Chitor in Mewar (r. 1484–1528), who had become a major force in Rajasthan, Central India and increasingly in the Duab.

Babur confronted and defeated the two most formidable rulers of these dynasties, Ibrahim Ludi in 1526 and Rana Sanga, in 1527 in victories that secured, for the moment at least, a Hindustan empire for the Timurids. In December 1528, he celebrated his achievement with a ceremony that proclaimed his triumph. What makes this celebration especially poignant is that following these triumphs and other successful campaigns, he seemed to realise the enormity of the task he had set himself in invading India, with large numbers of hostile Afghans still in the field and innumerable independent Hindu rulers dotting the landscape. In these years he was, as he admits, depressed, plagued by increasingly severe illnesses and desperately missing his old friends, many of whom had fled back to Kabul to escape India's climate. Babur also expressed his wish to return to the congenial and relatively carefree life he had created in Afghanistan and rule India from there. Yet, as he also admitted in a touching late poem, he was, due to his own ambition, trapped in Hindustan. By late 1530, Babur was exhausted and, as he told his young daughter, tired of rule. He died in December 1530 surrounded by his wives and children.

Endnotes

1   Eiji Mano, *Bâbur-nâma* (*Vaqâyiʿ*), (*Critical Edition Based on Four Chaqhatay Texts with Introduction and Notes by Eiji Mano*) (Kyoto: Syokado, 1995), f. 185b. (Afterwards cited as BN–M.) He quotes the saying in Persian, suggesting it came from a Persian language poet such as Saʿadi Shirazi, whose verse contain numerous useful aphorisms of this kind.

2   Babur once uses the term *Gurkhan* taken from the Turco-Mongol term *kurgan* or son-in-law, when he praises Humayun's first military victory in India in March 1526 as an *ish Gurkani*, 'a Timurid act.' Temür acquired this title after marrying a Chinggisid woman. BN–M, f. 263a.

3   The best English translation remains the carefully edited edition of Annette Susannah Beveridge, *The Bâbur-nâma in English* (London: Luzac, repr. 1969) (Afterwards cited as BN–B.)

4   BN–M, f. 339a.

5   Mirza Haydar Dughlat, *Tarikh-i Rashidi, A History of the Khans of Mughulistan*, ed. W. M. Thackston (Cambridge, Massachusetts: Harvard University, 1996) and Mirza Haydar Dughlat, *Tarikh-i Rashidi, A History of the Khans of Mughulistan*, trans. and ed. W. M. Thackston (Cambridge, Massachusetts: Harvard University, 1996) (Afterwards cited as TR.) and Annette S. Beveridge, *The History of Humâyûn* (*Humâyûn-Nâma*) (London: Royal Asiatic Society Oriental Translation Fund, 1902) (Afterwards cited as HN).

6   William Erskine, '*A History of India under the First Two Sovereigns of the House of Taimur, Babur and Humâyun*' (London: Longman *et al.*, 1854) (Volume 1), 519–23, citing the work of Mountstuart Elphinstone. *The History of India*, (London: John Murray, 1843), Volume 2, 117–19.

7   BN–M, f. 201a.

8   Reuben Levy, ed., *The Nasîhat Nâma Known as Qâbûs Nâma of Kai Kâʾûs b. Iskandar b. Qâbûs Washmgîr* (London: Luzac, 1951).

9   Abûʾl Fazl ʿÂllâmî, *The Âʾin-i-Akbarî*, trans. H. Blochmann and ed. D. C. Phillott (New Delhi: Crown Publications, repr. 1988) Volume 1, 112 and *The Akbar Nâmâ*, trans. H. Beveridge and ed. D. C. Phillott (Delhi: ESS ESS Publications, repr. 1987), Volume 1, 278.

10 BN–M, fs. 64a–b.

11 BN–M, f. 349a.

12 BN–M, f. 227b.

13 See BN–M, fs.120a–125a, for Babur's compelling description of these events, so astounding even to him that he attributed them to God's will.

14 For a beautifully illustrated introduction to this important work, see Maria Shreve Simpson and Louise Marlow, *Princeton's Great Persian Book of Kings: The Peck Shahnama* (Princeton: Princeton University Art Museum, 2015).

15 Sunil Kumar, *The Emergence of the Delhi Sultanate* (Delhi: Permanent Black, 2007), 102. Kumar includes an excellent discussion of the entire Ghurid slave apparatus, including the Turks' training and reputations as fighters, 78–105. They were the dominant military commanders of Mu'izzi dominions in North India, 77. See also his fascinating list of predominantly Turkic *ghulam*s in the reign of Iltutmish, the *ghulam* and successor to the Ghurids, 154–57.

16 Stephen Frederic Dale, *The Orange Trees of Marrakesh, Ibn Khaaldun and the Science of Man* (Cambridge: Harvard University Press, 2015).

17 For an informative discussion of al-Mawardi's ideas see Erwin I. J. Rosenthal, *Political Thought in Medieval Islam* (Cambridge: Cambridge University Press, 1968), 27–37.

18 *Sultan* literally means power or domination, which was not legitimised by Islam or any religious doctrine.

19 Peter Jackson, *The Delhi Sultanate* (Cambridge: Cambridge University Press, 1999), 57.

20 Kumar, *The Emergence of the Delhi Sultanate*, 226 and see 226–35 for Kumar's discussion of Iltutmish's religious policies and relations with the '*ulama*'.

21 Ibn Battuta, *The Travels of Ibn Battuta A.D. 1325–1354*, trans. C. Defrémery and B. R. Sanguinetti (Cambridge: Cambridge University Press for the Hakluyt Society, 1971), Volume 3, 674–83.

22 Ibid., 595.

23 For Husain Baiqara, see the excellent article by Hans R. Roemer in the *Encyclopaedia Iranica*, '*Husayn Bâyqarâ* 2012, Volume 12, Fasc. 5, 508–11.

24 Thomas W. Lentz and Glenn D. Lowry, *Timur and the Princely Vision, Persian Art and Culture in the Fifteenth Century* (Washington D.C.: Smithsonian Institution Press, 1989), 69–74, 109. This splendid volume is the best introduction to the nature and scope of the Timurid culture, which was essentially Perso-Islamic art and culture.

25 Ibid., 86.

26 Thierry Zarcone, 'Central Asian Influences on the Early Development of the Chishtiyya Sufi Order in India,' in *The Making of Indo Persian Culture*, ed. Muzaffar Alam, François 'Nalini' Devoye and Marc Gaborieau (Delhi: Manohar for the Centre Des Sciences Humaines, 2000), 99–117.

27 Vladimir Minorsky, '*La Domination de Dailamites*' Musée Guimet (Paris: Leroux, 1932), 21.

28 For the later Ghaznavids, who took refuge in the Punjab following the Oghuz Saljuq's migrations/invasion, see C. E. Bosworth, *The Later Ghaznavids: Splendour and Decay* (Edinburgh: Edinburgh University Press, 1977).

29 Sunil Sharma has written a lucid, knowledgeable and sympathetic account of Amir Khusrau titled *Amir Khusraw The Poet of Sultans and Saints* (Oxford: One World, 2005). See also Muhammad Wahid Mirza, *The Life and Times of Amir*

Khusrau (Delhi: Idarah-i Adabiyat-i Delhi, repr. 1974), 6–16, who believes Amir Khusrau's father's family were Turks, who possibly originated in Shar-i sabz, Temür's birthplace, and came to India during Chinggis Khan's campaigns in the early thirteenth century.

30   The Persian text is available in a scholarly edition produced by Muhammad Wahid Mirza, ed., *The Nuh Sipihr of Amir Khusrau (in 1318 A.D.)* (Jaipur: Historical Research Documentation Program, 1981), Volume 3, 151.

31   The *masnavi* in Persian is a poem of indeterminate length, often devoted to romantic or didactic subjects.

32   See Aditya Behl, *Loves Subtle Magic: An Indian Islamic Literary Tradition* 1370–1545 (New York: Oxford University Press, 2012), for an introduction to this fascinating devotional literature, often influenced by Persian models.

33   For an introduction to Nizam al-Din Auliya and a text of his conversations, see Bruce B. Lawrence, *Nizam Ad-Din Awliya: Morals for the Heart* (New York: Paulist Press, 1992). See also the account of these devotional performances that Regula Burckhardt Qureshi describes and carefully analyses in her work *Sufi Music of India and Pakistan, Sound, Context and Meaning in Qawwali* (Cambridge: Cambridge University Press, 1986).

34   The well-connected Barani wrote a number of important works including the *Ta'rikh-i Firuz Shahi* (1357). See Peter Jackson's discussion of Barani and other Sultanate era historians, *The Delhi Sultanate*, 49–60.

35   Kumar, *The Emergence of the Delhi Sultanate*, 314.

36   Quoted by Kumar in *The Emergence of the Delhi Sultanate*, 315.

37   Jackson, *The Delhi Sultanate*, 174.

38   For a summary of Afghan settlement and influence, see especially Rita Joshi, *The Afghan Nobility and the Mughals 1526–1707* (Delhi: Vikas, 1985), Chapters 1 and 2.

39   BN–M, fs. 270a–272a.

40   Rulers of the second major Delhi Sultanate dynasty (1290–1320), the Khilji or Khalji, may have been descendants of Turks long resident in and assimilated to society in Afghanistan.

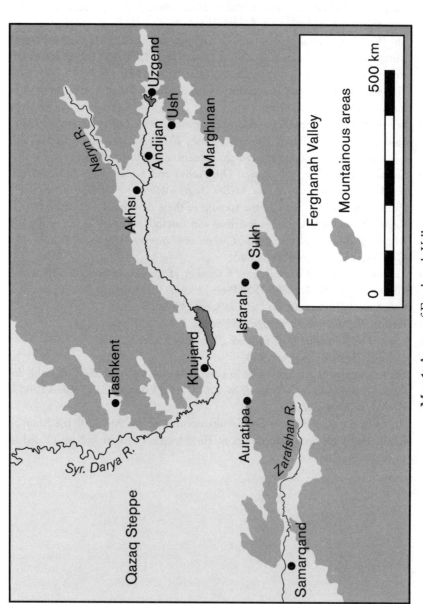

Map 1: A map of Ferghanah Valley

1

Qazaq: A Timurid Vagabond

Ferghanah and Samarqand

In 1488, the 5-year-old Zahir al-Din Muhammad Babur – the future founder of the Timurid-Mughal Empire of India – travelled more than 300 miles from his home in the Ferghanah Valley westward to the ancient Central Asian city of Samarqand, which was formerly the capital of the Turco-Mongol conqueror Temür (1336–1405). Babur, the eldest son of 'Umar Shaikh Mirza (d. 1494), a fourth-generation descendant of Temür, very likely left on his journey from his father's base at Akhsı. It was a Ferghanah town and citadel located high on the north bank of the Syr Darya River.[1] He was probably escorted on his trip by his mother Qutluq Nigar Khanım (d. 1505) – the second daughter of Yunas Khan (d. 1487), the recently deceased Khan of the Chaghatai Mongols and a direct descendant of Chinggis Khan (1162–1227). Babur was taken to Samarqand to be betrothed to his equally young first cousin 'Ayisha Sultan Begim – the daughter of his paternal uncle Ahmad Mirza (d. 1494), the ruler of Samarqand. He consummated the marriage eleven years later in 1500, noting the event with a single laconic sentence in his autobiography. 'Sultan Ahmad Mirza's daughter, named 'Ayisha Sultan Begim, whom my father and hers affianced to me, came to Khujand and I married her in the month of Sha'ban.'[2]

By his descent from both Temür and Chinggis Khan, Babur inherited an impeccable Central Asian, Turco-Mongol legitimacy. Since he was a patrilineal descendant of Temür, Babur was a Timurid, and the dynastic identity doubled by the marriage to his young cousin. He and his male relations derived their imperial ambitions from Temür, an Islamised member of the Barlas tribe – a Turkicised Mongol tribe – whose homeland was located near Kish, 48 miles south of Samarqand. While not a descendant of Chinggis Khan, Temür married into the Chinggisid line taking the title *Gurkan* or son-in-law, and he assumed the title Temür Gurkan. *Gurkanian* became the official dynastic name of the Timurids of Central Asia as well as their Indian descendants. Babur does not, however, use this term to refer to his own political lineage. He once alludes to himself as one of the *Timuriyeh Salatını*, 'Timurid Sultans', but more commonly, he refers to Temür's descendants, including himself, simply as Turks.[3] He does so, as will be seen, when he states his claim to Hindustan while narrating a raid on the western Punjab in 1519. Babur never uses the Persian term Mughal or, more accurately, Mughul – the Persian or Farsi term for Mongol – to identify his political lineage.[4] Despite his maternal Mongol descent, he repeatedly condemns the Mongol military culture, decrying its barbarism and political treachery, even while exploiting Mongol military skills that helped him win his first two critical Indian battles in 1526 and 1527. The mistaken use of Mughal to identify Babur's Indian dynasty is a later accretion, which became popular in the nineteenth century. It has probably contributed to, or even created the mistaken notion that Babur personified Central Asian Mongol barbarism.

Temür sought to replicate the Mongol ruler's conquests, and during his life, he mimicked Chinggis Khan's unrelenting ambition in campaigns of appalling barbarism. From the 1350s until his death in 1405, he campaigned first to extend his authority beyond Kish to Mawarannahr – the 'land beyond the river'. It is the Arabic term for the lands between the Amu Darya and Syr Darya Rivers known in Western sources as Transoxiana.[5] By 1370, he had subjugated most of this territory, and in the same year, he proclaimed himself sovereign of the Chaghatai line of Mongol Khans, implicitly claiming the former territory of Chinggis Khan's second son, who inherited his father's Central Asian provinces. In the following decade, Temür led successful campaigns north to Khwarizm on the Aral Sea and then east, crossing the mountains in 1380 to occupy Kashgar in the present-day Chinese Xinjiang province. Xinjiang was the homeland of Chaghatai Mongol tribes, including some of Babur's maternal relatives. In 1383, he burst out of Mawarannahr to the west, ravaging Iran, Iraq, Armenia and Georgia in a series of exceptionally ruthless campaigns, slaughtering tens of thousands and leaving behind his signature towers of skulls in the devastated cities of the region.

Between 1383 and 1394, Temür also fought a prolonged series of difficult battles with the Khan of the Golden Horde, prompting his invasion of the southern Russian steppes, eventually leading to a brief occupation of Moscow in 1395. Later, he returned east, and in 1398, marched swiftly into northwestern India and plundered Delhi of its treasure, elephants and artisans. After India, Temür returned west again, campaigning against the Turkic-Muslim Mamluks of Egypt, overrunning their Syrian possessions and briefly occupying Damascus in 1401, where he met and conversed at length with the philosophical historian Ibn Khaldun. Baghdad was occupied, sacked and its inhabitants slaughtered in the same year. In 1402, he moved quickly west into Anatolia to shatter an Ottoman army near Ankara, capturing Sultan Bayezid I, who remained a captive until his death a year later. Returning to his capital Samarqand in 1404, Temür planned an invasion of Ming China (1368–1644). In December 1404, he marched out of his capital for China, but died en route in February 1405 at Otrar in modern Kazakhstan.[6]

Temür did not, however, attempt directly to administer most of the territories he invaded, ravaged and plundered, with the exception of his homeland in Mawarannahr, Iran and its immediate western borderlands and Afghanistan. Following his death, it was these lands his son Shah Rukh (1377–1447), then governor of Khurasan, fought for and eventually gained control of by 1417–18. His triumph climaxed the internecine struggle that broke out among Timurid kin after Temür's death. This was the first in a history of violent succession conflicts that bedeviled all Timurid states, including the Timurid-Mughal Empire of Hindustan. Ruling from Herat, Shah Rukh and his son Ulugh Beg (1394–1449), who administered Mawarannahr for his father from Samarqand, dominated the Timurid world for nearly half a century. Their territories included Babur's Ferghanah Valley homeland. The valley was strategically and economically important as it bordered the Chaghatai Mongol territory to the east of the mountains in Xinjiang, and served as a commercial corridor linking China with Central Asia and beyond. Neither Shah Rukh, or his son Ulugh Beg, exhibited the world-conquering ambitions of Temür, nor did they campaign with his unrestrained ferocity. Still, they retained a Timurid dominance – if only fitful control of these lands – even as Qaraqoyunlu Turks, Uzbeks and Chaghatai Mongols threatened their fragile enterprise from the west, northwest and east.

The easternmost Timurid territory – the Ferghanah Valley – is a small but fertile alluvial valley situated within the modern state of Uzbekistan. Nearly 165-miles long and 65-miles wide at the centre, mountains enclose the valley on the north, east and south sides. These mountains, Babur reports, were largely impassable in the winter. The easiest approach to the valley then and throughout the year was from the west.[7] The earliest known reference to Ferghanah in historical sources occurs in Arrian's histories of Alexander the Great's campaigns, which allude to his construction of Alexandria Eschate, 'Alexandria the Farthest' in 329 BCE.[8] This Alexandria, built on or near an earlier Achaemenid Iranian settlement, was located along the southern bank of the Syr Darya River near the western entrance to the valley. In Timurid times, the settlement on this site was known as Khujand, the village or town where Babur finally married his young Timurid cousin in 1500. Alexander's troops may have settled not only in Alexandria Eschate, but possibly moved into Ferghanah as the valley was known in early sources of Han China (206 BCE–220 CE) as *Da-yuan* – two Chinese characters sometimes translated as 'The Great Ionians'.

In fact, it was Zhang Qian, the Han Chinese emissary to the nomadic Yuezhi tribal confederation, who compiled the earliest extant account of Ferghanah in 129 BCE. His account is the most extensive and informative description of the valley prior to Babur's detailed report, with which he began his autobiography more than 1500 years later. Zhang Qian reported to the Han Chinese emperor that:

> Dayuan lies southwest of the country of the Xiongnu [the nomadic enemies of the Yuezhi and the Han Chinese] some 10,000 Li southwest of China. The people are settled on the land, ploughing the fields and growing rice and wheat. They also make wine out of grapes. The region has many fine horses, which sweat blood; their forbearers are supposed to have been fouled from heavenly horses. The people live in fortified cities, there being some seventy or more cities of various sizes in the region. The population numbers several hundred thousand.[9]

By putting the Chinese state in contact with western Central Asia, Zhang Qian's diplomatic mission also led to the rise of what became known in the nineteenth-century Europe as the Seidenstrasse or Silk Road. This phrase refers to commercial exchanges along various routes that linked China with India to the south and Iran, Rome and the Mediterranean world to the west. Yet, while Chinese silk later gave its name to this commerce and these routes in the nineteenth century, it was the 'blood sweating, heavenly horses' he mentions that first attracted the attention of Chinese officials. Han Chinese rulers coveted steppe horses, which they needed to combat the incursions and invasions of the powerful Xiongnu pastoral nomads into Han territory. Consequently, following Zhang Qian's mission, they sent diplomatic missions to Ferghanah to acquire some of these celebrated animals. When unnamed rulers in the valley refused to part with any animals, Han officials responded by dispatching military expeditions from distant Xian that overwhelmed Ferghanah forces and compelled them to supply the Chinese with breeding stock.

Zhang Qian's mission brought Han China to Central Asia and the Ferghanah Valley, eventually leading to commercial exchanges of Chinese, Indian and West Asian goods. Just a few years before his mission a sub-tribe of the Yuezhi, known in Chinese as the Guishang, began the process that subsequently linked Central Asia with North India in a single state. At that time, the Yuezhi/Guishang had begun to move southwestward through Mawarannahr across the Amu Darya, gradually overwhelming the Bactrian Greek Kingdom of Mawarannahr, Afghanistan and northwestern Punjab. Bactria had earlier been a province of the Greek Seleucid state (312 BCE –64 BCE), which was Alexander the Great's easternmost political legacy. The Yuezhi/Guishang process of migration and conquest culminated a century later in the formation of the Guishang or Kushana Empire of Central Asia and northern India, which endured until the third century CE. The Empire evidently included the Ferghanah Valley as well as the town of Kashgar and eastern Xinjiang.[10] Controlling a land empire that extended from Central Asia to the Gangetic Valley, the Kushana Empire stimulated the earliest documented commercial and cultural interchange between China and India. This included Chinese silk exported to India, with Indian cotton, Buddhism and Buddhist artefacts exported to Central Asia and China.

Zhang Qian's account and the establishment of the Kushana state alerts readers to two important facts about the Ferghanah Valley in his time, which also held true for Babur's era. First, unlike most of the surrounding territory – home to pastoral nomads of various ethnicities – the valley's population was largely sedentary, perhaps partly settled with wine-loving Greeks. It was an agrarian society that supported multiple urban sites of indeterminate size mentioned in Zhang Qian's account. In Babur's days, as during the Han era in China, the Ferghanah Valley was home to settled inhabitants – by his time primarily Turks, Iranians and Mongols. Most of this population was composed of agriculturalists or inhabitants of the valley's modest urban settlements. His own base of Andijan in the eastern section of the valley was, he reports, populated entirely by Turks, all of whom spoke his native language Turki. According to Babur this Turkic dialect was identical to the language spoken by the outstanding Turki poet of Herat Mir 'Ali Shir Nava'i (1441–1501).[11]

Babur was never at any point in his life a barbarous, pastoral nomadic tribesman. He matured in a civilised urban environment. His character can be understood from his largely admiring portrait of his father 'Umar Shaikh Mirza, who presided over the modest but important urban settlement and fortress of Akhsı. Babur evidently spent his early childhood here before being sent to preside over a fortress of his own in Andijan, sometime before his 12th year. As Babur describes him 'Umar Shaikh acted politically like a Timurid, a member of the Turco-Mongol warrior class, whose profession was war and conquest. In his son's account, '[a]s Umar Shaikh Mirza was a Padshah of high ambition and great purpose he was always predisposed to conquest, (*mulkgirliq*)'.[12] He reports that his father led several unsuccessful campaigns against Samarqand, held by his elder brother Sultan Ahmad Mirza, and once fought and lost a battle with his father-in-law, the Khan of the Chaghatai Mongols – Yunas Khan. It was typical of this late fifteenth-century period, however, that Timurids and Chaghatai Mongols fought internecine battles with one another rather than campaigning outside their home territories.

In saying this about his father, Babur was not being critical, for he continues by characterizing 'Umar Shaikh in terms that make him appear as a Timurid ideal – a kind of perfectly balanced Turco-Mongol aristocratic warrior. Thus, he says his father was unpretentious or unceremonious (*bitakalluf*), generous, good-humoured, eloquent, sweet-speaking (*shirin zaban*), brave and manly (*shuja' u mardanah*) and a good swordsman. He was also, Babur says, a congenial person (*khush suhbat kishi*), and, like so many of his Turco-Mongol kin, a great drinker, although later in life he came to prefer the intoxicating sweet *ma'jun*. In this as in so many other respects, Babur later came to resemble 'Umar Shaikh Mirza.

If these traits defined Babur's ideal Turco-Mongol warrior, his description of 'Umar Shaikh's literary interests and religious practice illumined what he believed to be preferred traits of an urbane and pious ruler. His father was, he reports, learned (*rawan sawadi*), by which he seems to allude to his father's knowledge of Persian language writers – in his case, the romantic poet Nizami Ganjavi (1141–1209), the Iranian Anatolian Sufi poet Jalal al-Din Muhammad Rumi (1207–73), the prolific, multitalented Indo-Persian writer Amir Khusrau Dihlavi (1253–1325) and Abu'l Qasim Firdausi Tusi (c. 940–1020), the author of the great Iranian epic the *Shah Namah*.[13] Babur undoubtedly knew when he wrote the *Vaqayi'* that two of these writers, Nizami and Amir Khusrau, were the two Persian language poets most respected by the influential literati of Herat, the Perso-Islamic and Turkic cultural centre of the late Timurid world, which he visited in the late fall of 1506.[14]

Babur also admired 'Umar Shaikh's religious beliefs and practices. He was, as his son reports, 'In morals and manners' a faithful Hanafi Sunni Muslim (*Hanafi mazhabliq*), who never neglected the five daily prayers and often read the *Quran*. He was also a *murid* or disciple of the most influential Naqshbandi Sufi of the age, Khwajah 'Ubaidullah Ahrar (d. 1490), who often visited him and called him son. He displayed his composite identity as a Turco-Mongol and a Muslim by wearing a Mongol cap, a *börk*, except when he sat in court, when he exchanged it for a turban, which the Mongols and steppe peoples generally associated with Islam. Babur also emphasises that when 'Umar Shaikh ruled, he followed the Perso-Islamic ideal of the 'Just Sultan'. He illustrates this by telling how his father was just, *'adalat*, once carefully preserving the goods for the families of merchants who had died in a snowstorm as they traversed the passes between Khitai (China), and the Ferghanah Valley.

Babur too was a life-long Hanafi Sunni Muslim and a disciple of Ahrar. Like most of his Timurid contemporaries, he was literate in his native Turki, but also read and wrote Persian, the prestigious *lingua franca* of Mawarannahr. As his writing unmistakably demonstrates, Babur always preferred to reside among and rule over what he termed an *ahl-i ma'mur*, a settled or sedentary populace, rather than having to deal with *sahra nishin*, steppe dwellers or often simply pastoral nomads. He characterises *sahra nishin* with a number of derogatory adjectives:

sadiq (simple), *rusta'i* (rustic), *qazaqanah* (vagabond-like), or *turk* (a synonym for simple, rustic and vagabond-like). Even when his young Chaghatai Mongol uncle, known as Ahmad or Alacha Khan, came to Mawarannahr in 1502 from the Chaghatai Mongol homelands in Xinjiang to aid Timurids in their struggle against their joint Uzbek enemy, Babur gently criticised him. He reports that although he was a Muslim, Ahmad Khan displayed steppe traits, being 'rather simple, *rusta'i-raq* and rough-spoken, *darashtgui-raq idi'*. Visiting his uncle's tent he found melon rinds, grapes and saddlery thrown about in a *bitakallufanih* a dishevelled, careless or disorderly manner.[15]

Not only was the Ferghanah Valley historically, during Babur's lifetime, a region of sedentary agricultural and urban settlement, but it was in direct and constant contact with the great urban civilisations to the west and east. It served for nearly two millennia as one of the principal routes for Silk Road commerce. Merchants travelled from Chang'an, today's Xi'an, in north central China or more immediately from Kashgar in Xinjiang, through Ferghanah to Samarqand and then south and west to the great emporia of India, Iran and Byzantium. Traders and Buddhist pilgrims from South Asia and Afghanistan as well as Nestorian, Manicheans and Zoroastrians from Iran moved in the opposite direction.[16] Indeed, during the Kushana era and for several centuries afterward, Samarqand, which was Temür's capital, developed into a major Silk Road commercial *entrepôt*, as ethnically Iranian merchants from the city and surrounding region known as Soghdiana dominated this trade. Soghdians continued to participate in Silk Road commerce until at least the tenth century.

Commerce continued to flow along Silk Road routes in later centuries and was supplemented in the late fourteenth and early fifteenth centuries, when the Ming Chinese sent several missions to Samarqand, and the Timurids replied with at least one to China. The first Chinese delegation arrived in 1395. Others reached Herat in 1409, 1412 and 1417. A mission from Temür's son Shah Rukh, in Herat, arrived in the Chinese capital in 1421.[17] The overland commerce between China, Mawarannahr and South Asia never ceased, despite the later opening of the sea routes. In later Timurid times, it continued, albeit with merchants from different ethnic communities. From his earliest years, Babur would have seen merchant caravans moving east and west through the valley. Later in his autobiography when Babur describes Kabul, where he ruled between 1504 and 1525 before invading India, he describes Central Asian merchants he saw in the Afghan city, some of whom, he reports, came from Ferghanah, carrying Chinese goods.[18]

Still, despite its agricultural wealth, long history of agrarian and urban settlement and role in Silk Road commerce, Babur's Ferghanah homeland paled in historic, cultural, economic and political significance when compared with Temür's former capital Samarqand.[19] The lack of any surviving architectural monuments, either at Akhsı – the site of 'Umar Shaikh Mirza's capital, where only scattered pottery fragments testify to the site's earlier significance – or in Andijan – Babur's own base to the southeast, now exhibiting only faintest traces of surviving mud brick walls that once encircled this fortified settlement – reflects the modest size and resources of the Ferghanah Valley and its urban settlements. In military terms, Babur notes that the population of the valley in his day could yield only about 4,000 troops from its population. Samarqand, in contrast, situated to the southwest in the fertile Zarafshan river valley, was one of the oldest and most important cities in Mawarannahr.[20]

The site of Samarqand had been settled at least by the seventh century BCE. During the rule of the Achaemenid Empire of Iran (550 BCE–330 BCE), it became that state's easternmost administrative garrison and a likely early centre for the spread of Iranian culture into Mawarannahr. Later ravaged by Mongols, along with Bukhara, Balkh and other major cities in the region, it recovered its importance under Temür, who distinguished himself from militantly anti-urban Mongols by directing an ostentatious building program in the city. Using plunder and captives from his devastating campaigns, including captives taken in the Indian invasion of 1398, he constructed a splendid urban environment of architectural monuments and formal gardens in Samarqand. Here, he strove to legitimise himself to his predominantly Muslim audience by, among other gestures, publically playing chess with *saiyids* – men who claimed descent from the Prophet Muhammad.[21]

Anyone hoping to understand the type of society and state Babur envisioned when he descended into the plains of the Punjab from Kabul in 1526 ought first to read his loving description of Samarqand, later his even more elaborate, appreciative account of Herat – Shah Rukh's capital in Iranian Khurasan, and still later his critique of Hindustan. Babur may have been half Mongol, who grew up in modest Ferghanah towns of Akhsı and Andijan, but he wrote his autobiography as a sophisticated urbanite, who revelled in the physical pleasures and sophisticated Perso-Islamic religious and scientific culture of great cities of the eastern Islamic world. Whether or not he was awed by his visit to Samarqand at age five, writing as an adult he describes Temür's Samarqand, which he saw for the second time in November 1497 after his first occupation of the city. It was, he reports, one of the most pleasant cities in the inhabitable world.[22]

What made Samarqand in Babur's eyes such a 'fine' city was its importance as the great urban centre of the Mawarannahr region that, in his mind, included the ancient city of Bukhara. The population of these Central Asian cities was, he appreciatively reports, entirely composed of pious, observant Sunni Muslims, who historically included among their numbers, he argues, more important scholars than any other country.[23] Samarqand, in particular, possessed a splendid Timurid-created physical environment, imposing secular, religious and scientific architecture, gardens, fine *bazars* and rich meadows, which surrounded the city.

Among the *besyar 'ali imar'at*, 'very sublime buildings', erected by its Timurid Muslim rulers and their *beg*s or military elite, Babur especially admired two of Temür's structures – the Kök Saray, a four-story *kushk* or kiosk built within the ark or citadel, and the monumental stone mosque constructed by Indian stonemasons abducted from North India in 1398. The mosque featured a Quranic calligraphic inscription visible from a distance of 2 miles.[24] Temür's grandson Ulugh Beg, Babur reports, had left behind a *madrasah*, 'religious college', a *khanagah*, 'a Sufi hospice with an enormous dome', and an adjoining *hammam*, 'public bath'. Near this complex, Shah Rukh's son had also constructed a *masjid* or mosque, with wooden decorations arranged according to *khata'i naqshlar*, or 'Chinese designs', and a *qiblah* determined by *munajjim tariqi*, or 'astronomical methods'.[25] Babur's appreciative allusion to these methods referred to Ulugh Beg's patronage of mathematical and astronomical scholarship.

Timurid scientific culture had evolved to such an extent that during Ulugh Beg's rule in the first-half of the fifteenth century, Samarqand attracted scholars from throughout the eastern Muslim world, including Ottoman Istanbul. The astronomical research he patronised represented the Muslim revival of the Greek rationalist or philosophical tradition, which had been absorbed into the Islamic world from Greek texts translated during the cosmopolitan era of the 'Abbasid Caliphate (750–1258). At Ulugh Beg's observatory complex, scientists produced the *Zij-i Sultan-i Gurkani*. This work included an astronomical table and star catalogue, which by Babur's time had superseded the calculations that the Iranian Shi'i scholar Nasir al-Din Tusi (1201–74) had compiled for the Mongol Il-Khan rulers of Iran at their observatory near Tabriz in the thirteenth century.[26] Subsequently, Maharajah Sawai Jai Singh II replicated Ulugh Beg's observatory design in buildings he constructed in Jaipur, Rajasthan, between 1720 and 1738. The Rajput ruler also utilised Ulugh Beg's *Zij* tables when he composed his own astronomical study in 1733–34.

Babur's comments on these buildings and his informed allusion to Ulugh Beg's astronomical research are early entries in an autobiography that reveal him to be an individual who had matured in a society whose literate members embraced the urban Muslim cultural world. It was a highly Iranised Muslim culture in Mawarannahr. Apart from the Timurids' knowledge of Persian literature, art and architecture, Babur revealed an aspect of his cultural heritage by his praise for an important institution of Iranian civilisation – the formal garden. This was a geometrically precise landscape architectural tradition that was an integral element of Iran's pre-Islamic and Islamic society. Babur particularly valued formal gardens as sites for what he termed *suhbatlar* – social gatherings of the political and military elite, alcohol- or drug-fuelled social encounters with compatriots, featuring musical entertainments, literary recitals, political conferences and drunken debaucheries. He considered such social gatherings in these gardens to be a *sine qua non* of civilised life.

While describing Samarqand, he dwells on several gardens Temür built. One was the *Bagh-i dilkusha*, or 'Sweetheart Garden' with its avenue of popular trees leading to a *kushk* or kiosk decorated with paintings commemorating Temür's 1398 Indian campaign.[27] Five-year-old Babur may have first seen on its walls an account of his ancestor's lucrative plundering expedition to India, which left his descendants with a claim, however tenuous by the late fifteenth century, to a South-Asian empire. Nearby the 'Sweetheart Garden' was another smaller garden, which featured a small building known in Samarqand, and throughout Iran and Indo-Muslim world as a *Chini-Khanah*, a 'China House'. In this building, Temür displayed the porcelain an unnamed individual had brought from China – a valued Silk Road product and yet another example of the historic and continuous Chinese influence that was artistically manifested in Ulugh Beg's mosque. Other *Chini-Khanah*s were built in Timurid Herat, during its late fifteenth-century golden age, in Safavid Iran and in the Indian Deccan Sultanate of Golconda.[28]

The garden Babur most admired in Samarqand had been developed by one of the later Timurid *beg*s during the reign of Babur's uncle and Timurid father-in-law Sultan Ahmad Mirza. This *beg*, Darvish Muhammad Tarkhan, a maternal uncle of Sultan Ahmad Mirza, built a *charbagh*, or geometrically precise quadrilateral garden that Babur considered the model of urban garden landscape design. Of all the gardens built in and around Samarqand in the Timurid era, Babur writes:

> There were few equal to the *charbagh* of Muhammad Tarkhan in *safalıq*, *havalıq* and *maddinazarlıq* [charm, airiness and perspective].... In the *charbagh* lovely *narwanlar* [cypresses] and *sarv u sefidlar* [white cedars] have been planted *bileh siyaq* [with regularity] in rows. This is a perfect setting. Its one defect is that there is no large stream.[29]

Babur later applied the geometric norms and aesthetic principles of these gardens to those he constructed in and around Kabul between 1504 and 1525 and later in Agra as early as 1526. The same principles later determined the garden setting of the Taj Mahal.

Babur in Mawarannahr: 1494–1504

However much Babur recalled of Samarqand's architectural monuments and splendid gardens from his childhood visit, he did not dwell on the city's urban splendour when he opened his autobiography by describing the political tumult that engulfed him when his father died unexpectedly in Babur's 12th year on 8 June 1494. 'Umar Shaikh Mirza's death triggered a struggle among his Timurid and Mongol relatives for control of Ferghanah. In his opening sentence, Babur implicitly claimed to have inherited his father's authority, simply stating that in his 12th year during the month of Ramadan he became '*Padshah* [ruler] in the *vilayat* [province] of Ferghanah'.[30] As 'Umar Shaikh Mirza's eldest son he may well have assumed he would inherit the governorship of the province, but apart from his immediate family none of his Timurid or Chaghatai Mongol relatives recognised his authority in 1494. Instead, they mobilised troops and marched on Andijan with an evident intent to seize 'Umar Shaikh's Ferghanah province and either capture Babur or kill him.

His uncle and father-in-law, Ahmad Mirza of Samarqand, invaded the valley from the southwest, seizing several towns before camping outside Andijan. At roughly the same time, Babur's maternal uncle, the Chaghatai Mongol, Mahmud Khan of Tashkent, entered the valley from the northwest and besieged Akhsı, while his distant Mongol kinsman, the ruler of Kashgar Aba Bakr Dughlat (d. 1514), invaded Ferghanah by crossing the mountains from Xinjiang and occupying Uzgend at the extreme eastern end of the valley.[31] After relatively minor skirmishes, Babur's supporters were able to repulse the modest forces these three men led. Failing to take Andijan, Ahmad Shah retreated and died on his march back to Samarqand. Mahmud Khan, who fell ill during his march into the valley, returned to Tashkent, having been repulsed before Akhsı, while Babur's men attacked Aba Bakr Dughlat and chased him back over the mountains to Kashgar. The young Babur was able to retain control of the central valley, although he lost control of a number of small towns in the west.

This was the fragmented political world in which Babur manoeuvred as he sought to survive and prosper as a young but ambitious Timurid in 1494. Like his Timurid relatives, he sought to reconstitute Temür's state around his own person, but initially he and his men merely sought to consolidate their hold over the modest territory left to them in the Ferghanah Valley. After the initial danger of his relatives' incursions passed, members of his late father's household and commanders left Akhsı for Andijan implicitly recognizing the young Babur's new status. These included Babur's paternal grandmother Shah Sultan Begim, Jahangir – one of his two younger brothers, the '*haram* household' and 'Umar

Shaikh's *beg*s, his principal military staff, who now along with individual *yiğit* or young individual warriors, shifted their loyalty to 'Umar Shaikh's son. He reports that his father's *beg*s and *yiğitler*, his principal commanders and individual warriors, had all rallied to him in these first few dangerous months. Now, probably advised by the cleric and Naqshbandî Sufi Khwajah Maulanah Qazi, he organised his government by reappointing or rewarding these men. The outlying towns of Ush to the extreme southeast, Marghinan to the west and Akhsı – 'Umar Shaikh's capital – were assigned to three important individuals. The remainder of 'Umar Shaikh's men were appointed to head districts (*wilayat*), or given land (*yir*) or offices (*mauja*) or stipends (*wajh*).[32]

In describing these events in the opening pages of his autobiography, Babur introduces his readers to the turbulent social and political environment of the Ferghanah Valley and Mawarannahr in the late fifteenth century. He never steps back from his detailed narrative to identify and analyse the nature of the almost indefinably complex dynamics of this political milieu, which his audience of literate Turki speakers would have known from personal experience. Nonetheless, in his opening and subsequent account of events of these years, he offers reflective readers a wealth of data that reveal much about this Turco-Mongol dominated atomistic political situation, overlaid with a veneer of Persianate artistic and literary culture.

In contrast with the first half of the century when Ulugh Beg governed, however imperfectly, the entire Mawarannahr region on behalf of his father Shah Rukh, three major political claimants and thousands of individual Turks and Mongols, *beg*s and *yiğit*s manoeuvred for advantage there in the 1490s. Members of three lineages – Timurids, Chaghatai Mongols and Uzbeks – dominated the struggle for control of the region. Representing the Timurids were four brothers, who descended from Temür's third son Miranshah. These were Ahmad Mirza, the nominal ruler of Mawarannahr, but in reality, a man who controlled only Samarqand and its immediate hinterlands including Bukhara; 'Umar Shaikh Mirza, Babur's father, who presided over the Ferghanah Valley; Mahmud Mirza (d. 1495), who held lands in the region known as Badakhshan along the upper Amu Darya; and Ulugh Beg Kabuli (d. 1502), the ruler of Kabul and its environs in eastern Afghanistan. The Chaghatai Mongol and Babur's maternal uncle Mahmud Khan (d. 1509) held Tashkent, sometimes aided by his brother, Ahmad Khan (d. 1504), who was based east of the mountains in Aqsı in the present-day Xinjiang Province of China. Both Timurids and Chaghatai Mongols were threatened by the third contender for power in Mawarannahr – Shaibani Khan, the Chinggisid leader of the powerful Turco-Mongol Uzbek tribal confederacy that originated to the north in the Qipchaq steppe.[33] The Uzbeks had been raiding Timurid territories for decades before they began moving on the principal Timurid power centres in Mawarannahr and Iranian Khurasan in Babur's time.

Neither Timurids nor Mongols cooperated among themselves or with each other for shared dynastic ends. Realistically only dynamic, ruthless leaders, such as Temür or Chinggis Khan, could enforce common effort among the disparate armed groups inhabiting Mawarannahr. In this atomised or individualistic political situation of the 1490s when no such dominant figure had emerged, each Timurid and Chinggisid Mongol either imagined or claimed political legitimacy. Kinship ties meant something, but they did not ensure political loyalty. This was especially true when brothers were sons of different mothers, each of whom had his own household.

In Babur's case, not only did Ahmad Mirza, his uncle and father-in-law, attack Andijan, but his younger half-brother Jahangir (b. 1485), who had joined Babur in Andijan after 'Umar Shaikh's death, later challenged his brother's authority in Ferghanah.[34] Similarly, Babur's maternal or Chaghatai Mongol relatives attacked or supported him as circumstances or personal interests dictated. Like Ahmad Mirza, Mahmud Khan of Tashkent had marched into Ferghanah in 1494, but later, he loaned his nephew Mongol troops to help Babur recover his fortunes in the turbulent years that followed. Still later when Babur's fortunes turned for the worse, Mahmud Khan turned his back on his young Timurid nephew, lending troops to Jahangir and his Mongol allies.

Only Shaibani Khan Uzbek commanded a coherent, disciplined and consistently loyal tribal military force in Mawarannahr during this period. Timurids and Chaghatai Mongols in Mawarannahr competed for power with fragile retinues composed of their family's hereditary followers, sometimes numbering no more than a core group of 200 or 300 men, augmented as their fortunes rose, with coalitions of military entrepreneurs, seeking short-term advantage in their service. The core retinues consisted of relatives, sometimes clerics and Turkic and Mongol warriors with hereditary or long-term family service. These men usually controlled small contingents of their own, which they might pledge to one or another Timurid *Mirza* or Chinggisid *Khan*, depending on political circumstances.

Two such men who played pivotal roles in Babur's early campaigns were two non-Chinggisid Mongols, both 'great *begs*', important warriors, possessing their own armed retinues, previously in his father's service. These men were: Sultan Ahmad Tambal, a man initially loyal to Babur, and 'Ali Dust Tagha'i, also one of

Babur's original loyalists, who first betrayed and then reunited with him, only to equivocate as Babur's fortunes rose and precipitously fell in the last years of the century. Babur mentions dozens of other such men, whose constantly shifting loyalties were determined by their ruthlessly realistic pragmatism born in the political chaos of the age.

This was the political reality Babur faced as he tried to consolidate his authority in and around Andijan with a series of minor raids and skirmishes in the spring summer and fall of 1495. In addition, he tried to strengthen his position with diplomacy as he took time to visit Mahmud Khan, his Mongol uncle in Tashkent, whose attempt to seize Akhsı in 1494 can be attributed to his long rivalry with Babur's father. Given Mahmud Khan's earlier rivalry with 'Umar Shaikh Mirza it is not surprising that Babur came away from the meeting with nothing more than kind words from a man he nonetheless described as a person like 'his father and elder brother', his relation, his *tuqqan*. In fact, Babur alludes to the enmity between his father and Mahmud Khan, and reports that he visited his uncle solely for the purpose of gaining some prestige the visit might bring him in his political struggles.

It is doubtful if Babur gleaned any public benefit from his brief encounter with his Mongol uncle, although it is understandable that he thought it worth the trouble of visiting, given the multiple political claimants and power centres in Ferghanah. He never alludes to this meeting again, perhaps because in June or July 1496, his attention was diverted by the news of political chaos in Samarqand, which offered him the possibility of seizing Temür's capital, the goal of every ambitious young Timurid.

Succession struggles among Sultan Ahmad Mirza's kin had precipitated the collapse of authority in the city. After Ahmad's Mirza's death on his march back from Andijan in 1494, his chosen successor, his brother Sultan Mahmud Mirza, who had earlier ruled Badakhshan, died within a year. He left Samarqand to his 18-year-old son Baisunghar Mirza, two of whose brothers quickly challenged him. Learning of these events, Babur decided to leave Andijan and Ferghanah behind and exploit these divisions among his cousins to seize Samarqand for himself. 'Given a capital like Samarqand', he once remarks in one of his engaging autobiographical asides, 'why would a person wish to waste time in a place like Andijan'.[35] Later in the *Vaqayi'*, he similarly compared the choice between wealthy India and impoverished Kabul.

Babur joined with Baisunghar Mirza's two contending brothers to besiege Samarqand in the fall of 1496 and again, after a winter's pause, in the spring and summer of 1497, finally entering the beleaguered city in November 1497.[36] Taking

Samarqand was every Timurid's dream, but Babur later describes this success as a pyrrhic victory, for the city these three young men occupied was in desperate straits after their prolonged siege. Its inhabitants lacked food and could not plant new crops in the surrounding fields and gardens so late in the year. In these conditions, many men in the disparate coalition of perhaps 600 to 800 Turks and Mongols Babur had laboriously assembled began dissolving almost immediately. One who abandoned him, the Mongol, Sultan Ahmad Tambal, either seized or allied with Babur's younger brother Jahangir. With his own troops, plus this young Timurid for legitimacy, Tambal returned to the valley to besiege Andijan, evidently hoping to become a kingmaker of sorts in Babur's modest appanage.

When he had left Andijan to march on Samarqand, Babur claims that the fort, with his mother and grandmother in residence, was amply staffed with men. Now, however, responding to his family's plea for help, he abandoned Samarqand in February or March 1498, leaving the city to one of his nominal allies.[37] He turned back towards the valley, but shortly after leaving the city he learned that 'Ali Dust Tagha'i, one of his father's former *begs*, had opened Andijan's gates to his fellow Mongol Sultan Ahmad Tambal. With his now badly depleted remaining force of about 200 to 300 men, Babur decided to take refuge in Khujand. This was the town at the western entrance of the Ferghanah valley, where two years later he would consummate his marriage with his young Timurid cousin, Sultan Ahmad Mirza's daughter. The town was, he writes, 'a miserable place', that could scarcely hold even his small force.[38] After his arrival there, he heard that Ahmad Tambal had murdered his former tutor, the wealthy, distinguished cleric and Naqshbandi Sufi disciple, Maulanah Muhammad Qazi, who had helped to organise the defence of the town in Babur's absence.[39]

Recording his response to these devastating events, Babur offers readers an evocative personal memory that is unique in the literature of the pre-modern Islamic world. This passage, like his many later emotional asides, gives his work the humanistic substance that has attracted so many readers, illustrating why Babur's text is legitimately considered an autobiography and not just a political memoir. Writing as usual in his native Chaghatai Turki, he describes his turbulent emotions when he learned of his tutor's murder by remarking: 'Since I had known myself, *ta özümni bilip idim*, I had not known such grief and affliction',[40] later adding, 'I involuntarily wept'.[41] Apart from his startling portrait of a weeping Timurid, Babur's use of the reflexive Turki pronoun *özüm* is also significant because it indicates that in his 15th year, he saw himself as a youth who had come of age, a maturation accompanying puberty. This reading of the text is also suggested by a similar phrase found in modern Turkish. He had probably 'known' or seen himself as an adult since his 12th year, given the traditions of Turco-Mongol and Afghan societies at this time.

However distraught, Babur recalls that he quickly recovered his aggressive spirit. His mother and grandmother were allowed to join him – generosity to women captives being one of the very few courtesies of internecine Turco-Mongol conflicts. He once again contacted his Mongol uncle in Tashkent for help to resume his attempt on Samarqand and was loaned 4,000 or 5,000 troops, but upon hearing Shaibani Khan was raiding nearby, they refused to go further than Auratipa, about 80 miles due east of Samarqand. Babur disconsolate, returned back to Khujand. Despite this new setback, he told himself, which he frankly observes, that it was unthinkable for a Timurid to do nothing when he was 'ambitious to rule and desirous of conquest',[42] and so he visited the Khan personally to ask for another loan of troops to try to retake Andijan. His uncle, in Babur's opinion 'a poor soldier but a decent man', then lent him 7,000 or 8,000 men, and sometime in late May or June 1498, he rode out southeast for Andijan. However, this campaign too ended almost as soon as it began, for his Mongol troops argued that beyond occupying the Khujand, they had too few men to carry out new campaigns. Agreeing to this, Babur reluctantly returned once again to 'miserable' Khujand sometime in the late summer or early autumn.

Despite his own sovereign ambitions, Babur was reduced to desperate straits in the autumn of 1498, camping in Khujand with fewer than 300 men. It was the beginning of a period he characterises as his first *qazaqlıqlar* or *qazaq* years. He and other Timurids or Chinggisids used the term to describe throneless, vagabond times, when they wandered about as little more than ambitious brigands in the political wilderness, bereft of supporters, territory and authority.[43] Nothing conveys this reality of Turco-Mongol politics in Mawarannahr better at this period than Babur's candid account of the next year and a half, as he tried to revive his fortunes.

Despising Khujand, he began by petitioning a prominent Mongol – Muhammad Husain Kurkan Dughlat, who controlled nearby Auratipa, east-southeast of Khujand – if they could 'borrow' the town of Pashagar for the winter. The town had previously 'belonged' to Khwajah Ahrar (d. 1490), the prominent Naqshbandi Sufi who had exercised outsized influence among the Timurids until his death in 1490.[44] During the winter, Babur and his men spent time subjugating minor forts in the vicinity of Pashagar, where, he pointedly remarked, all the villages were fortified because both Mongols and Uzbeks had ravaged the area, an allusion to the chaotic conditions that prevailed in this region of late fifteenth-century Mawarannahr. Yet, raiding this thinly-settled mountainous region could not have yielded much value of any kind, as by spring Babur was, in his own account, paralysed with indecision. Eventually, he and his men simply retreated eastwards up to summer pastures near Auratipa.[45] There, writes Babur, they stayed for some time, stunned into bewildered indecisiveness by their seemingly hopeless situation.

Then, as happened so frequently in this era of transitory personal loyalties and fluid, ever-shifting political allegiances, Babur's fortunes unexpectedly improved. 'Ali Dust Tagha'i, who had welcomed Sultan Ahmad Tambal and Jahangir into Andijan, unexpectedly and inexplicably apologised to Babur for his betrayal, and offered him the town of Marghinan, located west of Andijan. With his 240 men, including some Mongols he borrowed from his uncle in Tashkent, Babur marched swiftly eastwards over more than 150 miles of difficult terrain. He took possession of Marghinan from 'Ali Dust Tagha'i, after the Mongol opened the gates and sought and received Babur's pardon. Babur's return precipitated a series of popular uprisings against the increasingly unpopular Ahmad Tambal, who he reports, had oppressed the local population in eastern Ferghanah.

The most important of these incidents occurred in 'Umar Shaikh's capital of Akhsı, when what Babur condescendingly describes as a 'mob', led by a prominent citizen, rose up and forced Tambal's men to take refuge in the citadel. Just then, some of Babur's commanders, leading his uncle's Mongol troops, confronted and killed seventy or eighty of Tambal's men, who had rushed to Akhsı to relieve the besieged troops in the citadel. News of this victory prompted a Mongol officer of Ahmad Tambal, who held the Andijan fort, to switch his allegiance to Babur, who quickly left nearby Marghinan to re-establish control in the town in June 1499. Four or five days later, Babur personally led troops 40 or 50 miles from Andijan to Akhsı to expel the supporters of Tambal, who were entrenched in the citadel. After occupying it and the town, he left behind one of his own commanders as governor.

Writing in India about these events so many years after the incident, Babur interrupts his numbingly detailed narrative of events to reflect on this first *qazaqlıq* period in his young life – another retrospective reflection of the kind that enriches his autobiography. While doing so, he also includes passages of political commentary that gives the *Vaqayi'* another dimension as a *nasihat*, or advice, treatise. In his case, it was an unusually personal and compelling type of a 'mirror for princes' literature, in that it was a mirror held up specifically to reflect his own turbulent life. Abu'l Fazl, Akbar's minister and historian, thought of the work in these terms, writing in the *Akbar Nâmah* that the *Vaqayi'* '...is an Institute for all early sovereigns and a manual for teaching right thoughts and proper ideas'.[46] As he narrates events, Babur does indeed suggest numerous 'right thoughts and ideas' to his sons, descendants and other readers of the autobiography.

After recounting the betrayal of Sultan Ahmad Tambal and 'Ali Dust Tagha'i, and the havoc which Mongol troops inflicted on Andijan and the surrounding countryside, he pauses to denounce Mongols. More precisely, he viscerally attacks troops of the Mongol *ordu,* or horde – not his own Chaghatai relations – as a class apart. Even though he just had broken out of his *qazaqlıq* malaise with the help of borrowed Mongol troops, he attributed Tambal's betrayal and his Mongols' depredations to their very 'Mongolness' – their essential nature – and not to personal idiosyncrasies or political circumstances. *Yamanlıq* and *buzuqchiluq,* 'viciousness and destructiveness', he insisted, were always to be expected from the Mongol horde. Babur also implicitly demonises them as barbarians by alluding to their treatment of his 'Muslim' subjects, thus invoking for his readers the emotive images Muslim historians commonly used when they described the appalling havoc Mongol invasions had wrought on eastern Muslim lands.[47] In earlier pages, he had already distanced himself from such 'Mongolness' for his readers by emphasizing his growing attention to orthodox Islamic practices, such as dietary restrictions and the regular performance of late evening prayers.[48] Then to drive home the point that Mongol actions in 1498 were due to their 'shameful' natures, he points out that not only had they rebelled against him four or five times during his life, but that they had repeatedly betrayed their own khans as well.[49]

What makes Babur's portrayal of these Mongols particularly memorable is that he follows his bitter condemnation of their actions and character by describing, what he later realised was a disastrous decision to take revenge on some Mongol troops, who remained behind near Andijan, after their leaders had fled. These horsemen had plundered people in Babur's Andijan region, stealing their clothing, horses and food. Considering that he had not imprisoned or otherwise retaliated against these men, he thought it only just that his own men should be allowed to reclaim their possessions and strip these Mongols in turn, and he ordered them to do so. It was a hasty and disastrous decision, he recounts with regretful hindsight, for the same Mongols joined in a subsequent attack against him, which later led to Babur's second expulsion from Andijan. He learned from this episode that:

> In conquest and government, though many things may have outside appearance of reason and justice, yet 100,000 reflections are right and necessary as to the bearings of each one of them. From this single incautious order of ours, what troubles, what rebellions arose! In the end, this same ill-considered order was the cause of our second exile from Andijan.[50]

Babur's reflection concludes his account of this first *qazaqlıq* period of his life. He had retaken Andijan and Akhsı and was no longer, therefore, a political vagabond.

Yet, this success gave him no respite in his struggle for survival in the turbulent late Timurid world. In the following year, not only did a detachment of his men suffer a serious defeat, but in the summer of 1499, Sultan Ahmad Tambal and Babur's brother Jahangir reappeared a mere 2 miles to the east of Andijan, intending to retake the town. In August 1499, they eventually abandoned their efforts, but in the next year, Babur was entangled in a series of inconclusive engagements with Tambal or his supporters. Tambal's forces then included Mongol detachments provided by Babur's Mongol uncle in Tashkent, who, in Babur's opinion, was persuaded to turn against his nephew by several of Tambal's relatives, who served in high positions in Mahmud Khan's retinue. Babur's own dismal fortunes may have also influenced his uncle's decision to abandon his nephew.

Then sometime in late February 1500 'Ali Dust Tagha'i, still riding with Babur, but apparently loyal to Tambal, joined with another of Babur's nominal followers to force him to make peace with Tambal and Jahangir. Meeting at Bishkharan, a village northeast of Akhsı, Babur reports that after Jahangir and Tambal offered their 'obeisance' – a meaningless theatrical act – he ceded Akhsı and its surrounding districts to them. He was to retain Andijan and its nearby territories. The three men then jointly agreed to march on Samarqand, and after taking the city, Babur was to rule there, giving Andijan and evidently the entire Ferghanah Valley to Jahangir and his Mongol allies or captors. Following this agreement, which included a prisoner exchange, he returned to Andijan early in March 1500. Writing later in life, he vented his anger about this agreement, bitterly denouncing both Tambal and 'Ali Dust Tagha'i for forcing it upon him. Both men, he writes, were *mardak*s – vile, base individuals – an insulting Persian term he frequently applies either to upstart commoners or, in this case, to ambitious, but politically presumptuous men who lacked Timurid or Chinggisid blood and, therefore, possessed no recognisable dynastic legitimacy.[51]

Back in Andijan once again, March 1500 marked the end of, what in retrospect can be seen as the first chapter of Babur's political life, the 6-year-period that began with his father's death in 1494, when he was thrust into the brutally individualistic political world of the late Timurid era. It was marked by his return to Andijan, following the disasters of the occupation of Samarqand and the following *qazaqlıq* years, his partial recovery of the Ferghanah appanage and persistent conflicts with Sultan Ahmad Tambal, which concluded with the partition agreement of February 1500.

The period of March 1500 also appears to have been a denouement in this intense social and emotional period in Babur's young life, for sometime later in the month he left Andijan and rode back to Khujand where he consummated the marriage with his Timurid cousin, 'Ayisha Sultan Begim. Babur presumably brought his wife back to Andijan after meeting her in Khujand and it was there presumably, where because of 'modesty and bashfulness', he visited his new bride only occasionally. Babur confesses that he gradually lost interest in his young wife, and only visited her when his mother would scold him for ignoring her. He did see her often enough to father a daughter, but the child, born during Babur's second occupation of Samarqand, died within infancy and 'Aisha Sultan Begim left him shortly thereafter, egged on, he says, by his wife's older sister.[52]

Perhaps Babur lost interest in 'Ayisha Sultan Begim because during this interregnum in Andijan, he fell deeply in love with a boy named Baburi, an infatuation that raises many unanswerable psychological questions. Whatever emotions or social restraints stimulated Babur's feelings, he relates this episode in emotionally-affected prose, depicting a distant and unresolved infatuation, which also led him to produce endearingly adolescent Turki and Persian romantic verse. Interestingly, he describes his response to what seems to have been repeated encounters with Baburi by remarking that out of 'modesty and bashfulness' he was tongue-tied when he met Baburi in the *bazar*. Babur reports that he was incapable of even having a conversation with the young man, who aroused in him the novel emotions of 'desire' and 'love'. 'I conceived an uncommon feeling for him', he writes in a Turki verse. 'Still worse,' Babur reports, 'I made myself madly infatuated with him.'[53] Babur describes what is easily recognised as typical youthful self-absorption, when he reports that overwhelmed with emotion he often wandered 'like a madman around Andijan or outside in the hills and steppe'. Using Persian, whose verse contained thousands of images of distraught lovers a writer might appropriate or imitate, Babur wrote: 'May no person be as ravaged, lovesick and humiliated as I'.[54]

Samarqand Redux

With his compelling account of marital tensions and emotional upheavals, Babur offers readers additional glimpses of a recognisable humanity. These reflections do not so much offer insights into distinct personality traits as they reveal memories of recognizably common human experiences. Such vivid emotional recollections are difficult to encounter in any pre-modern Islamic, Central Asian or south Asian text from this or earlier eras. As is the case with his angry critique of Mongol troops, Babur's record of these memories distinguish his autobiography from the one-dimensional political narratives and sycophantic eulogies of pre-modern historical works devoted to events of this or earlier eras in Central Asia, the Islamic world or India. Still, Babur did not write a deeply psychological autobiography, for after revealing personal asides in the text he always quickly resumes his account of political struggles. This narrative represents the underlying purpose of a discretely self-referential work that documents and celebrates the drive and persistence that characterised his ultimately successful attempt to form a new Timurid empire.

In this particular instance, he abruptly turns from his engaging personal recollections to describe the events that led to his second brief occupation of Samarqand. In May or June 1500, Babur learned of a renewed turmoil in Samarqand when a group of Mongols, known as Tarkhans rebelled against Babur's cousin and the nominal ruler of Samarqand, Sultan 'Ali Mirza, and invited Babur to reoccupy the city.[55] Having also 'heard' that Khwajah Yahya Ahrari, the son of the Timurid's revered Naqshbandi Sufi, Khwajah Ahrar, supported him in Samarqand, Babur left Andijan. He did so even though he doubted the loyalty of some of his own men, and Sultan Ahmad Tambal continued to threaten his control of eastern Ferghanah.

Yet, as Babur approached the city, Shaibani Khan Uzbek, having just occupied Bukhara, took Samarqand as well and murdered Sultan 'Ali Mirza. Shortly afterward Uzbeks, presumably at Shaibani's orders, also killed Khwajah Yahya Ahrari and two of his sons, most likely because of the Ahrari Naqshbandis' close ties with Timurids. Almost simultaneously with these events Babur's habitually unreliable commander 'Ali Dust Tagha'i betrayed him once again by openly defecting back to Sultan Ahmad Tambal. Then the Tarkhans, who had invited Babur to Samarqand, suddenly abandoned him and joined forces with one Khusrau Shah. He was a Qipchaq Turk, not a Timurid or a Chaghatai, who had come to dominate Badakhshan after the Timurid Mahmud Mirza had been called to rule Samarqand in 1494, only to die a year later. Recalling these new multiple calamities, Babur wrote that at this moment 'we were deprived of city and province, uncertain as to whether to leave or to remain' in the Samarqand region.[56] He was reduced, once again, to a *qazaqlıq* state, that of a throneless Timurid vagabond.

Babur recalls thinking how, in his desperate straits, he might save himself and the estimated 240 'good and bad' men he led or cajoled into remaining with him, considering that Shaibani Khan manoeuvred in the Samarqand area with an estimated 3000 to 4000 Uzbek horsemen. Additionally, he feared for the safety of his wife, mother and close relatives, who had left Andijan shortly after him in May or June 1500. They had taken refuge first in Auratipa, a day's march east of Samarqand, probably because they feared to remain in Andijan with Sultan Ahmad Tambal nearby. One of the courses that Babur considered was, to cross the mountains to Xinjiang, or in his terms, Moghulistan, to enlist the help of his young, *kichik*, Chaghatai Mongol uncle Ahmad Khan.[57] Eventually abandoning this idea, he and his men circled around Samarqand to the south, suffering new desertions and a loss of pack animals as they moved ahead. Babur nonetheless decided to stage a surprise attack on Uzbek-held Samarqand, which was lightly garrisoned with 500 or 600 troops. Calculating that the Uzbeks would not have had time to consolidate their control of this historically Timurid city, Babur opted for a *coup de main*, and took the city by surprise a few days after Khwajah Ahrar, who had died 10 years earlier, came to him in a dream and assured him of victory.[58]

With this improbable success, Babur had, as he writes, restored the honour of the Timurid dynasty, reclaimed Samarqand 'for our [dynastic] family', and at age 19, surpassed all Timurids with his achievement, even outdoing the twice-noble Sultan Husain Baiqara of Herat (d. 1506).[59] Husain Baiqara, the 'high-born' emperor who had descended from two Timurid lines, had occupied Herat, Shah Rukh's capital, in 1469, and presided over a florescence of Timurid artistic and literary culture in the city, which even Ottomans in distant Istanbul admired. Writing so many years later in India, at a time when he had indisputably surpassed the achievements of every Timurid, living or dead, Babur in a powerfully crafted passage of formally polite apologetics says that when he trumpeted his achievement, he did not intend to diminish anyone. Nonetheless, he insists what he had written about his achievement was the 'truth', the truth that he outshone Husain Baiqara, who, when he seized Herat, took it not from a formidable foe, but from a drunken, inexperienced boy of 18 – Yadgar Muhammad Mirza. Despite his youth and inexperience, Babur had triumphed over Shaibani Khan, an experienced and formidable enemy.

Babur may reasonably have felt he told the truth by exalting his achievement in this second seizure of Samarqand, and he reports that commanders of many nearby forts affirmed their allegiance, and writers, such as the Herat poet Mullah Banna'i, eulogised his achievement. With his wife, mother and family arriving from nearby Auratipa, and his daughter born shortly afterwards, he must have felt elated. Yet, such ebullient emotions quickly dissipated. Not only did his daughter die within a month, but also this victory, while momentarily impressive, was in reality yet another pyrrhic triumph. Babur could not long sustain his occupation of Samarqand, considering Shaibani Khan's superior forces and his inability to persuade most '*khan*s, *sultan*s, *amir*s and border lords' to rally to his side by sending troops to defend Timurid Samarqand.

Shaibani Khan, after withdrawing from the city to winter in Bukhara, reappeared in the spring of 1501, and his horsemen confronted Babur's troops, who had ridden out of the city to meet them at Sar-i pul – a point just to the northeast, but south of the Zarafshan River. Shaibani Khan's disciplined cavalry, which, as Babur noted later, could charge, wheel and retreat in strict formation, overwhelmed Babur's relatively small, less cohesive force that by then included as many as a thousand Mongols of various lineages, who had come in from the countryside.[60] The Uzbek chief used a *tulghamah* flanking manoeuver against Babur, a manoeuver Babur himself employed successfully in India, a quarter of a century later, against Afghans and Rajputs. Typically for this type of warfare, as Babur's force disintegrated, clusters of his ostensible Mongol allies began plundering his core group of loyalists as soon as the pitched battle turned against them, prompting Babur in his account of the battle to denounce anew the 'habits of these wretched Mongols'.

Babur and a few of his men then fled back behind the walls of Samarqand, where they endured an Uzbek siege of the city in the ensuing months that drove the defenders into a state of nervous exhaustion and forced inhabitants to slaughter dogs and donkeys for food and feed their horses mulberry leaves. Babur, desperate, sent out pleas for help, including one to Sultan Husain Baiqara, the twice-noble-Timurid ruler of Herat, who rather than coming to his troubled kinsmen's aid sent an envoy to the powerful Shaibani Khan. Shortly after Husain Baiqara's death, the Uzbek would occupy Herat and murder two of Husain Baiqara's sons, as he sought to eradicate Timurid progeny.[61] Babur's remaining troops, including some of his most prominent *beg*s, now fled the city in small groups. 'A sort of peace was made' with Shaibani in July 1501, apparently giving Babur a kind of safe conduct. One midnight, Babur with his mother and a few loyal men, leaving behind his sister Khan Zada Begim, who had been somehow betrothed to Shaibani with her mother's consent, fled the city before Samarqand fell.[62]

Yet, whatever guarantee Shaibani had offered him, Babur fled as a hunted fugitive with a small retinue, at first wandering about disoriented in the maze of irrigation channels, plots and lanes that surrounded the city in a crazy quilt assortment. In his flight, Babur fell from his horse, and, he reports, he was dazed in a kind of dream-like state until evening.[63] By morning, he and his companions finally found their way clear of Samarqand's environs and took refuge in a small village. Some women who had been left behind in the panic gradually struggled out of the city on their own and joined Babur, his mother and a few others. His aunt, Mihrnigar Khanım, and Chaghatai Mongol grandmother, Aisan Daulat Begim, were allowed to leave the city – Mihrnigar Khanım fleeing to Tashkent and his grandmother joining Babur at the village of Dikhkat near Auratipa with her small retinue of ill-nourished and exhausted servants. Babur must have been familiar with this village from his earlier visits to this region, and he probably knew that its inhabitants pastured an estimated 40,000 sheep, which could feed his ragtag band. He decided to spend the winter of 1501–02 here.

Once again a *qazaq*, a throneless, powerless political refugee, Babur, now more desperate than ever, decided yet again to visit his Mongol uncle in Tashkent, who, he hoped, would give him a province or district to govern. '*Umidvar idim*', Babur writes of his desperation, *kim Khan dadam ri'ayat ve 'inayet maqamida bulub*, 'that my uncle in his condescension and graciousness', *vilayet ve parganah bergayelar*, 'would grant province or district'.[64] His uncle promised his nephew the town of Auratipa, despite the fact it was occupied by Muhammad Husain Mirza Dughlat, the husband of one of Babur's maternal Mongol aunts, who, not surprisingly, refused to give up the town when Babur visited him. Muhammad Khan may well have promised Babur the city merely to rid himself of his importunate, perennially needy, unfortunate kinsman. Amid this travel to and from Tashkent, Babur was at least able to visit Khwajaka Khwajah, the eldest son of the deceased Naqshbandi Shaikh Khwajah Ahrar.[65] Khwajaka Khwajah had been able to leave Samarqand and escape the fate of his younger brother and nephews, whom Uzbeks killed shortly afterwards. Returning to the village of Dikhat, Babur spent the winter with a handful of followers, female relatives and servants.

Unable to return even to Andijan, which Ahmad Tambal had once again occupied with Jahangir, Babur spent a miserable winter sometimes wandering for days, *yalang ayaq*, barefoot in the hill country, on one occasion riding to the Khujand area with a few men to oppose a raid of Shaibani Khan who had come out from Samarqand. In this extremely severe winter, when even fast-flowing rivers froze, several of Babur's men perished from the terrible cold before Shaibani Khan retired, but the Uzbek chief returned to the Auratipa area in the spring of 1502.

At this juncture, the future founder of the great Mughal or Timurid-Mughal Empire of South Asia paused to have a verse carved into the rock near a tomb and spring, an act, which from the evidence of the autobiography, was meant to convey the pathos of his perilous situation. The verse, taken from the Iranian poet Sa'adi's work, the *Bustan*, alludes to Jamshid, a legendary king of pre-Islamic Iran, and reads:

> I heard that the fortunate Jamshid inscribed on a stone at a
> fountain-head:
> At this spring many like us who boasted,
> Passed away in the twinkling of an eye.
> With valor and might we seized the world
> And yet we did not take it with us to the grave.[66]

Then tired of wandering 'penniless and homeless' and 'mountain to mountain' in the Auratipa highlands, Babur again returned to Tashkent on 16 June 1502 to visit his Mongol uncle. Based on his recent experience, Babur could not have hoped for much from Mahmud Khan, who on this occasion largely ignored him. He passed most of his time in the town by visiting some relatives, including his maternal grandmother Shah Begim, while also using this brief period of leisure and relative security to write more poetry and to improve his knowledge of Turki prosody. He had already let his readers know how ambitious he was to be recognised as a poet, for he reports that in 1500, during his second occupation of Samarqand, he had scribbled several verses of his own on a letter he sent to Mir 'Ali Shir Nava'i in Herat, the great Turki literary figure of the era.[67]

While Babur cannot have relaxed or ceased even for a moment to worry how he might repair his shattered political prospects, he opens his narration of this interlude by discussing the quality of a Turki *ruba'i*, or quatrain, he had written earlier. Still unsure of his command of prosody – he had not yet learned, he recalls that 'ta' and 'da' were interchangeable for rhyme – he recited it before his uncle, hoping for some literary advice. He discovered, though, that Mahmud Khan, who had written some *ghazals* and was 'good natured', or *khushtab'*, was not a knowledgeable writer. Apart from technical questions of prosody, Babur's quatrain is worth reading because it seems to have been alluding to his desperate political situation in it.

> No person cares for a man in peril.
> No person gladdens the exile's heart.
> My heart has found no joy in this exiled state.
> Certainly no person takes joy from exile.[68]

This is the first of many verses and passages in the *Vaqayi'* when Babur evokes the idea of exile, or *ghurbat*, which represents a recurring theme in his life, in which he repeatedly endured exile – from Andijan, Samarqand, Ferghanah and then finally, by his own choice, from Kabul – until he was, poetically enough, reburied in Kabul after his death in India.

The verse did not unsurprisingly, persuade Mahmud Khan to rally to Babur's side, who, in despair at his wretched, powerless situation, resolved to abandon Mawarannahr and flee to Khitai, North China, where his young Chaghatai uncle Ahmad Khan, controlled territory in the Aqsu region of Xinjiang. Just as he was considering this idea, Ahmad Khan himself arrived with somewhere between 1,000 and 2,000 horsemen, 'adorned in Mughal/Mongol fashion with red caps', *börklar*, long coats of Chinese satin and Chinese armour.[69] The 'Young Khan', Babur's 'Khan Dada', as he now calls him, had responded to Mahmud Khan's earlier request for troops following Shaibani Khan's occupation of Samarqand.

The Ferghanah Denouement

Ahmad Khan's arrival in Tashkent marked the denouement of Babur's struggle for political and personal survival in Mawarannahr, which concluded 2 years later in his flight from the region and the Uzbek extermination of the remaining Timurids there. At first, his young uncle's arrival momentarily resuscitated Babur's fortunes, as he found himself as part of an alliance with his Mongol relatives. Yet, they led their first assault, not against Shaibani Khan, but Ahmad Tambal, whose previously close relations with Mahmud Khan seemed to have completely ruptured. Tambal still held Andijan, and the threat of his expanding power in eastern Ferghanah may have prompted the Mongol brothers' campaign. As they entered the valley with an estimated and probably exaggerated force of 30,000 horsemen, many fortresses pledged their allegiance to Babur and the allies occupied Ush at the extreme eastern end of the valley. Babur then moved to reoccupy Andijan with a detachment of Mongol troops lent to him by Mahmud Khan, but Tambal in a dawn raid surprised his unguarded camp and badly wounded Babur, who retreated to Ush with his few surviving troops.

Blaming his defeat on his lack of combat experience, Babur could only listen and agree as Mahmud Khan transferred Ush and other forts in eastern Ferghanah to Ahmad Khan. Babur was to have Akhsı, and after the allies retook Samarqand, Babur was to rule from that city, with Ahmad Khan controlling the entire Ferghanah valley. In retrospect, this imagined partition of territory represented a poignant moment in the history of Timurid Mawarannahr, for none of the elements of the plan were realised, although the Mongol brothers began besieging Andijan. Babur then rode to Akhsı at the invitation of Tambal's brother, who then held the fortress there, and, in Babur's opinion, wished to separate him (Babur) from his allies, the Mongol Khans. A cascading series of disasters followed.

Babur was allowed to enter the outer gate of the Akhsı fortress, where his younger brother Jahangir Mirza, according to Babur a 'fugitive from Tambal', now arrived with his retinue.[70] To counter Babur and his Mongol kinsmen, Tambal himself now pledged his loyalty to Shaibani Khan and invited him into Ferghanah. The Uzbek Khan's appearance forced Mahmud and Ahmad Khan to raise the siege of Andijan and retreat eastward out of the valley. This in turn freed Tambal to march northwest to Akhsı to relieve his brother and confront and defeat Babur once again, after Babur, in what he admitted to be another inexcusable military lapse, failed to post guards at his camp.

Babur was driven from Akhsı with eight others and eventually fled by himself into the nearby hills with Tambal's men closely pursuing him. It was now winter and Babur, shivering with cold after two nights in the open, recalled that he prepared himself for death, alone in an abandoned garden near the small village of Karnan, saying to himself: 'if a man lives a hundred years or a thousand years he will come to an end'.[71]

Yet, Babur somehow survived this final debacle in his decade-long struggle to survive and prosper in Mawarannahr, although missing pages of his autobiography make it impossible to understand just how he managed to extricate himself from danger. Still when he fled to Karnan, some of his men were near, and Jahangir Mirza still led half of Babur's small surviving force somewhere to the north. Eventually, Babur found a way to reunite with his uncles in the late winter or spring of 1503, and fought with his Mongol kin when Shaibani Khan defeated them in June 1503.

The Khans were captured. Ahmad Khan died a year later in unexplained circumstances, and Shaibani Khan murdered Mahmud Khan and his five sons 6 years later. Babur escaped once again, this time fleeing into the hill country, just at the edge of the mountains, due south of Khuqand, where he stayed 'in great misery' for nearly a year in and around the village of Sukh.[72] Then in the month of Muharram/June 1504, at age 23, he abandoned the valley and with a party of no more than 300 men, his mother, younger brothers Jahangir Mirza and Nasir Mirza and two small tents, he made his way south through the Hisar Mountains to the Amu Darya River.

Originally, Babur had thought to take his small retinue to Herat, Sultan Husain Baiqara's capital in Khurasan, but as he moved south with his fellow refugees through the mountains, he gradually changed his mind.[73] He began to hear rumours that Khusrau Shah, the Qipchaq Turk now ruling Badakhshan, was losing control of his Mongol troops as Shaibani Khan's Uzbeks began sending probing detachments south from Mawarannahr. At the village of Qabadian, located in the southern plains of modern Tajikistan, just north of the Amu Darya, he received an emissary from Khusrau Shah's brother Baqi Chaghaniani, who proposed an alliance. Baqi Chaghaniani then greeted Babur after he had crossed the river. As both men moved south towards Bamian, Baqi told him that Khusrau Shah's retainers would soon join Babur's service. Pausing at Ajar, a village in the present-day Bamian Province, his younger brother Jahangir, like Babur before him, was married to his Timurid cousin, the daughter of Sultan Mahmud Mirza, an engagement concluded 14 years earlier.

At this time, one after another of Khusrau Shah's Mongol horsemen rode out to join Babur, followed by 3,000 to 4,000 heads of Mongol households and then by Khusrau Shah himself, who was fleeing south into Afghanistan as Shaibani Khan's forces were said to be marching on Qunduz in the northeast. Climaxing the defections of all Khusrau Shah's Mongols, a remarkable scene was enacted one day in late August 1504. Khusrau Shah himself knelt before and surrendered to Babur while his remaining troops, with their 700 or 800 coats of mail and occasional pieces of porcelain, left his side and joined Babur.

Apart from revealing Babur's sudden transformation from a pitiful refugee into a formidable leader of thousands of Mongol troops, the events of the spring and summer of 1504 determined the direction of his future Timurid *mulkgirliq* ambitions, as well as exhibiting one of the important truths of late fifteenth-century politics. Khusrau Shah's defecting Mongol troops drew him away from Khurasan as a refuge to lowland Tajikistan and northeastern Afghanistan, shifting his focus from Husain Baiqara's Herat to Kabul. Babur may also have preferred Kabul to Herat because it offered him a chance to rule a Timurid outpost, rather than residing as a refugee in Herat as Husain Baiqara's guest. He may also have been influenced to prefer impoverished Afghanistan to wealthy Khurasan after reading Husain Baiqara's pleading letters, which he received as he fled south from Ferghanah.

This 'twice-noble' sultan begged Babur to help him fortify the defences of his territories in Khurasan against Shaibani Khan's advances, rather than mustering his own men and meeting the Uzbek Khan in battle. Babur despaired of Timurid fortunes when he read these importuning letters, and in writing them to Babur, Husain Baiqara revealed that the last and most important Timurid dynastic line had fallen into a kind of irredeemable languor. Babur saw this for himself when 2 years later he visited Herat just after Husain Baiqara's death, and sadly observed that the great ruler's sons displayed a debilitating, frightening passivity.

Apart from events and considerations that led Babur to turn away from Khurasan towards Kabul, these events surrounding the collapse of Khusrau Shah will remind thoughtful readers of Babur's autobiography that Timurids, Chaghatai Mongols, Uzbeks and dozens of lesser, but ambitious Mongols and Turks, displayed a ruthless pragmatism as they competed for power in this political environment. When Khusrau Shah surrendered to Babur, he told him that his Mongol detachments had deserted him and returned four times before. As Babur had already spoken with bitter distaste of Mongol disloyalty, treachery or simple self-interest in Ferghanah, he cannot have been surprised that the Mongols, who joined him in 1504, deserted him later.

Yet, what is perhaps most notable about Babur's transformation from hunted and haunted refugee to commander of thousands of Mongol troops – however untrustworthy – is that it demonstrated the power of dynastic legitimacy. Individual Mongols and even Khusrau Shah's brother joined him although at that moment he was impoverished and powerless, a *qazaq* in every sense of the word. Considering Babur's brief and catastrophic political career from 1494 to 1504, he was still a

Timurid *Mirza,* and the apparent aura of that lineage attracted men to his cause or, more accurately, to his person. Perhaps Mongols also saw Khusrau Shah as an ineffectual leader, but what did they know of Babur as a military commander, other than that he had lost battles to Ahmad Tambal and Shaibani Khan Uzbek. They may not have been aware that Babur himself was at fault for at least two of these defeats. Babur attributed the reversal of his fortunes to God's omnipotence. 'How wonderful is his power', he writes, that 'without a battle or a skirmish in the presence of two hundred or two hundred and forty wretched, impoverished men such as ourselves [Khusrau Shah] became so contemptible, weak, helpless and exhausted that he no longer controlled his retainers, his property or his life'.[74]

Babur now marched south towards Kabul in late September with men of his newly acquired Mongol troops quarrelling among one another and plundering the inhabitants as they passed. With Uzbek raiders pressing him from behind, after a debate he and his men decided to move on to Kabul before winter set in and lay siege to the city. Babur's newly acquired Mongols must have intimidated Muqim Arghun, who then held Kabul, although Babur gives the impression that they were more of an undisciplined rabble than an army. Still, with the offer of safe passage for himself, his family and their retinues, Muqim Arghun offered to surrender the city, which Babur's uncle Ulugh Beg Kabuli had held until his death 2 years earlier.

During the negotiations, social order began to disintegrate within the city, which Babur quelled by killing six or seven people. Within a day and without a fight, he took possession of the city in late September or early October 1504, where he was able to rebuild his shattered political fortunes over the following two decades. While he continued for many years to plan a return to Mawarannahr to conquer Samarqand and occupy the Timurid homelands, the powerful Uzbek confederation made this impossible. After taking the city once again in 1511, but failing again to hold it, Babur finally accepted the logic of his situation and sought to establish a new Timurid state in Hindustan.

Endnotes

1   See Beveridge's appendix 'The Site and Disappearance of Old Akhsï' in *The Bâbur-nâma in English*, Appendix A, i–v. The site, built on multiple mud brick strata of ancient habitation, raising it well above the river, is now largely deserted, but it is covered with a scattering of potsherds.

2   BN–M, f. 75a.

3   BN–M, f. 34a.

4   The Persian word is spelled and pronounced *mughûl*, a term that is always rendered *Mughal* when applied to the Timurid-Mughal dynasty of India.

5   Mawarannahr refers to western Central Asia, known to Iranians as Turan. In Western classical sources, the Amu Darya is called the Oxus and the Syr Darya the Jaxartes. In these sources, Mawarannahr is known as Transoxiana. Geographers, such as the German scholar W. Rickmer Rickmers, sometimes refer to the region between the Amu Darya (Oxus) and Syr Darya (Jaxartes) as the *duab*, the region between these two *-du*, rivers *-ab*. See Rickmer's book *The Duab of Turkistan* (Cambridge: Cambridge University Press, 1913).

6   For a precise account of these campaigns and a description of the reach and depth of Timurid authority in the first half of the fifteenth century, see Chapter I of Beatrice Forbes Manz's work *Power, Politics and Religion in Timurid Iran* (Cambridge: Cambridge University Press, 2007), 12–48. See also her instructive map of Timurid territories in this era, 18–19.

7   See Beveridge's informative notes on Babur's opening account of Ferghanah in her carefully edited English translation of Babur's autobiography: *The Bâbur-nâma in English*, 1–12. For an introduction to the valley's long history of sedentary agrarian and urban settlement, stretching from 1600 BCE to the present, see Abdulkakhor Saidov, Abdulkhamid Anarbaev and Valentina Goiyacheva, eds., 'The Ferghana Valley: Pre-Colonial Legacy', in *Ferghana Valley*, ed. Frederick Starr (London and New York: Routledge, 2015), 3–28.

8   Arrian, *Alexander the Great, The Anabasis and the Indica*, trans. Martin Hammond and ed. John Atkinson (Oxford: Oxford University Press, 2013), 102 & 296 n. 1.3.

9   Sima Qian, *Records of the Grand Historian: Han Dynasty II*, trans. Burton Watson (New York: Columbia University Press, 1961), 233. Zhang Qian drafted his report upon his return to the Chinese capital Chang'an in 125 BCE. For his mission and information on Dayuan, Ferghanah and Chinese interest in Ferghanah horses, see also Étienne de la Vaissière, *Sogdian Traders: A History*, trans. James Ward (Brill: Leiden and Boston, 2005), 25–29 and references to Ferghana(h) in his Geographical Index.

10 See A. D. H. Bivar, 'Kushan Dynasty I. Dynastic History', *Encyclopædia Iranica*, accessed on 8 December 2014, http://www.iranicaonline.org/articles/kushan-dynasty-i-history.

11 BN–M, f. 2b. See Chapter 2 for a discussion of Nava'i, with whom Babur once corresponded.

12 BN–M, f. 5b.

13 BN–M, f. 7a.

14 Evgeniĭ Eduarovich Bertels, *Izbrannye Trudy, Navoi i Dzhami* (Moscow: 'Nauka,' 1965), 31.

15 BN–M, fs. 103b and 108b. Sedentary populations to the west and to the east considered the Chaghatai Mongols of Xinjiang to be uncouth tribesmen. For insight into nomadic–sedentary relations between Chaghatai Mongols and their cousins, the rulers of the Mongol or Yuan dynasty of China, see John Dardess, *Conquerors and Confucians: Aspects of Political Change in Late Yuan China* (New York: Columbia University Press, 1973).

16 See Edward H. Schafer, *The Golden Peaches of Samarkand* (Berkeley: University of California Press, 1963) for Indians in China during the later Tang era (616–907). In the Tang era as well as the Kushana period, Soghdian merchants from the Samarqand region probably dominated the commerce between Mawarannahr and India.

17 For these missions and routes to and from Herat and China, see A. B. Buriev, who discusses the evidence of the Timurid geographer and historian Hafiz-i Abru (d. 1430) in his essay 'Svedeniya Hafiz-i Abru O Vzaimootnoshinyakh Sredneĭ Azii S Kitaem v XV v' (Information of Hafiz-i Abru about the Relations of Central Asia with China), in *Iz Istorii Srednei Azii i Vostochnogo Turkistana* XV–XIX vv (From the History of Central Asia and Eastern Turkistan), ed. B. A. Litvinskii (Tashkent: 'Fan': 1937), 24–37; and Yolanda Crowe, 'Some Timurid Designs and Their Far Eastern Connections,' in *Timurid Art and Culture* (Leiden: Brill, 1992), eds. Lisa Golombek and Maria Subtelny 169–70. Ming Chinese sources contain considerable information on the Chinese missions, which include descriptions of Samarqand and other Central Asian and Iranian sites.

18 Annette Susannah Beveridge, *The Babur–Nama in English*, 202. In the nineteenth century, various Afghan tribes traded between India and Mawarannahr. They have generally been designated as *Powindah*s. One of these ethnically complex tribes was the Luhani or Nuhani, concentrated in the Ghazni region, whose members traded as far as Tashkent, Kashgar and Yarkand. See H. W. Bellew, *An Inquiry into the Ethnography of Afghanistan* (Graz, Austria: Akademische Druck-u. Verlagsanstalt, repr. 1973), 28, and J. A. Robinson, *Notes on Nomad Traders of Eastern Afghanistan* (Quetta, Pakistan: Nisa Traders, repr. 1978).

19 De la Vaissière describes the agricultural wealth and urban growth of the Samarqand region known as Soghdiana in the fifth and sixth centuries. *Soghdian Traders: A History*, 104–06. For important information on the economy, artisan and mercantile classes of Mawarannahr in Babur's day, see especially R. G. Mukhminova, *Sotsial'naya Differentsia'tsiya Naseleniya Gorodov Uzbekistana v.*

XV–XVI vv. (Social Differentiation of the Population of the Cities of Uzbekistan in the XV–XVI Centuries) (Tashkent: Fan, 1985.)

20 All the extant copies of Babur's *Vaqayi'* begin with his survey or gazetteer of Ferghanah, fs. 1b–24a. He subsequently includes similar gazetteers of Kabul and Hindustan as prefaces to his narrative of events in those regions.

21 Ruy Gonzalez De Clavijo, *Court of Timour at Samarcand AD 1403–06*, trans. and ed. Clements R. Markham (London: The Hakluyt Society, 1859), 141–42.

22 BN–M, f. 44b.

23 BN–M, f. 45b.

24 BN–M, fs. 45b–46a.

25 BN–M, f. 46b.

26 Of the many sources on Ulugh Beg's observatory see V. V. Barthold, 'Ulugh Beg,' in *Four Studies on the History of Central Asia*, Volume 2 (Leiden: Brill, repr. 1963), 129–34; Lentz and Lowry, *Timur and the Princely Vision*, 144–53; Bernhard du Mont, 'Ulugh Beg: Astronom und Herrscher in Samarkand,' *Sterne und Weltraum* Nos. 9–10 (2009): 38–46. For Timurid astronomy in South Asia, see G. R. Kaye, *The Astronomical Observatories of Jai Singh* (Calcutta: Government Printing Office, 1918).

27 BN–M, f. 46a. De Clavijo describes this garden, which he visited as Spain's ambassador to Temür's court. *Narrative of the Embassy of Ruy González de Clavijo to the Court of Timour at Samarcand A.D. 1403-6*, 136. The Uzbek Babur Foundation has erected a similar structure just outside modern Andijan, with paintings illustrating Babur's career.

28 In Herat, the *Chini-Khanah* was located in the garden built by Mîr 'Ali Shir Nava'i, the Turki poet and cultural patron of the city, during the reign of Sultan Husain Mirza Baiqara. See Chapter 2, for the discussion of Herat culture in that era and also the work of Bernard O'Kane, *Timurid Architecture in Khurasan* (Costa Mesa, CA: Mazda, 1987), 12, cited by G. A. Bailey, 'The Dynamics of Chinoiserie in Timurid and Early Safavid Ceramics,' in *Timurid Art and Culture*, eds. Lisa Golombek and Maria Subtelny (Leiden: Brill, 1992), 189.

29 BN–M, f. 47b.

30 BN–M, f. 1b.

31 For a detailed introduction to Central Asian history from Chinggisid to Timurid and Uzbek times, see, Nicola Di Cosmo, Allen J. Frank and Peter B. Golden, eds., *The Cambridge History of Inner Asia: The Chinggisid Age* (Cambridge: Cambridge University Press, 1989). This volume contains a number of excellent maps.

32 In this passage, *vilayat* must mean district or *tuman* rather than province and while *wajh* seems to refer to a stipend, Babur later uses the term *wajhdar* to describe men who were granted territorial assignments in India.

33 For the Uzbeks, see Yuri Bregel, 'Uzbeks, Qazaqs and Turkmens,' in *The Cambridge History of Inner Asia, the Chinggisid Age*, eds. Di Cosmo, Frank and Golden, 221–36.

34 Babur rarely mentions Nasir Mirza (b. 1487), his second, younger half-brother, during his narrative of the Ferghanah decade.

35 BN–M, f. 78a.

36 BN–M, f. 44b.

37 BN–M, fs. 52b–53a.

38 BN–M, f. 58.

39 BN–M, fs. 53b–54a.

40 BN–M, fs. 54a–55b.

41 BN–M, f. 55b.

42 BN–M, f. 55b.

43 See Joo-Yup Lee's study of the *qazaqlïq* idea in his book *Qazaqlïq, or Ambitious Brigandage, and the Formation of the Qazaqs* (Leiden & Boston: Brill, 2016) and Maria E. Subtelny's discussion of this term, which evidently entered Turco-Mongol vocabulary in the fourteenth century, in her work *Timurids in Transition, Turco-Persian Politics and Acculturation in Medieval Iran* (Leiden and Boston: Brill, 2007), 28–32. Babur also uses the term *fatrat* or interregnum as a synonym for *qazaqlïqlar*.

44 Babur mentions how disgracefully Khwajah Ahrar's descendants were treated after the Naqshbandî Shaikh's death. f. 23. Nonetheless, his youngest son, Khwajah Yahya, living in Samarqand, was actively involved in Timurid politics in Babur's early years and, Babur writes, perhaps in wishful thinking, that Yahya hoped that he would return to Samarqand. BN–M, fs. 59b & 78b.

45 BN–M, f. 60a.

46 Abu'l Fazl 'Âllami, *The Akbar Namah* trans. H. Beveridge (Delhi: Ess Ess Publications, repr, 1987), I, 273.

47 BN–M, f. 64.

48 BN–M, f. 25a.

49 BN–M, f. 64b.

50 BN–M, fs. 64b–65a.

51 BN–M, fs. 74a–b.

52 BN–M, f. 20a.

53 BN–M, f. 75b.

54 BN–M, f. 75b.

55 *Tarkhan* was originally a high Mongol military rank, but at this period it designated an aristocratic clan of Mongols. Subtelny, *Timurids in Transition*, 71 n. 151.

56 BN–M, f. 81a.

57 Ibid.

58 BN–M, f. 83b.

59 BN–M, fs. 85a–86b.

60 BN–M, f. 90 for Babur's description of Uzbek discipline and manoeuver.

61 BN–M, f. 94a.

62 BN–M, f. 95a. Beveridge notes that this marriage had taken place before the city fell to the Uzbek chief. BN–B, 147, n. 3. See also *Humayun Namah*, f. 3b where Babur's daughter Gulbadan Begim, writes that Shaibani Khan said this marriage would lead to peace with Babur. Babur clearly did not believe it to be so.

63 BN–M, f. 95b.

64 BN–M, fs. 96b–97a. Here Babur uses *vilayat* to mean province and the Indian term *parganah* to mean district. In his Kabul section he consistently uses *tuman* for district.

65 BN–M, f. 96b.

66 BN–M, f. 99a. A. Mukhtarov discusses this description and others by Babur in his article 'Inscriptions with Babur's Name in the Upper Reaches of the Zarafshan,' *Afghanistan* No. 25 (September 1972): 49–56.

67 BN–M, fs. 86b–87a.

68 BN–M, f. 100a.

69 BN–M, fs. 102b–103a.

70 BN–M, f. 11a.

71 BN–M, fs. 118a–118b.

72 The village/town is located on modern maps of Uzbekistan.

73 BN–M, f. 120a.

74 BN–M, 124b.

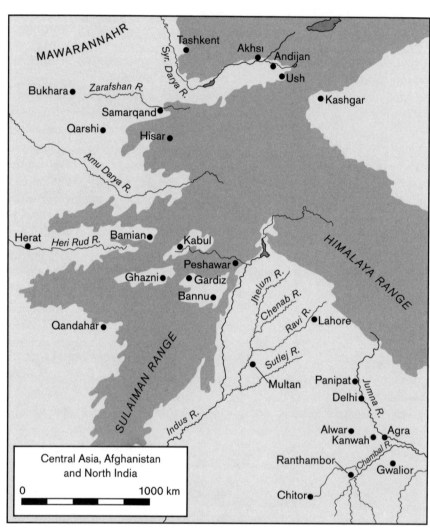

Map 2: A map of Mawarannahr, Afghanistan and Hindustan

2

Padshahliq, Governance, in Kabul

Babur's account of his 22 years in Afghanistan, which breaks off in 1508 and resumes in 1519, first of all shows a man recently transformed from a refugee to a ruler by the power of legitimacy, struggling to survive in the face of further Uzbek assaults in an impoverished Kabul province, which was populated by a contentious maelstrom of Afghan tribes. Gradually, he achieved a measure of control and stability in Kabul and the city's immediate hinterlands, and despite the many alarms and excursions of the following years, he came to love the city and its mountainous environs. The irony of his Afghan life is that, while he ruled in Kabul for more than two decades, he always viewed his occupation of the city as a temporary necessity. During the first decade, he hoped to use it as a base to return north and restore Timurid rule in Samarqand. When that attempt failed in 1511, he gradually turned his gaze to the southeast, and after 1514, Kabul became a staging ground for the probing attacks on India that culminated in his invasion and victory over the Ludi Afghans at the Battle of Panipat in April 1526.

Yet, not only did Babur mature in Kabul, where he enjoyed a considerable degree of stability for the first time in his young life, but these were his years of great personal and intellectual accomplishment. While ruling the city, he fathered eighteen children with four wives, wrote a considerable body of Turki poetry, composed an ambitious verse treatise on Islamic law, and finally, abandoned his childhood abstinence. It was also during these two decades that he created a congenial life for himself, revelling in alcohol-fuelled *suhbatlar*, the convivial gatherings of friends, poets, artists and musicians, that came to represent for him the good life, a life lived as much as possible in the aesthetically pleasing context of the formal Persianate garden. It was the civilised norm he had hoped to enjoy in Samarqand and briefly experienced in Herat when he visited the great Timurid city in 1506. He longed to experience this life again after his victorious campaigns in India, but once there, he failed to find respite and longed to return north, to what had become for him his Afghan home.

Timurid State Formation in Kabul

In retrospect, Babur's seizure of Kabul in the fall of 1504 might appear to mark a definitive break with the first decade of his political life – the struggle for ascendency and subsequently for survival in Mawarannahr. At the time, however, and for many years later, he valued the Afghan city primarily as a relatively safe haven, where he could regroup and prepare for a renewed campaign to seize Samarqand from the Uzbeks. Kabul was shielded in the north from major Uzbek attacks during at least half of the year, due to winter snows and spring floods, and in 1504, at least the Timurid Sultan Husain still controlled the western approaches to the city from his capital of Herat, with his territory extending, Babur notes, from Balkh in the northeast to Bistam in the west, and Khwarizm in the north to Qandahar and Sistan in the southeast.[1]

Otherwise Babur had little use for the Kabul *tuman*, the city and district, or the broader Kabul *vilayat,* or province, as the nucleus of a new Timurid State, because both city and province were impoverished and nearly ungovernable. He dismissed Kabul city as a 'trifling place' remarking: 'What revenue there is from Kabul is from the *tamgha*' (customs dues). These commercial taxes probably generated the largest percentage of the city's income, and Babur suggests as much when he emphasises how important it was as a trading centre. Goods were sold there from Anatolia, Iraq, Iran, India and China.[2] He describes the Kabul *vilayat* with its fourteen *tumans*, or districts, as a 'trivial province, with a poor agrarian economy'.[3] Based on knowledge accumulated over more than two decades, he reports that the city and province's total revenue from agriculture, nomads and trade – *vilayat, sahra neshin* and *tamgha* – equalled only 8 *lac*s or 800,000 *shahrukhis*, or approximately 33,000 pound sterling in nineteenth-century values.[4] In contrast, the revenue from Agra alone in 1526 was 29 *lac*s.[5] The revenue from Timurid-controlled Hindustan territories in that year was staggering compared to the resources of Afghanistan or even, almost certainly, Mawarannahr.

Besides eastern Afghanistan's poverty, Babur had also to contend with the region's tribal countryside, inhabited by Turks, Mongols (Mughuls), Arabs, Hazarahs and, most of all, Afghan or Pashtun tribes. In explaining the reason in December 1506, when he was enjoying the pleasures of Herat, he had to leave the city and return to Kabul, Babur writes that the 'not yet desirably subjugated country of Kabul…[was] full of a turbulent and ill-conducted medley of peoples and hordes, Turks, Mughuls, clans and nomads, *aimaq u ahsham*, Afghans and Hazarahs'.[6] He noted that 'eleven or twelve languages' were spoken in the province. It is not possible to determine exactly how much territory in and around Kabul his Timurid uncle Ulugh Beg Kabuli had effectively controlled at the time of his death in 1502. Apparently, it did not include any trans-Indus districts or Peshawar located near the eastern entrance to the Khyber Pass.

The problem of ruling eastern Afghanistan is exemplified by the territorial control of the formidable nineteenth-century Afghan ruler, Ahmad Shah Durrani.

In 1809, the well-informed British-Indian official Mountstuart Elphinstone estimated in his work on Kabul that Ahmad Shah's authority was limited to the plains around towns, the areas inhabited by Tàjiks or Iranians and the 'foreign [non-Afghan] provinces of the state'. Elphinstone went on to remark: 'An ordinary monarch might endeavour to reduce the tribes [Afghans] to obedience by force; but one Afghaun king [Ahmad Shah Durrani] has already had the penetration to discover that it would require a lesser exertion to conquer all the neighbouring kingdoms, than to subdue his own [Afghan] countrymen'.[7] Babur quickly came to this realisation in the early sixteenth century and wrote, 'Kabul [*vilayat*] is... of the sword [and] not of the pen', a wonderfully succinct way of saying that Afghan tribes were independent, and did not pay taxes or tribute unless they were forced to do so.[8] In search of an economically viable kingdom and in face of independent Afghan tribesmen, he too eventually opted for the wealthy plains and relatively compliant farmers of Hindustan.

Over two decades, Babur developed a comprehensive knowledge of the geography, population, flora and fauna and economic resources of Kabul city and its province. He summarised its information for his descendants in his autobiography and in a separate Turki verse composition on Islamic law called the *Dar Fiqa Mubaiyan* or *Mubin*, which he wrote and dedicated to his young son Kamran in 1521 or 1522.[9] The gazetteer-like section of his autobiography favourably compares with nineteenth- and twentieth-century British surveys of Indian districts in its range and depth. Both, this section and his verse composition, reflects his analytical intelligence as well as his desire to bequeath a comprehensive body of knowledge to his descendants to help them govern Afghanistan and Hindustan.

Yet, while Kabul city and province were both impoverished and politically fractious, and if Babur was to return to Mawarannahr and re-establish Timurid rule in Samarqand, he had no other choice but to consolidate his authority there to survive and even prosper. While momentarily safe in the fall and winter of 1504–05, he could not realistically depend on the loyalty of the thousands of Mongols who had defected to him from Khusrau Shah, and he possessed no funds beyond whatever unreported coins he might have discovered in Kabul's treasury. He was immediately faced with the problem of feeding his Mongol horsemen, newly arrived refugees from Uzbek-controlled Mawarannahr, along with his small retinue of immediate relations and Andijan retainers.

Desperate for supplies, one of his first acts late in the fall of 1504 was that he stripped 30,000 donkey loads of grain from the districts around Kabul and Ghazni. Writing later in India, he expressed regret for the amount of grain he seized remarking that he had not known the extent of the Kabul harvest and later learned that by seizing so much grain. he had devastated the two provinces.[10] Both, his admission and one he makes later in the text about a ruinous effect of a grain levy he assessed in a mountainous district in eastern Afghanistan in 1519, startles the readers of political autobiographies of almost any era, unprepared for a ruler's revealing self-censure.

The 'sword not pen' rule for Afghan revenue collection in the countryside may not have applied to farmers in easily accessible lowland areas near major towns such as Kabul and Ghazni. At least Babur suggests as much in his account, for he does not mention any difficulty in gathering this grain. He writes very differently when he describes his attempt to extract resources from tribes in the hills or other remote areas, which he calls *chapquns* or raids. He describes many of these raids in the narrative of his Kabul years, as he tried to feed his men and assert his authority. His men undertook the first raid against the Sultan Mas'udi Hazarahs in late 1504 to enforce tribute in kind – payment of sheep and horses. These Hazarahs, he reports, had been raiding the roads near Ghazni and Gardiz, so this *chapqun* also appears to have served a second purpose as a kind of ad hoc pacification mission along a critical trade route.[11]

While this raid did not, Babur concedes, turn out well, it represented an early aspect of his state formation. Thus, he attempted to enforce some degree of control over the countryside, and tried to prevent tribal raids on the roads carrying the commerce that was vital to the survival of the otherwise impoverished Kabul regime. Just a year later in February 1506, he personally led a more ambitious and rewarding *chapqun* against another Hazarah clan. These were the 'Turkman Hazarahs, located northwest of Kabul in a snow-covered valley near Bamian on the main route north to Badakhshan and the Amu Darya River. Giving highway robbery as the reason for the raid, Babur and his men seized 400 or 500 sheep and 25 horses and killed 70 or 80 Hazarahs, who had taken refuge in a cave.[12] He led another *chapqun* against these same Hazarahs the following year, implicitly demonstrating how little these periodic campaigns achieved.

When he marched out to steal animals and to bludgeon tribes into submission, and when *chapquns* slaughtered enough people, beating even ferociously independent Afghan tribesmen into resentful submission, the raids constituted a means of transforming tribes into what he terms *ahl-i ma'mur*, or 'settled inhabitants'. Once settled, tribes could be taxed rather than raided in the future. Babur, like his draconian ancestors Temür and Chinggis Khan, left behind what he terms 'minarets of skulls' to terrorise Afghan tribes and others who resisted. Knowledge of Babur's Afghan *chapquns* is not of much help in understanding how he later dealt with the relatively quiescent peasants of the riverine Punjab and the Hindustan heartland. The information does, though, alert readers to Babur's mentalite as an ambitious Timurid who wanted to construct a stable sedentary state in the Kabul region.

He expanded his raids beyond Kabul's environs in January 1505 because he still desperately needed more supplies for the estimated 20,000 Mongols he had acquired on his march south to Kabul, as well as the 'clans and hordes' who had drifted in from Samarqand to join him there.[13] After 'consulting with people', quite likely Indian or Afghan merchants, who knew the country, he decided to launch an extensive raid along the western Indus plains – his first foray into the territory he explicitly identifies as Hindustan.[14] Leaving frigid Kabul behind, he, his brother Jahangir and Khusrau Shah's brother Baqi Chaghaniani, conducted four months of raids into the Bangash district south of Peshawar. They entered an exotic 'hot country' that Babur describes as 'a different world', with its different grasses, different trees, different birds, different animals and people with different customs.[15]

Perhaps because of its length, he describes this incursion as a *yurush*, a campaign, rather than just a *chapqun*. Learning that the Indus plain was populated and easy to cross, he and his men decided to move south from Bannu, along the foothills west of the Indus. Here, they murdered a group of Afghan merchants and stole their goods: sugar, textiles, horses and 'aromatic roots' – possibly asafoetida. Now on 21 March with 'Id al-Fitr, the end of Ramadan on the lunar religious calendar and *Nau Ruz* on the Iranian solar calendar coinciding, Babur reports composing a Turkic *ghazal*, a lyric poem, typically portraying unrequited love, but enlivened here by commemorating the two festivals – one Islamic and the other Iranian or Zoroastrian – while camping on the banks of the swollen Gumal River. In the *matla'*, or opening couplet, Babur cleverly plays on the metaphorical significance of the moon as the face of the beloved, the subject of so many lyrical poems devoted to unrequited love.

> On seeing the new moon with the beloved's face,
> People are joyous at the festivals.
> As for me separated from thy face and brows
> The festivals are sad.[16]

This is one of Babur's earliest 'Kabul' poems, the first of many *ghazal*s and *ruba'iyat*, or quatrains, he wrote during these decades. He eventually collected these in his *diwan*, which later in India, he proudly distributed to relatives and comrades.

Afterwards, he and his men rode further south, seizing more cattle as they went, before turning back west at the Sarwar Pass for a difficult and nearly disastrous march along a rain-swollen river to Ghazni.[17] If Babur had not appreciated the relative wealth of South Asia earlier, this *yurush* revealed to him its prosperity. During his Kabul days he repeatedly plundered these border regions, but as his political interests evolved subsequent raids increasingly assumed the character of probing expeditions that prefaced his final invasion in 1525–26.

Apart from *chapquns* and what they implied about Babur's unspoken assumption of legitimate Timurid claims on Hindustan, in 1504, he also moved quickly to establish an administration in eastern Afghanistan. He kept Kabul city and its district (*tuman*) as *khalisah*, that is, demesne or state land, and retained it throughout his life, in part for the nostalgic reason that it had served as his base for the later conquests in India.[18] Otherwise, he assigned towns and districts to his two brothers and gave administrative assignments, land grants or offices to members of his family, unnamed loyal Andijan members of his retinue and Baqi Chaghaniani, who had brought the Mongol troops to Babur's side as he fled south to Afghanistan.

He assigned Jahangir Mirza to Ghazni, the bleak fortress city 91 miles to the south-southwest, the capital of the earlier Ghaznavid Empire (984–1187). He appointed his second half-brother, Nasir Mirza, to some unspecified districts in Lamghanat, one of Kabul's eastern *tumans* or districts, located about 49 miles east of Kabul, the district where Babur later constructed a garden in Adinapur. Babur gave nearby Pamghan (Paghman), 'the best place in Kabul', to Shah Begim, his maternal or Mongol grandmother. Then, to reward Baqi Chaghaniani, he appointed him as his 'Lord of the Gate' – his aide-de-camp or principal advisor – and made him the *darughah*, or governor, of the city and controller of Kabul's *tamgha*, the city's custom duties, Kabul's most important source of revenue.

In appointing his brothers and Baqi Chaghaniani to important districts and positions, Babur tried to stabilise his modest new state with the most logical choices, his own kin and the man who had rescued him from his powerless penury and supplied the Mongol troops he used to overawe Muqim Arghun before Kabul in October 1504. Yet, he writes that within a short time of his making these assignments, both his half-brothers and Baqi Chaghaniani betrayed him by revealing their own sovereign ambitions. Babur says that Nasir Mirza, who he barely mentions in the Ferghanah narrative, immediately began acting like an independent ruler as soon as he arrived in the Lamghanat region. Instead of accompanying Babur on his *yurush* into India in January 1505, he launched an attack on a nearby fortress and when that failed, he returned to his district and spent the winter drinking with his men.

Later in 1505, hearing that people in Badakhshan had rebelled against the Uzbeks, Nasir Mirza accepted their invitation to join them. In May 1506, after marching north with some of the Mongols who had come to Kabul with Babur, he defeated an Uzbek force. However, his apparent ambition to establish some kind of Timurid regime there collapsed, when the *beg*s of Badakhshan rebelled against him in the spring of 1507. He fled back to Kabul in tatters with seventy or eighty followers, where, Babur reports, he gracefully received his younger brother.[19]

While Babur was ready to excuse his Timurid half-brother for his military adventures, he was less charitable when it came to the political ambitions of a Qipchaq Turk, even one as important to him as Baqi Chaghaniani. He writes that from their first encounter, Baqi had been 'mean, miserly and malicious', refusing to share even a few of his thousands of sheep with Babur's exhausted, starving retinue as they retreated past Hisar towards Afghanistan. Later, when made *darughah* in Kabul and given control of the *tamgha*, Babur reports, he assumed royal airs and had kettledrums beaten before his gate – a royal act – even while formally acknowledging Babur as his *Padshah*, his sovereign. Worst of all, during the march back to Ghazni after raiding the Indian borderlands, he offered to help make Jahangir Mirza *Padshah* in Babur's place. In this case, Jahangir promptly reported Baqi's plot, acting, as Babur notes, as a younger brother should. Even then, Babur tolerated Baqi Chaghaniani's mean-spirited character and this treachery for some time before dismissing him in the latter half of 1505, apparently doing so without any opposition from the Mongols he had helped bring to Kabul.[20] Baqi Chaghaniani decided to go to India, perhaps the only alternative open to him, but after traversing the Khyber Pass, Afghans captured and killed him.

In these days, Babur's relations with the oldest of his half-brothers Jahangir were complex, as indeed they had been earlier in Ferghanah. He comments more often on his relations with him, than he does on any other relation. He is adamant though, in rejecting the notion that either a brother or even a son could ever be a co-ruler.[21] In his narrative of 1504, he refers to past disputes between himself and his brother over 'kingdom and retainers'. Even then, that comment only raises anew the question of whether Jahangir acted independently in Ferghanah after Babur's first occupation of Samarqand.

It was then, while still little more than a boy, that he and Tambal had occupied Andijan. On several occasions, Babur writes that Tambal *Jahangir ni alib kilib*, Tambal took or brought Jahangir', from one place to another. Yet, when Tambal and Jahangir met Babur in 1500 to partition Ferghanah, it seems possible Jahangir could have left Tambal and re-joined his brother. He did later 'escape' from Tambal in 1503, but how and why only then? Did the Mongol's vaunting ambition and brutal tactics drive him away, or did the threat of Uzbek expansion threaten him? It is impossible to understand more about these brothers' previous relations, but in 1504, as Babur and his band during their flight south paused briefly at Ajar in Afghanistan to celebrate Jahangir's wedding, Babur reports that Jahangir had become a 'companion' with a '*tuqqanlıq ve khidmatgarlıq*', or 'familial and deferential manner'.[22]

In the *Vaqayi'*, Babur shows that he expected deference from both his younger brothers, and writes on several occasions that kinship was, or should have been, a tie that bound close relatives. Jahangir did remain at his side until May or June 1506, when, upon hearing of Sultan Husain Baiqara's death, he briefly seems to have considered leaving Babur to join with the Sultan's sons to form a new regime in Herat. He left Kabul, returned to Ghazni and marched north to Bamian, where he evidently hoped to persuade some of Nasir Mirza's Mongols to join him. Yet, Babur himself made a forced march to Bamian and persuaded Jahangir, who had made little headway with these Mongols, to re-join him. Eventually, both men marched together to Herat, with Jahangir later conveniently dying on the return trip to Kabul, thus sparing Babur from further competition with this brother.

Sultan Husain Baiqara's Herat

The news that the man he called the 'twice-noble' Timurid, Sultan Husain Mirza Baiqara, had died on 5 May 1506 climaxed another turbulent year for Babur in both personal and political respects. In June or early July 1505, his mother Qutluq Nigar Khanım had died of a fever. While he and his closest *beg*s mourned her at a house just outside Kabul, built by his Timurid uncle and former ruler of Kabul Ulugh Beg, Babur received news that his 'young' Chaghatai Mongol *dada* Ahmad Khan and maternal, or Chaghatai Mongol, grandmother Aisan Daulat Begim had also recently died. Just at this moment, his maternal, grandmother Shah Begim, his maternal aunt Mihr Nigar Khanım and Muhammad Husain Kurkan Dughlat – the former ruler of Auratipa in Ferghanah – arrived from Khurasan and learned of these deaths, triggering a fresh emotional outburst of mourning.[23]

On 5 July 1505, as Babur was about to lead an expedition to Qandahar to wrest the strategic city from Muqim Arghun, whom he had forced from Kabul the previous year, he came down with a severe fever, perhaps an illness caught from his mother. Next an earthquake that was followed by a series of severe aftershocks levelled many villages around Kabul. In Pamghan, northwest of Kabul, every house was destroyed. In nearby Tipa, Jahangir barely escaped with his life when the roof of the house, where he was staying following the mourning period, collapsed. Sick and distracted by the earthquake, Babur abandoned the Qandahar campaign, opting instead for a series of raids. It was during this period that Baqi Chaghaniani was dismissed and left for India.

During these events, Sultan Husain Mirza in Herat sent an emissary to Babur asking for help in repelling the Uzbeks, who, having consolidated their hold on Mawarannahr, were advancing towards the city. Babur writes that he felt he had to help the great ruler, the de facto Timurid leader, who, he says, had inherited Temür's authority. 'It was right...for us to start for Khurasan...when a great ruler, sitting as Sultan Husain Mirza sat, in Timur Beg's place, had resolved to act against such a foe as Shaibani Khan and had called up many men and had summoned his sons and *beg*s. If there were some who went on foot it was for us to go even if on our heads.'[24] Subsequently, he learned during his march west that Husain Mirza had died in May 1506 as he marched north to confront Shaibani Khan, Babur nonetheless pressed on towards Khurasan. 'Despite this news', he writes, 'we set out for Khurasan, anxious for the reputation of this *khanehvadih*, this [Timurid] dynasty', then adding, without explanation, that he also had other reasons for going to Herat.[25] Those reasons may have been nothing more or less a desire to see the famous city, the Timurids' de facto capital and cultural centre of the eastern Islamic world.

It was not until 26 October 1506 that he met a number of Sultan Husain Mirza's sons at a Murghab River crossing 110 miles northeast of Herat in western Afghanistan. Nearly all Husain Baiqara's sons had assembled and marched north to relieve Shaibani Khan's siege of Balkh in north-central Afghanistan. Camped at the Murghab, where one has to imagine splendid tents and horses of individual Herat *mirzas* and their households spread over the areas near the river, they had sent an emissary to Babur as he rode west, and he joined them in what seemed to offer a rare opportunity to forge a common anti-Uzbek coalition. Arriving at the camp, he was enthusiastically welcomed by an 'amazing crowd', a splendid first meeting for Babur with so many Timurid princes.[26]

Yet, writing so many years later about these *Mirza*s during the month he spent with them before riding on to Herat, Babur expresses varying degrees of disappointment and frustration with their behaviour. Firstly, after meeting one of them, Abu'l Muhsin Mirza, who had joined the gathering after riding south from Merv, Babur was offended that two of Abu'l Muhsin's younger brothers had failed to accompany him when he rode out from camp to formally welcome Babur. Still Babur excused their behaviour, reasoning that their delay was due to drowsiness brought on by the previous night's '*aish u 'ishrat*, debauchery and revelry', rather than being an intentional slight. Then with another older brother, the co-ruler of Herat Muzaffar Mirza, offering apologies for this indiscretion, they all rode to the riverside camp. Muzaffar Mirza's brother and fellow co-ruler Badi' al-Zaman Mirza awaited them there with an elegant feast. Also attending this meal was Zu'n-Nun Arghun, the father of Muqim Arghun, whom Babur had chased from Kabul, and 'Abd al-Razaq Mirza, the son of the last Timurid ruler of Kabul, Ulugh Beg Kabuli.

Babur writes that this meeting and the elegant dinner that followed, including *sherbet* served in gold and silver cups, was *suhbat yok* – not a companionable gathering – primarily tensions over matters of rank and status. In particular, he felt then and at later gatherings that Badi' al-Zaman Mirza was discourteous, failing to acknowledge Babur's status in the now shrunken Timurid world. While not alluding to his disastrous campaigns in Ferghanah, Babur writes that although

'I was young my place of honour [among Timurids] was great. Twice I had taken the ancestral capital Samarqand in battle. No one', he continued, 'had fought with this foreign enemy [the Uzbeks] for the *khanehvahdih*, [the family/dynasty], as I had done. It was unconscionable to delay in showing me respect'.[27]

Babur also seems to have been surprised that his cousins served this dinner according to the *törah* or *tore*, the Chinggisid Mongol customary code.[28] Noting that while his ancestors had scrupulously adhered to this code in all things, including feasts, he nonetheless notes that this code, this Chinggisid *törah*, was not a '*nass qati*', a 'definitive ruling'. It did not, that is, have Quranic legal force. Therefore, this particular custom did not have to be obeyed, although as a matter of polite conduct, Babur thought it was still reasonable or polite to follow ancestral rules.[29] In saying this Babur, as he had done in Ferghanah, again distanced himself from his Mongol heritage by reminding readers of his Islamic faith, as he implicitly does when he reports that when he later attended several of Badi' al-Zaman's elegant drinking parties, he did not drink, and he was not pressured to do so by his hosts.

Still, questions about etiquette and Chinggisid custom were overshadowed in Babur's mind by his astonishment at his hosts' extraordinarily casual attitude about confronting Shaibani Khan Uzbek, the looming threat to what remained of the Timurid world. He notes that it had taken Husain Baiqara's sons three months to form a coalition, mobilise their troops and reach the Murghab. As an explanation and scornful critique, he goes on to say, '*Bu mirzalar agarcheh suhbat ve suhbatarayılıqda ve ikhtilat ve amizesh da turi idilar*', 'These *Mirza*s, although companionable and sociable in conversation and friendship', '*vali sipahılıq riv ve rankidin yarak ve mardanehliq ve jang ve jedeldin qiraq idilar*', 'but were strangers to military affairs and strategy, courage, battle and war.'[30] Babur goes on to mention that during this strange month-long interregnum at the Murghab River crossing, the *Mirza*s learned that 400 or 500 Uzbeks were raiding a district little more than 50 miles away and he asked to lead a force against them. The *Mirza*s, he indignantly reports, neither sent a force against the Uzbeks nor would they allow Babur to do so, as it would impugn their honour.[31]

By late November, the Herat *Mirza*s, having taken no military action, decided to return to Herat. By this time, Shaibani Khan had occupied Balkh and retired to Samarqand having heard mistakenly that the Timurids were on the march. With winter approaching, the campaigning season was drawing to a close, so they decided to resume, or begin, their operations the following spring. They persuaded Babur to accompany them, even though he felt he should return to Kabul, which was still not effectively pacified, before the snows made travel impossible through the shorter, but mountainous, route he intended to take. Unable to refuse such important men, he finally agreed to join them because he also desired to see this uniquely beautiful city that Husain Baiqara had embellished in so many ways.

Following the *Mirzas* by a few days, Babur arrived in Herat on the 2nd or 3rd of December. He immediately began a social round of visits, first by meeting a number of his paternal aunts, daughters of his Miranshahi Timurid paternal grandfather Abu Saʻid Mirza, the ruler of Samarqand between 1451 and 1469. Each of these Timurid ladies lived in her own set of tents, which Babur moved between, showing respect by bending the knee before each of them. He spent his first night in the tent of Payandah Sultan Begim, a wife of Husain Baiqara and daughter of Abu Saʻid, before taking up residence two days later in the former house of ʻAli Shir Navaʻi, the Turki poet and acknowledged Maecenas of Heratʻs literary, artistic and musical culture. Living in the poetʻs house must have meant a great deal to Babur as he had exchanged letters with the great man in 1500, even inscribing one of his early Turki couplets on the back of his correspondence, a sign, one of many in the autobiography, of his own literary interests and ambitions.[32]

In reporting on his nearly month-long sojourn in Herat, Babur reveals more of his profound appreciation of urban, Perso-Islamic high culture. He also records his corresponding assessment of whether the Turco-Mongol and Iranian elite of the city possessed the traits he considered to represent civilised men. (Women are briefly mentioned, but usually only in passing as wives, concubines or daughters.) He does this through his biographical sketches of Husain Baiqara and his family, military and administrative elite and stars of the cityʻs cultural firmament, which make up most of his account of this period. In compiling these sketches, he also clarifies why the Timurid world was on the verge of collapse in 1506, by adding to the observations he has made about his Timurid cousins while partying on the banks of the Murghab.

He spent part of his time in the city acting like a tourist, visiting more than fifty buildings, structures and gardens, content just to mention their names rather than, as in Samarqand, describing each one in detail. Herat contained too many marvels and presumably many of his readers were familiar with them.[33] He also waited on Badiʻ al-Zaman Mirza every few days in the Bagh-i jahan ara, the ʻWorld-Adorning Gardenʻ. Both he and Jahangir spent many evenings in the city partying with the Badiʻ al-Zaman and his brother and co-ruler Muzaffar Mirza.

It was also during his visit that he met a future wife, Maʻsumah Sultan Begim, the youngest daughter and another first cousin of his deceased paternal uncle Sultan Ahmad Mirza of Samarqand. She had come to Herat sometime before Baburʻs *qazaqlïq* times in Andijan. Babur gives two accounts of his encounter with this girl during a visit to her mother, a member of the Arghun clan. He first says that he was attracted to her, but he later reports it was she who was attracted to him.[34] In an event after some days, it was 'arranged' she would later join him in Kabul, which she did in the late summer of 1507.[35] Before she arrived, he wrote a Turki *ghazal,* which he presumably sent to her as it contained the following couplet, playing on the word *shah,* which poets commonly used to address to their beloveds. He wrote: 'If you travel on the road to Kabul, Let me offer myself to you O Shah.'[36]

Soon after his arrival Muzaffar Mirza invited him and Jahangir to the White Garden, where Khadijah Sultan Begim, another daughter of his paternal grandfather Abu Sa'id Mirza, also dined with them. After eating, Muzaffar Mirza took Babur and his brother to a wine party at the *Tarab-khanah,* or 'pleasure-house', an elaborate *kushk.* Here, they sat in a room on the second storey, which Abu Sa'id had decorated with paintings, depicting his battles and wars, just as Temür had decorated a *kushk* in Samarqand with paintings commemorating his campaigns. They sat here while the *saqilar,* the 'cup-bearers', filled cups, which the other guests drank, as if the wine were the 'water of life', until they were intoxicated.

Babur noting that even when his father had urged him to drink wine, he had not sinned, *irtikab qilmas idim,* as he then followed the religious teachings of his childhood tutor Khwajah Maulana Qazi, whom Sultan Tambal had murdered in Andijan. Now, even though Babur wanted to drink, he could not as it would offend Badi' al-Zaman for drinking with his brother and not with him. Later, after the evening prayer, the gathering moved to another house in Muzaffar Mirza's winter quarters, *qishlaqi,* where 'Janak recited in Turki, two slaves of the Mirza's known as Big Moon and Little Moon, did offensive drunken tricks... The party was warm till night...'[37] (Illustration 1).

When Badi' al-Zaman heard Babur had first feasted with his brother, he invited him to a party of his own in the Bagh-i jahan ara. There, with weeping willow trees brought in and decorated with strips of gilded leather, probably in imitation of Timurid or Mongol tradition, he enjoyed another feast.[38] With some chagrin, he tells how he revealed his provincial upbringing to his cousins, by being unable to carve a roast goose placed before him. Badi' al-Zaman rescued him and carved it himself. His cousin was, in Babur's words, 'unrivaled in such matters'. Carving was only a small sign of the Herat Timurids *pur zarafat,* their 'refined manners' or urbane sophistication. These traits included 'quiet, delicate and melodious' poetry recitals, conducted to the accompaniment of the *nay* or flute and the *chank* or *chenk,* a hammer dulcimer, harp or Jews harp, and elegant dancing. Knowing that Herat fell to Shaibani Khan less than seven months after he left the city, almost exactly a century after Temür died, Babur's account of such Timurid refinement conveys the fin de siècle atmosphere of Husain Baiqara's brilliant but doomed city.

Babur indeed blames the Sultan for creating the conditions that led to the atrophy of Timurid power and the consequent Uzbek occupation of Herat in June or July 1507.

The Perfect Timurid

Babur's biographical sketch of Sultan Husain Baiqara introduces his catalogue of noteworthy *begs*, administrators, scholars, artists, musicians and poets who lived in Heri or Herat during the Sultan's rule there from 1469 to 1506. He avoids such hagiographies as a court historian might produce, and instead entertains – or instructs – his readers with critical, individualised portraits, peopling Herat with distinct, complex personalities. His characterisation of these notably idiosyncratic Turks, Iranians and Mongols seems like a casting call for a Shakespearean drama – comedy, history or tragedy – in his attention to their physical peculiarities, personal quirks, talents and depravities. His opening portrait of Husain Baiqara is especially compelling, for having earlier referred to the Sultan as the 'twice-noble' Timurid, who presided over the florescence of Herat culture, Babur offers his readers a largely acerbic assessment of the man. He only alludes to Husain Baiqara's political stature as a ruler, while taking much more trouble to describe the great man's physical peculiarities, personal habits and multiple literary, moral and military failings. Sultan Husain, he begins:

> Was 'slant-eyed …and lion-bodied, *shir andam*, being slender from the waist downwards. Even when he was old and white bearded he wore lively colored red and green silk…. When he first took Heri he considered reciting the names of the Twelve Imâms [of the Shi'ahs] in the *khutbah* [the Friday prayers]. 'Ali Shir [the poet] and others prevented it. Afterwards all his important acts were done according to the law [Sunni *mazhab*]. He could not perform the prayers due to pain in his joints and he kept no fasts.
>
> He was a pleasant and good natured person, somewhat temperamental as were his words …. After taking the throne he was abstinent for six or seven years. Afterwards he was lost to drink…. This was the situation with his sons, all the soldiers and the town. They all pursued pleasure and debauchery to excess. He was a brave and courageous man…. He had a poetic temperament [and] also composed a *diwan*, writing in Turki, using Husaini as his *takhallus* [pen-name]. Some of his couplets are not bad; but they are all in the same meter. Although he was a great ruler by virtue of both age and state, yet like youths he kept fighting-rams, flew pigeons and fought cocks.'[39]

Babur later supplements this character sketch with two other telling observations, one praising the cultural florescence in literature, art and music that occurred in Herat during Husain Baiqara's rule, and a second explaining the consequences of the Sultan's dissolute life. 'Sultan Husain Mirza's time was a wonderful age,' Babur reports, 'in it Khurasan, and especially the city of Herat, was filled with learned and extraordinary men. Whatever a person put his mind to, he desired and aspired to bring that work to perfection.'[40] Echoing this assessment the sixteenth-century Ottoman historian Mustafa Ali saw Husain Baiqara's Herat 'as the perfect political and cultural environment, one in which rulers were not only inclined, but duty-bound to surround themselves with the learned and talented'.[41] Yet, Babur also tells readers that the cultural splendour of Husain Baiqara's age took place amidst the steady atrophy of state power.

Babur lamented that after Husain Baiqara took Herat 'his only concern by day and by night was comfort and pleasure', adding that his men similarly indulged themselves. 'In him, in his sons and in tribe, *il* and horde, *ulus*, vice and debauchery was very notorious.'[42] Babur thought it to be particularly telling that 7 or 8 years after Husain Baiqara's death no sons and only one grandson, Muhammad Zaman Mirza, survived him, a fact he uses to document the debauchery of the dynasty and its followers.[43] He concludes with a harsh assessment of Husain Baiqara's rule and an implicit explanation for the eventual and almost effortless Uzbek conquest of Khurasan. Babur well understood the swift Uzbek triumph after meeting Husain Baiqara's sons on the Murghab and then partying with them in Herat.

Due to the debased state of the Husain Baiqara and his men, Babur argues, 'the trouble and labor of campaign, *laskarkeshlik* and conquest, *jahangirlik* was not sustained. Consequently the *naukar* [supporters] left and the *vilayat* [province/state] declined.'[44] In what amounts to an implicit illustration of the Sultan's deteriorating power, he writes that Husain Baiqara directed his last successful campaigns against his rebellious sons in the 1490s, at a time when he also launched attacks on Qunduz and Hisar. Babur, expressing his dismay, bemoans the fact that 'a great *Padshah* like the brave Sultan Husain Mirza' retired from these campaigns without accomplishing anything.[45]

It was just after his Herat sojourn that Babur described the Chaghatai Mongol-led coup against him in Kabul, insisting: 'It is the truth that is written… I have revealed all the known faults and virtues of kinsmen and strangers.'[46] Still, his characterisation of Husain Baiqara is a very stark portrait of an internationally known Timurid, who is never elsewhere described in such intimate and caustic terms. Is Babur offering a balanced critique, or does his critical tone resound so loudly due to his own barely controlled anger over the bankruptcy of the Sultan's court, which compromised his admiration for Herat's cultural florescence during

Husain Baiqara's reign? What might it tell his readers about his autobiographical intent and his own self-image, ambitions and biases?

Firstly, had he, and in literary terms, decided not to praise Husain Baiqara, but to bury him – and if so why? Did he wish to contrast favourably his own career with that of this 'twice noble' Timurid? Was this simply another *nasihat namah* or Mirror for Princes-type of passage meant to educate his sons and grandsons about the dangers of moral lassitude and military passivity, just as he had earlier warned readers to beware the inherent treacherous natures of Mongols? His son Humayun's lack of aggressiveness and self-indulgence bothered him both before and after he occupied Hindustan.[47] Readers, who were rulers, could hardly have missed the point of his scathing critique of Husain Baiqara's dissolute indolence. Yet, Babur's alcoholic grandson Jahangir, who was known to have read the text, neither mentions it nor appears to have been moved by Husain Baiqara's example to shake off his prolonged alcoholic haze.

What else were Babur's descendants meant to take from his portrait of Husain Baiqara? Was this just another proof of Babur's honesty? Were they supposed to appreciate his sensitive understanding of human nature, and, in his critique of Husain Baiqara's verse, respect his knowledge of Turki prosody? Whatever his motives, when they later read his account of the Sultan, they could not have misunderstood his insistence on the importance of dynamic militarism, Sunni orthodoxy and hostility to Shi'i practice, concerns he repeats in his portraits of other individuals.

It is reasonable to ask similar questions and glean more information about Babur's social and cultural ideals when considering his character sketches of members of Husain Baiqara's inner military, clerical and literary circle. The question that arises from all these portraits, Husain Baiqara's and others, is: What qualities did Babur consider to comprise the perfect man, not the *murshid-i kamil*, the prefect Sufi *shaikh* or *pir*, but the perfect Timurid?

One approach to this question is to recall how Babur describes his father 'Umar Shaikh Mirza'. Thus, taking Babur's account of his father 'for all in all' readers might reasonably think Babur never saw his like again – in Ferghanah, Samarqand, Kabul, Agra, or even among the luminaries in Herat. After all, he portrays his father as a generous, affable and eloquent individual, who was a companionable person, *khush suhbat kishi*, a good swordsman, an aggressive and ambitious – if largely unsuccessful – campaigner, a pious Hanafi Muslim and devout Naqshbandi Sufi *murid*, literate in classical Persian, who read verses well, *khub abyat odkur idi* and a just Sultan. As Babur describes him, few among Husain Baiqara's military entourage, administrators, scholars, writers or artists, could measure up to his father's plentiful cache of human virtues.

Babur does not describe Husain Mirza's most important sons in detail, other than to discuss his encounters with them at the Mughab River crossing, his enjoyment of their parties in Herat or to report what he learned later about their failure to mount a defence against Shaibani Khan Uzbek shortly after he returned to Kabul. He takes considerable trouble, however, to evaluate the virtues and failings of important *beg*s, scholars, writers and artists. He often summarises these men's careers, undoubtedly matters of compelling interest for an aspiring ruler and his heirs, as well as recording his impressions of their characters and talents. He thus offers readers considerable insight into the qualities he admired in these men, as well as revealing more of the humanistic complexity of Timurid society.

A considerable number of Husain Baiqara's most important *beg*s were members of Temür's Turkicised Mongol Barlas clan and as such a fair guide to the Turco-Mongol ethos of Herat at this period. Babur's description of four of these men offers some sense of their different characters. 'Muhammad Baranduq Barlas, for example, 'was a very intelligent person, a very commanding person! He much loved the hawk such that… if a hawk died or was lost [it would have mattered more] than if one or another son had died or broken his neck'.[48] Muzaffar Barlas, another member of the clan,

> …was with the Mirza in the *qazaqlïqlar* [Husain's "guerrilla" days before taking Herat in 1469]. I do not know why [Babur writes critically in his most reflective, advice mode], but for some reason he was much favored. His honor was such that in those guerilla days it was arranged the Mirza would take four *dang* (sixths) if any country was conquered, and he [Muzaffar Bârlas] would take two *dang*. This is a strange arrangement. When would it be right in governance to make even a loyal person a partner in rule? Even with a younger brother or son such an arrangement would be impossible; how then with his own beg should it be possible. Upon taking the throne he repented this arrangement, but it was too late. That evil minded little man, *tireh maghaz mardak*… also sought to govern. The Mirza did not act with judgment. In the end it is said he [Muzaffar Barlas] was poisoned. God knows the truth of the situation.[49]

Jahangir Barlas was a third member of this large tribal group. He had earlier served Babur's uncle Ulugh Beg Mirza in Kabul, afterwards joining Husain Baiqara in Herat. He was a man, Babur writes, 'whose movements and postures were elegant and graceful. He was an entertaining person. He knew the rules of hunting and hawking very well [so] most of those matters the Mirza assigned to him'.[50] A fourth, Islim Barlas,

...was a simple, *turk*, person and understood hawking, (*qushchilik*) well and did some things beautifully. Drawing a bow of from 30 to 40 batmans strength, he would shoot his arrow right through the target.... He did many remarkable [such feats]. He was continuously in attendance and was at every *suhbat* [every entertainment].[51]

A particularly important member of Husain Baiqara's inner circle, at this time, was Zu'n-nun Arghun, the father of Muqim Arghun, who held Kabul when Babur arrived before the city in 1504. Following Husain Baiqara's death, he became 'lord of the gate' to the Sultan's son, Badi' al-Zaman Mirza. Babur had met Zu'n-nun at the Murghab River crossing. 'He was a brave man,' Babur writes, '... There can be no question about his bravery, but he was a bit crazy. Otherwise he would not have accepted flattery as he did.' Babur reports that he took seriously the praise of some *shaikhs* and *mullahs*, who called him 'The Lion of God' and predicted he would defeat the Uzbeks.' Instead, they captured and executed him when he staged an ill-considered charge against Uzbek forces. Babur concludes his elaborate character sketch of Zu'n-nun Arghun by saying 'he was a *pak mazhab kishi, a* deeply orthodox person, [who] did not neglect prayers but indeed performed extra ones', adding, 'He was very mad for chess...,' Babur concludes critically, as he often does in his biographical sketches, by adding, without comment, that Zu'n-nun's character 'was marked by avarice and stinginess'.[52]

A well-connected member of this class was Darvish Beg, *'Alishir Begning tuqqan inisi,* that is, 'a full younger brother' of the poet, Mir 'Ali Shir Nava'i. He governed Balkh for a time and while there he did good [unspecified] *beg*-like actions [but] he was a very stupid and dishonorable person'. Later when he was dismissed, he joined Babur in Qunduz as Babur prepared to attack Uzbeks in Hisar in 1510. Babur found him 'twisted and stupefied, incapable of acting like a *beg*'. He attributed the man's status among Husain Baiqara's *beg*s to his brother's influence.[53]

Another man whom Babur knew personally, after meeting him at a *suhbat* in Herat, was known as Saiyid Badr, 'Sayyid Full-Moon', whom he describes as

> a very powerful and extremely graceful person. He was an admirably honorable individual. He was an outstanding dancer, [and] danced distinctively, apparently that was original dancing. He was always attendant upon the Mirza [and] was perpetually his wine companion and fellow celebrant.[54]

Saiyid Badr was the sultan's 'boon companion', who attended all the *suhbat* entertainments, the kind of parties Babur experienced in Herat.

Another man of this *beg* class was Khwaja 'Abdullah Marwarid. 'At first he was chief judge, *sadr*, but subsequently became an intimate court *beg*. He was a person full of accomplishments; he was unequalled on the zither… He wrote in several scripts, best in *ta'liq*. He produced elegant compositions, *insha'*, was an excellent conversationalist and wrote good verse with the penname, the *takhallus*, Bayani, "Expression." Compared with his other accomplishments,' Babur concludes, 'his verse was inferior, but he understood poetry well. He was a filthy sodomite. He suffered from venereal disease due to disgraceful debauchery.'[55] Once again Babur startles the reader by punctuating a seemingly positive personality sketch with a lacerating criticism.

Another *beg* Babur knew personally was Sayyid Hasan Aughlaqchi – a Mongol who later served with Babur in Samarqand in 1511. 'He had a little verse but recited well. He understood the astrolabe and astronomy well. He was excellent company and a good conversationalist, but he was a poor drinker.'[56] Babur then concludes by saying, 'There were [also] a few Turkmân *beg*s, whom the Mirza welcomed with great favor. One of the first to come was 'Ali Khan Bayandar [an Aq Qoyunlu Turk from Iran]. Asad Beg and Tahamtan Beg, an elder and younger brother, were others. Badi al-Zaman Mirza took Tahamtan Beg's daughter and with her had Muhammad Zaman Mirza…'.[57]

Regarding Husain Mirza's Chief Justices (*sudur*), 'One was Mir Sar-i Barahnah (Bare-head). He was from a village in Andijan and probably was not a real *saiyid*, [not a genuine descendant of the Prophet].[58] He was a very agreeable companion, good-natured and well-spoken. Among the learned and poets of Khurasan, his judgments and rulings were esteemed and carried weight. 'He produced a worthless thing', Babur remarks about one of his poems, 'as a response to the story of Amir Hamza, a false and bizarre story, contrary to nature and reason'. A second *sadr* was Kamal al-Din Husain Gazurgahi.

> Although he was not a Sufi, he was mystical. He assembled such mystically-inclined persons in 'Ali Shîr Beg's presence and went into raptures and the ecstasies of *samâ'* [singing or chanting]. He was probably better born than most. His respect was probably due to his good birth, since he had no other quality. He had a composition titled *Majalis al-'ushaq* ("Assemblies of Lovers")…It is mostly profane, extraordinarily weak, mainly false and also tasteless…It was this same Kamal al-Din who flattered Zu'n Nun Arghun with the title "The Lion of God".

This flattery encouraged him, Babur implies, to think so highly of himself that he later charged Shaibani Khan's army with a small force, resulting in his capture and death.[59]

Apart from *beg*s and *sudur*, Babur discussed the traits of ministers and revenue experts, religious scholars, poets, artists and musicians. While he identifies only two men with technical revenue knowledge, he praises one of them, Majd al-Din Muhammad Khwafi, as an individual who brought order to Husain Baiqara's chaotic finances and introduced radical reforms in Herat's revenue administration. Majd al-Din, a man of the Tajik or Persian administrative class, dominated Husain Baiqara's regime at two different periods, 1472–78 and 1487–90.[60] The son of an important treasury official under the former Timurid ruler of Herat Shah Rukh, Majd al-Din was first given extraordinary powers in 1472, three years after Husain Baiqara had seized Herat.

As Babur puts it, 'At first in Sultan Husain Mirza's Diwan [revenue office] there was a want of order and a lack of method and great extravagance and waste. Neither was the peasant prosperous nor was the soldier grateful'. Majd al-Din, he reports, told the sultan, 'If the Mirza agrees to strengthen my hands and not oppose my influence from this time the situation will be such that the peasant will be prosperous, the soldier grateful and the treasury full.' Majd al-Din took control of the entire province of Khurasan and, Babur reports, succeeded in making 'the peasant content, the soldier grateful, the treasury full and the country prosperous and populous'. He did this in the face of opposition of all of the *beg*s and dignitaries, led by 'Ali Shir Nava'i.[61] Forced from office once and then reappointed, rivals later accused him of embezzlement, and in 1490, they had Majd al-Din arrested, tortured and later killed as he travelled to Mecca, the fate of many disgraced or dismissed officials in sultanate regimes.

As for scholars, artists and musicians, Babur writes: 'In Sultan Husain Mirza's time Khurasan and especially Herat swelled with a population of learned and exceptional men'. He prefaces his individual portraits by briefly mentioning one of the two most famous writers in the city Maulana Nur al-Din 'Abd al-Rahman Jami (1414–92), a contemporary and friend of Mir 'Ali Shir Nava'i. He was a Naqshbandi Sufi and extraordinarily prolific poet, who is usually regarded as the last great poet of classical Persian verse. Babur says of him, first alluding to his religious knowledge, including Sufism, and then to his poetry: 'He was first in his day for his exoteric and esoteric knowledge. His verse is famous'.[62] Jami was such a towering figure that Babur says he felt unable to do justice to his stature, adding that he has mentioned Jami at the beginning of his section on Herat's intelligentsia and artists only as a kind of blessing for what follows.

What initially follows is Babur's appreciation of religious scholars, beginning with the former Shaikh al-Islam of Khurasan – Saif al-Din Ahmad. Saif al-Din was one of the victims of Shah Isma'il Safavi's murderous purge of Sunni officials when he occupied Herat in 1510, shortly after defeating and killing Shaibani Khan Uzbek. Saif al-Din was a descendant of the well-known Iranian theologian Sa'd al-Din Mas'ud Khurasani Taftazani (1322–90), whose works were widely known in Ottoman Sunni Muslim circles. Saif al-Din, Babur reports, was 'a very learned person. He knew the Arabic sciences [Quran] and revealed sciences [Islamic theology] well. He was an exceedingly pious and devout person. Although he was a Shafi'i [instead of a Hanafi] he respected [all] legal schools, *mazahib*'.[63]

Of nine other *'alim*s, most, like Saif al-Din, Babur praises for being 'very learned' in one respect or another, some in both exoteric and esoteric sciences, '*ulum-i zahir* and '*ulum-i batin*, some for their knowledge of philosophy, logic and rhetoric, *hukmiyat*, *'aqliyat* and *kalam 'ilmi*, and some for their religious writings. Perhaps because of these men's professions Babur finds fewer deviant personalities and less to criticise, although he suggests that Mir 'Ata'ullah of Mashad, *mazhabıda inhirafı bar ikandur*, 'may have turned away from the faith', often his way of suggesting someone had Shi'i sympathies. Otherwise he records personality quirks, such as Mir Murtaza's fanatical devotion to chess, or Mir 'Abdullah Ghafar's 'casual, unceremonious personality'.[64] He also includes an appreciation of Qazi Ikhtiyar, 'an excellent *qazi*, who wrote a Persian treatise on jurisprudence, *fiqh*'. He asked Babur to demonstrate the special script, *khatt*, he had developed, a hint of Babur's scholarly bent, which he demonstrates throughout the *Vaqayi*'. It is remarkable he could turn to such arcane scholarly pursuits amid his tumultuous life he had lived before meeting Qazi Ikhtiyar in Herat.[65]

He is most critical of Mir Muhammad Yusuf, Saif al-Din's successor as Shaikh al-Islam, who 'later [in life] became obsessed with the military and command. Apart from these two things', Babur writes, 'his conversation lacked wisdom and his pen lacked understanding. Although he had no success in either [of these military pursuits], these two ambitions had the [unexplained] consequence for him, losing his house and his home, his property and his life'. Then Babur concludes: 'He may have been a Shi'ah,' raising the question what he meant by his earlier vague reference to Mir 'Ata'ullah's possible spiritual deviation.[66]

Then there were the poets, artists and musicians, the very men who made Herat the cultural capital of the Perso-Islamic world in the late fifteenth century. It was these men whose verse, paintings and compositions Babur alluded to when he wrote that Husain Baiqara's reign was a 'wonderful age'. Poetry was the art Babur most admired and practiced. As his survey of the Herati military, religious and scholarly elite reveals, many literate members of Timurid society wrote verse, or like 'Umar Shaikh Mirza, they read or recited it. Babur mentions twelve poets, and two of them in particular – Jami and Nava'i, made major contributions to Persian and Turkic literature, which made them famous throughout the eastern Islamic world from Istanbul to Delhi.

Babur again briefly alludes to Jami, but merely says he was the greatest of the Herati poets, and does not attempt, for reasons he gave earlier, to summarise his achievements. It is easy to understand why he was reluctant to try to describe the work of an individual, whose wide-ranging literary, religious and scientific writings could not be easily summarised and which even Babur, despite his genuine literary interests, may not have found time to read, although he had read one of Jami's early work – the *Suhbat al-ahrar* – as he later alludes to the poem's metre.[67]

Still the least well known of the great 'classical' Persian language poets, Jami collected his many *ghazal*s, *ruba'i*s and *qasidah*s into three chronologically ordered *diwan*s: *Fatihah al-shabab*, or 'The Beginning of Youth', *Wasitah al-'iqd*, 'The Middle of the Necklace', and *Khatimah al-hayat*, 'The End of Life'. He also wrote an epic the *Haft Awrang*, or 'Seven Thrones', two parts of which are a written in response to Nizami's philosophical poem *Makhzan al-asrar*, 'The Storehouse of Mysteries'. Jami was also known to be a deeply committed Naqshbandi Sufi, whose piety suffused many of his verses, and as a scholar of multiple talents, who wrote on scientific subjects, Arabic grammar, Persian prosody and once simply, just his love of books.[68]

'Ali Shir Beg Nava'i, the other star in this literary firmament, was a childhood friend of Husain Baiqara and a literary and spiritual companion of Jami. Babur speaks with equal if not greater praise of this writer, both as a writer and as a patron of the arts. While earlier poets in Mawarannahr or Iran had composed in Turki, Nava'i, more than anyone else, established a 'classical' literary tradition of a language Western scholars generally call Chaghatai Turkish. Babur considers Nava'i under the heading of Husain Baiqara's *beg*s, since, unlike Jami, he was intimately involved with the sultan's administration. "Ali Shir Beg Nava'i,' he writes, 'was not his *beg* but his boon companion. They had been classmates together in childhood… There was not a person who was his equal. For verse written in the Turki language none have written as much or as well'.[69] He wrote six books of poems (*masnavi*), compiled four *diwan*s and several prose compositions, including one extolling Turki over the dominant literary language Persian.[70]

Yet, however much he admired the great man, Babur was not reluctant to critique his work. He found Nava'i's work on prosody *bisyar madkhul*, 'very confused', and thought that while some of the poet's *ruba'iyat* were not bad, most of his Persian language verse was 'feeble and vile'. This comes from Babur, whose own juvenile Persian verse was mediocre at best! Still he felt that 'in music' Nava'i composed some 'good things', including some fine 'airs and preludes'. Equally important for Babur, who was after all staying in Nava'i's former house while in Herat, the poet was a superb educator and patron of the accomplished and artistic.[71] He was responsible, Babur argues, 'for the development of Ustad Qul-i-Muhammad the lutanist, Shaiki the flautist, and Husain the lutanist, [who] became famous musicians... It was through his effort and supervision that Master Bihzad and Shah Muzaffar became so famous and celebrated in painting'.[72]

Outshone by these stars stood a galaxy of less influential Herati writers. Banna'i, a *takhalus* or pen name, sparks interest because he had met Babur during his second occupation of Samarqand in 1500–01, travelling there from Herat, after he had exchanged insults with his literary rival, the powerful Mir 'Ali Shir. In his *ghazal*s, Babur writes of Banna'i, 'there is grace and ecstasy. He organised a *diwan*. There are also *masnavi*s. One of his *masnavi*s, in the *mutaqarib* meter on the topic of fruits, is useless and worthless... He composed beautiful music. One song among these is called *Nuhrangi, Nine Variations*, characterised by nine themes and the song's variation on the note *rast*'.[73]

In Babur's pantheon of Herati poets, none ranked as highly as Jami, Nava'i and, to a lesser degree, Banna'i. Most of the others he either damns with faint praise or dismisses with acerbic critiques. One such individual was Saifi Bukhari, whom Babur considered a pedant. 'He reveled in his *mullah* status and to prove it he used to give a detailed list of books he had read.' He wrote no *masnavi* and of his two *diwan*s, Babur notes without further comment, 'one of them was completely written for craftsmen... There is a Farsi prosody. In one respect, it is very short; in another respect it is very long: brief in the sense it omits things that ought to be included, long in the sense that it details simple matters... It seems he was bad drinker and a poor drunkard'.[74]

'Abdullah the *masnavi* writer was another poet... Hatifi was his *takhallus*. There were tasty *ghazal*s, although the taste was not appropriate. There is Turki verse of his, which is not bad. Later, he went to Shaibani Khan and was treated with complete favour. He wrote a Turki *masnavi* in Shaibani Khan's name in the *raml masaddas makhbun* measure, the *Suhbat* measure [of Jami]. It is feeble and vile, '*sust u farud*. The person reading Muhammad Salih loses faith in his verse. This is one of his nice couplets.'

> The country of Ferghanah has become Tambal's [the fat man's]
> It made Ferghanah the Tambalkhanah [the house of the fat man.]

'They also call Ferghanah vilayat Tambal Khanah,' notes Babur, alluding to his former nemesis Sultan Ahmad Tambal, before concluding: 'Muhammad Salih was a malignant, tyranical and heartless person.'[75]

Another interesting writer was Hilali (New Moon), who was alive when Babur visited Herat. His

> *ghazal*s were melodious, elegant and somewhat affecting. Correct and graceful though his odes are, they make little impression... There is a diwan [and] a *masnavi* in the *khafif* meter titled "Shah and Darvîsh." Many couplets are quite acceptable but the *masnavi*'s subject and plan are very useless and bad... Hilali has made the lover a *darvish*, the beloved a king. The couplets concerning the king's act and words depict him as shameless and abominable... It is reported Hilali had a very good memory and had memorised thirty to forty thousand couplets, and most of two Quintets [of Nizami and Khusrau Dihlavi].[76]

Finally, Babur evaluates twelve Herati artists and musicians, beginning with Sultan 'Ali of Mashhad, a calligrapher, who was an outstanding writer of *naskhta'liq* and copied books for Husain Baiqara and Nava'i, 'writing every day'. Babur notes, 'thirty couplets for the Mirza and twenty for 'Ali Shir'. He briefly mentions two painters Bihzad and Shah Muzaffar, but he adds little to his earlier comment that they owed their prominence as 'distinguished artists', to Nava'i's patronage. His scant treatment of their work suggests he had little interest in the Persian-style miniatures these men produced. Babur confines his comments to praise for Bihzad's very delicate, *nazak*, painting, and criticism that the artist 'drew beardless faces poorly... Bearded faces he drew well'.[77] Shah Muzaffar, Babur mentions even more briefly. While noting this artist died young, he remarks that Shah Muzaffar 'produced fine portraits and painted hair especially delicately'.[78]

Babur seems far more appreciative of music, perhaps because he composed music himself. He previously praised Banna'i for his masterful compositions. *Suhbats* usually featured music, whether in solo performances or to accompany poetry recitals and Babur writes enthusiastically of several musicians, displaying his technical knowledge of instruments and musical modes. He repeats his earlier praise of the dulcimer, the *kanun* playing of the 'vicious and shameless' Khwäjah 'Abdullah Marwarid, and adds also his appreciation of the lutanist, Quli Muhammad, another beneficiary of Mir 'Ali Shir's patronage. He adds that Quli Muhammad was not only a superb artist on the *'oud*, but also played the guitar, *ghicak*, beautifully and 'added' three strings to it. He also wrote' Babur further remarks, 'superb instrumental preludes, *pishrau*' but Babur carefully notes that praise applied only to his preludes.[79]

Husain was another *'oud* player, who 'played with taste and sang delightful things... His sole fault, *'eib*, was this. He was incredibly boastful, *naz*, about playing'. Then there was 'Ghulam Shadi (Slave of Recitation), the son of Shadi the reciter... Though he played instruments, he played them less well than others.

There are excellent themes (*sut*) and beautiful airs (*naqhsh*) of his; no one in his day composed such excellent airs and fine themes.' Finally, Babur mentions a wrestler, who seems to have personified for him the florescence of the arts in Herat during Husain Baiqara's rule. 'An unrivaled man,' *binazir ildin*, Babur writes, 'was the wrestler, [*pahlavan*], Muhammad Bu-Sa'id. He was chief amongst wrestlers, also wrote verse, composed themes and airs, one excellent air being in four-time, *chargah*, [and] he was a wonderfully congenial person, *khush suhbat kishi*. It is extraordinary that such accomplishments are combined with wrestling'.[80]

In his portraits of Husain Baiqara and the military, administrative, scholarly, literary and artistic elite of Herat, Babur offers a remarkable tableau of complex individuals. In doing so, he reveals more about his personal biases and cultural preferences than can be found in any pre-modern literature of the Islamic, Persian or Turki world. He admires effective administrators, jurists and learned clerics, but devotes most of his attention to *beg*s, men of his own class, and to the artistic and literary elite. Of *beg*s Babur writes approvingly of simple but talented individuals he calls *turks*, that is, rustics, who were good archers and horsemen. Yet, most of all he praised men who resembled his father in different ways: sophisticated, talented individuals who were 'intelligent and leader-like', 'gay hearted and elegant', 'strong, graceful and well-mannered', 'comrades in wine and pleasure', men who were 'full of accomplishments', men who might be chess fanatics, write poetry and even play the dulcimer.

Such individuals – and in Babur's personal sketches they seem to be true individuals – conformed in varying degrees to his unstated ideal of a Turco-Mongol warrior aristocrat. They were men, like his father, this seemingly-perfect Timurid man, who combined '*beg*-like' military skills with social polish and cultural sophistication. These were men who fought well, but who also had pleasant tempers, the ability to drink companionably, converse amiably and, perhaps most of all, men who possessed the ability to practice the cultured arts: writing verse in various metres, playing instruments and even composing music. Separately, he praised talented and influential poets, effective administrators, accomplished religious scholars and talented artists and musicians. All these men – clerics, bureaucrats, *beg*s, poets, artists and musicians – comprised the complex population of this most sophisticated Turco-Mongol, Perso-Islamic sedentary society, lived among splendid buildings and delightful gardens. This was Babur's preferred world, the cultural world of great cities, the civilised world.

In describing *beg*s and others, Babur also catalogues an entire encyclopaedia of character faults he found offensive in some men, including those he otherwise admired, but typically saving such critiques, often unexplained, for the end of his portraits. In this way, he fulfils what he promises in the text just after describing his return to Kabul, that is, to appraise everyone fairly. Thus, he reveals that certain individuals were 'bad drinkers' and speaks contemptuously of braggarts, inexcusably bad poets, pretentious scholars, incompetent strivers, grasping, avaricious men, sinful individuals afflicted with wasting diseases and some who were simply muddle-headed military incompetents. In writing of them, Babur reveals a human aspect of the Herat society, hardly recognizable in the panegyric accounts written from afar or later by historians such as the Ottoman scholar and official Mustafa Ali. Perhaps he was excessively critical of human failings, but in these sometimes-devastating character sketches, Babur completed what for modern readers feels very much like a realistic, that is, truly humanistic, cast of idiosyncratic individuals. In doing so, he has produced an autobiography of almost novelistic subtlety when it comes to the dramatis personae of the Turco-Mongol, Perso-Islamic world at this time.

Return to Kabul

However much Babur enjoyed himself in Herat, by late December he grew increasingly restless and worried. He wrote later about the political situation in Kabul, although now he apparently had no news about trouble in the city. His cousins, for all their hospitality, had not bothered to arrange winter quarters for him and it had begun to snow in the mountains. Finally, on 24 December, using the pretext of finding winter quarters outside the city, he rode out, with some of his men not joining him until a month after he reached Kabul. As snow fell, some suggested they should travel via the longer but easier southern road through Qandahar. After much squabbling though, he decided to take the central route through the mountains, a disastrous decision, which almost cost him and his men their lives in the deep snow and cold of Afghanistan's winter. In one of the most self-serving, mean-spirited passages in the *Vaqayi'*, Babur blames this decision on the advice of one of his men, Qasim Beg Qauchin, rather than taking responsibility for it himself. He does this even though Qasim Beg, a member of a prestigious Andijan military family, was one of his most loyal and long-serving supporters, who, in other contexts, Babur praises more than any other man apart from his father.[81]

Suffering, Babur writes, more 'great alarm and hardships' than at any time in his life, he composed an opening couplet of a poem to express the perilous journey, as he and his men had to trample down drifts to advance even a mile or two a day during the worst part of the journey from the Herirud River valley over the mountains.

> Does there remain for me unseen, any cruelty or oppression of fate?
> Shall my wounded heart yet know unknown pain or suffering?[82]

Many of his men suffered terribly during a blizzard; two lost both their legs to frostbite, another both arms before they finally descended from the Zirrin Pass.

Around mid-February, a month and a half after leaving Herat, they arrived at Hazarah territory near Bamian. Nearby, they encountered an encampment of Turkmen Hazaras, 'thieves', *rahzan ve sarkashlar*, Babur writes, whose horses and sheep they seized.

As they were plundering the Hazarahs, Babur learned that several men in Kabul, fellow refugees from the Uzbeks, had persuaded the Mongol troops, still in the city, to install Wais Mirza, the son of his long deceased uncle Mahmud Mirza, as ruler of Kabul, claiming that the Herat *Mirzas* had taken Babur prisoner. Leading this coup were Muhammad Husain Dughlat, previously the ruler of Auratipa in Ferghanah, and Sultan Sanjar Barlas, a nephew of his maternal aunt, Shah Begim. She was a wife of the Chaghatai Mongol and Babur's maternal grandfather, Yunas Khan and the mother of Ahmad Khan of Mughulistan. However, having failed to take Kabul's citadel from Babur's loyalists, they were unable to put up much resistance when Babur suddenly arrived and, after a brief skirmish, captured all three men. He spared their lives, and later Wais Mirza re-joined Babur in an attack on Qandahar. Babur nonetheless writes bitterly of their betrayal, which he attributed to a conspiracy of his maternal or Chaghatai Mongol relatives, although Wais Mirza had a paternal Timurid descent. Nonetheless, Babur expresses a deeply felt grievance against his mother's kin, who, he says, had never helped him or his mother during their *qazaqlïq* days in Ferghanah. Yet, he had welcomed them to Kabul, he reports, out of respect for their *tabaqah*, their lineage. It is in this context that he writes at length about his intention to accurately describe events, insisting he always told the truth in his autobiography – about both relatives and others.

Fin de siècle Herat

Following Babur's powerful and moving description of the suffering, he and his men endured on their return journey from Herat and his account of the inept rebellion in Kabul, he offers his readers a kind of charming antidote by narrating a sightseeing excursion to the mountains. It is a preface to what became a later theme of his Kabul life, a life he came to love so much that he regretted ever leaving Kabul's cool forested countryside and its cascading streams for the hot, humid and arid plains of Hindustan. On this occasion, he and some men took time to ride north from Kabul to see the wildflowers in the *Gulbahar* or 'spring-flower' hills there. Later, he would delight in viewing fall colours in the same area.

Riding along the Baran River, known to a local unnamed poet as *jinnat* or paradise, Babur expressed his affecting pleasure in the natural beauty of the area – an aesthetic emotion he always experienced when visiting the riverside, by completing another *ghazal*, with the opening line of the *matla'*, reflecting something of his delight. 'Petal upon petal, my heart is like a rosebud,' but translated more artfully by Annette Beveridge, seemingly echoing the Scottish poet Robert Burns, as 'My heart, like the bud of a red, red rose, Lies fold within fold aflame.'[83] Few of his contemporaries or founders of other empires are remembered, as Babur is for his sensitive appreciation and literary evocation of nature, which he invokes many times over in his subsequent narrative.

The evident pleasure he took from this pastoral interlude was abruptly shattered when he learned that Shaibani Khan had overrun Khurasan, meeting only feeble opposition from Timurid forces. He writes that he heard Shaibani Khan had crossed the Murghab River in May or June on his way to attack the Timurid princes in Herat. Hearing details of events from refugees who fled to Kabul, Babur reports that the co-rulers of Herat, Badi al-Zaman Mirza and Muzaffar Mirza, along with Muhammad Baranduq Barlas and Zu'n-nun Arghun, had camped in a meadow east of Herat, as if preparing for battle, but they had done nothing to prepare for an Uzbek attack. He particularly blamed Zu'n-nun Arghun, who had been so close to Husain Baiqara, for the indecent denouement of the Herat Timurids. When Zu'n-nun and the *Mirzas* heard of Shaibani Khan's crossing of the Murghab they did nothing, Babur writes, neither collecting more troops nor forming a battle formation with the men they had. Zu'n-nun, who, Babur says, had long believed the flattery of courtiers in Herat, who had burnished his echo by praising his courage, charged Shaibani's army of an estimated 40,000 to 50,000 horsemen with no more than 150 of his men. He was captured and beheaded.

The Mirzas, Babur's refined cousins, who carved fowl so well, then retreated to a nearby fortress with their mothers, sisters, wives and treasure and Husain Baiqara's haram. Yet, rather than fortifying it, they soon fled westward leaving their families behind to be captured by the Uzbeks. On 27 May 1507, Shaibani Khan took Herat itself, virtually without a fight, thus bringing Husain Baiqara's brilliant Timurid cultural moment to an inglorious end. Herat's vice-regents fled: Badi al-Zaman Mirza to Azerbaijan, where he was captured by Ottoman forces and taken to Istanbul; Muzaffar Mirza went to Astarabad, near the Caspian, where he is lost to Babur's narrative. Two of the younger Mirzas, whose hangovers had caused them to be dilatory in welcoming Babur at the Murghab River crossing six months earlier, were captured near Mashhad, and, after embracing one another, were beheaded seated together on the ground by Shaibani Khan's forces.

While Babur does not reflect on the implications of the Uzbek victory, it had one major positive, long-term consequence. It left him as the single surviving Timurid prince of any consequence. Still in the summer of 1507, it was not obvious that he would long survive. His most immediate concern was to protect himself against the Uzbek juggernaut, as Shaibani Khan in Herat now threatened his impoverished refuge in Kabul. The fear that Uzbeks would swiftly overrun the entire region led Babur to think of establishing some kind of base in central Afghanistan at Qandahar, then held by Zu'n-nun's sons, Shah Beg and Muhammad Muqim. Having received friendly letters from Shah Beg and an actual invitation, he claims, to come to Qandahar from Muhammad Muqim, whom he had chased from Kabul in 1504, Babur decided to march west. He was thinking, he writes, to join the Arghun brothers in some ill-defined action to be decided upon when he arrived. However, as he approached the city, writing again to suggest an anti-Uzbek alliance, the brothers, he says, reneged on their earlier invitation, insulting him by placing their seal on a letter in a manner, which indicated they considered him a person of inferior status. Due to their rude reply, Babur writes, 'they forfeited their dynasty, their family and their treasure'.[84]

Babur confronted the Arghun's forces on the outskirts of Qandahar with, he says, only half of the 2,000 men who had ridden with him from Kabul. The others had gone off to forage for food, still in short supply in Kabul. Without waiting for them, Babur confronted the Arghun brothers and their estimated 4,000 to 5,000 troops in what he proudly characterises as a 'first-rate' battle formation. His elaborate description of his battle order, lists of its principal commanders and account of the actual conflict is important, for it represents the first of his three elaborate reports of pivotal battles. He followed this with vivid accounts of the Battle of Panipat, north of Delhi in 1526, and the epic struggle at Kanwah near Bianah, Rajasthan, in 1527. In his narrative, Babur supplies some of the most detailed battle plans and descriptions of combat in histories of the eastern Islamic world at this period.

Unlike his earlier reports of self-inflicted losses in Mawarannahr, in describing the battle of Qandahar, Babur congratulates himself on his organisation and tactics, which produced his first significant military victory. He begins by saying, 'Although our men were few, I had an excellent ordered and arranged battle plan, a *yasal*'.[85] He reports first on the battle order, with troops being divided into 'tens and fifties, each ten or fifty under a commander who knew the position in the right or left of center'.[86] With himself at the centre of a circle, *bui/boy*, of at least thirty-two young braves, *yiğitlar*, none of whom, he says, were great *begs*, *ulugh beglar yok*, the formation comprised three major sections, all led or staffed by Timurids.

His younger brother Nasir Mirza was formally in command of the vanguard or forward detachment, the *irawul*, which included several important *begs*, among them Sayyid Qasim Jalair, the Lord of the Gate, or *Ishik Aga*, and Shir Qul-i Mughal, the Qaraghul, or 'scout', who had helped to suppress the attempted coup in Kabul.[87] Babur assigned commands of the right and left wings, prestigious positions in Turco-Mongol warfare, to important *begs*. Two of the most important members of the right wing, or *baranghar*, were Wais Mirza, who had plotted against

Babur in Kabul but had been pardoned and now returned to his service, and Sherim Taghai Kunji Mughul. Sherim Taghai was a maternal or Mongol relative, Babur's great uncle, an Andijan loyalist at critical periods. Apart from Sherim Taghai and another Taghai, the right wing also included an important detachment of Mongols. The *yasal*'s left wing, its *javanghar*, was led by two important men, 'Abd al-Razzaq Mirza, the son of Ulugh Beg Kabuli (d. 1502) and therefore a Miranshahi Timurid, and Qasim Beg Quchin, so recently criticised for suggesting the mountain route to Babur as they left Herat. He later became Humayun's guardian. Two of Qasim Beg's sons, Tingri Birdi and Qambar 'Ali, also served in the left wing.

Babur's *Yasal* or Battle Order

	Irawül	
	(vanguard)	
javanghar	ghol	baranghar
(left wing)	(centre)	(right wing)
sol qol		ong gol
(left arm of centre)	khâsah tâbin	(right arm of centre)
	(imperial guard)	
sol yan		ong yan
(left side of guard)		(right side of guard)
	bui/boy	
	(command circle)	
sol		ong
(left of bui)		(right of bui)
	chağdavul	
	(Rear detachment)	

In Babur's account of the battle, the Arghuns began this open-field cavalry battle by assaulting his left wing and attacking his vanguard, forcing it back upon Babur's core circle of young troops. His right wing, heavily staffed by Mongols, then successfully attacked the Arghuns' left, apparently outflanking their troops and forcing them to abandon the field. This manoeuvre, known as *tulghamah*, was a well-known Turco-Mongol cavalry tactic, which Uzbeks used against Babur outside Samarqand in April 1501. Babur's use of it here presaged similar and critical Mongol flanking manoeuvres in his subsequent three major victories, against Uzbeks in 1511, Afghans in 1526 and Rajputs in 1527.

Muqim Arghun, however, on the right continued fighting until Babur, with a relatively small force of about 1,000 men, had the battle drums, the *negarets*, beaten, causing Muqim to abandon the field. Both he and his brother fled in different directions leaving Qandahar open to Babur. His men discovered in the fortress two separate treasuries, one belonging to each Arghun brother containing what Babur describes as an astonishing wealth of coins, silver *tankas* and a wealth of camels, masses of silk and cotton cloth and an enormous wealth of material goods of all kinds. Muqim must have brought some of this treasure from Kabul, when Babur forced him out of the city in 1504. His wealth may partly explain why Babur was so impoverished during his first years in Afghanistan.

After the victory, in a cynical act of realpolitik, Babur appointed his young brother Nasir Mirza to command Qandahar. Leaving him in Qandahar at Qasim Beg's urging to face the Uzbeks, he retreated along the Kabul road, taking the time to portion out the vast quantity of coins among his *beg*s, for their support and the pay of their retainers. We returned to Kabul, he reports, 'with masses of goods and treasure, great honour and reputation'.[88] How fortunate this must have seemed, for on his return, he finally was able to marry Ma'suma Sultan Begim, Sultan Ahmad Mirza's daughter, whom he had met the previous December in Herat. Somehow, amid the Qandahar campaign, someone had brought her out of Herat. This happy event was followed a few days later by the arrival of news that Shaibani Khan, urged on by the Arghun brothers, who had fled to his camp, had left Herat and laid siege to Qandahar.

Reflecting that the experienced Qasim Beg Quchin had given him good advice and without alluding to the perilous situation of his younger brother, Babur ratifies Qasim Beg's advice to flee back to Kabul by quoting unidentified Persian verse, an aphorism, which celebrates the wisdom of old age. It read: 'Whatever the youth sees in the mirror, The old person sees it in the baked brick'. Shaibani Khan's siege of Qandahar, Babur writes, frightened him and his men in Kabul, and his report on a council they held throws a brilliant autobiographical light on the uncertain, ad hoc process of Timurid empire-building in early sixteenth-century Afghanistan.

> The *beg*s were summoned [and] a council held. These were among the matters discussed, that such a foreign people as the Uzbeks and such an old enemy as Shibani Khan had seized all the provinces of Timur Beg's descendants. Of Turk [Timurid] and Chaghatai, [Mongol] who survived in corners and on the margins, they either willingly or unwillingly joined the Uzbeks. I alone remained in Kabul, the enemy very strong, ourselves extremely weak. Neither reconciliation nor resistance was possible. In the face of such power and strength we had to think of some place for ourselves.

> Given this brief opportunity it was imperative to get further away from this
> powerful enemy. Either the Badakhshan side or the Hindustan direction
> had to be chosen. It was imperative to decide on a direction.[89]

Babur and his men resolved the panic and indecision gripping them by opting
for India. They abandoned Kabul, very much as they had left Qandahar, in the
hands of another possible sacrificial lamb, in this case 'Abd al-Razaq Mirza, Ulugh
Beg Kabuli's son, an individual who might have reasonably claimed to be the
rightful Timurid heir to the city. Babur also gave Husain Baiqara's nephew, Wais
Mirza, and his grandmother Shah Begim permission to try their Timurid luck
in Badakhshan, as Shah Begim was descended from the ancient rulers of this
northern Afghan and southern Tajikistan territory. Babur's maternal aunt Mihr
Nigar Khanim, a blood relative, he points out, went with them, over his objections.

The Timurids fled from Kabul in September 1507 with no supplies, harassed
by Afghans, 'thieves' in Babur's words. The Afghans had, he said, prayed for such
an opportunity, a likely reflection of their hostility to his plundering and punitive
expeditions against them. After fighting their eastward way to Adinapur, the
modern Jalalabad, they had to find food, and learned the nearby Mil Kafirs had
large stocks of recently harvested rice. They rode into the nearby Kafir territory
and seized enough grain to provision themselves, killing the Kafirs who resisted
them.[90]

Sometime later, Babur decided against going to India. He does not explain his
reasons or link his decision with the news he heard about this time that Shaibani
Khan had unexpectedly abandoned his siege of Qandahar to rescue his *haram*,
captives of a rebellious commander in a fortress near Herat. Now in mid-winter
Babur made his way back to Kabul, ordering the date to be cut into a rock at the
pass where they crossed over from Lamghanat *tuman* to the Kabul region. He
gave Nasir Mirza Ghazni, where his brother had fled during the Uzbek siege, and
granted the valuable Ningnahar *tuman* to 'Abd al-Razaq Mirza. Astonishingly, for
the times when loyalties were so fragile, Ulugh Beg Kabul's son had not tried to
claim Kabul for himself during this brief interregnum.

Babur, who had thus survived yet another possible calamity, celebrated his return
to Kabul by having himself titled *Padshah*, an imperial Iranian title, reflecting his
sense of status as the only surviving Timurid ruler, as well as suggesting his future
ambitions. Mongol Khans had sometimes used this title, but as Babur remarks,
none of the Timurids, who were universally acknowledged only as *mirzas*, had
never assumed it. Then on 6 March 1508, his son Humayun was born, with his
birth celebrated by a feast five or six days later and typically with celebratory

verses, one by a 'minor poet', in Babur's estimation, as '*Sultan Humayun Khan*' and '*Shah-i firuz qadr*' (Shah of Victorious Power).

Around this time also Babur commemorated this titular inflation by having an inscription cut into a rock south of Kabul. According to his grandson Jahangir, who visited the city in June 1607, the place was then known as the *Takht-i Shah*, the Throne of the King, while the inscription read: 'The seat of the king, the asylum of the world, Zahir al-Din Muhammad Babur, son of 'Umar Shaikh Gürgan, May God perpetuate his Kingdom'. By inscribing Temür's title *Gürgan*, or son-in-law, Babur publicised his own and his father's Timurid heritage. Babur later had the same title inscribed on his coinage. Jahangir, who describes the scene where, he reports, Babur used to sit and drink wine, ordered a second basin cut in the rock that would hold wine and had his own name engraved on this stone terrace, along with that Temür, in this case Temür's honorific 'Sahib-i qirani', the Lord of the Auspicious Conjunction, a title also adopted by Jahangir, but trumpeted more assertively by his son Shah Jahan.[91]

The seeming idyll of the immediate aftermath of Babur's return to Kabul was shattered by a rebellion of many of Khusrau Shah's Mongols, troops which Babur had acquired as he fled south from Ferghanah in 1504. Joining them were 2,000 or 3,000 Turkmen, some of whom had fought with him at Qandahar. Those who reported the uprising to Babur did not know if 'Abd al-Razaq Mirza was initially involved, but he had left Ningnahar and come to Kabul at this time. Babur's young cousin Haidar Mirza, who took refuge with him in 1509, reported that 3,000 of Khusrau Shah's Mongols rebelled against Babur and 'raised Abd al-Razzaq to the throne'.[92] Babur later executed him for his suspected part in this uprising.

Babur himself records only how he first learned of the rebellion, since his autobiography breaks off in May 1508 and does not resume until 1519. Lacking his richly detailed, reflective and emotion-laden narrative for these years, it is necessary to rely on Haidar Mirza's personal account for the three years he spent with Babur between 1509 and 1512 and the occasional reference to Babur's in a few scattered sources. He describes Babur's suppression of the rebellion, which featured him fighting and defeating five of the rebel's champions.[93] The rebellion, however, passes into insignificance in Haidar Mirza's narrative when he records the victory the new Safavid ruler of Iran Shah Isma'il Safavi, won over Shaibani Khan on December 1510. At news of his Uzbek nemesis' defeat, Babur immediately left Kabul for the north, where he planned to join Wais Mirza and plan an attack on the still formidable Uzbek forces that remained in Mawarannahr, hoping that if he was victorious, he could then move on to Samarqand.

Endnotes

1   BN–M, fs. 165b–166a.

2   BN–M, fs. 159a and 129a.

3   BN–M, fs. 128a and 129b. For a survey of Kabul from Akbar's era to the collapse of Timurid-Mughal rule in the early eighteenth century, see Farah Abidin, *Suba of Kabul Under the Mughals: 1585–1739* (Delhi: Partridge, 2014).

4   BN–M, fs. 140a–b. Erskine estimates the value of the *shahrukhi* at 'nine pence half penny'. *A History of India Under the First Two Sovereigns of the House of Taimur, Bâber and Humâyûn*, 414n. See also his appendix 'Amount of Bâber's Revenues,' 540–46 and Stephen F. Dale, *The Garden of the Eight Paradises, Bâbur and the Culture of Empire in Central Asia, Afghanistan and India (1483–1530)* (Leiden and Boston: Brill, 2004), 334–35 for a discussion of Indian and Timurid coinage.

5   BN–M, f. 292b.

6   BN–M, fs. 187b–188a.

7   Mounstuart Elphinstone, *An Account of the Kingdom of Caubul and its Dependencies in Persia, Tartary and India* (London: Longman *et al.*, 1815), 173 and 176.

8   BN–M, f. 144b.

9   See BN–B, 437–38, for a discussion of this text.

10   BN–M, f. 144b.

11   In his nineteenth-century ethnography of Afghanistan, H. W. Bellew alludes to the 'Hazarah proper' as opposed to the use of the application of the term Hazarah 'to all divisions of the Aimâc [Aimâq]' or nomads. H. W. Bellew, *An Inquiry into the Ethnography of Afghanistan* (Graz, Austria: Akademische Druck-u. Verlagsanstalt, repr. 1973), 34. In later centuries, this name was used exclusively for Persian-speaking Shi'i Muslims living in central Afghanistan, the region surrounding the Bamian Buddhas later destroyed by the Taliban. Babur gives little information about the specific tribes he calls Hazarahs.

12   BN–M, f. 160a–160b.

13   BN–M, f. 144b. While Babur names some individuals who joined him in Kabul, he does not systematically identify or quantify the different groups, which arrived after he took the city. It would have been natural for Timurid loyalists and their Chaghatai Mongol kin to flee Uzbek control for the new Timurid state, as they did later after his victories in India.

14   BN–M, f. 145a.

15   Ibid.

16   Babur dates this verse to 1505, but he may have written it or part of it a year earlier. See the analysis of the verse in Dale, *The Garden of the Eight Paradises, Bâbur and the Culture of Empire in Central Asia, Afghanistan and India (1483–1530)*, 272–74.

17   BN–M, fs. 149b–150a.

18 Babur states he kept the Kabul *vilayat* or province for himself, but he must refer only to the immediate Kabul *tuman* or district, since he assigned parts of the province to family members or retainers. See BN–M, f. 128a passim and Beveridge's notes on the Kabul section.

19 BN–M, fs. 202b and 203a.

20 BN–M, fs. 159a–b.

21 BN–M, f. 170b.

22 BN–M, 121b.

23 BN–M, f. 157a.

24 BN–M, fs. 162b–163a.

25 BN–M, f. 184b.

26 BN–M, f. 186a.

27 BN–M, f. 187a.

28 For an explanation of the term, see the entry 'tore' in Reşit Rahmeti Arat, ed., *Vekayi: Babur'un Hâtıratı*, 656–57.

29 BN–M, f. 186b.

30 BN–M, f. 187b.

31 BN–M, f. 187b.

32 BN–M, f. 87a.

33 Terry Allen provides a detailed survey of Timurid Herat's monuments and gardens, with references to Babur's visit, in his book *A Catalogue of the Toponyms and Monuments of Timurid Herat* (Cambridge, MA: Aga Khan Program for Islamic Architecture, 1981).

34 BN–M, fs. 20a and 191b–192a.

35 BN–M, f. 191b.

36 Dale, *The Garden of the Eight Paradises: Babur and the Culture of Empire in Central Asia, Afghanistan and India (1483–1530)*, 274.

37 BN–M, fs. 189a–190a.

38 Eiji Mano discusses the 'willow trees' passage in his article *The Weeping-Willows Passage in the Bâbur-nâmâ*, Proceedings of the 27th Meeting of Haneda Memorial Hall (Kyoto: Institute of Inner Asian Studies, 1993), 28–35.

39 BN–M, fs. 164a–165a.

40 BN–M, f. 177b.

41 Cornell H. Fleischer, *Bureaucrat and Intellectual in the Ottoman Empire: The Historian Mustafa Âli (1541–1600)* (Princeton: Princeton University Press, 1986), 71.

42 BN–M, fs. 166a and 169b–170a.

43 BN–M, f. 169b–170a.

44 166a.

45 BN–M, f. 165b.

46 BN–M, f. 201a.

47 See Chapter 4, for more details.

48 BN–M, f. 170a.

49 BN–M, fs. 170a–b.

50 BN–M, f. 172a.

51 BN–M, f. 173b.

52 BN–M, f. 172a–173a.

53 BN–M, f. 173a.

54 BN–M, fs. 173a–b.

55 BN–M, f. 175a.

56 BN–M, fs. 175a–b.

57 BN–M, f. 175b. Muhammad Zaman Mirza was the last surviving male heir of Sultan Husain Baiqara.

58 BN–M, d. 176a. *Sudur,* the plural of *sadr,* can connote a judge, a minister or an important official.

59 BN–M, fs. 176a–b.

60 Maria Eva Subtelny discusses this man's policies and his conflict with the Turco-Mongol elite, including Mir 'Ali Shir Nava'i, who reacted angrily and ultimately successfully in opposing his centralising reforms. See Maria Eva Subtelny, *Timurids in Transition*: Turko-Persian Politics and Acculturation in Medieval Iran, 79–99, and in her article 'Centralizing Reforms and its Opponents in the Late Timurid Period', *Iranian Studies* 21, No. 1–2 (1988), 123–51.

61 BN–M, fs. 176b–177a.

62 BN–M, f. 177b.

63 BN–M, f. 177b.

64 BN–M, fs. 178b–179a.

65 BN–M, f. 179a. The script was believed to be lost but it is discussed by the Turkish scholar Ali Alparslan in his article on the Quran Babur copied using the script. 'Babur' un icad ettiği/Babur yazısı/ve onunla yazılmış olan Kur'an' Türkiyat Mecmuası Dergisi 18 (1976): 161–68. The prolific Soviet scholar S. A. Azimdjanova published photographs of the script in her presentation 'Novie Svedeniya o 'Khatt-i Baburi,' at the XXVI Congress of Orientalists in Moscow, 1963. I am indebted to Anshuman Pandey for bringing Azimdjanova's presentation to my attention in his online presentation, ISO/IEC JTC1/SC2/WG2 N4130 L2/11-341 2011-09-16, in which he includes photographs of Babur's script.

66 BN–M, f. 179a.

67 BN–M, fs. 179a and f. 346a.

68 Still one of the best introductions to Jami's work is the Soviet era scholar Bertel's *Izbrannye Trudy, Navoi i Dzhami*, 209–73.

69 BN–M, f. 170b. See Bertel's, *Izbrannye Trudy, Navoi i Dzhami*, 1-208 for a superb introduction to Nava'i's work.

70 See Mir ʿAli Shîr, *Muhâkamat al Lughatain*, trans. and ed. Robert Devereux (Leiden: Brill, 1966).

71 BN–M, 170b–171a.

72 BN–M, f. 171a.

73 BN–M, 179b–180a.

74 BN–M, f. 180b.

75 BN–M, f. 181a. *Tambal means fat.*

76 BN–M, fs. 181a–b.

77 BN–M, f. 181b.

78 BN–M, f. 182a.

79 For a sophisticated appreciation of Timurid era music, largely taken from Babur's *Vaqayiʿ, see* John Bailey, *Music of Afghanistan: Professional Musicians in the City of Herat* (Cambridge: Cambridge University Press, 1988), 12–15.

80 BN–M, f. 182b.

81 BN–M, f. 14a.

82 BN–M, f. 193b. Babur refers to these verses as a *matlaʿ*, the opening couplet of a *ghazal*, which he evidently completed later. In the Turkish translation of his *diwan* or verse collection, it appears as the opening lines of his forty-ninth *ghazal*. See Bilal Yücel, *Babur Dîvânı*, 147.

83 Dale, *The Garden of the Eight Paradises, Babur and the Culture of Empire in Central Asia, Afghanistan and India (1483-1530)*, 276–77.

84 BN–M, f. 208a.

85 BN–M, f. 209a.

86 The Turkish scholar Reşit Rahmeti Arat gives the best information and illustration of the Turco-Mongol *yasal* or battle order in his modern (1943) Turkish translation of Babur's autobiography. See his *Vekayi Babur'un Hatıratı*, 664–66. He takes much of his information from Babur's text.

87 Babur mentions several individuals who served as his Lord of the Gate, but reconstructing the dates of the men who held this critical post is difficult.

88 BN–M, f. 212b.

89 BN–M, f. 213a.

90 Kafiristân, the 'stan' or country of *kafir*s or unbelievers, which became known after the inhabitants' later forcible conversion to Islam as *Nuristan*, the 'stan' of light or Islam, is a mountainous region, whose inhabitants George Scott Robertson describes in his 1896 work, *The Kafirs of the Hindu-Kush* (Karachi: Oxford University Press, repr. 1974).

91 Jahangir, *Tûzuk-i Jahângîrî or Memoirs of Jahângîr*, trans. Alexander Rogers and ed. Henry Beveridge (Delhi: Munshiram Manoharlal repr. 1978), I, 108.

92 TR, II, 204.

93 TR, II, 137.

3

Mulkgirliq: The Act of Kingdom-Seizing

Samarqand Redux

Babur's third and last attempt to reclaim Samarqand for himself and the Timurids was made possible by Shah Isma'il when on 2 December 1510, the founder of the new Safavid state defeated and killed Shaibani Khan Uzbek near Merv. This city in modern Turkmenistan was approximately 150 miles northeast of the Iranian city of Mashhad. Babur learned of Shaibani Khan's death when his Miranshahi Timurid cousin, Wais Mirza, sent a messenger with the news also telling him that 20,000 Mongols – previously subjugated by the Uzbeks – had arrived in Qunduz.[1] According to Haidar Mirza, Babur, always 'the Padshah' in his text, immediately left Kabul for Qunduz, taking the route with no high passes because it was winter. He reached Bamian and celebrated Ramadan on 1 January. He arrived at Qunduz in late January, where Wais Mirza and the Mughul troops greeted him.

In 1507, Wais Mirza had earlier gone to Badakhshan with Shah Begim – Babur's maternal or Mughul grandmother – when Shaibani Khan Uzbek seemed poised to march on Kabul from Qandahar. He had been living, what Haidar Mirza describes as a 'miserable life' in the isolated Badakhshan fortress of Zafar, harassed by Uzbek marauders and surrounded by hostile Badakhshan natives.[2] After he heard about Shaibani Khan's death and sent his messenger to Babur, Wais Mirza went to Qunduz. He apparently hoped to assemble a joint anti-Uzbek campaign with Babur that might improve his own political fortunes and those of his displaced relatives, who had suffered badly after the Uzbek triumph in Mawarannahr.

It is impossible to say how many loyal troops Babur brought with him from Kabul. He had earlier commanded about 2,000 when he marched on Qandahar, but he had suppressed the recent revolt in Kabul with only 500 men. Whatever his force, sometime later that winter, Babur, Wais Mirza and some of the recently arrived Mongols crossed the Amu Darya, intending to attack the two Uzbek governors of Hisar. Yet, when they prepared to stage an attack on the camp of one of the Uzbeks, Hamza Sultan, they discovered that he had already fled. Failing to engage the Uzbeks after much confused manoeuvring, Babur and his cousin eventually retired to Qunduz.

At this juncture, Babur's older sister, Khanzada Begim, arrived in Qunduz. She was sent by Shah Isma'il, who recognised her after his victory in Merv. Babur had left her behind in Samarqand after he fled the city in 1501, married to Shaibani Khan under unexplained circumstances. The Uzbek had married her, but shortly afterwards, distrusting her, in Haidar Mirza's telling of the affair, he married her off to an influential saiyid, who had died alongside Shaibani Khan in the battle with the Safavids.[3] About this time, Haidar Mirza, who had travelled with Babur from Kabul to Qunduz, received a message from his uncle Sa'id Khan, also previously a refugee with Babur in Kabul, that he succeeded in joining some Mongol troops in Andijan and had expelled Uzbek forces from the valley.[4] Haidar Mirza writes that this new information energised the Timurids and their Chaghatai kin to think that they might expel the Uzbeks from Mawarannahr.

Given this news and the prospect of finally returning to Samarqand, Babur and Wais Mirza crossed the Amu Darya a second time to confront the Uzbek governors of Hisar, about 120 miles to the north. At this time, their combined forces included approximately 3,000 of the 20,000 Mongols who had come to Qunduz. According to Haidar Mirza, these particular men were among his deceased father's hereditary Mongol retainers.[5] Babur's forces were also strengthened by an Iranian detachment, which arrived after he had sent Wais Mirza on a mission to the Safavid Shah with pledges of *ita'at u inqiyad*, 'fealty and submission'. This act began his entanglement with Shah Isma'il and Shi'i Islam. Babur's 'fealty and submission' meant he recognised Shah Isma'il's sovereignty in Mawarannahr, which, by later evidence, also included his formal acceptance of Shi'i Islam as a state religion after he occupied Samarqand. Thus, when he took the city, Shah Isma'il's name and not Babur's was read in the Friday prayers, and the Shi'i profession of faith, *Shahada, 'Ali wali Allah* was stamped on coins, including his own coinage.[6] Babur makes clear his personal revulsion of Shi'i and their 'heretical' faith throughout his autobiography, but if Paris would be well worth a Mass for Henry IV in 1593, Samarqand was evidently worth at least an outward profession of Shi'i faith for Babur in October 1511 – the month he eventually entered Samarqand.[7]

With Wais Mirza, Haidar Mirza, his newly acquired Mongol troops and the Safavid contingent, Babur marched north to face a formidable Uzbek force at the Pul-i Sangin – the stone bridge over the Surkhab River due east of Hisar. It was the site where Temür had once won a major victory. After the armies faced each other across the river for a month, the superior Uzbek force crossed the river downstream to outflank Babur's troops. This drove him to retreat with his outnumbered contingent into the mountainous terrain on the left bank of the river. The Uzbeks concentrated their attack on the left wing, defended by Wais Mirza, who was nearly overrun before the commander of the Mongol contingent from Qunduz intervened to save him. Here, as in Babur's battles at Qandahar and against Afghans and Rajputs in India, Mongol tactics and contingents ensured victory.

The battle ebbed back and forth during the day but, near evening, Babur, who had not been involved with the fierce fighting on the left wing, decided to make camp for the night. The Uzbeks facing Babur's men also began to retire to the river for the evening. Seeing this, the Uzbeks fighting Wais Mirza and the Mongols turned to retreat, precipitating a chaotic melee in the Uzbek centre. This allowed Babur's men to counterattack and 'by the time of the evening prayer', three Uzbek Khans were captured and brought before Babur, and, in Haidar Mirza's words, 'what Shaibani Khan had done to the Mongol Khaqans [in Ferghanah], the Chaghatai Sultans [Babur and Wais Mirza's forces] now did to them'.[8]

Afterwards Babur and his forces regrouped at Hisar, where they were joined by Iranian reinforcements and unspecified troops 'from all parts of the world', generating a total new force, Haidar Mirza estimated, of nearly 60,000 men.[9] It seems unlikely that Babur had anything like this number of men at his disposal, and Haidar Mirza does not report that he, or anyone else, was assigned to count units of the expanded army. Whatever was their actual size, Babur, Wais Mirza and Haidar Mirza marched northward to assault the Uzbeks at their principal bases in Samarqand and Bukhara. At their approach, Uzbek forces in both cities retreated into the Turkistan desert. Babur then gratefully dismissed his Iranian allies and re-entered Samarqand for the third and last time on 8 October 1511. Haidar Mirza describes his ecstatic reception by the entire populace of the city, 'from great to small...from merchant to peasant', a welcome that in Haidar Mirza's account soon turned to bitter disappointment when Babur had the Shi'i profession of faith read in Shah Isma'il's name.[10]

Writing three decades after these tumultuous events, Haidar Mirza offers the sole, first-person account of what was known about Babur's motives and the consequence of his actions. He implies that Samarqand residents had known that Babur had outwardly agreed to Shah Isma'il's terms in exchange for his help. He explains this as an act of realpolitik, saying that 'in the time of necessity... [Babur] donned the clothes of the Qizilbash', using the common Turkish name 'Redheads' for the Iranian Shah's largely Turkic tribal followers, who wore special turbans symbolising their Shi'i allegiance. Perhaps, Babur actually adopted the Safavid turban. Haidar Mirza argues that the populace expected Babur to 'renounce this schism which verged on heresy', and replace these clothes with 'the crown of Muhammad's tradition'. Instead, he says, Babur 'procrastinated and dissimulated with the Qizilbash', shattering the expectations of the – presumably – mostly Sunni populace in the city.[11]

The question that Haidar Mirza left unanswered is the degree to which Babur's public adoption of Shi'i Islam in exchange for Safavid military aid contributed to his later defeat by 'Ubaidullah Khan Uzbek near Bukhara in the spring of 1512. The reports of Shah Isma'il's murder of Sunni leaders in Herat in December or January 1510 must have been widely known in Mawarannahr by this time. The Safavid Shah's especially ferocious assault on the Sunni Naqshbandî Sufi order must have also caused consternation for Timurids and Timurid loyalists, considering their reverence for Khwajah Ahrar and other Naqshbandî Sufi *shaikhs*. Babur himself would have seemed especially hypocritical because he was by birth and profession a disciple of the Naqshbandî leader. Finally, the Sunni Uzbek loyalist Ruzbihan Khunji, who was in Samarqand when Babur arrived, writes bitterly of these 'heretics', and claims he convinced 'Ubaidullah Khan to campaign against Babur. The unanswerable question remains: Did the revulsion of the Sunni residents in Samarqand contribute directly to Babur's military defeat?

Haidar Mirza, who was nonetheless ill in Samarqand during this battle, writes with unfeigned astonishment that Babur, with a large force he estimates, probably wrongly, at 40,000 men, could have lost the Battle of Köl-i-Malik in May or June 1512 to what he characterises as 'Ubaidullah Khan's *pur-rikhtih* or 'rag-tag' force of approximately 3,000 Uzbeks.[12] Yet, even if Babur had 10,000 men, he could have presumably defeated the Uzbeks. The Safavid historian Hasan-i-Rumlu attributes the Uzbek victory to the heroism of twenty men and a trap sprung by the Uzbek commander.[13] Haidar Mirza in his later astonishment at the Timurid defeat could only attribute Babur's loss to God's demonstration of his omnipotence. He does not, interestingly, ascribe the defeat to the anti-Shi'i hostility of the Samarqand populace, or the Sunni beliefs of the broader population of Mawarannahr. Probably, it is most reasonable to assume that once again, as in Babur's loss to Shaibani Khan at Sar-i-pol in 1501, Uzbek military discipline and manoeuvrability and the unwieldy nature of the Timurid coalition explain his defeat in 1512.

Babur now briefly returned to Samarqand before turning back to Hisar with the recuperating Haidar Mirza in tow. He once again sought the help of Shah Isma'il, who sent him a commander Mir Najm, with a reported 60,000 troops, another figure that must be taken with a grain of salt, as Haidar Mirza, who supplies the figure, had left Babur's side to join his uncle in Andijan before the new Iranian troops arrived. Another estimate by Hasan-i Rumlu is that Mir Najm brought only 12,000 horsemen, a far more reasonable number.[14] Still, Babur and his Iranian allies felt confident enough to return northwest and overrun the Uzbek-held fortress of Qarshi near Samarqand. Following a massacre, a *qatl-i 'am*, or 'general slaughter', of some 15,000 inhabitants, apparently ordered by Mir Najm, he and Babur turned towards Bukhara and the fortress of Ghizhduvan. Uzbek forces defeated them there, killing Mir Najm and most of his troops.

Once again Babur fled back to Hisar with the remainder of his troops and family members. Ruzbihan Khunji, commemorated this retreat in an insulting Persian *ghazal*, two lines of which read:

> From Samarqand's gate that pathetic army again
> Fled to Hisar, hidden under a *chadar*.
> Babur, fortunate to have been a Sunni,
> Now through calculation became a friend of heresy.[15]

In Hisar, Babur experienced a revolt of some of his recently acquired commanders, probably confirming his long-held mistrust of Mongol troops. He was forced to abandon that fortress and flee south across the Amu Darya back to Qunduz, while his former allies plundered Hisar. They so devastated the city that one of the Mongol Khans, Mir Ayyub Begchik, previously with Babur in Andijan and at Qandahar, later regretted the Mongol destruction, telling Haidar Mirza, 'I frequently pleaded with God quickly to call down a calamity so that the Muslims [of Hisar] would be released'.[16]

Apparently Babur still hoped to return to Mawarannahr, for he spent the next two years wandering around the Qunduz region, unremarked by any historian. However, he never again crossed the Amu Darya in force, leaving Samarqand to the Uzbeks. By 1514, he had returned to Kabul. Surprisingly, Nasir Mirza, who had been left in charge of the city for these several years, peacefully returned to his district of Ghazni. By 1519 at the latest, Babur turned his attention to the conquest of Hindustan. Babur's descendants retained a revanchist ambition for the Timurid homelands. In 1607, Jahangir wrote in his autobiography that 'I had made up my exalted mind to the conquest [of] …the hereditary kingdom of my ancestors'.[17] Yet, he, in his years of alcoholic and drug-induced torpor, never mounted an expedition. His son Shah Jahan, far more ambitious and active, dispatched forces to Balkh between 1645 and 1648, but was unable to hold that city, much less move across the Amu Darya to march on Samarqand.

Little is known about Babur's state of mind between 1514 and 1519, the date when his autobiography resumes. He seems to have been preoccupied with Afghan affairs, rather than either Mawarannahr or Hindustan. Sometime in 1517 or 1518, he returned briefly to northern Afghanistan, where he had appointed Husain Baiqara's grandson and last surviving heir – the 21-year-old Muhammad Zaman Mirza, recently married to Babur's 9-year-old daughter – as governor. In the same year, Babur made another attempt to re-take Qandahar from Shah Beg Arghun.[18] When the autobiography resumes on 3 January 1519, he reports being engaged in yet another of the never ending attempts to pacify his Afghan territories. By March, however, he makes several entries in his autobiography that indicates Hindustan that had at last become the focus of his Timurid *mulkgirliq* ambitions.

The Indian Expeditions

In January, Babur and his men began a sustained campaign to subjugate Pushtun tribes in the region northeast of Adinapur.[19] The powerful and influential Yusufza'i Pushtuns were his principal target, but he began an attack on 3 January with a well-fortified fortress of Khahr, which he calls Bajaur, about 100 miles east-northeast of Kabul, now included within Pakistan's Northwest Frontier districts.[20] Over a two-day period, he staged a concerted attack, featuring for the first time, the use of *tufang* or matchlock weapons.[21] Derided with obscene ridicule by its defenders, who had never seen firearms before, Babur's men used them to kill up to ten men on the ramparts of the fort on the first day. On the second day, one of his men twice fired something Babur calls a *firingi*, a light cannon. At this stage, however, gunpowder was a minor and preliminary factor in a pitched battle featuring Babur's men letting fly blizzards of arrows as others scrambled up ladders to attack the defenders with sword and lance. After three hours, they prevailed and then massacred an estimated 3,000 captives – an act, Babur justifies, citing their enmity and unexplained 'heretical customs'.[22]

After sending news of the victory to Kabul and northern Afghanistan, Babur and his men rode down the valley from the fort, where on 11 January they erected a 'minaret' or tower of skulls, followed the next day by a wine party and seizures of corn to feed the army. Later at Kahraj, they demanded 4,000 ass-loads of rice, which he admitted ruined the local populace, who were unable to pay the full amount.[23] This was followed by a series of other raids to seize corn and a pause to conclude a marriage to the daughter of a Yusufza'i chief to conciliate some clans of this tribe. In early February, further marches eastward aimed at pacifying Yusufza'i and Mohammadi Pushtuns. Later in mid-February, after taking the time to destroy a tomb of a 'heretic *qalandar*', he paused to consume some of the intoxicating confection *ma'jun* on the tomb's picturesque hillside. He expressed his delight at this aesthetically appealing natural perspective, as he had done earlier for gardens in Samarqand and Kabul.

Following this pastoral interlude, Babur decided to march southeast to Bhirah, across the Indus, just below the Salt Range on the east bank of the Jhelum River. By doing so, he penetrated into what he terms 'the borderlands of Hindustan'. He was responding, he reports, to his men's complaint that they had acquired nothing, no significant plunder so far in their *yurush*. He thought they might acquire something with a rapid strike further east, perhaps recalling the wealth they plundered during their incursion on the west bank of the Indus in 1505. Yet, as Babur narrates the march on Bhirah, he reveals that a spontaneous raid for plunder somehow became in his mind an ad hoc *mulkgirliq* act, a Timurid imperial invasion to seize territory in India. His narrative is fascinating because of its confusing account of his abrupt decision to begin occupying Indian territory, and even challenging the reigning Ludi Afghan government of Delhi in the name of Timurid legitimacy. More than anywhere else in his autobiography, his account of these events suggests a distortion due to a conflation of political ambition and imperfect memories of complex events.

In describing his march towards Bhirah and arrival outside the city, Babur makes a number of crucial but confusing comments about his intentions. He notes first that he had thought of conducting a Hindustan *yurush* – an Indian campaign – ever since he came to Kabul, but had not done so for various unexplained reasons. In writing this, he cannot mean to imply that he had been thinking of invading India since December 1504.[24] Not only had he sought to recover Samarqand in 1511 and remained in Badakhshan until late 1514. He had also written that he decided to march on Bhirah because his men longed for plunder and he thought a brief Indian *yurush* might yield something. Yet, when Babur later describes fording the Indus on 17 February on his way to the city, he gives a completely different impression. He indicates that he had decided to begin the subjugation of India. Babur writes that 'Taking Hindustan was always being considered', and because Bhirah and the nearby towns of Khushab, Chin-ab and Chiniut 'had once been territories of the Turk [Temür/Timurids]... we thought of them as our own'.[25] Finally, he adds to the confusion of these statements in a parenthetical remark that the original idea to march on Bhirah was not even his plan. It had been suggested to him, he writes, by one Langar Khan, whose maternal uncles held territory along the Salt Range near the city.[26] This in turn raises the unanswerable question of Langar Khan's motives: was he encouraging Babur to plunder his relatives or supplant them?

In trying to make sense of Babur's narration of the move across the Indus to Bhirah, it may be wise or at least prudent to assume that – given his description of the initial attack on Bajaur and the planned assault on the Yusufza'i Pushtuns – the decision to move east was initially driven by his men's frustrations. Babur evidently chose Bhirah due to Langar Khan's advice. His precipitate decision to treat the Bhirah raid as an invasion of India, which many of his men had actually opposed, may have been the product of three factors. First, as a descendant of Temür, Babur believed he inherited a legitimate right to claim Hindustan. Second, there was the grim reality of his situation in Kabul. He knew that impoverished and impossibly contentious Afghanistan was no place to realise *mulkgirliq* ambitions. Third, by December 1514, when he finally returned to Kabul from the north, he must have finally concluded it was impossible for him to return north and overthrow the well-entrenched and militarily-formidable Uzbek forces in Mawarannahr and re-establish a Timurid state at Samarqand.

As Babur's forces approached Bhirah he issued an order, which by itself testifies to his decision to suspend the *yurush* in favour of an occupation – a territorial seizure. Thus, even though while in camp on 19 February, he was aware of the nearby flocks and herds of local hill men; instead of plundering their animals, as he had done in similar situations in the past, he ordered that the local people be treated well. Then, two days later as they descended the Hamatatu Pass to the Indus plain, Babur broadcast his political intentions when he ordered a messenger sent ahead to the people of Bhirah to announce: 'These *vilayatlar* have belonged to the Turk from of old... [and so know] we care for these lands and people. There shall be no plunder and pillaging'.[27] The 'Turk' collectively refers to Temür and his Timurid descendants in Samarqand, and especially those in Herat. Thus Babur now claimed the authority of the deceased Husain Baiqara as the legitimate Timurid overlord of the Punjab.

On 21 February, Babur and his men moved in military formation – left, centre and right wing – towards Bhirah to meet emissaries from the city offering presents and submission. Babur and his men dismounted east of the city on the banks of the Jhelum. They did not allow any harm, he is careful to note, to come to its people.[28] He added, to drive his sovereign point home: 'Temür Beg, coming into Hindustan, upon leaving, several of these countries such as Bhirah, and Khushab and Janab and Chiniut belonged to Temür Beg's descendants and their dependents'. Finally, to conclude this episode, he announced on 23 February that the people of Bhirah were being assessed, in lieu of being plundered, a *mal-i aman* or 'security' levy or tax of 400,000 *shahrukhis*. He notes that the next day, he slit the noses of some of his warriors who had been harassing Bhirah inhabitants and executed others.[29] Thus, the Bhirah episode represents the first, albeit preliminary, attempt to found a Timurid state in Hindustan.

The sequel followed when on 3 March Babur sent a messenger to Sultan Ibrahim Ludi in Delhi and Daulat Khan Ludi – the governor of Lahore – saying, without a trace of diplomatic politesse, 'We want the territories that have long been dependent on the Turk'.[30] In asserting his claim as a Timurid to be the legitimate ruler of Hindustan, or at least northwestern India, Babur undoubtedly had in mind merely not Temür's 1398 raid and brutal sack of Delhi, but also the sovereignty Shah Rukh of Herat theoretically enjoyed in Hindustan, even if it was only sporadically enforced until his death in 1447.

Timurid Herat was an authority recognised by the Saiyids, who were rulers in Multan and then Delhi, following the political chaos bequeathed by Temür's invasion, as well as by Muslim rulers in Malwa and even in distant Bengal. The Timurid governor of Kabul independently reminded Indians of continued Timurid power in the 1420s and 1430s by staging several incursions into the northwest and even occupying Lahore briefly in 1432/33.[31] Timurid authority in India had, however, all but evaporated following the deaths of Shah Rukh and Ulugh Beg in 1447 and 1449. Their deaths occurred almost precisely at the time the Sayyids were pushed aside by the Ludi Afghans, who had been one among many Afghan lineages Sayyid rulers and the Tughluqs before them had recruited to bolster their authority. Three Ludi sultans ruled Hindustan between 1451 and 1526, bringing even more Afghans into the country. They had somewhat revived Delhi's prominence as the formidable centre of Muslim authority in Hindustan. Their impressive tombs in Delhi still remind visitors of their ambitions and achievements.

Babur cannot have been surprised when Daulat Khan refused either to meet with his messenger or to send him on to Sultan Ibrahim Ludi. Still it prompted him, writing many years later, when warring with Afghans in the Gangetic Valley, to write: 'These Hindustan people and especially Afghans are bereft of intelligence and wisdom and lost to council and plan'.[32] Regardless, before he would have learned of Daulat Khan's contempt for his claims, Babur announced his *mulkgirliq* ambitions to the world when on 4 March he learned of the birth of a son and named him Hind-al, 'The Taking of Hind', pointedly noting he chose the name because his son was born during the 'Hindustan campaign'.[33]

He must have been aware that he was in no position to forcibly assert his claims on Hindustan at the moment. Thus, Babur did not follow this demand by trying to mobilise a larger army. Instead, the next morning of 5 March, he rode to the river where he got a boat and began drinking *'araq* with thirteen of his men. They drank this fermented date-palm juice until mid-morning prayer, when he and some of the men decided they preferred the intoxicating confection *ma'jun*. After riding back to camp during the evening prayer, Babur described some inebriated joking among him and his men. He commented that *'araq* and *ma'jun* drinkers should not mix because those who had been drinking wine begin talking wildly about the *ma'junis.* He reported that despite his attempts to calm things down, a disgusting uproar became so intolerable that the party was ended.[34]

The next two days of 7 and 8 March, Babur briefly returned to the business of government by appointing a governor of Bhirah and another for the nearby Janab *vilayat.* He chose a long-term loyalist appropriately named Jalal al-Din Hindu Beg Qauchin as governor of Bhirah. He was a man from a Central Asian Turkicised-Mongol clan or military unit, who supported Babur throughout his later career, fighting with him at Panipat against the Ludis and again at Kanwah against the Rajputs. Eventually Babur appointed him along with several others to be a companion of Humayun.[35] During this period, he also sent a man to nearby Khushab to demand that territory – one he had identified as being long dependent on the Turk. As in Bhirah, Babur's claim on Khushab meant an assessment, part of which his agent returned with on 12 March. Khushab was then assigned to Langar Khan, 'the prime mover and cause', as Babur remarks, of the Bhirah expedition. Other *beg*s and 'the Turk[ish] and local troops of Bhirah' were assigned to help Hindu Beg govern at Bhirah.[36]

He followed this administrative business with several days of drunken and drug-infused *suhbatlar* or gatherings on 10 and 12 March. The first lasted the entire day and is memorialised in a miniature painting from Akbar's era, titled 'Babur returns to camp, drunk on horseback'. It was based on Babur's own testimony that after drinking he did not recall riding back to camp late one night. The second featured a shoreline excursion among orchards of blossoming trees and sugarcane fields, followed by a boat trip on the Jhelum, consuming *ma'jun,* which made him and his men drowsy. They slept in the boat and returned to the camp at dawn. The next day featured another Jhelum boat excursion drinking *'araq,* accompanied by six musicians.[37]

Two days later, on 13 March, with the Indian hot season coming on, they began their march back to Kabul. Babur left behind a momentarily subjugated Bhirah, whose briefly cowed Afghan and Hindu inhabitants threw off Timurid rule almost as soon as he left the city. They chased out Hindu Beg, who was not able to make his way back to Kabul until late April. In his autobiography, Babur concedes that Hindu Beg had been left with little support, but he says no more about what the loss of his first occupation of trans-Indus territory meant to him at the time.[38] His treatment of Bhirah inhabitants, appointment of a governor for the town, and naming of his son Hind-al unmistakably testify to his imperial designs on Hindustan in 1519 – whenever those ambitions had formed in his mind. Yet, the almost casual and ad hoc nature of the Bhirah expedition and precipitate collapse of Babur's authority in the town and surrounding region may explain why he fails to comment on this failure, which was his first attempt of *mulkgirliq*, 'an act of kingdom seizing' in Hindustan. He also does not allude to these events in his narrative for the remainder of 1519.

What was remarkable about Babur's narrative of his nearly three-week return march to Kabul, where he finally arrived on the evening of 3 April, is its unremarkable description of events. It is a laconic record of the everyday life of an ambitious Timurid momentarily at least untroubled by larger issues or immediate threats. The return began with an assault on the fort of a Kakar headman, in the hills between Bhirah and the Indus on 14 March. Babur failed to capture the man and tried to reconcile with him on 18 March, giving *khilat*s (robes of honour) to a relative, who came to Babur's camp. He also gave him a sword to be taken to the Kakar chief. The following day, Babur notes that he counted the number of camels in his camp at 520 and reports discovering the *sambhal* or spikenard plant for the first time. He reached the Indus on 21 March, where he stole a merchant's barge filled with corn needed to feed his men. After crossing the Indus, over four days from 21 March to 24 March, he appointed one of his men to the territory between Bhirah and the Indus. He held a tiger hunt on 25 March, lost his valued hunting hawk on 26 March and, on the same day, used money taken from Bhirah to reward six loyal Dilazak Afghans who had accompanied him to Bhirah. On 29 March, Babur had lunch in one of his favourite gardens, the Bagh-i vafa, the Garden of Fidelity, at Adinapur. The next day, he met his son Humayun in Kabul city. There he drank for much of the next two days – first on 2 April at a house and the next morning and afternoon in a boat in the Violet Garden – before entering the citadel in the evening.

Bazm u Razm 1519–20

The bawdy denouement of this first, if impromptu Indian campaign, the several *'araq* and *ma'jun* parties that followed in and around Bhirah, and the many more such *suhbatlar* that enliven Babur's narrative of the remainder of 1519, before his autobiography breaks off again for 6 years, calls to mind the Persian phrase *Bazm u Razm*, 'feast and fighting'. The phrase evokes a leitmotif of Iranian warrior culture – and indeed the warrior culture of other pre-modern societies – including ancient Greece.[39] After refusing wine at the elegant parties of his Timurid cousins in Herat, Babur had taken to drinking wine and eating the intoxicating confection *ma'jun*. He rejoiced, it seems clear from his enthusiastic recollections, in the inebriated camaraderie he had shared only as an observer in Herat. Having begun taking wine or *ma'jun*, he enjoyed many intoxicating *suhbatlar* gatherings throughout the spring and summer of 1519.

During these months, he mentions Bhirah but once again in his autobiography. The next time was when Babur reports that Hindu Beg Qauchin finally returned to Kabul on 26 April, after being forced to flee the town by hostile inhabitants. Hindu Beg brought with him two Hindu prisoners, who, after paying large ransoms, were given horses and honorary robes and allowed to leave. Otherwise, Babur's entries for this period have the quality of an unrevised diary, briefly recording notable events amidst descriptions of innumerable *suhbatlar*. For example, on 13 April, Sultan Husain Mirza Baiqara's eldest daughter Sultanım Begim arrived, having earlier taken refuge in Khwarizm, below the Aral Sea, during what Babur refers to as her *qazaqlıq* days – an evident allusion to her flight from Khurasan after the Uzbek conquest of Herat.

Greeted with great respect by Babur, who always describes how he 'bent the knee' during his respectful acknowledgement of Turco-Mongol female relatives, she was assigned the *Bagh-i Khilwat* or 'Private Garden' for a residence.[40] The arrival of such a distinguished individual was notable. While Sultanım Begim was not the first refugee from Uzbek-held territories to arrive in Kabul, she was one of the most prestigious. Her decision to take refuge in Kabul testified to Babur's status in 1519 as the sole Timurid ruler and the asylum of Timurids and Chaghatai Mongols and their followers fleeing Iran and Mawarannahr. Many others followed, first to Kabul and later to Agra and Delhi, following Babur's victory over the Ludis in 1526.

Seven days later on 20 April, he and some men rode out of Kabul about 50 miles into the Pamghan Range, northwest of the city, to a spring called Khwajah Sih-yaran, or 'Three-Friends'. Khwajah Sih-yaran was located just below Istalif, where Babur's mother had been buried in June 1505. It was also near the site of a house of the former Timurid ruler of Kabul, Ulugh Beg Mirza. Babur and his entourage rode into this mountainous terrain, celebrated by him and later European travellers for its entrancing forested landscape and fruit orchards, planning to have a party.[41] They first stopped at a *qazi*'s house in the evening, where they thought to begin drinking, but after the cleric objected, they postponed their *suhbat angizi*, 'social gathering', and moved on the next day, 21 April, to Khwajah Sih-yaran. The next day, they rafted along the river surging down from Istalif, where Babur saw for the first time a *dang*, or Adjutant-bird, at the home of professional bird catchers, who caught these birds for sale in Khurasan. On the 24th, if not earlier, they had a wine party by the spring at the time of the mid-day prayer. They left for Kabul the next day, but were too drunk to continue their journey. They had to stop on the way to sleep and reached the Charbagh garden in Kabul only around midnight.

Babur's abbreviated account of this excursion, is amplified by his deeply appreciative descriptions of the tree-lined Istalif river and Khwajah Sih-yaran spring in his earlier Kabul gazetteer. It offers thoughtful readers a clear understanding of his ideal physical and social environment. Kabul may have been a miserably-poor and politically-contentious city and province, unsuitable as the base of a Timurid empire, but Babur never ceased to marvel at the enchanting landscape of the nearby Pamghan range. Speaking of Istalif particularly, he writes:

> Few places are known to have a village like Istalif. There are orchards on both sides of the great river flowing through the village [and] small pleasure gardens. The water is cold; ice is not needed. It is generally pure. In this village is the garden known as Bagh-i kalan, the Great Garden that Ulugh Beg [the Timurid ruler of Kabul] took by force. Having given value to its owners I took it. Outside the garden are plane trees. The area beneath the trees is green, shady and pleasant.[42]

His desire to be buried in Kabul reflects his enduring love of its high mountain valleys, bisected by cascading streams, lined with trees bedecked with flowers in spring and ablaze with brilliantly coloured leaves in the autumn.

As for the gardens, he ordered them to be constructed in the mountains and around the city. They reflect the formal Persianised Timurid garden aesthetic he relished in Samarqand. Geometric symmetry was the defining design trait of such gardens and Babur's own constructions.[43] He admired the naturally-growing native trees and flowers of high mountain valleys, but when it came to gardens, he and Timurids generally defined beauty by the precise and symmetrical ordering of nature. For example, after he purchased Ulugh Beg Mirza's garden, he decided to alter the *bisiyaq*, the 'irregular' *arıq* or small stream, flowing through it. 'I ordered,' Babur writes, 'the *arıq* to be made *siyaq*, "straight" and regular. It has [now] become a very fine place'.[44]

Timurids appreciated gardens even more if they featured scenic perspectives, *maddinazarlıq*, such as the pleasing view Babur praised in Muhammad Tarkhan's hillside garden in Samarqand. As a young man in 1496, Babur had built not an actual garden, but a porch, overlooking the town of Ush in the western Ferghanah Valley, where many gardens planted with violets, roses and tulips lined the river that flows from Ush out into the valley to Andijan.[45] This was the first of many such viewing platforms he later constructed in gardens near Kabul and in Hindustan. As for the Khwajah Sih-yaran spring below Istalif and its newly straightened stream, Babur had sometime earlier ordered the spring to be enclosed in a ten-by-ten stonework with symmetrically designed platforms on each side, placed so that visitors could overlook the surrounding *arghawan* or Judas trees. On the occasion of this outing, he reports that a day after they arrived, he and his men constructed a large round seat and surrounded it with newly planted sycamores.[46]

Timurid devotion to geometric precision in garden design and buildings is not merely an interesting cultural preference, which can be compared to Chinese and Renaissance European garden designs. It is another cultural trait that helps to distinguish Babur, Husain Baiqara and their Timurid kin from their pastoral nomadic Mongol relations and also from Indians. If *hendesi*, or 'geometrical', represented their watchword in landscape architecture, *ma'mur*, 'inhabited' or 'cultivated', expressed their preference for ordered, prosperous agrarian societies. Babur sometimes uses the verb *ma'mur kardan*, 'to settle', when he describes suppressing and forcibly sedentarising troublesome Afghans. He also preferred to see that societies adhered to the *shari'ah*, the 'straight path' of Sunni Islam. Although Muslim clerics, like the *qazi* they encountered as they rode out of Kabul, may have thought the habits of hard-drinking Turco-Mongol Muslims to be as socially *bisiyaq* as the Istalif garden stream.

If Babur's comments about garden construction illustrate his devotion to Timurid *hendesi*, or geometrical aesthetics, his repeated references to wine parties in gardens also help readers to understand a central fact about his social life and Timurid warrior society in general. In referring to the 'entertainments' that enlivened his life and many pages of the *Vaqayi'*, he typically refers to them as a *suhbat*, or as in this case, a *suhbat angizi*. *Suhbat* is a term that connotes far more than just a meeting or gathering. In Babur's frequent use, the term or phrase implies gatherings enlivened with wine, music and verse – featuring conversation and social engagement, friendship and camaraderie. Related words and phrases amplify these associations. *Suhbati* is a comrade; *suhbat jui* means seeking one another's company, while, perhaps most significantly, the phrase *suhbat-yaftah* is a synonym for someone who is comfortable in society or well-bred, and based upon Babur's evidence, it would apply to many members of Husain Baiqara's court.

Babur does not take the trouble to describe the April gatherings in detail. In narrating events later in the year, he includes details of several *suhbatlar* that lasted for days and continued as he and his men moved about the countryside, sometimes stopping in gardens, at others times reclining on hillsides or visiting homes. Later in India, he found the absence of such social gatherings among Hindus to be one of the several things, including the weather and many aspects of Hindu culture, that made him want to retreat to Kabul and rule Hindustan from there. As will be seen, Babur and some of his *begs* regarded both the Indian environment and its culture as *bisiyaq*, or 'irregular'.

Interspersed with excursions into the mountains, Babur carried on the affairs of the state – of an Afghan State – by trying to bring some order to the countryside and extract funds or food out of the Afghan tribes. On 31 May, still suffering from a fever for several weeks, he received Malik Shah Mansur, the chief of the important Yusufza'i tribal confederation, who had been with Babur at Bajaur, and whose daughter Babur had married on 28 or 29 January to conciliate the Yusufza'i 'horde'.[47] Malik Shah, writes Babur, paid his respects, *malazamat*, thus formally accepting at least some degree of subordination. In return, he and six of the chiefs who accompanied him were given silk coats, but also told that the Afghan farmers of Bajaur and Sawad must produce 6,000 ass-loads of rice as their revenue payment. By this act, Babur slightly improved Kabul's authority over the Afghan countryside, making the transition from 'sword' to 'pen' revenue collection.

Perhaps Babur later felt self-conscious when writing about his ceaseless round of *suhbatlar* in the spring of 1519, for he mentions that he appointed a Quran-reader on 23 June to read verses in his presence. Still, he describes wine parties, but little else of importance for the following three weeks, except the arrival of envoys from Shah Shuja' Arghun from Qandahar and Muhammad Zaman Mirza from Balkh. Both men expressed their loyalty by bringing gifts, illustrating Babur's relative security in Kabul at this moment. Babur had chased Shah Shuja' and his brother Muqim from Qandahar in 1507, but the Arghun had returned to the city sometime before 1519. He was a nervously insecure, if nominally independent ruler there, but was constantly fearful that Babur might return. Now in 1519, he sent Babur, as a present, a *tipuchaq*, or specially-trained horse, perhaps with the hope of deflecting Babur's perennial desire to take or re-take Qandahar.

The Timurid Muhammad Zaman Mirza, now Babur's feudatory and later ally in India, was Husain Baiqara's grandson and the former Herat ruler's last surviving male heir. He had been captured and surprisingly spared by Shaibani Khan, and had later found his way to Balkh, accompanied by the historian Khwandamir, who was with him during part of this period. Married to Babur's daughter Ma'sumah Sultan Begim, he continued to serve Babur in Balkh until sometime before Babur left Kabul to confront Ibrahim Ludi. Now in 1519, he held northern Afghanistan for Babur along with the Miranshahi Timurid Wais Mirza, who remained in Badakhshan. At this moment, he confirmed his loyalty by sending Babur tributary payment as well as a horse.[48] He is not listed among Babur's commanders at Panipat, but nonetheless received a gift of 15 lacs of coin when Babur distributed the Ludi treasury after the battle. Afterwards, he served Babur during the Hindustan campaigns, but later caused Humayun no end of political trouble after he succeeded Babur in 1530.

This interregnum of partly enforced inactivity was broken in late July when Babur returned to the Sisyphean task of subjugating, or at least temporarily intimidating Afghans in and around Kabul. In this instance, he attacked the 'Abd al-Rahman Afghans of the Gardiz region, about 60 miles south of Kabul and 45 miles due east of Ghazni. His account of what he alternatively terms a *chapqun,* or a *yurush,* illustrates better than any of the pacification and state-building exercises in Afghanistan describes how little control he had been able to achieve in the mountainous regions so close to Kabul and Ghazni. Babur's comments should have been an instructive lesson for others – British, Soviets and Americans – who have tried to control Afghans in these mountainous regions.

Denouncing these Afghans for failing to continue making their tribute on time, and damaging caravans, Babur led a raid near Gardiz. It resulted in the death of 40–50 Afghans fighting on foot, whose heads were then piled into a minaret. Yet, apart from stealing some sheep and other goods, Babur achieved nothing from this raid other than temporarily intimidating members of an Afghan tribe. The raid was symptomatic of Babur's relations with the powerful Pushtun tribes throughout his residence in Kabul. From the evidence of the autobiography, he undertook raids as ad hoc attacks in response to particular tribal issues, failure to pay tribute or attacks on merchant caravans. He never suggests that he developed a comprehensive plan to pacify the region. Indeed, when writing of the isolated *tuman* of Bangash, located about 120 miles east-southeast of Kabul and south of the Safid-Kuh Mountains, he indicates that he just could not be bothered to bring its Afghan inhabitants under control. He never pacified it because, he says, he was too busy conquering Qandahar, Balkh, Badakhshan and Hindustan.[49] In this particular Gardiz raid in July 1519, his only reward was to go sightseeing on the Rustam Plain with a few men, where they saw for the first time the *pushkal* or monsoon rain clouds piled up against mountains to the south.[50] It is a sight he may have recalled when writing this section of his autobiography in 1527 or 1528 in India, where the arrival of the monsoon rains in June or July is always greeted with an outpouring of joy and relief.

Babur's autobiography, which covers the period from late July 1519 until it breaks off again for 5 years in late January 1520, continues the *razm u bazm* pattern of the time. After returning to Kabul on 31 July, he seems to have spent most of his time until early September taking part in moveable feast entertainments. These began on 11 August as they rode into the Pamghan Range, stopping at Istalif on the 12th, where they took *ma'jun,* followed by a *chaghir suhbati,* a wine party. The entertainments continued at Khwajah Sih-yaran on 14 August, where Babur mentions a *chaghir majlisi.* They then decamped to Gul-i Bahar, about 76 miles due north of Kabul on the Panjshir River, where he held another *chaghir suhbati,* followed the next morning by a *sabuhi,* or morning drink. He returned to Kabul on 19 August.

On 8 September, he and his men left Kabul to attack the Yusufza'i, in the Parashawar/Peshawar region, with the limited goal of just keeping them under some measure of control. Marching due east from Kabul and stopping briefly in the Bagh-i vafa garden he constructed in 1508 at Adinapur, they reached the Khaibar on 27 September, but found that the Yusufza'is had fled. Shortly afterwards, he heard news of Sa'id Khan Chaghatai, Babur's Mongol cousin, who had taken refuge with him in Kabul in 1508 and had later gone to Ferghanah to fight the Uzbeks, where he had been joined by Haidar Mirza. Babur learned to his surprise that Sa'id Khan had arrived in Kashgar and that he was about to invade Badakhshan.[51]

Abandoning their plan to provision Peshawar, which he mentions in passing, Babur and his men crossed back eastward through the Khaibar and decided to raid the Khizr Khail Afghans, who had been harassing his troops and stealing their horses. They seized the Khizr Khail's goods and some of their small children. This raid persuaded the nearby Waziri Afghans, who, Babur complains, had never offered *piskish*, or tribute, to offer him 300 sheep. Some of the Khirilchi and Samu Khail tribes also decided to submit to Babur's authority. He levied an assessment of 4,000 sheep on these Afghans, dismissed them with ceremonial robes and appointed 'collectors', thus here also marginally extending his authority. In this case, he was, however, still collecting *mal*, or property, as tribute rather than *kharaj*, or assigned collections, from these and most other Afghans at this time. He rarely says that he extracted coin from Afghan territories, once only mentioning that he received sixty *altıns*, or gold coins, from a Tajik or Persian-speaking village in Nijrau district, northeast of Kabul.[52] These Tajiks are likely to have merchants who were able to remit such an amount in cash. Otherwise, Babur collected tribute or assessments in kind, as animals or crops (Illustration 2).

On 14 October, Babur returned to at the Bagh-i vafa garden, just in time to see its trees in their brilliant fall colour.[53] Concern for Badakhshan faded when Babur learned that Sa'id Khan had withdrawn from the region after making Mongol claims to the border areas between northern Afghanistan and Kashgar. Sa'id Khan's envoy reached Babur a week later in Kabul. Instead of marching north, he and his men then spent seemingly idyllic three or four days in the garden, admiring the brilliant fall foliage of the pomegranate trees and eating the fruit. The garden's oranges, he reports, were not quite ripe but he nonetheless distributed fruit from one or other tree to certain individuals. 'This was the particular time,' Babur writes, 'that we were delighted with the Bagh-i vafa'.[54] On 17 October, Babur and his men resumed their march back to Kabul. It was interrupted with wine parties at Jagdalik on 18th and Quruqsai a day later, where they killed a sheep and ate *kebabs* and drank all day long, which made his men very drunk. They returned to Kabul at midnight of 19 October. A few days later, they resumed their entertainments at sites in and around Kabul throughout the remainder of the year.

They again visited Istalif on 30 October, as part of an extended excursion to view the fall harvest in the mountains. They ate *ma'jun* that day and drank wine the next, in an entertainment that lasted throughout the day. Reporting that 'we took the morning draught', *sabahi subuhi qılduk*, Babur says that the following morning they moved on to nearby Bihzadi, 15 miles northwest of Kabul, where they admired the fall foliage and drank until the evening prayer. After returning to Kabul sometime after 1 November, Babur resumed this *suhbat* life with seemingly undiminished enthusiasm on 14 November. Then, he and his companions began a three-day movable feast, which Babur describes in greater detail than any other *suhbat* or *majlis* of the year.

It began with Babur riding up into the hills alone to the house of a local villager, Tardi Beg Khaksar, a man 'whose shortness was known', and from his name a man probably employed in digging *karizes*, or irrigation channels.[55] Giving Tardi Beg 100 *shahrukhi* coins 'I myself brought with me', Babur remarks, he sent Tardi to buy wine, announcing he wanted to have what he terms a *halvat u levendanehsuhbat*, 'a private and casual gathering'.[56] After Tardi Beg returned with wine, which they drank, two men who heard about the drinking, but not about Babur, also appeared.

Later, Tardi Beg told Babur that a local woman, Hul Hul Anigah, wanted to drink wine with him. Babur replied he had never seen a woman drink wine. This was another example of the social distance between Temür's tribal traditions, where women commonly and openly drank with men and the somewhat more restrained Islamised social conventions of Babur's day.[57] He told Tardi Beg to invite her. 'We also invited', he reports, 'Shahi a *qalandar* [a wandering Sufi] and one of the *kariz* men', an irrigation channel worker, 'who played the *rabab* [an ancient Afghan stringed instrument]'. Together they all drank sitting behind a *kariz* until evening prayer, and later, drank again at Tardi Beg's house until the bed-time prayer. Then 'I lay down', Babur writes, '...Hul Hul Anigah came [and] made [unstated] offensive requests. By feigning drunkenness', he adds, 'I finally escaped her'.[58]

Around midnight, Babur, Tardi Beg and one of the uninvited guests rode off to the Istalif area, which they reached, *farz vaqtida*, at the first prayer, when they ate some *ma'jun* and viewed the harvest. At sunrise, they dismounted at a garden in Istalif and ate grapes and slept for some time, before a man whom Babur knew, 'Ata Mirakhur', the Master of Horse, brought a jug of fine wine. They rode on to another garden, with beautiful fall foliage, enjoyed another *suhbat*, where they were joined by Khwajah Muhammad Amin. He had earlier served with Babur during his first foray into Hindustan in January 1505 and had been with Nasir Mirza's forces in Qandahar, when it was besieged by Shaibani Khan. After being joined by several other men, who had ridden up from Kabul, they drank until the bed-time prayer.

At dawn, they rode east to the *Bagh-i padshahi*, the 'Royal or Imperial Garden', at nearby Astarghach, where they viewed the lovely fall leaves, with one tree exhibiting a regular display of five or six leaves on each branch, which appealed to Babur's Timurid geometric aesthetic. No painter could have equalled the scene, he remarks, alluding to this natural symmetry.[59] On Tuesday, 17 November, rode to Charbagh of Kabul, and on Thursday, finally entered the fortress. Two days later they held another *suhbat* at the Chinar Bagh, the Plane Tree Garden in Kabul.

Babur briefly alludes to his conduct of state affairs in late November and early December, with three men visiting him for unexplained reasons in Kabul. Taj al-Din Arghun, a member of the Arghun clan that previously held Kabul and still held on to Qandahar, visited him, as did two of Babur's men he had left to administer districts in or near Bhirah. One came from Bhirah, the other from a nearby Indus district. In this brief reference, it is possible to detect faint early traces of the administrative origins of Timurid rule in India, although nothing more is known about his governance of these areas.

The remainder of Babur's staccato-like diary entries for December 1519 and January 1520 are almost exclusively given over to accounts of the *suhbat* life and hunts in and around Kabul. These were initially concentrated in an area of Tajik or Persian speakers living in the isolated, mountainous Nijrau region. Apart from assigning a modest tribute for the Nijrau inhabitants, Babur and his men indulged in *ma'jun* consumption, 'morning draughts', drinking on rafts and a five- or six-day visit to the Bagh-i vafa garden, where the oranges were maturing well and spring blooms were developing. Babur punctuates his narrative of two weeks of these entertainments between 23 December and 6 January with the engagingly candid admission that he had been drinking excessively. He explained that he drank so much because he had taken a vow to return to 'obedience', *ta'ib*, of Muslim abstinence in his 40th year, and he had only 1 year of indulgence remaining (Illustration 2).

Having candidly explained this to his readers, Babur describes how he returned enthusiastically to his pleasures the next day in the Bagh-i vafa. After taking his *subuhi* and then sobering up, *hushyar bulub*, he ate *ma'jun* while listening to a musician play a five-line, five-time piece. Stimulated by the music and also probably mellowed by *ma'jun*, Babur suddenly felt an urge to compose, which, he remarks, he had not done for some time. He composed *baghladim*, a four-part piece. Three days later, still in the garden, Babur kept up his seemingly manic pursuit of pleasure, writing approvingly of someone's suggestion during their *subuhi* that anyone who speaks like a Sart, a Persian-speaking town dweller, should drink a cup, while anyone who speaks like a Turk should drink a cup.[60] After sunrise, everyone retired to the shade of the orange trees to drink. Leaving the garden on 11 January, he and his men continued along his indulgent, pre-renunciation path for at least another two weeks, interrupted only when Babur broke one of his front teeth. This is not shown in the imagined miniature portraits included within the illustrated manuscripts of Babur's *Vaqayi'* commissioned by Akbar in the later sixteenth century. Babur's *Vaqayi'* itself breaks off at this point, not to resume until he rides out from Kabul to invade Hindustan in December 1526.

The Literary Life

Babur's seemingly untroubled life during much of 1519 also gave him the opportunity to pursue his literary interests, and in mid-December, he finished copying the *ghazallar* and *abyatlar*, the odes and couplets of Mir 'Ali Shir Nava'i's four *diwans*. Nava'i titled and dated these four collections of Turki verse according to periods of his life, very much like the phases of life verses Jami had written. Nava'i's were titled: (1) *Miracles of Childhood*, (2) *Rarities of Youth*, (3) *Wonders of Middle Age* and (4) *Useful Advice of Old Age*.[61] As an aspiring poet, Babur would have copied the great man's verses as young Iranian and Turkic writers did traditionally to master the metrical forms and metaphorical language of their illustrious predecessors. It would also have been natural to focus on the *ghazal*, the most prestigious and popular verse form, which was used to measure the talent of writers. A poem of four to fourteen couplets, in a variety of metres, the *ghazal* was outwardly a love plaint, addressed to absent or indifferent lovers, but adaptable to an infinite variety of subjects. Babur wrote his first complete *ghazal* in 1502 and may have written as many as twelve of these poems during his tumultuous life between 1502 and 1505, but he had enjoyed little leisure during those tumultuous years. He wrote most of his verse during his Kabul years.[62] Some he quotes in whole or in part in his autobiography. When he cites only a few lines of a poem, its complete text can be usually found in his *diwan*, which also contains most of his oeuvre.

Several of Babur's early *ghazals* typify the generic verses devoted to frustrated infatuations. These have no discernible autobiographical meaning beyond the author's attempt to demonstrate his mastery of the form and possibly also his creative, innovative metaphorical language. The opening lines of his altogether ordinary eighth *ghazal* serve as an example, when he writes: 'She who seemed to me a soothing beloved, She was more than cruel and less than kind'.[63] In a few examples, though, Babur's verses have either an apparent or obvious autobiographical meaning. It is also easier to detect connections between literary art and life in his case. This is because, first he sometimes dates his poems, second, due to Babur's unusual practice of arranging verses chronologically in his *diwan*; and third, because he uses his own name, not a pen name as the *takhallus* in his *ghazals*' final couplets.

An example is his forty-sixth *ghazal*, which he wrote in April or May 1507, after he visited the *daman*, or piedmont of the flower-strewn hills near Gulbahar, the 'Rose' or 'Flower of Spring' village north of Kabul. After quoting an unnamed poet's Turki couplet, which praised Kabul and Gulbahar during springtime, he reported competing the poem, whose four opening lines evoke the anguished apprehensions of a lover.

> Petal upon petal, my heart is like the rosebud,
> If there would be even a thousand springs, it would not open.
> If I wished to pass through the garden without the one
> Whose brow is like a bow,
> The flowering cypress would be like an arrow
> For the eye and a fire for the heart.

Then in the poem's final four lines Babur wrote:

> Finding ease in the pleasure of union is difficult,
> While relinquishing life due to the pain of separation is easy.
> Turning round her/his head, I have died grief stricken, O Babur.
> Let my bier encircle that fairy-world.[64]

Here, Babur, inspired by the natural beauty of a hill covered with wild tulips, responds by producing an altogether generic *ghazal* describing the metaphorical garden of Persian verse. Only because he describes the moment in his autobiography do we know what inspired the verse.

It is rare to be able to establish a connection between Babur's verse and life as clearly as in this case and that is especially true for his many *ghazals*. It is easier to understand the existential context of his writing in many of his shorter poems. Three verses he wrote during this 1519 interregnum are unmistakably linked to specific events during this period. He completed one *du-bayti* or two-couplet verse about 19 January, just a few days after he sent his long-time Ferghanah loyalist Khwajah Kalan to govern the recently captured fortress of Bajaur. The poem, which Babur sent to his now departed compatriot, contains the same imagery of separated or inconstant lovers found in *ghazals* and exemplifies how writers used this vocabulary to evoke genuine male friendship as well as metaphorical infatuations.

Such was not my pact and covenant with the beloved/friend.
Finally he chose parting and inconstancy to me.
What could someone do against the caprice of fortune.
Finally it forcefully separated lover/comrade from beloved/companion.[65]

A second short poem, a *ruba'i*, or quatrain, was probably written in the spring of 1519, based on its placement in his *diwan*, three quatrains before another *ruba'i*, which he dates to June 1519. In this Turki verse, he evokes the *suhbat* entertainments that filled his life during the year.

Ramadan came and I a pious wine-sot.
'Id arrived and with it remembrance of wine
Neither fasting nor prayer [but] years, months,
Nights and days with wine and *ma'jun*, crazy and drunk.[66]

The June 1519 *ruba'i* Babur wrote during a brief time when he was declined to drink because he was recovering from the fever that he had contracted two weeks earlier. It celebrates a gathering he held *Chanar Baghning eshiki-da*, 'at the gate of the Plane-Tree Garden', just after he had celebrated the marriage of the children of two of his compatriots. He and his friends gathered at a small white arbour, to be joined by Ghiyas the Buffon, Tardi Muhammad Qipchaq and Mullah, the librarian. Alluding to this gathering as a *majlis* rather than a *suhbat*, Babur says he then composed an impromptu *ruba'i* addressed to the grandson of Zu'n-nun Arghun, who was at that moment hosting another *suhbat* at his house nearby.

Friends who are at the banquet, are a beautiful garden
Although they gave us no leave to attend
If there is ease in that gathering
A hundred thanks the gathering is not troubled.[67]

A final poem, which Babur wrote in July 1519, represents an intriguing conclusion to this first phase of his literary life. Few of his verses can be dated to the period between 1520 and 1525, but it seems likely that he wrote more verses and that these were lost, along with this five-year narrative gap of his autobiography. He addressed it to Pulad Sultan, the son of the Uzbek leader in Samarqand. It is curious that he would send what he describes as a *qit'ah* or fragment to an Uzbek and also interesting that he would copy it on the outside of the *diwan* or collection of his poems – the first of two collections he mentions. He finished the second diwan in Agra in 1528. *Qitah*s represented occasional verses, free poetic expressions that were not expected to adhere to rigid norms of other forms, particularly the *ghazal*.

Nava'i, Babur's idol as a Turki poet, indulged in the form because it allowed him a freedom of expression, 'a garden', he wrote, 'for resting the mind'.[68] Whether Babur had read Nava'i, or simply was familiar with the commonly known form, he included a large number of such 'fragments' in the final or Indian section of his second *diwan*. This fragment reads:

> O breeze, if thou enter the sanctuary of that cypress
> Remind his/her heart of the wound of separation.
> May God have mercy; he/she does not recall Babur
> God grant mercy to his/her heart of steel.[69]

Did Babur mean to address this verse to Pulad Sultan, the son of his avowed enemy, the Uzbek ruler of formerly Timurid Samarqand? Or was it intended for Pulad Sultan's mother, who may have been Babur's half-sister, Mihrban(u)?[70] Not only is the sanctuary of the poem the *harim*, the sacred women's quarters, but Babur refers to the 'wound of separation', an unusual sentiment for an Uzbek he had never met, but a natural emotion to express to a relative he had not seen since his youth. Nonetheless, the fourth and final line also includes a word play on the Uzbek's name, as Pulad means steel, so conceivably Babur intended the verse for both mother and son in inventive and subtle ways.

Babur's reputation as a poet, which at the time would have depended almost entirely on the quality of his *ghazals*, now rests with modern critics on the extant *ghazals* he wrote before sending this *diwan* to Samarqand in July 1519. He is only known to have written one *ghazal* between 1520 and 1530. He does not enjoy an exalted poetic reputation. Babur's *ghazals* are significant not as literary monuments, but instead they are important for his autobiography as further evidence of his literary ambitions and cultured personality. In any case, he may have abandoned poetic composition following his long residence in Kabul because of the pressure of consolidating his victories in 1526 over the Ludi Afghans and his equally important triumph the following year over the formidable Rajput, Rana Sanga'. Otherwise, apart from one *ghazal* and a single *masnavi*, the extant poems from his Indian years consist entirely of occasional poems, *qitahs* and *ruba'is*.

In contrast to the predominantly formulaic *ghazals*, these verse fragments are nonetheless exceptionally important for their emotional content. They are openly existential, as he reminds his readers at the end of his second or Rampur *Diwan* from 1528, where Babur asked readers to remember him when he wrote: 'Each time you read these words, reading them, think of me'. Otherwise, he was ensuring that readers would certainly remember him as he evidently spent his free time between 1526 and 1530, amidst campaigns and increasing illness, writing the

Vaqayi'. These verses form an emotional counterpoint to his autobiography, as he conveys powerfully rendered conditions of loneliness, sickness and old age. These are made more poignant by his sense of being an exile, triumphant, but isolated in a country, whose society and customs he disliked and its very geography caused him to regret being unable to return to the gardens, fruit and climate of Kabul and Istalif.

Mulkgirliq: The Battle of Panipat

When Babur's autobiography breaks off in January 1520, he remained the Padshah of Kabul, an imperfectly subjugated, impoverished territory of independent or autonomous Pushtun tribes. Additionally, he exercised authority over, if not direct control of, Badakhshan and Balkh south of the Amu Darya or Oxus river. Wais Mirza and Muhammad Zaman Mirza governed these contiguous regions, with Babur's son Humayun, who had been appointed to succeed Wais Mirza in Badakhshan after the Mirza's death sometime in 1520 or 1521. Lacking the information of his autobiography for the years 1520 through 1525, it is not possible to examine Babur's strategy, but he must have understood the reality of his political situation far better than any later student of his affairs. Uzbeks blocked him in the north from retaking the Timurid homelands, while the Safavids controlled the Iranian plateau, and in 1520 at least, exercised authority over Qandahar, nominally ruled once again by the Arghuns. Ludi Afghans still dominated large parts of Hindustan from the Indus to the western Gangetic Valley, but in the 1520s, the Ludi state began to fragment, which offered Babur the opportunity to finally realise his imperial Timurid imperial ambition.

In 1519, at Bhirah, Babur boldly asserted his right to rule Hindustan as a descendant of Temür, and in a certain respect, his victory over the Ludis in 1526 was made possible by Temür's destruction of the splintering remnants of the Delhi Sultanate in 1398. Temür left a power vacuum in Hindustan that was ineptly filled by two weak dynasties, the Saiyids and Ludis. The so-called Saiyid dynasty was founded by one Khidar Khan, one of the provincial rulers who had emerged in the final days of the last sultan of Delhi – Mahmud Shah Tughluq (1396–1412/13). Khidar Khan, who claimed descent from the Prophet Muhammad, hence his title, had become the ruler of Multan in the 1390s, but, having been deposed by a rival, joined Temür as he approached the Indus region in October 1398. Following Temür's sack of Delhi and the further fragmentation of Muslim rule in Hindustan, Khidar Khan fought his way to the Delhi throne in 1414. He ruled precariously over what then amounted to a city-state, threatened by Muslim rivals and renascent Hindu principalities. Khidar Khan had ruled formerly as a feudatory of the Timurid Shah Rukh in Herat, who sent him the traditional *khilat*, or ceremonial robe.[71] Khidar Khan, like other competing North Indian Muslim rulers, exerted very little direct authority over his own territories, which in his case led him to recruit Afghans, including the Ludi chief Islam Khan. His nephew Bahlul Ludi (1451–89) was given Lahore in the early 1440s and gained control over the entire Punjab by 1448. The last Saiyid ruler abandoned Delhi in the same year. In 1451, having made two unsuccessful attempts on Delhi, Bahlul Ludi entered the city and founded the first Afghan dynasty in Hindustan.

Bahlul Ludi, a member of the larger, powerful Ghilza'i Afghan tribal confederation, founded the state in 1451 that Babur had claimed for the Timurids in 1519 at Bhirah. Delhi sultans had increasingly recruited Afghans during the thirteenth century, despite their uncivilised crudity, unbridled ferocity and, from the perspective of other Indian Muslims, bizarre appearance. His state, while more substantial than his Saiyid predecessors, functioned as a Pushtun tribal oligarchy, rather than the centralised military despotism that the Delhi sultans, such as Ala al-Din Khalji (1296–1316) and Muhammad bin Tughluq (1324–51), had controlled in the fourteenth century. Bahlul consciously ruled as a Pushtun tribal primus inter pares, rather than as a sultan, dividing Hindustan's agrarian wealth and campaign booty among his Afghan tribal compatriots.[72]

His successor Sikandar (1489–1517) began the transition to a more centralised, authoritarian state, and his measured policies of strengthening Ludi authority were continued, but more ruthlessly implemented by the last Ludi ruler, Ibrahim (1517–26). His ferocious attempt to subordinate the largely independent Pushtun tribes, and create a monarchical state provoked family and tribal resistance. The dissention Ibrahim's actions caused within the Ludi clan, combined with the rising power of the Rajput Rana Sanga' of Mewar in Rajasthan, to create the unstable political situation that gave Babur the opportunity to realise his *mulkgirliq* ambitions in Hindustan.

The Conquest of Hindustan

Babur never indicates he had a comprehensive plan to invade India, before his autobiography and poetry too break off in January 1520. One can infer that the ease with which he had initially occupied Bhirah in 1519 inspired him to make subsequent probing actions deeper into India, which he did the following year in 1520, penetrating as far as Sialkot, 72 miles north of Lahore before returning to Kabul. At the same time, he had to worry about holding the Amu Darya or Oxus boundary in the north. Still, with Wais Mirza at Qunduz in Badakhshan and the Baiqara Timurid, Muhammad Zaman Mirza, married to Babur's daughter in Balkh, he could have considerable confidence in his ability to fend off Uzbek raids. When Wais Mirza died in 1520 or 1521, Babur appointed Humayun, then age 13, to succeed him and travelled north with him and his mother Mahim Begim to Qunduz. Humayun remained there until he joined his father in November 1525 for the assault on the Ludis.

Throughout these years Babur continued to covet Qandahar, the valuable trading centre and strategic gateway for the approaches to Kabul. The city and fortress had also become, what it was to continue to be in later centuries – the informal boundary between Timurid-Mughal Kabul and Safavid lands to the west. Any ruler in Kabul would have wanted to control Qandahar for both economic and political reasons, but without his autobiographical explanations it is difficult to know why he returned from the Lahore area in 1520 to launch another attack on the city. At this moment, it was held by the friendly and deferential Shah Shuja' Beg Arghun. Babur had made an abortive move on Qandahar in 1517, but retired to Kabul without actually attacking the city. Now in 1520 after returning from the Punjab, he marched west and besieged it. As he did so, he disingenuously carried on discussions about the fate of the Qandahar with Safavid officials in Herat. With so little information, much of it contradictory, it is impossible to understand the military and diplomatic considerations that led him to suspend operations in 1520 or 1521. He returned in 1522 having finally gained control of Qandahar in September 1522, when the governor of the fortress gave him the keys to the city. Babur assigned it to his son Kamran who in 1525 still held the city. All the while Shuja' Beg Arghun, who had been caught between the Safavids and Babur, had been hedging his bets by establishing a power base in the Sind. He now fled to Sind, where his descendants would be confronted again by the Timurids later in the century, by then emperors of Hindustan ruling from Agra.

With Humayun and Muhammad Zaman Mirza in the north and Kamran in Qandahar, Babur was more secure in Kabul than he had ever been in the past and was well positioned to exploit the opportunity, which Daulat Khan Ludi, the governor of Lahore, suddenly offered him. Daulat Khan, whose son and representative in Delhi, Dilawar Khan, had just returned to the Punjab after witnessing the torture and murder of twenty-five Afghan tribal leaders. He offered Babur an alliance and opened talks by sending Dilawar Khan to Kabul, who petitioned Babur for help. Babur joined Daulat Khan and Ibrahim's aged uncle 'Alam Khan with the goal of overthrowing Ibrahim. They allied without formally agreeing who would then rule in Ibrahim's place if he were deposed. In the fall of 1523 Babur returned to the Punjab to meet and defeat a Ludi army sent from Delhi. Now in January 1524, he occupied Lahore and appointed his own men to administer the city and nearby fortress before he continued campaigning south-southeast towards Dipalpur.

Daulat Khan came to resent Babur's pre-emptory assertion of Timurid authority, which caused Babur to break with him. Babur retreated to Lahore and shortly afterwards returned to Kabul, where he soon became preoccupied with an Uzbek siege of Balkh. In his absence, 'Alam Khan and Dilawar Khan staged what Babur describes as a pathetically incompetent assault on Delhi. After relieving Balkh, Babur returned to Kabul sometime in 1525, after 'Alam Khan and Dilawar Khan had retreated to the Punjab. Perhaps, it was after his return when he decided to organise a decisive campaign to overthrow Ibrahim Ludi. Without describing his decision in the *Vaqayi'*, he merely reports that he set out on 17 November. with a field army of unstated strength, to conquer Hindustan. It is implicit in his later narrative that when he began this campaign he abandoned the idea of an alliance with Daulat Khan, for he treated him as his enemy when Babur returned to the Punjab.

Choosing his words with care as his narrative resumes in 1525, Babur describes leaving Kabul on his way to India. In this passage, he does not describe this expedition as a *chapqun* or a *yurush*, but a *safar*, a journey or expedition. In both Persian and Turki *safar* can convey the idea of a state of war. With this in mind, Babur's opening sentence ought to be understood to mean: 'On Friday, the first of the month of Safar of 932 A.H.... [we] marched with a resolve [for taking] Hindustan'.[73] His description of the nearly six-month-long march constitutes another valuable contribution to the understanding of the practice of early sixteenth-century warfare (Illustration 2).

Just a few days after leaving Kabul, a messenger arrived with 20,000 *shahrukhis* of gold *ashrafis* and silver *tangahs* taken from the revenues of Lahore, which Babur forwarded on to Balkh, presumably to ensure the continued loyalty of Muhammad Zaman's garrison in this distant border region.[74] Babur rode east to the Bagh-i vafa garden of happy memory in Adinapur, which he reached on 25 November and where he impatiently waited for Humayun. He had earlier ordered his son to leave Badakhshan to join the expedition, but Humayun did not arrive until 3 December. His delay could have been due to the slow progress of Badakhshan foot soldiers he brought with him, or more simply because he might have paused in Kabul to visit his relatives.

Babur takes time out from his narrative to recall once again the '*hadd u hudud wa safa u latafat*, 'boundary and extent and the charm and delight' of the garden, where he and the army, *charik*, stayed for a week, drinking on 'drinking days' and enjoying *ma'jun* at *suhbatlar* on alternate days. Meanwhile, Babur wrote letters to Humayun, criticising him for his delay. His son had finally arrived just after

Babur had taken his morning draught, and they marched out the same evening, and three days later, paused to take a raft on the Kabul river, drinking as they went. After joining the army that evening, they rafted again the following day, but lost track of the army, which they found the next day. During this rafting Babur and his men amused themselves with a verse competition since, he reports, several of these men were poets. He recalls someone quoting a Persian couplet, the first line of which read:

What can a person do with the love of any coquette?

Babur then said that the poets among them should compose verses on this model, which they did while Babur says he spontaneously recited the following two lines whose last three words faithfully echoed the original: *che kunad kas*, 'What can a person do'.

What can a person do with a senseless [intoxicated] person like you?
What can a person do with every ass-hole she-donkey.[75]

Babur reports that he aimed this bit of ribald humour at a man named Mulla 'Ali Jan, who, he says, was often the butt of jokes. He then admits with some chagrin that he habitually composed spontaneous scatological verse, 'good or bad', 'however empty and harsh the verse might be', and says that he had actually repented, *ta'ib*, from doing so shortly after he composed his versified Turki treatise on Islamic law, the *Mubin* in 1521 or 1522. He concedes he had completely forgotten his oath at this moment on the raft when he targeted 'Ali Jan with his verse and was punished for it, he thought, when he fell ill a few days later, coughing and spitting up blood. To punctuate his sense of regret, Babur quotes an undated Turki poem, which he may have written later in Agra. It reads:

What shall I do with you o tongue,
Due to you my insides are bloody.
Even if you speak such joking verse well,
It is at once shameful and false.
If you speak and will not be tainted by this sin, *bu jurm*,
Turn your reins from this field.[76]

Here, we have Babur reminding his readers once again of his reflexive piety – a Turco-Mongol, who rarely alludes to praying in a mosque, still conscious of and sometimes observant of – the moral precepts of Islam.

The army's march as moveable feast continued when the army reached 'Ali Masjid in the Khyber Pass, the scene of battles during the First and Second

British–Afghan wars in the nineteenth century. The narrowest part of the Khyber, which Babur knew from his previous expeditions, now sparkled with camp-fires, which illumined the night. It was a sight, he writes, that had always stimulated drinking – and now did so again! The next day he rode out and took *ma'jun*, while fasting the entire day. Reaching Bigram/Peshawar on the 10th, the report of a rhino nearby triggered a hunt, which led to the killing of three animals.

At Peshawar he began to organize the *safar* by appointing *beg*s and *ichki*s to supervise clerks who were assigned to count all of the men who were with the army as they crossed the Indus, which they did on Saturday, 16 December. The clerks counted 12,000 men, 'great and small, good and bad, *naukar*s and non-*naukar*s, retainers and non-retainers. These included Badakhshanis, Hazarahs, Afghans and Mongols in addition to his Andijan Turco-Mongol loyalists. Later, Babur reveals that he did not know at this point how many of these men were actually troops as many of the 12,000 men counted were merchants and servants. After he crossed the Indus, some Ludi troops also joined him, but their numbers are not known and their loyalty was not surprisingly suspect. Even before the Panipat battle, he did not seem to be sure precisely how many troops he commanded.

Safely crossing the Indus, the Hindustan campaign began in earnest. Babur heard – probably mistakenly – that his former ally, the very aged Daulat Khan and his son Ghazi Khan had collected 20,000 to 30,000 men to oppose him. He had earlier expelled Babur's men from Lahore, understandably angry that Babur, whose help he had sought, had implicitly claimed sovereignty for himself. Marching south-eastward along the foothills to Sialkot, about 60 miles march north of Lahore, Babur reached the town on 29 December. He had retained Sialkot and nearby Buhlulpur even after his men had been expelled from Lahore. It was then he heard that 'Alam Khan's attack on Delhi had failed. The following day the army marched out southeast to capture Daulat Khan and his son but heard that the Afghan army had fled. After crossing the Beas River, he finally came upon Daulat Khan and a few supporters at the fort of Milwat. After a grandson of Daulat Khan came out to ask for terms, Babur pointedly replied, as he candidly puts it, 'with a morsel of a promise and threats and encouragement and menace'.[77]

Daulat Khan surrendered to be humiliated by Babur, who, using his favourite epithet *mardak*, denounced him as a *qari mabhut mardak*, an 'old stupified little man'. He forced Daulat Khan to kneel in front of him and, with a Hindustani translator at hand, Babur reviled him as a feudatory, whom he had earlier rescued and rewarded only now to be betrayed.[78] He was, Babur reports, only able to mumble a few words in response to Babur's accusation that he had seized 'our provinces'. In this situation, he could not remind Babur that he had originally invited him to the Punjab, not expecting to lose his base of Lahore, for which

Babur had compensated him with some lands that reduced him to the level of a petty landlord.

In dramatising this scene, in which he insults Daulat Khan with contemptuous and probably feigned outrage, Babur records for his readers, with unusual clarity and force, the gritty reality of his Timurid dynastic arrogance. He then sent Daulat Khan, his *khailkhanih*, that is, his chiefs and clan families to the fort of Malot in the Salt Range, but Daulat Khan died along the way. Babur distributed valuable books found in Ghazi Khan's residence – Ghazi Khan having escaped into the hills – to Humayun and Kamran in Qandahar. Then, on 10 January, after his Andijan compatriot Khwajah Kalan arrived with several camels of Ghazni wine, he and his men had a *suhbat*, at which some drank wine and others drank *araq*. After that, Babur began his march to the south to confront Ibrahim Ludi.

Babur now pauses in his day-to-day narrative of the campaign to preface his account of the battle with Ibrahim Ludi, with a passage that conveys his grandiose objective or later sense of achievement. He wrote it in an atypical and florid formulaic style that could have been composed by a Timurid court historian. 'Placing the foot in the stirrup of resolution', he writes, [and] 'putting the hand on the rein of God's will, he would move against Sultan Ibrahim, son of Sultan Sikandar, son of Bahlul Ludi Afghan, who at that time held the throne of Delhi and the country of Hindustan'.[79] Then reverting to his plain narrative style, he reports making a new appointment to Balkh and, more engagingly, mentions sending gifts seized at Milwat to his younger children and households in Kabul. About two days later, 'Alam Khan Ludi having failed to defeat Ibrahim Khan at Delhi, now arrived as a bedraggled refugee in Babur's camp. He was, from Babur's description, received now as a petitioner rather than an ally.

As Babur's army moved southeast across the northern Punjab in late January and February, he began to decorate Hindustan with Timurid or Perso-Islamic institutions, starting with his favourite, the *charbagh* – the symmetrical, four-part garden. Just after passing Sirhind, nearly due north of Delhi, the army camped at the headwaters of the Ghaggar/Kakar river, which Babur described with the kind of enthusiasm he had earlier reserved for Istalif and other rivers in the Kabul *tuman*. He remarks that apart from its great rivers, possibly alluding to those of the Punjab, this was the one 'flowing water', *aqar su,* in Hindustan, by which he seems to mean the kind of turbulent mountain stream along which he and his men liked to repose on their frequent excursions from Kabul to Istalif. He found the upper reaches of the Ghaggar area to be *latif u khush hava wa munasib yerlar,* 'lovely, with pleasant air; pleasant places', and ordered that a *charbagh* be built at the mouth of the valley below. Just then, Babur received word that Sultan Ibrahim was on the march, along with Hamid Khan, one of his officials from Hisar Firuzah, about 100 miles north of Delhi.[80]

The 18-year-old Humayun was deputed to deal with the official from Hisar Firuzah, Hamid Khan. Given a formidable force of experienced men, including 'the entire right wing of the army', *tamam baranghar kishi*, as well as some Hindustan '*begs* and braves of the centre', *guldun ichkilardın ve yiğitlardın*, Humayun marched out on 26 February to confront Hamid Khan. In Babur's telling, his son outmanoeuvred the Afghan commander, whose army dissolved, allowing Humayun to capture 100 to 200 men, half of whom were beheaded on the field and the other half brought back to Babur's camp with seven or eight elephants.

Returning to the camp on 5 March, Humayun was feted for this victory in his first battle, and Babur ordered his matchlock men, to shoot the remaining prisoners, 'as an example', *siasat jihatı*. Babur thought Humayun's first battle, his first Timurid action, *ish Gurkhanı,* 'was a very good omen'.[81] Humayun thought so himself, for he later noted in the margin of his copy of the *Vaqayi'* in 1554 or 1555, that he shaved for the first time after the battle, an act of filial piety, as Babur mentioned shaving for the first time in his autobiography.[82]

Now in March, usually a time of constantly sunny days in North India, but with the hot season approaching, Babur moved south towards Delhi, sending messengers back to Kabul with news of Humayun's victory and dispatching agents forward to determine Ibrahim Ludi's movements. Learning that the Ludi Sultan was slowly moving north a few miles at a time, but spending a few days in camp after each march, Babur continued forward and reached the Jumna River on 15 March. Fording the river, the army came to Sarswa, where they took *ma'jun*. Babur thought the town had an appealing spring, which he describes as 'not a bad place', and jokingly notes that he 'gave' it to his Kabul drinking companion and *kariz* worker Tardi Beg Khaksar, just because the *beg* had praised it.[83] Apparently waiting for more news of Ibrahim's movements, Babur built a platform on a boat and rode on it two marches downstream, when news came that Ibrahim's advanced force of some 5,000 to 6,000 men was nearby. He sent Chin Temür Sultan, the son of Babur's maternal or Mongol uncle Ahmad Khan, three other men, the entire left wing of the army and two other men from the centre. On 2 April, they met and defeated Ibrahim's force, which they then pursued and, just opposite Ibrahim's camp, unhorsed many of them, capturing sixty to seventy men, who were brought to Babur's camp and killed, once again as a *siasat* or warning.[84]

Now with the entire army marching in battle formation of *baranghar, javanghar* and *sol*, right, left and centre, towards Ibrahim's camp, a count was made of the number of troops and was found to be less than estimated earlier. Babur does not record the total, but it is likely his force did not exceed 8,000 men. His daughter, Gulbadan Begim, writing her memoirs late in the century, who had access to Babur's work, says, probably based on eyewitness reports, that he had only 6,000 to 7,000 *kar-amadani* or 'serviceable troops' at Panipat.[85] He estimated Ibrahim's force at an improbable 100,000 and 1,000 elephants, the heavy but sometimes unreliable armour of Indian armies. His estimate of Ibrahim's *charik*, his army, was almost certainly inaccurate and very likely grossly exaggerated.

Studying Babur's relatively well-documented earlier battles reveals that he often did not know the strength of his own forces, especially when allied troops were involved. It would have been unlikely that Babur had an accurate account of Ibrahim's army, although he would have been given some reports on the Ludi sultan's strength. There is also the question as to whether Ibrahim could possibly have assembled these many troops and elephants at a time when his state was coming to pieces. It is, nonetheless, almost certain that Ibrahim's army far exceeded the number of Babur's modest force. Thoughtful readers may also consider that Babur had good reason to exaggerate the numbers involved, considering the scope of his achievement. In any event, by 12 April, Babur's army confronted Ibrahim Ludi at the town of Panipat on the west side of the Jumna, slightly more than 50 miles north of Delhi. By this time, the daily temperatures in North India would probably have reached into the low or middle nineties.

Babur's account of the Battle of Panipat, the only extant eyewitness account, represents one of the most complete first-person records of a decisive battle in the early modern history of the Islamic world or Asia. It is only equalled, and perhaps surpassed, by Shaikh Zain's later description of the Battle of Kanwah with Rana Sanga' the following year. As a backdrop to his detailed narrative of the battle itself, Babur critiques Ibrahim Ludi's military skills as well as revealing the uncertainty of his own men. He unfavourably and caustically compares Ibrahim's generalship to the sophisticated operations of the Uzbek Khans he had faced in Mawarannahr, saying to one of his commanders it was ridiculous to suggest the Ludi sultan was comparable to them and that he was a poor planner and lacked aggressiveness.[86] Babur further remarks that Ibrahim was too much of a miser to pay for additional troops, although the latter critique hardly seems relevant if Ibrahim truly fielded anywhere close to 100,000 troops at Panipat. If his numbers, and elephants, were only half Babur's estimate, he ought to have been able to overwhelm Babur's small force.

His own troops, Babur freely admits, included some men who were very 'apprehensive and doubtful' before the battle, but, he adds, writing of course after the victory:

Anxiety and fear were baseless. As God has predestined in eternity nothing else was possible. Yet it was also impossible to fault them, for they were right. They had come a journey of two to three months from their homeland and had to deal with strange people. We neither knew these people's languages, nor did they know ours.[87]

In making this observation, Babur also unintentionally suggests a partial explanation for the cohesion of his army. The situation differed radically from that of his early battles in Mawarannahr, where men so often abandoned commanders and retired to their nearby estates or switched sides, because they could easily take service with other Timurids or Chingissids. Hindustan did not offer those opportunities to frightened, vacillating or ambitious Turco-Mongols, who could not speak Hindustani. The very foreignness of India probably helped to ensure their loyalty.

As for the actual battle, Babur established a line with Panipat on his right flank and ditches dug by him and bordered with branches on his left. It seems likely from his description of the actual fighting that his victory was due to several factors that must have distinguished his battle formation, weapons and tactics from that of the Ludis. Prior to the battle, he carefully prepared his line, more carefully than he had at any other conflict described in his autobiography. Unlike the Battle of Qandahar in 1507, an open-field cavalry attack against a relatively small Arghun force, in April 1526 he prepared an elaborate line to face a formidable and numerically superior Ludi army that had just earlier easily fought off 'Alam Khan Ludi's assault at Delhi.

At Panipat, Babur adopted an Ottoman Turkish model, as advised by Ustad 'Ali Quli, an Iranian who may have been present at the Battle of Chaldiran in 1514, when Ottoman forces destroyed an Iranian army led by Shah Isma'il Safavi just west of Tabriz.[88] He ordered carts and had them tied together in the *Rum dasturi*, 'the Roman or Ottoman manner', every 20 or 25 feet with foot soldiers perhaps Badakhshanis or Afghans, who fought on foot-holding shields in between. Standing behind them were the vulnerable matchlock men, who would have needed their protection and time to reload. At intervals of an arrow shot, perhaps 100 to 150 yards, there were spaces that allowed cavalry to ride through to join the battle.

As had been true at the Battle of Qandahar, Timurids and Chaghatai Mongols commanded most of the major sections of the army. Humayun commanded the right wing with Muhammad Sultan Mirza Baiqara, Sultan Husain Baiqara's grandnephew, on the left wing. Chin Temür Sultan, the Chaghatai Mongol and son of Ahmad Khan led the right flank of the centre, along with the young boy Sulaiman Mirza, the son of Babur's cousin Wais Mirza of Badakhshan – his

long-time Ferghanah companion. Nizam al-Din 'Ali Khalifah led the left flank
of the centre. Another Ferghanah loyalist Khusrau Kukultash commanded the
centre, with the less well-known Muhammad 'Ali Jang-jang. On the extreme edge
of the right and left wings were flanking detachments charged with *tulghamah*,
encircling or enveloping manoeuvres.[89] Mongols constituted and commanded at
least one and probably both of these latter detachments.

As Babur and only Babur describes how the battle unfolded, he reports that as
the two armies faced each other, Babur's men raided the Ludi lines multiple times
after 12 April and staged one unsuccessful night attack. He reports that Ibrahim
did not respond until the 20th, when he led his forces out of their lines at dawn,
moving rapidly forward, then stopping as they saw Babur's line and examining
his formation and line of carts. Ibrahim would not have previously fought a battle
against a foe that used Ottoman tactics and possessed Mongol cavalry. He was,
however, likely to have had some knowledge of firearms, from reports of Babur's
earlier battles, if not from other sources.

Whatever Ibrahim saw and understood, Babur says that once the Ludis began
moving forward they could not remain stationary, but that they were now unable
to resume their earlier swift forward charge. He says nothing about Ibrahim's
use of his elephants, the intimidating heavy armour of traditional Indian armies.
Babur implies that after pausing, the Ludis slowly resumed their approach towards
his lines while he sent Mongol flanking detachments to the right and left sides of
Ibrahim's rear. As the Mongols engaged with showers of arrows, he sent his left
and right wings forward.

The enduring question about the battle was whether Babur's firearms played a
decisive role in his eventual victory. He does not mention the fire of his matchlock
men, but he does say that two types of cannon, *Farangi* and *zarb-zanan Rumi*,
were used; *Farangi*s from the centre and *zarb-zanan* from left of centre. Based on
his description, it seems doubtful these weapons were decisive. Babur writes that
the *Farangilar* fired a few times, while the *zarb-zanan* got off 'good shots', but he
does not suggest that they won the day. His narrative leaves the impression that
he won the day for two reasons. First, his Ottoman battle array caused Ibrahim to
halt his advance and forfeit the effect of a shock assault. Second, by successfully
outflanking Ibrahim's army, Babur's Mongol troops forced both wings of the
Afghan army to press in upon their own center, causing catastrophic confusion.
He reports that his 'right, left, centre and turning parties' surrounded Ibrahim's
troops, who were so hemmed in that they were unable to make more than a few
small charges on Babur's right and left before falling back under showers of arrows.
By noon, about 4 hours after the battle began, when the sun was one spear over the

horizon, the Timurids were victorious, with Ibrahim and an estimated 15,000 to 16,000 Afghans killed and many men and elephants captured. Babur says nothing about his own casualties.

Humayun and a number of others were immediately ordered to ride to Agra that same afternoon to secure the Ludi treasury, while Babur sent his brother-in-law Mahdi Khwajah and the Baiqara Timurid Muhammad Sultan Mirza to seize the second treasury in Delhi. Babur marched slowly south to the outskirts of Delhi, where he indulged in a kind of religious and political ritual, where he personally linked himself with Muslim India's spiritual and imperial past. He visited graves of Sufi shaikhs and former rulers. On the 24th, he circumambulated the tomb of the important Chishti Sufi Nizam al-Din Auliya (d. 1325) – a major pilgrimage site (Illustration 4). He followed this the next day by a visit to another but less well known Chishti shaikh, Khwajah Qutb al-Din (d. 1235), but perhaps known to Babur because he was a native of Ush – the town at the eastern end of the Ferghanah valley, where Babur had erected a viewing platform. Next, he stopped at the tombs of Sultanate rulers Ghiyas al-Din Balaban (d. 1286), Sultan 'Ala al-Din Khalji (d. 1316), and the tombs and gardens of the first two Ludi sultans, Bahlul and Sikandar. Following this excursion, he and his men returned to camp outside the city and boarded a boat, where they drank *araq*. Then, he appointed a *shiqdar* and a *diwan*, governor and financial administrator in Delhi, the first appointments of his Timurid state in Hindustan.

On Friday, 27 April, while Babur remained in camp, Shaikh Zain Khwafi, one of the versifiers on the raft on 8 December, and a few others went to Delhi to have Babur's name included in the *khutbah*, the congregational prayer, thus formally declaring his Hindustan sovereignty. The next day he set out for Agra, taking the time for a tour of Tughluqabad, the palace and fortifications in South Delhi erected by the Tughluqs, the dynasty founded by Ghiyas al-Din Tughluq who overthrew the Khaljis in 1320. He reached the outskirts of Agra on 4 May, allotted a generous land grant to Sultan Ibrahim's mother, and, on 10 May, entered the city and rode to the *manzil*, the residence of Sultan Ibrahim.

Interrupting his narrative with his arrival in Agra, Babur stops to summarise his *Hindustan hawası*, 'ambition/desire/lust for Hindustan', and measure his achievement against earlier Muslim invaders and rulers of India. His account is the most indulgently self-serving section of the *Vaqayi'*. He begins:

'From the date 910 [a.h.], when Kabul was subdued, from that date to this there has always been a desire for Hindustan. Sometimes because of *begs*' foolishness; sometimes because of the desertion of older and younger brothers, *"agha ve eynı"* a *yurush* on Hindustan was not practical and its territories, *mamaliki*, remained unconquered. Finally, no obstacles remained [and] none of the *beg*s of lesser status would speak a word against this design.[90]

Continuing, Babur writes that in 1519 he stormed Bajaur in 44 to 66 minutes and after massacring the population, *ilini qatl 'am qilib*, went on to Bhirah. At Bhirah, he reminds his readers, he had not plundered, *talan u taraj*, but levied a ransom on its people and then returned to Kabul. 'From that year until the year 932', Babur concludes, 'we sent the army to Hindustan, and the fifth time, God, May He be Exalted, *Tengri ta'ala*, in wisdom and mercy, made such an enemy as Sultan Ibrahim, defeated and worthless, and [left] such a country as Hindustan accessible and conquered for us'.[91]

While Babur partly reprises the demonstrably-false assertion he had made in the 1519 Bhirah narrative that he had constantly planned to move on to Hindustan since he arrived in Kabul in 1504, he now blamed unnamed *beg*s and relatives for delaying the invasion for 21 years. He does nonetheless accurately date the first stroke of his *Hindustan hawası*, his 'desire for Hindustan', at Bhirah. He does so without reminding readers that he had agreed to one of his men's suggestion for the strike across the Indus because the army had failed to gain much booty from the assault and massacre at Bajaur. He is certainly not the last autobiographer to imply his political career unfolded as a logical, seamless plan, despite evidence to the contrary. Otherwise, his account is notable because he ultimately ascribes his Panipat victory to God's plan, in contrast to what he earlier wrote about his defeat of the Arghuns before Qandahar. Not only does he make this ritualistic gesture, but when he invokes God in this passage, he uses the name of the Turco-Mongol deity *Tengri*, 'the blue sky' of Central Asian pastoral nomadic societies. He uses this word for God throughout the *Vaqayi'* far more often than the Arabic-Islamic Allah, which occurs only thirty-four times, often in Quranic quotations and frequently in the writings of clerics or scholars he quotes, such as his companion Shaikh Zain.[92]

Most of the time he invokes *Tengri* either after a death – he or she 'went to God's mercy' – or as a ritualistic statement after a victory – 'by God's grace' or 'God brought it right'. Many times he uses *Tengri* as a synonym for Allah in the phrase *Allah ta'ala*, 'God Most High', and occasionally he uses it specifically in an Islamic theological context as when he writes: 'What God (*Tengri*) has fixed in eternity cannot be changed'. As Babur was undeniably a Hanafi Sunni Muslim – someone who clocked his daily affairs according to the times of the five daily prayers – his religious language seems to be merely the natural expression of a member of the Turki-speaking military class, who had grown up in Mawarannahr. His vocabulary nicely illustrates his composite cultural personality, evident in other contexts as well. It is ratified anew when he follows this passage by comparing himself favourably with *dısharı*, those from the outside of Hindustan, who, 'from the time of the *Hazrat Rasalat*, the Honoured Prophet, have conquered or ruled India.

Babur's list of these 'external' conquerors included Mahmud of Ghazni, Muhammad of Ghur and himself. His achievement, he argues, was far greater, although in the following description his ego is subsumed, rhetorically at least, to his faith – in *Tengri*! After all Mahmud of Ghazni controlled Khurasan and dominated Khwarizm and Samarqand, and he only had to face independent Hindu rajas rather than a *padshah* who ruled the entire country. Shihab al-Din Ghuri, according to the thirteenth-century historian Minhaj al-Juzjani's history, the *Tabaqat-i-nasiri*, which Babur cites, led 120,000 men into India, also against independent rajas.[93] In contrast, Babur writes, he commanded only 1,500 to 2,000 men when he took Bhirah, and *naukar* (troops), *saudakar* (merchants) and *chakar* (servants) equal to a total of 12,000, when he defeated Ibrahim.

'Dependent on me', Babur writes, were the territories of Badakhshan, Qunduz, Kabul and Qandahar, but none of these countries, he pointedly remarks,

> was profitable... Then too all of Mawarannahr was possessed by Uzbek Khans and *sultan*s, an ancient enemy whose troops numbered 100,000. Moreover, Afghans possessed the Hindustan country from Bhirah to Bihar and Sultan Ibrahim was *Padshah*... In these conditions and with such strength...we placed our trust in God the most High, *Tengri ta'ala*... We do not pretend that this happiness [of the conquest] comes from our own strength and power but from *Tengri*'s kindness and compassion.[94]

Perhaps Tengri, the overarching steppe sky, had indeed protected its Timurid and Chaghatai sons.

Endnotes

1   TR, II, 158. Haidar Mirza's account is confusing, as he says that Wais Mirza's envoy told Babur that Uzbek forces had also fled from Merv and come to Qunduz, which was not the case.

2   TR, II, fs. 112a–112b.

3   BN–M, fs. 8b, 95a and TR II, f. 118a.

4   TR, II, 160 and 163. It is difficult to determine the date when Haidar Mirza's uncle, Sa'id Khan, left Babur for Mawarannahr. He was in Kabul until December 1510, when the news arrived there of the Battle of Merv, but he had reached Andijan before Babur crossed the Amu Darya a second time. He apparently accompanied Babur to Qunduz and left from there with some of the 20,000 Mongols who had earlier arrived in Qunduz.

5   TR, II, 161.

6   In his account of these events the historian Khwandamir, who lived mainly in Herat and wrote for the Safavids before he emigrated to India and met Babur in 1528, reports that Babur agreed to acknowledge Safavid sovereignty in these traditional terms. Ghiyâs al-Dîn b. Humâm al-Dîn al-Husaini Khwândamîr, *Habîb al-siyar fî akhbâr afrâd bashar* (Tehran: Intishârat-i Kitabkhânah-i Khayyâm, 1954), Volume IV, 524. Timurid-Mughal historians usually gloss over or deny this, but numismatic evidence and the eyewitness account of Haidar Mirza confirm Babur's concession. For the coins, see Stanley Lane Poole, *The Coins of the Moghul Emperors of Hindustan in the British Museum* (Delhi: Inter-India Publications, repr. 1983), 5. Very few of these coins survive.

7   Edmund H. Dickerman, 'The Conversion of Henry IV: Paris is Well worth a Mass in Psychological Perspective,' *The Catholic Historical Review* 63, no. 1 (January, 1977): 1–13. The story, but not Henry's conversion, is apparently apocryphal.

8   TR, II, f. 120b.

9   Ibid.

10 TR, II, fs. 121a–121b.

11 TR II, f.121b.

12 TR, II, f. 125b. Yet Khwândamîr describes the Uzbek force as 'immense'. *Habib al-siyar*, Volume 3, 525.

13 Hasan-i Rûmlû, *Ahsan al-tawârîkh*, ed. 'Abd al-Husain Navâ'î (Tehran: Intishârat-i Bâbik, 1978), 167–70.

14 Hasan-i Rûmlû, *Ahsan al-tawârîkh*, 170.

15 Fadlullah b. Rûzbihân Kûnjî-Isfahânî, *Sulûk al-mulûk* (Tehran: Intishârat-i Khwârazmî, 1983), 60.

16 TR, II, fs. 126b–127a and see also TR, Volume 2, f. 144a–b, for information on this Mongol clan.

17 Rogers (trans.) and Beveridge (ed.), *The Tûzuk-i Jahângîri or Memoirs of Jahângîr*, Volume 1, 89.

18 BN–B, 429.

19 For discussions of Afghan tribes, see, among many other sources, the works by British Imperial era writers, among them: Bellew, *An Inquiry into the Ethnography of Afghanistan*; Major Henry George Raverty, *Notes on Afghanistan and Baluchistan* (Quetta: Nisa Traders, repr. 2nd ed. 1982), Volume 2; Captain J. A. Robinson, *Notes on Nomad Tribes of Eastern Afghanistan* (Quetta: Nisa Traders, repr. 2nd edition, 1980); G. T. Vigne, *A Personal Narrative of a Visit to Ghuzni, Kabul, and Afghanistan* (Lahore: Sang-e Meel Publications, repr. 1982).

20 It is not easy to locate these sites on modern maps, but Bajaur is located northeast of the Kunar Valley in modern Pakistan. See the map of Kafiristan in Robertson, *The Kafirs of the Hindu Kush*, following 658 and Annette Beveridge's notes on 367 to 373.

21 For a discussion of Timurid-Mughul firearms, including the *tufang*, see Andrew de la Garza, *The Mughal Empire at War* (London and New York: Routledge, 2016), 37–38.

22 BN–M, f. 218a.

23 BN–M, f. 219b.

24 He does actually suggest something of the sort when he refers to his 1505 expedition and says that despite his *dai'iyah*, his 'desire', to enter Hindustan, the now deceased but still reviled Baqi Chaghaniani had persuaded him to raid down the west bank of the Indus. BN–M, f. 225a.

25 BN–M, f. 223b.

26 BN–M, f. 229b.

27 BN–M, f. 224a.

28 BN–M, f, 224b.

29 In the same way, Temür had made *mal-i aman* levies on cities that he spared from being sacked. It was essentially a form of protection money. See H. R. Roemer, 'Timur in Iran', in *The Cambridge History of Iran: The Timurid and Safavid Periods* (Volume 6), eds. Peter Jackson and Laurence Lockhart (Cambridge: Cambridge University Press, 1986), 54.

30 BN–M, f. 226b.

31 See Peter Jackson's brief account of Muslim rulers in Delhi following Temür's campaign in *The Delhi Sultanate*, 321–25.

32 BN–M, f. 226b.

33 BN–M, f. 227a. Hind-al from the Turkic verb *almaq*, meaning to take, occupy or conquer.

34 BN–M, fs. 227a–228a.

35 It is not known how this Central Asian warrior came to be called 'Hindu'.

36 BN–M, f. 229b.

37   BN–M, fs. 228b–229a.

38   BN–M, f. 235b.

39   See 'Razm u Bazm' in Eleanor Sim's elegant volume, *Peerless Image: Persian Painting and its Sources* (New Haven and London: Yale University Press, 2002), 91–126 and the record of the exhibit *Bazm and Razm: Feast and Fight in Persian Art* at the Metropolitan Museum of Art in New York City, 17 February–31 May 2015.

40   BN–M, f. 234b–235a.

41   Istalif and its immediate area includes a group of villages that were famous for crafts, fruit and wine grapes. The village and surrounding area is described with photographs and house plans by Albert Szabo and Thomas J. Barfield in their volume *Afghanistan: An Atlas of Indigenous Domestic Architecture* (Austin, Texas: University of Texas Press, 1991), 197–215.

42   BN–M, 136b.

43   For a lavishly illustrated history of the geometrically precise Iranian garden model, see, among many other sources, Mehdi Khansari, M. Reza Moghtader and Minouch Yavari, *The Persian Garden: Echoes of Paradise* (Washington, DC: Mage, 1998).

44   BN–M, f. 136b.

45   BN–M, fs. 2b–3a.

46   See BN–M, fs. 136b–37a and f. 235a. It is not exactly clear when Babur ordered a formal garden made at Khwajah Sih-yaran, perhaps in 1505 after his mother's death. He describes the round platform being constructed during his visit on 22 April.

47   BN–M, f. 220a–b.

48   BN–M, f. 238a.

49   BN–M, f. 139b.

50   The summer monsoon reaches the Gardiz and Ghazni area from the southeast. See the climatological map of Afghanistan in Szabo and Barfield, *Afghanistan: An Atlas of Indigenous Domestic Architecture*, 253.

51   BN–M, f. 244a.

52   BN–M, fs. 248b–249a.

53   BN–M, 245a.

54   BN–M, f. 245a.

55   Beveridge suggests this in one of her many erudite and invaluable footnotes, 417. n.1.

56   BN–M, f. 247a.

57   For a description by the European traveller Clavijo see his work, Ruy González de Clavijo, *Embassy to Tamerlane, 1403-1406*, trans. Guy Le Strange and eds. E. Denison Ross and Eileen Power, (New York and London: Harper, 1928), 244–45.

58   BN–M, f. 247b.

59 BN–M. f. 248.

60 BN–M, f. 249b. Babur uses the term Sart to refer to urban inhabitants, whether they spoke Persian or Turki. Turk has a number of meanings, but when he uses it to refer to people generally it means a rural Turki speaker.

61 Ludmila Serikova, Aziz Kayumov and Temira Saidullaeva, *Alishir Navou* (Izdatelstvo TSK Kampartii Uzbekistana, 1963), 9–153.

62 His first *ghazals* are discussed by Stephen F. Dale, *The Garden of the Eight Paradises: Babur and the Culture of Empire in Central Asia, Afghanistan and India*, 269–70.

63 Ibid., 272.

64 Ibid., 276–77.

65 See Beveridge's alternative translation. 372, n. 2. As she notes the poem is full of word play, principally playing on the meaning of *ba-jaur*, 'with force' for Bajaur, the fortress, in the final line.

66 Bîlal Yücel, *Bâbur Dîvânı* no. 297, 255 and Dale, *The Garden of the Right Paradises: Bâbur and the Culture of Empire in Central Asia, Afghanistan and India* (1483–1530), 281–82.

67 Bîlal Yücel, *Bâbür Divânı*, no. 162, p. 256 and Dale, *The Garden of the Eight Paradises, Babur and the Culture of Empire in Central Asia, Afghanistan and India* (1483–1530) 282–83.

68 Bertels, *Izbrannye Trudy, Navoi i Dzhami*, 95.

69 Yücel, *Bâbür Divânı*, no. 407, p. 283 and Dale, *The Garden of the Eight Paradises, Babur and the Culture of Empire in Central Asia, Afghanistan and India* (1483–1530) 283–84.

70 Beveridge suggests that Mihrban(u) was the intended recipient. BN–B, 402 n. 3.

71 For a summary of the last days of the Delhi Sultanate and the bewildering political chaos that followed Taimur's invasion and sack of Delhi see Jackson, *The Delhi Sultanate*, 311–25.

72 John F. Richards provides a lucid summary of Ludi financial and political practices in his article 'The Economic History of the Lodi Period: 1451-1526,' *JESHO* 8, no. 1 (August 1965), 47–67.

73 BN–M, f. 251b.

74 The value of these coins was substantial, possibly as much as 1000.00 pounds sterling in nineteenth-century values. See BN–B, 446, n. 5.

75 BN–M, f. 252b. I am indebted to Professor Ranin Kazemi of San Diego State University for his useful suggestions regarding these verses.

76 BN–M, f. 253a.

77 BN–M, f. 258a.

78 BN–M, f. 258b.

79 BN–M, f. 261a.

80 BN–M, fs. 261b–212a.

81 BN–M, fs. 262b–263a.
82 See Beveridge's note to this effect. BN–B, 466, n. 1.
83 BN–M, fs. 263a–263b.
84 BN–M, f. 264.
85 HN, f. 9b, 12.
86 BN–M, fs. 264a–265b.
87 BN–M, f. 264b.
88 Noted by Annette Beveridge, BN–B, 469, n. 1.
89 BN–M, f. 266a. Babur uses the word *tulghamah* as both a noun and a participle. It is derived from a Middle Turkic word, which means to circle, encircle or go around and so on and was used in Uighur Turkish and Chaghatai. See Martti Râsânen, *Versuch Eines Etymologischen Wörterbuchs De Türksprachen* (Helsink: Suomolais-Ugrilainen, Seura, 1969–71), Volume 1, 486.
90 BN–M, f. 269a.
91 Ibid. I have followed Arat's modern Turkish translation for the sentence that reads: 'From that year until 932 [a.h.] we sent the army to Hindustan'. Arat, *Vekayi Babur'un Hatirati*, f. 269a.
92 Babur's use of these two terms may be traced in Volume 2 of Mano's superb text of the *Vaqâyi'*, 'Concordance and Classified Indexes'.
93 See Kumar's multiple references to Juzjani in his work *The Emergence of the Delhi Sultanate* and for the Ghaznavid and Ghurid invasions, Kumar's Chapter 2: 'The Sultanates of North India: the Mu'izzi Maliks in Hindustan'. The number 120,000 is patently absurd.
94 BN–M, f. 269b and 270a.

4

Padshahliq, Governance, in Hindustan

'Hindustan is vast, populous and productive.' With this sentence Babur introduces the Hindustan Gazetteer section of the *Vaqayi'*. Like Babur's earlier gazetteer of the Kabul region, this gazetteer prefaces the political and military narrative of the following years. It introduces his Turki-speaking readers to the kingdom he had just seized from Ibrahim before he resumes the narrative by describing the distribution of the Ludi treasury in Agra. Yet, the two gazetteers are substantially different. His survey of the Kabul region of eastern Afghanistan reflects the detailed knowledge of its *tuman*s or districts he acquired over two decades. It is not only vastly more detailed and precise than his survey of Hindustan, but in the gazetteer and the subsequent narrative of his Afghan decades, Babur also reveals his love for the region, where he later asked to be buried.

In contrast, Babur's account of Hindustan, where he lived for only 4 years, is much briefer – his appreciative survey of its exotic flora and fauna constitutes the greatest part of the section. Otherwise, it is distinguished by his largely dismissive critique of the environment and society of the Hindustan he had, in his own words, so long desired. Later, he translates this critique into deeply emotional verses of regret that he wrote in India after the conquest. In part, he reacted as a homesick Timurid in both the critique and verse. He and his compatriots found Hindustan to be both strange and also deeply repugnant in many different respects. Compared with 'our countries', he writes in Turki and presumably alluding to Mawarannahr, it is an 'extraordinary country,' *gharib mamlekati*. Babur further writes that everything about it is different: 'its mountains, rivers, jungles and deserts, its people and their tongues, its rains and its winds are all different... Once the water of Sind [Indus] is crossed, everything is in the Hindustan way: land, water, tree, rock, people and horde, opinion and custom'.[1] Nor was he alone in experiencing northern India as a profoundly foreign country. Some of his most loyal and long-serving *beg*s abandoned him within months of the Panipat victory to return to Afghanistan.

Babur may not have cared for the Hindustan he had so long desired, but following his victory at Panipat in April 1526 he set about trying to realise his ambition of subjugating a country he did not control. At that time, his state comprised a swath of territory from Kabul through Lahore down to Delhi and Agra, but little else. During the following months, he began working to extend his influence to districts immediately around Agra, but found it difficult as he faced a hostile populace. Babur had not, after all, overwhelmed the Ludis with a massive barbarian horde, which he might have used to envelop large parts of the countryside. He occupied Delhi and Agra with fewer than 10,000 troops, leaving most of Hindustan still controlled by a complex medley of Afghan and Hindu rulers of varying strength. As he gradually expanded his influence in the Duab region and on the borders of Rajasthan, he quickly came to appreciate the great danger he faced from resurgent Afghan forces gathering to the east in the Gangetic Valley and the openly aggressive intentions of the powerful Rana Sanga' of Chitor. Yet, even as he manoeuvred to counter these threats, marked by his second major victory at the epic Battle of Kanwah with Rana Sanga' in March 1527 and by subsequent campaigns against Afghans in the east, he began modifying what he considered to be Hindustan's bleak environment in Istalif's appealing image by constructing formal Persianate gardens in Agra and other nearby towns. By December 1528, he had succeeded well enough in his goal of pacifying the Punjab and the Duab, and modifying the region's unsatisfactory environment by formally celebrating the creation of a Timurid empire. This event was made more satisfying by the migration of hundreds of Timurid and Chaghatai Mongol refugees who enthusiastically joined Babur to enjoy the relative safety and surpassing wealth of Hindustan.

Vast, Populous and Productive

Babur does not dwell at length on Hindustan's geographical extent or population density except to say that 'on the east, south and even on the west it ends at the great enclosing ocean…', while emphasising the immensity of Hindustan's population. Remarking that 'the country's pleasant thing is that it has a limitless number of workmen of every kind and', he alludes to the existence of castes, 'a fixed group, *jam*', for every kind of work'.[2] He reports that most of Hindustan's inhabitants were pagans, called Hindus, but says little about Muslims, apart from his circumambulation of Sufi shrines in Delhi after Panipat and a passing reference to his name being pronounced in a Delhi mosque. Apart from references to Afghan enemies, he does not give his Turki readers any idea about the size or ethnic complexion of the Indo-Muslim population or allude to the historic migration of Turkic and Iranian Muslims, which intensified during the Mongol invasions of Mawarannahr, Iran and Afghanistan in the thirteenth century. Nor does he ever comment on relations between Muslim and Hindu inhabitants.

Babur does mention that Hindustan had been ruled by the sultans of Delhi since 1206, and briefly describes the five most important Indo-Muslim rulers in 1526. As someone concerned with contemporary governance, he does not discuss the legacy of three centuries of Muslim rule in establishing an institutional Islamic infrastructure of mosques and financing the growth of an indigenous '*ulama*' or clerical class. Most notably, Babur does not praise an Indian city or celebrate Hindustan's Indo-Muslim civilisation as he had done earlier for Samarqand and Herat and their cultures. Babur does not name any major Indo-Muslim literary and historical scholars, such as the outstanding Persian language poet and Chishti Sufi disciple Amir Khusrau Dihlavi (1253–1325), whose verse Babur's father knew, or the prolific Persian language historian of the Delhi Sultanate era Zia al-Din Barani (1285–1357). His Hindustan gazetteer is so abbreviated because when he wrote, he simply did not know even a fraction of what he had learned about the Kabul region over 20 years. He explicitly acknowledges this at the end of the section when he reports that he has written what is known, and that in the future he will relate, *taqrir qildum dur*, other important information as it becomes known.[3] What he does make known with absolute clarity is that he valued Hindustan for the same reason earlier invaders coveted the country – its productivity and its extraordinary wealth. His appreciation of India's wealth echoes the understanding of previous invaders and is nicely expressed by seventeenth-century Safavid poet Ashraf Mazandarani who wrote:

> Whoever comes to Hindustan from Iran imagines,
> That in India gold is scattered like stars in the evening sky.[4]

Babur writes that he valued five things about Hindustan: its numerous craftsmen, its refreshing air following monsoon rains, the system of calculation and categories of measures and the fact that it was a large country awash in gold and silver coins.[5] Its wealth, he pointedly mentions, was arithmetically reflected in its numbering system, which included such high values as *lacs* (100,000), *crores* (10,000,000) and even greater amounts that were needed to calculate the monetary value of the country's agricultural and commercial economy. His knowledge of India's wealth, which contrasted with Kabul's relative poverty, was fully documented when he distributed the coin of the Ludi's Agra treasury. He gave Humayun 70 *lac*s, 7,000,000 coins, or approximately 56,000 or 57,000 pound sterling, in nineteenth-century values, along with a separate uncounted treasure house and the extraordinary 'Mountain of Light' diamond. This stone was apparently the *kuh-i nur* Humayun took from the family of the former Rajput ruler of Gwalior, Bikramajit Rajah, who had been killed fighting as a tributary of Ibrahim Ludi. Major *beg*s were allotted between 10 and 6 *lac*s of coins, while appropriate gifts were given to every element of the army. Merchants and religious students who accompanied the army as it crossed the Indus also received substantial gifts.

He gave other substantial sums to family members and important individuals who remained in Afghanistan: 17 *lac*s to Kamran, 15 *lac*s to Muhammad Zaman Mirza and large amounts of gold and silver coins, jewels and slaves to all his relations. His daughter Gulbadan Begim writes almost rapturously about the largess each 'royal' woman still in Kabul received: a dancing girl, a gold plate full of jewels – ruby and pearl, cornelian and diamond, emerald and turquoise, topaz and cat's eye...trays full of *ashrafi* coins.[6] He sent other gifts to *beg*s and common soldiers who remained outside Hindustan, with special payments made to individuals in Samarqand, Khurasan, Kashgar in Xinjiang and Iraq. Shaikhs, probably Naqshbandi Sufis, in Samarqand and Khurasan were given offerings, which were also sent to Mecca and Medina. Finally, every person in the Kabul region and a village in Badakhshan, called Varsak, received a single *shahrukhi* coin.[7] Babur gave away so much wealth that the Iranian historian Ferishta (1560–1620) later referred to him as a *qalandar*, an impoverished, wandering Sufi.[8]

Readers of Babur's autobiography, who study his entire Hindustan gazetteer will soon realise that he preferred to rule a state that combined Kabul's environment and society and Hindustan's lavish resources. After longing for Hindustan while in Kabul, he now devoutly wished for Kabul while in Hindustan. Apart from citing wealth as one of the few things he liked about North India, he criticised nearly every other aspect of the region, ranging from its climate, topography, cities and gardens to its customs and culture. 'Hindustan', Babur writes, 'is a place with little appeal'. The climate alone was oppressive, prompting him to remark: 'We were oppressed by three things in India, first by its heat, then by its strong winds and also by its dust'.[9] Just the topography seemed to depress him. He disliked the tedious flatness of the Gangetic Valley, the drab sameness of its cities and the region's ragged, unplanned gardens. 'The greater part of Hindustan's territories is a level plain.' He writes, undoubtedly recalling Istalif, its mountain torrents, flower-strewn hillsides and delightful shaded gardens. 'Its towns and countries are extremely unpleasant, *asru bisafa dur*. All its towns are one and the same... Its gardens have no walls and... there is no running water in their gardens or residences [which] are without charm, *safa*, air, *hava*, proportion, *andam* and symmetry, *siyaq*'.[10]

Babur expanded the indictment of Hindustan with a comprehensive critique of the country's Hindu society.[11] He seemed to consider that his victory at Panipat had rewarded him with a poisoned chalice. Its people, he writes...

> Are not handsome, *husn*. They have no convivial society, *ikhtilat u amizish*,
> no social intercourse, *amad u raft*, no character or genius, *tab' u idrak*,
> no urbanity, *adab*, no nobility, *karm*, no chivalry, *muruvat*. In the skilled

arts and crafts, *hunar ve ish*, there is no symmetry, order, straightness and
rectangularity, *siyaq*, *andam*, *rajah* and *gunya*. There are no good horses, no
good dogs, no grapes, muskmelons or first-rate fruits, no ice or cold water,
no good bread or cooked food in the bazars, no public baths, *hammam*s,
no religious colleges, *madrasah*s, no candles, no torches or candlesticks.[12]

Babur's catalogue of complaints reveals several things about his reaction to North
India, ranging from the relatively petty to the deeply meaningful. Hindustan's
lack of grapes, melons, fruits and bread and cooked food in the *bazar*s may be
put down simply to homesickness. Perhaps, his inability to find good dogs might
be taken slightly more seriously, if in fact he missed watchdogs for his camps.
The absence of good horses was, however, more serious, for India, like China, did
not raise good cavalry animals. Just as Chinese officials looked to Ferghanah and
elsewhere in Central Asia for its 'blood-sweating horses', so later Indian Timurids
looked to Mawarannahr for cavalry mounts. Their import later represented one of
the largest foreign expenses for the Timurid-Mughal Empire.

His further critique also signified that Babur found Hindu culture and society to
be fundamentally inferior to the Persianised, Islamised Turco-Mongol life he had
known in Mawarannahr and Afghanistan. Here, he expresses a simple, unadorned
racism in finding Hindus unattractive, lacking in *husn*, beauty or elegance, and
concluded that their cultural was inferior. It exhibited no character or genius, no
adab or urbanity, the belletristic politesse he saw in Husain Baiqara's Herat *beg*s.
They neither possessed any nobility or chivalry, thinking perhaps of his father,
or the individual *beg*s he met in Husain Baiqara's capital. Apart from his earlier
violent encounters like stealing from merchants along the Indus, Babur does not
seem to have familiarised himself with Indians of any particular class at this time.

Even then, Babur thought that Indian crafts, like their gardens, were badly or
carelessly made, lacking, among other qualities, in *siyaq* or symmetry and *gunya* or
rectangularity. The latter word was a Greek geometrical term, which, like so many
mathematical knowledge and languages, had been absorbed into Arabic and Islamic
culture. Babur may possibly have learned it during his Kabul days or from a Herat
garden architect, Mirak-i Saiyid Ghiyas, who arrived in India a year before Babur's
death.[13] In fact, his commitment to classic Greco-Islamic geometrical design – or in
Hindustan, its lack – helped him to define the boundaries between his and Hindu
society. He applied this standard not only to gardens and crafts of all kinds but to
buildings, as when he surveyed the buildings of Gwalior in 1528, whose raja had
died fighting with Ibrahim at Panipat. He thought the buildings within Gwalior
fort to be *gharib* or strange and *lokpalok ve bisiyaq*, ponderous and irregular – once
again invoking *siyaq* or symmetry and proportion as geometric standards.[14]

Yet, even more important to him was the compelling fact that Hindu caste society was antithetical to the social ideal Babur repeatedly extolled in the *Vaqayi'* when he has described his delight in the occasion and society of the *suhbat* or the social *majlis*, the *iikhtilat u amizesh* and *amad u raft* of Persianised Turco-Mongol life. Few things bothered him more in India, in Hindu India, than a society based on social separation, a culture that did not celebrate, as he repeatedly did in Mawarannahr, Herat and Kabul, social gatherings of diverse individuals. His terms *ikhtilat u amizesh* connotes conversation, social intercourse and friendship, while *amad u raft*, literally coming and going, alludes to the exchange of visits. In his society, men at least would also have met one another when they frequented communal institutions, the *hammam* or public bath and the *madrasah* or theological college. In Hindu India, the exclusivity of temple worship was paralleled by the restrictive norms of social intercourse.

In reacting as he did, Babur expressed an outsider's surprise and dismay with Hindu social separation or isolation, which was observed by Megasthenes, the Greek-Seleucid ambassador to the Mauryan court at Patna in the third century BCE. He is quoted as saying that '...other things they do which one cannot approve: for instance, that they eat always alone, and that they have no fixed hours when meals are to be taken by all in common, but each one eats when he feels inclined. The contrary custom', Megasthenes pointedly remarks, 'would be better for the ends of social and civil life'.[15] Eating and drinking together was a social value Babur embraced. He would have applauded what the first-century CE Greek writer Plutarch said when he wrote about meals: 'We do not sit at table only to eat, but to eat together'.[16] The seventeenth-century Pushtu poet and tribal chief Khushal Khan Khattak expressed this idea even more pointedly when he wrote:

> What one consumes in solitude,
> Will fill the gut and nothing else;
> What one consumes in company,
> And sociably, is the true feast.[17]

In the eleventh century CE, the Kwarezmian Iranian al-Biruni (973–c. 1050), a Greco-Islamic mathematician, scientist and later a student of Sanskrit, wrote an encyclopaedic work on Indian civilisation titled *Tahqiq ma li'l Hind me maqula fi 'aql aw mardhulah*. Generally, but misleadingly known simply as the *Kitab al-Hind*, the *Book of India*, the original Arabic title more accurately indicates al-Biruni's bias as an Iranian Natural Philosopher, trained in Aristotelian thought, and the title indicates that he wrote a critical study of India. When translated, it read *'A Verification of What is Said on India, Whether Rational or Ridiculous'*, and in it he approached the study of India with what he termed the 'geometrical method' – the Aristotelian logical process of moving from induction to use deduction to critically scrutinise Brahmanical Hinduism, as well as employing empirical observations to analyse the Indian landscape. He anticipated Babur's later astonishment and dismay when he wrote of Indians:

> First, they differ from us in everything, which other nations have in common... Many Hindu customs differ from those of our country and of our time to such a degree as to appear to us simply monstrous. One might almost think they had almost intentionally changed them into the opposite, for our customs do not resemble theirs, but are the very reverse..." When they eat, al-Biruni writes, "Hindus sit one by one on a tablecloth of dung...[and regarding *adab*, al-Biruni wrote about Hindus' lack of social graces that] "They spit out and blow their noses without any respect for the older ones present.... [and] If one of them hands over a thing to another, he expects that it should be thrown to him as we a throw a thing to the dogs.[18]

Al-Biruni was, like Babur, a Central Asian Muslim, who had spent time in Afghanistan at Mahmud of Ghazni's frigid court. Just as Babur invoked Greco-Islamic geometric norms to critique Indian gardens and buildings, al-Biruni promoted the geometric intellect and used Greco-Islamic logical assumptions and methods to critique the Brahman society and Sanskrit texts – which he too thought was very *bisiyaq*.

Homesick in Hindustan

Whether Babur's Turco-Mongol and Afghan *beg*s and *yiğit*s or warriors expressed their reaction to India with the same sophistication and detail as Babur did when he wrote the Hindustan gazetteer nearly 2 years after Panipat, many wanted to abandon Hindustan and return to Afghanistan within a few months after the victory. In part at least, they suffered from the oppressive pre-monsoon heat and dust of the North Indian plain. Late April, May and early June, before the great monsoon clouds pile up in the north – if indeed they do – it can be an exhausting and enervating experience in northern India. Babur remarks that 'it was the hot time', *isig vaqtları idi*, adding that it was especially hot in 1526. The heat intensified the Timurid army's senses of being overwhelmed with the chaotic social situation in the summer of 1526. 'For these reasons', he laments, 'most of the *beg*s and groups of the *yiğit*s lost heart and were not content to stay in Hindustan'.[19]

Recalling the complaints of his men in 1527 or 1528, Babur wrote a reflective but bitter commentary denouncing what he felt to be the betrayal of men who had joined him to invade Hindustan. It was bad enough, he notes, that recently promoted *beg*s of little status, who had, he implies, all agreed on their common purpose, should now betray his trust. Yet, some senior officers, he writes, behaved far worse. He was particularly upset that one of his closest friends and long-serving officers, Khwajah Kalan – the son of one of his father's men whom Babur had appointed to govern Bajaur in 1519, desperately wanted to leave Agra to return to Kabul because he could not endure the climate.

Attempting to prevent the threatened dissolution of his army, Babur called a conference with all his *beg*s, and in a scene reminiscent of Alexander the Great's purported attempt to persuade his men to advance further into India, 'I said', he writes, possibly polishing the vocabulary he may have used: '*Saltanat ve jahangirliq*, government and conquest, are not realised without implements and weapons. *Padshahliq ve amirliq*, kingship and nobility, are impossible without *naukar and vilayat*, retainer and province. We have struggled for several years, seen difficulties, traversed immense territory, exposed ourselves and the army to the perils of war and slaughter. *Tengri 'inayati bile*, "with God's favor" we have overpowered so many such enemies, seized such vast countries.... Should we have remained in Kabul subject to impoverished misfortune? "By speaking these reasonable and justifiable words," he continues, we dissuaded vacillating men from leaving.'[20]

Well, he failed to persuade everyone. Since Khwajah Kalan had no heart to stay in Hindustan, Babur gave him the Ghazni and Gardiz *tuman*s in Afghanistan and a *parganah* near Patiala in the southeastern Punjab, worth 3 or 4 *lac*s. Khwajah Kalan was also entrusted with guarding Kabul and he later became the *de facto* governor of the city. Babur also assigned three others to accompany him to bring gifts to Timurids and Chaghatai Chinggisids in Kabul. Before Khwajah Kalan left, but not until late August, he was unable to mask his feelings about India and wrote a couplet on the wall of his house in Agra, which reads: 'If I should safely cross the Sind (Indus), My face be blackened if I long for Hind.' Babur thought the verse in poor taste, considering he had to remain behind in India. It was, however, clever, as blackened meant disgraced, but probably also alluded to the association Iranians and Central Asians made between black, dark and night and India or Indians.[21] Babur responded tartly to his friend, who nonetheless remained a friend, with a Turki *ruba'i*, the first verse he mentions writing in India.

> Voice a hundred thanks Babur, that the merciful Pardoner,
> Gave thee Sind, Hind and many a kingdom.
> If you cannot tolerate the heat,
> And wish to see the frigid side, there is Ghazni.[22]

Ghazni, located high on a hill southwest of Kabul, was known for its bitterly-cold winter weather. Still, Khwajah Kalan did not regret leaving India for he responded with a literary parting shot, a Turki *ruba'i* of his own. In it, after complementing Babur's verse, he wrote 'everything in India was upside-down'.[23] He might just as well have added that for Turco-Mongols the country and its society was *bisiyaq*.

As this and other poems attest and as Perso-Islamic literary culture affirms, literate individuals openly expressed their feelings most commonly in verse. In these lines, Babur reveals that he experienced Khwajah Kalan's departure emotionally as a personal abandonment of a close friend. In January 1520, he had recalled him from his recent appoint to Bajaur because, as Babur twice recalls within the text, he was a *musahib*, a friend or companion, or as he says later in the text, he was 'a long-time cordial companion'.[24] Assigned to Ghazni, he had joined Babur's army on December 1526 and fought in the right wing when Babur assigned the army to accompany Humayun's attack on February 1526. Khwajah Kalan served as a prominent commander again, perhaps second in command to Humayun at Panipat, and accompanied Humayun after Panipat to seize the Ludi treasury in Agra.

Babur never saw his friend again after he left India for Kabul and Ghazni but they continued to correspond. In a long letter, he wrote to Khwajah Kalan on 10 February 1529 concerning affairs in Kabul. He expresses how much he longed to see his friend and tells him that he hoped to be able to return to Kabul as soon as conditions allowed. 'We have,' Babur writes, evoking the *suhbat* culture he had so enjoyed while in Kabul, 'a boundless and infinite nostalgia for those places'.[25] His longing intensified throughout the Indian years, when he consolidated the empire while feeling ever more intensely an exile.

Politics

In the summer and fall of 1526, however, Babur immediately turned to the task at hand, expanding Timurid control of Hindustan beyond his Delhi–Agra axis. If consolidating power in and around Kabul had seemed daunting to him, securing control of the variegated political topography of North India was no less challenging. Still, as he pointedly reminded his homesick *begs*, ruling wealthy Hindustan promised considerably more reward than governing impoverished Kabul. As is true of other sections of his autobiography, his day-to-day narration of events during the next 4 years offers readers the opportunity to understand something of the gritty realities of empire building in this era. On the other hand, readers themselves must be willing to reflect on and analyse Babur's narration to make sense of his situation, while narrating pauses to explain his policies and tactics while narrating events in excruciatingly minute and often confusing detail.

To begin with, it is important to recall what is often described as a conquest of India in 1526, represented a single military victory by a relatively small force over an already badly-weakened Afghan tribal state. Panipat gave Babur prestige, the occupation of Delhi and Agra and a considerable treasury, but it did not come with control over a quiescent countryside, although Lahore and parts of the Punjab, previously taken, seem to have remained secure in these early years. Some Afghans supported Babur during this period. Most prominent was Dilawar Khan Ludi, Daulat Khan Ludi's son, who had visited him in Kabul and on 10 January met him in camp as Babur moved south towards Panipat. Dilawar Khan later fought with him at the Battle of Kanwah with Rana Sanga'. Three other former Ludi officers, who had been campaigning against anti-Ludi Afghans in the Ganges Valley, also joined him. Around 11 July, Babur assigned them large cash awards to be taken from the revenues of Jaunpur, Awadh and Ghazipur as he tried to stabilise his eastern front.[26] In Agra, as Babur clarifies after Panipat, he was surrounded by a hostile countryside with Afghan remnants of the Ludi State holding many fortresses and *parganah*s – the Indian term – as he notes, for *tuman*s.

After Panipat, Babur learned how much effort was required to pacify his conquest, remarking,

> When we came to this Agra there was exceptional hostility between our people and the people roundabout. Its soldiers and peasants ran from our people. Apart from Delhi and Agra all the places had strengthened the fortresses and refused to submit.[27]

As Babur had emptied the Agra treasury with his lavish gifts and rewards, it was impossible to send his men out into the countryside. His list of nine hostile rulers, mainly but not exclusively Afghans, reveals those he felt were most threatening. It is a list that explains the immediate military and political manoeuvres he took to secure his position after Panipat. The nine included Qasim Sambhali in Sambhal, Nizam Khan in Bianah, Muhammad Zaitun in Dhulpur, Tatar Khan Sarang-Khani in Gwalior, Husain Khan Nuhani in Rapri, Qutb Khan in Etawah, 'Alam Khan Kalpia in Kalpi and Hasan Khan Miwati in Miwat. Hasan Khan, Babur claimed, was the principal nearby source of *sharr u shurr*, 'trouble and mischief'. He was a Hindu convert to Islam, and therefore, in Babur's eyes, a *mulahhad mardak*, a 'heretical little man', whose family had ruled the hill country along the Delhi–Agra road for more than a century.

Then there was a coalition of Afghan tribes, whose men had rebelled against the Ludis years earlier and now held Qanauj and territory to the east. Unlike the commanders of the fortresses near Agra, none of whom claimed to be political successors to Ibrahim Ludi, this latter Afghan force seemed to present the greatest immediate danger to his nascent state, for their khans had elected Bihar Nuhani as their *padshah*. Omitted from this list was Rana Sanga', the powerful Rajput ruler of Mewar, who ultimately proved to represent Babur's principal rival for a North Indian empire and with whom he fought a climactic battle in March 1527.

Between June and August, Babur was preoccupied with this perilous situation, short of money, surrounded by hostile rulers, concerned about the Afghan force near Qanauj, which was a three days' march from Agra. As summer and the monsoons merged into fall, he became increasingly worried about Rana Sanga'. He began to pacify the region by appointing some of his own commanders to seize some of the outlying fortresses. They took Sambhal, due east of Delhi in late July or early August. Around this time, he also planned a campaign to take the important fortress of Bianah, west–southwest of Agra in Rajasthan. He dispatched a messenger to Bianah with a clever Persian poem warning its commander Nizam Khan, *Ba Turk setizah makan ay mir Bianah*, 'Do not contend with the Turk, O Mir of Bianah'.[28] However, his Turks, some 250 to 300 unnamed men, leading some 2,000 unidentified 'Hindustanis', did not march on to the fortress until early December. Then in late July or August, two long-time Timurid commanders were ordered to occupy cities to the southeast and south of Agra. Babur sent Mahdi Khwajah towards Etawah and ordered Sultan Junaid Barlas to take Dhulpur.

After these first few months, when he acted to expand his control around Agra, but without reporting whether Babur had a broader strategy in mind, he called what amounted to a war council. In late July or early August, he summoned his 'Turk *amirs*' and 'Hindustan *amirs*' – no longer *begs*, but they are now called *amirs* in Indian parlance. He presented his men with a chance to discuss strategy. The Afghans to the east, he told them, have crossed the Ganges with 40,000 to 50,000 men and taken Qanauj, while Rana Sanga' has captured Kandar in Rajasthan. Given that the monsoons were coming to an end, he said that they should attack either the 'rebels', meaning the Afghans who had taken Qanauj, or the pagan, Rana Sanga'.[29]

Seeing that dealing with nearby forts was easy – though Babur had only occupied a very few at this point – and could be overawed and cowed if major opponents were defeated, he argued that Rana Sanga' was not only quite distant, but thought that the Rajput chief was less of an immediate threat than the Afghans in Qanauj. After reporting that all present agreed with him, he says that Humayun then spoke up and volunteered to lead the eastern campaign. At

this juncture, Babur, showing how seriously he took the Afghan threat, recalled
the forces that had been sent with Mahdi Khwajah against Etawah and Sultan
Junaid Barlas against Dhulpur, and ordered them to join Humayun at Chandwar
between Agra and Etawah to pursue Afghan forces.[30]

With Humayun on the march as of 21 August and Khwajah Kalan finally
away for Kabul on 28 August, Babur decided to construct a garden, a possible sign
he was reconciled to stay and fight, perhaps to even live in Hindustan whatever
the remembered charms of Afghanistan. Prefacing his account of the garden's
construction and repeating one of his earlier critiques of India's landscape, he
remarks that he was continually reminded of one of Hindustan's greatest defects
– 'there was no running water', *aqar suyı yoktur*. He meant by this that the flat
North Indian plain lacked the sparking mountain streams of the Istalif region.
Crossing the Jumna, he went looking for a suitable site outside of Agra. Yet, while
he found the terrain so *bisafa u kharab*, so unpleasant and desolate that he could
not imagine building a *charbagh*, a four-part garden, there, no other land near Agra
was suitable. He resigned himself to making a virtue of necessity, or in this case,
making a Timurid garden from scrubland.[31]

Construction began with a well, which would provide water for the hot bath,
followed by a large enclosed tank and a *talar*, a pillared porch, in front of an
outer residence, and then a private house, or *khilwat-khanah*, with a garden and
subsidiary buildings. Finally, the hot bath was then added, something incredibly
important, he emphasises, in Hindustan with its heat, violent winds and dust.
With that, Babur enthusiastically concludes. 'In unpleasant and disorderly Hind
planned and well-ordered gardens were laid out…'[32] He had begun literally to
straighten out a small bit of Hindustan in his preferred Afghan and Central Asian
or Iranian image. Abu'l Fazl, the chronicler of Babur's grandson, during Akbar's
reign, lauded this landscape architecture in his late sixteenth-century work, the
'A'in-i Akbari, the *'Institutes of Akbar'*. He wrote probably paraphrasing Babur,

> Formerly people used to plant their gardens without any order, but since
> the time of arrival in India of the emperor Bâbar, a more methodical
> arrangement of gardens has obtained; and travellers nowadays admire the
> beauty of the palaces and their murmuring fountains.[33]

Babur also applauded how many of his men, who acquired land on his side of
the river followed suit setting the precedent for the riverside gardens of Agra that
proliferated during the reign of Shah Jahan.[34] He particularly mentions two of his
important *begs* who built gardens at this time. These were Saiyid Nizam al-Din 'Ali
Khalifa, one of the two sons of Junaid Barlas – a man who had been with Babur

in his Ferghanah days and served in the battles at Bajaur in 1519 and Panipat in 1526, and Shaikh Zain Khwafi, who, by his *nisba*, was a native of or descended from a family in Khwaf – a city near Nishapur in Iranian Khurasan known for its scholars. Both men, writes Babur, laid out 'regular and elegant gardens with tanks'. He notes with clear pleasure that Hindustanis, having never seen anything like these gardens, now referred to this area as Kabul.[35]

He remained in Agra throughout the rest of the year, preparing for a siege of Bianah by ordering the construction of a large mortar – finally successfully tested the following February – conducting business, including receiving his Iranian envoy, who had returned from the Safavid court in Iran, and threatening or negotiating with a variety of nearby rulers and fort-holders as he tried to extend his influence in the regions surrounding Agra. As most of his *beg*s and best *yiğit*s were serving with Humayun or had been assigned to plunder areas around Bianah, Babur could not launch major expeditions at this time.

He was able to dispatch small forces against certain Afghan groups, as he did successfully on 21 November, and in November or December, he was able to establish control over some strategically important centres by exploiting the insecurity of local fort-holders who feared Rana Sanga' more than they did him. He was able to take over the formidable Gwalior fortress south of Agra, when its commander Tatar Khan, fearing Rana Sanga' and harassed by local rajas, offered the fortress to Babur. Even though he later changed his mind, the few men Babur dispatched from Agra were able to occupy the fortress. At this time, Muhammad Zaitun in Dhulpur, also apparently fearing the Rajput chief, offered his fortress to Babur and came to Agra, where he received a few *parganah*s as compensation.[36] Even more significant at this time in the late fall, Nizam Khan, the commander of the strategically important Bianah fortress in Rajasthan, panicked because of Rana Sanga's approach and offered it to Babur's men.

By late November and December, therefore, Babur already knew from the news of Rana Sanga's movements, as well as the panic of commanders in Gwalior, Dhulpur and Bianah, that he could no longer enjoy the self-indulgent interlude that followed Panipat and that he must act. On 30 November, he had learned that Husain Khan Nuhhani had fled as Humayun approached his Afghan forces near Ghazipur, just down river from Varanasi. Given this news, he immediately ordered his son to return to Agra to prepare to confront Rana Sanga'. Humayun, who had appointed Timurid officers to Jaunpur and Awadh, did not return to Agra until 6 January, when he met his father in the Garden of the Eight Paradises.

In the interim, Babur had survived what he reports as an attempt by Ibrahim Ludi's mother to poison him. Perhaps she did plot his death, as he and some of his men fell ill. They all survived and recovered after three days. Babur responded by having his delinquent taster cut in pieces and ordered the cook, who he says poisoned the food, to be skinned alive. Of two women implicated, one was thrown under an elephant and another shot. He stripped Ibrahim's mother of her goods and slaves and sent her under guard to Kabul, while he ordered her infant grandson to be taken to Kamran in Qandahar.[37]

The Battle of Kanwah

Rana Sanga' had corresponded with Babur when he was still in Kabul and the Rajput had proposed, Babur writes, that Babur should take Delhi while he, Rana Sanga', would seize Agra. Reporting on these negotiations, Babur then simply notes that he had taken both Delhi and Agra, while Rana Sanga' had not given any sign of moving. He does not say whether he meant his seizure of Agra to be a *fait accompli*. Nor does he consider in these passages of the *Vaqayi'* that Rana Sanga's apparent inaction after Panipat did not necessarily imply that he had abandoned his earlier plans to take the former Ludi capital. By the time Humayun returned to Agra on 6 January, or just shortly thereafter, Babur knew for certain that the Rajput was in fact advancing toward Agra. Babur probably did not act earlier because Humayun and the core of the army remained downriver, after frightening off the Afghan coalition near Qanauj, but even after his son returned, he did not immediately take action, perhaps because of heavy rains. While it rained, the Timurids enjoyed many *suhbatlar* sessions in Agra.[38]

Not until 11 February did Babur finally move to the plains outside of Agra, where he spent three days assembling his army. He began by excluding from the campaign any Indian *amir*s he had recently enrolled in his service – men who had joined him after losing their fortresses – as he did not trust them. Instead, he sent them off on other missions away from Agra. Thus, Babur still led a predominantly Central Asian army when he confronted Rana Sanga' and a grand coalition of Rajput rulers at Kanwah.

It seems from his narrative that Babur did not fully appreciate the danger Rana Sanga' posed to him until the 11th or shortly thereafter, for it was then when he received reports that a detachment of Rana Sanga's forces had savaged Timurid raiders sent out from recently occupied Bianah. Later, some of Babur's men praised the man now known to be a fierce and warlike *kafir* – the first time Babur uses the Arabic term for non-Muslims in the *Vaqayi'*. Babur finally left Agra on the 14th and initially intended to camp near a reservoir or tank at Sikri, the site of the great sandstone city his grandson Akbar later constructed. He sent out scouting parties to find Rana Sanga's army, and Rajput detachments badly defeated one of them as they rode from Sikri in the direction of Kanwah, killing many Timurids. Babur continued moving cautiously forward in search of Rana Sanga's principal forces and finally made a preliminary camp near a lake and had his Ottoman military advisor, Mustafa Rumi, who had served as a gunner at Panipat, begin constructing defensive lines in the Ottoman mode.[39] More than three weeks elapsed before these defences were ready.

At this juncture, 500 reinforcements for Babur's force arrived from Kabul, including a maternal grandson of Husain Baiqara, along with an astrologer and a water-carrier, who had previously been dispatched to Kabul and who now returned with three camel-loads of 'reasonable Ghazni wines'.[40] Reporting on the poor morale in his army after the initial loss of men in his skirmishing detachments, Babur writes that his troops became even more dispirited because the newly arrived astrologer predicted that the Timurids would be defeated if they fought at the present astrological moment. Resolute, writes Babur, in his intention to fight, he nonetheless decided on 25 February as he rode out around the camp that he would renounce the sin of alcohol. He did so as a dramatic gesture to hearten the troops and ordered that the recently arrived Ghazni wine should be salted to make vinegar.

Shaikh Zain, who first appears in Babur's narrative of the poetry contest aboard rafts drifting down the Kabul River in December 1525, produced an elaborate *farman* in Persian the following day – 26 February.[41] Without any explanation on Babur's part, Shaikh Zain had become his resident intellectual, both cultured, *adib*, and pious, *'alim*. Persian was presumably his native language and in this instance, he did himself proud by producing a florid, Quran-laced document lauding this renunciation on the eve of a battle between the Holy Warriors of the army of Islam and the infidel.

The Shaikh argued that the coming *jihad* ought to be prefaced by the still greater struggle, the *jihad-i akbar*, against sensuality. Drinking vessels were then dashed to pieces, presaging, Shaikh Zain hoped, the destruction of the gods of the *kafir*s. He announced that in these *mamalik-i mahrusah*, these sovereign dominions, alcohol was forbidden. Finally, the *farman* said that as a thank-offering the *tamgha* tax on Muslims will be abolished. A Mongol levy and not canonical tax for Muslims, the *tamgha*, often became a popular target of pious Muslims. [42]

Nonetheless, Babur recalls that his men were morose and downhearted by past events, an obvious illusion to the military defeats they had just suffered. Still, he reports, almost as an aside, that Nizam al-Din 'Ali Khalifa, the Barlas Turk, who had served him so well at Bajaur and Panipat, had taken effective charge of the preparations for the battle. To stem his men's dark mood, Babur summoned all his *beg*s and *yiğit*s and, apparently, began by quoting Persian and Turki verses. The first

Persian lines reminded his listeners of the transitory reality of life: 'All who come
into the world will die, That which is enduring and lasting is God'. Then, after
citing a Turki quatrain with similar sentiments he quotes a passage from Firdausi's
epic eleventh-century work, the *Shah Namah*, to the effect that 'it is well for me
to die with a good name; I must have the name, as the body is certainly death'.
Babur then made his men take an oath on the Quran not to waver in the face of
the coming battle.[43]

While Babur was trying to bolster his men's resolve, his nascent empire was
coming to pieces around him as Afghans and other Hindustanis, who had learned
of his multiple military losses to Rajputs, seized the opportunity to reclaim their
holdings. He wrote: 'Terrible news came every day from every side'.[44] His control
of towns or fortresses he had so recently garrisoned evaporated. Afghans took
Rapri and Chandawar, southeast and east of Agra, and Koil, just east of Aligarh.
In Sambhal, his commander deserted. Hindus besieged Gwalior, and the man sent
to reinforce it instead fled to his own *parganah*. Many Indians who had previously
joined Babur's promising enterprise now deserted him.[45] Babur must have realised
that even if he survived a losing battle with Rana Sanga', Timurid Hindustan
would cease to exist, and he would have to flee back to Kabul. He writes that
he ignored these events – he was powerless to do otherwise – and continued
preparing for the coming battle.

Babur's force marched from camp on 13 March, but did not reach
the eventual battlefield until several days later. The battle itself began on
17 March. Unfortunately, he left it to Shaikh Zain to describe the conflict in a
Fath Namah, a Proclamation of Victory. Readers accustomed to Babur's unadorned
Turki prose instead have to thread their way through the Shaikh's high literary
Persian *adabi* style, which frames the battle as a titanic struggle between Muslims
and infidels, Islam and heresy, good and evil. Nonetheless, the proclamation is
something of a rhetorical triumph for this courtly genre. Not only did Shaikh
Zain write elegant prose, interspersed with telling Quranic passages, but as a
fighter himself he produced an immediate, detailed and compelling picture of the
ferocity of the Timurid–Rajput clash.

Completed only 12 days after the battle on 29 March, the Shaikh gives readers
what seems to be a meaningful sense of the ebb and flow of a truly epic struggle.
While he does not finally explain the Timurids' victory, he does supply enough
information for readers to at least infer why Babur's men triumphed against Rana
Sanga's formidable Rajputs, whose tenacious fighting qualities had unnerved so
many of them. Unfortunately, he does not estimate the numbers of the Timurids'
forces, but considering Babur commanded only 7,000 or 8,000 troops at Panipat,
it is unlikely that he had more than 10,000 men at Kanwah. Shaikh Zain

calculates that Rana Sanga' and the ten Rajput chiefs who had joined him may have mobilised more than 200,000 men. However, he based his estimate solely on the revenue that each of their territories was estimated to produce. Rana Sanga's lands, he writes, yielded 10 *crores* of unspecified revenue, which ought to have enabled him to mobilise 100,000 cavalrymen. Despite the unreliability of such figures, it is likely that Babur's force was once again seriously outnumbered, as had been true at Panipat.

Shaikh Zain notes that the Kanwah Battle began between nine and ten in the morning as the forces of 'light and darkness' confronted each other. Babur's army seems to have arrayed very much as had been at Panipat. At least, Shaikh Zain lauds the Timurid line of carts as an imitation of 'the *ghazis of Rum*', the Ottomans, although he does not include details of the formations as Babur had done for Panipat. Despite this, what the Shaikh depicts of the field and the actual clash ought to be taken seriously, as he served in the formation to the left of centre. Babur commanded from the centre of the classic Turco-Mongol *yasal* formation, initially at least behind the line of carts. Chin Temür Sultan, his Chagatai or maternal Mongol cousin, served on the right, while 'Alam Khan, the son of Bahlul Ludi, served on the left. Humayun commanded the right wing, while Mahdi Khwajah, Babur's brother-in-law, served in the left with Muhammad Sultan Mirza, a Baiqara Timurid.

The battle began on both wings of the armies, with the Rajput left wing attacking the Timurid's right, which counter-attacked, driving the Rajputs back nearly behind the centre of their line. Mustafa Rumi then brought the chained carts forward and, writes the Shaikh, 'broke' the Rajput cavalry ranks with *tufang and zarb-zanan*, matchlocks and light cannons. He reports that wave after wave of Rajput troops then attacked, with a series of ferocious Rajput assaults on the Timurids' left wing. At this point, the flanking units on this wing, reinforced by Nizam al-Din 'Ali Khalifa among others, performed their traditional *tulghamah* flanking manoeuvre to the rear of the Rajput line. As the battle continued, Babur issued an order to send out the *tabinan-i khasa-i padshahi*, the royal guard, from behind the carts out to both the right and the left of the centre, leaving the matchlock men behind the carts. Meanwhile, Babur's artillery chief, Ustad 'Ali Quli, who, in February, had successfully tested his new mortar, fired large stones at the Rajputs and these, along with the *tufangs and zarb-zanan*, killed many of the enemy. Babur then ordered the matchlock men and foot soldiers out from behind the carts into the midst of the battle. At this juncture, he ordered the carts protecting the centre to move forward and he himself evidently rode directly into the battle, energizing his troops.[46]

Despite these manoeuvres, Shaikh Zain writes that 'between the first and second prayers' the ferocious combat continued, even as the Timurids accomplished what they had done at Panipat to Ibrahim Ludi, forcing the enemy on the left and right wings in upon the centre. Flanking units had apparently accomplished this with their *tulghamah* manoeuvre as they had at Panipat, although the Shaikh does not say this. Nonetheless, apart from Shaikh Zain's report that the left flanking detachment had been ordered into action, there is a compelling evidence that after the battle, Babur generously rewarded the commander of the right flanking detachment – a Mongol named Tardika – with a grant of a 15 *lac*s stipend and the town of Alur/Alwar, which Babur did not then control 'because he had done better than the others'.[47] He is one of the few individuals Babur explicitly singles out for such praise.[48]

Otherwise Shaikh Zain suggests, without exactly saying so, that when the Rajput wings had been collapsed onto the centre, victory was in sight. He writes that at that moment, Rana Sanga's troops made final desperate attacks upon both the right and left wings of the Timurid line, penetrating deep into the left, but says that they were repulsed with showers of arrows. He implies Rajputs now realised their situation was hopeless. Whether Shaikh Zain understood his enemy this well, the Rajputs did abandon the field, leaving mounds of dead, which Timurids used to construct their traditional, grisly monuments to victory, *minaret*s of skulls. Among the dead, who had fallen either to *tir u tufaq*, bow and gun, he lists seven rajas or chiefs, who had commanded, he asserts, a total of 33,000 cavalrymen.[49] Rana Sanga', however, survived and fled the field.

Babur now added the title of *ghazi*, frontier warrior, to his titles inscribed on the *Fath Namah* and then, characteristically, just below his signature or seal he wrote a Turki quatrain with a refreshingly frank message.

> I am become a desert wanderer for Islam
> Having joined battle with infidels and Hindus,
> I readied myself to become a *shahid*.
> God be thanked I am become a *ghazi*.

In the first line, Babur presumably alludes to the Rajasthan desert as he has written he invaded India to satisfy dynastic ambitions. His victory did encourage him to present himself for the first time, echoing the Ottomans, as a heroic Muslim fighter on an Islamic frontier and not just a displaced Timurid in search of a satisfactory kingdom. Afterwards, he began using the title of *ghazi*, having it inscribed on his seal and currency. A coin minted in Lahore in 1529/30 reads *Zahir al-Din Muhammad Babur Padshah Ghazi*. Shaikh Zain further encouraged the view of Babur's victory as an Islamic one, when, using the *abjad* numerical values of Arabic letters, he produced chronogram: *Fath-i Padshahi Islam*, Victory of the Emperor of the Faith.[50]

The victory itself may be seen as a moment in Indo-Muslim military history when gunpowder weapons began to exert a significant effect on the outcome of a battle. In Babur's previous major battles – at Sar-i Pul against Shaibani Khan's Uzbeks in 1501, at Qandahar against the Arghuns in 1507, at Hisar against the Uzbeks in 1511 and at Panipat against the Ludis in 1526 – guns do not seem to have played a pivotal role, despite the common but undocumented assumption that these new weapons insured his victory at Panipat. At Kanwah, however, guns seem to have been an important if not the only cause of the Timurid victory.

If readers tenaciously thread their way through verbal thickets of Shaikh Zain's prose, they will notice the repeated firing of a large mortar and the unusual tactic of bringing Timurid matchlock men out from behind their defensive position behind the carts directly into the field of battle. Perhaps, their fire directly into the Rajput line explains why Rana Sanga' directed his last attack on the two wings rather than the centre. Even then, Shaikh Zain uses the phrase *tir u tufaq*, 'arrow and gun', in accounting for the Rajput dead, which seem ＿ ＿ ＿e equal weight to archery and firearms. Yet, while noticing the increased ＿ ＿tance of guns and artillery, it is still important to remember that the Tu＿ ＿gol *tulghamah* or flanking manoeuvre seems to have turned the tide at ＿ ＿ as well as earlier at Panipat. Based on Babur's testimony, *uṣbu tulghan＿ ＿ctly* this flanking manoeuver', of Shaibani Khan at Sar-i Pul, outside S＿ ＿qand a quarter of a century earlier in April 1501, had won the battle for the Uzbeks, forcing Babur to abandon the city a short time later. It was a well-established Mongol manoeuvre.

Following the Battle of Kanwah, Babur and his men pursued the fleeing Rajputs, unhorsing one after another as they approached Rana Sanga's *ordu* or camp about 4 miles from Babur's own camp. Stopping beyond the camp, he sent some men to pursue Rana Sanga'. They failed to capture the Rajput, prompting Babur to reflect he should have gone himself, but he returned to his camp for evening prayer.[51] The denouement of the day's tumultuous struggle involved Babur excoriating the astrologer – 'a very contemptuous and disagreeable person' – who had predicted a Timurid loss. He exiled the unhappy man from his dominions.

Leaving camp the following day on 20 March, Babur and his men rode to Bianah, along a road strewn with the dead, and two days later held a council of both 'Turk and Hind *amirs*' to decide whether they should pursue Rana Sanga' into his territory. They decided against it given the lack of water and the heat. Rather than riding into the desert, Babur turned to subjugate nearby Miwat, whose converted

Hindu chief, Hasan Khan, had caused him such trouble in the days after he first took Agra the previous year and who had joined and died with Rana Sanga'. He had been killed, Babur notes, with a matchlock at Kanwah. Alluding to the fact that the early Muslim rulers in India had never really brought this territory under their control, he met with a representative of Hasan Khan's son near the latter's fort at Alur. He accepted the son's submission and granted him some unidentified territories, presumably elsewhere, for it was just afterwards that he granted Alur to the Mongol Tardika for his work on the right flank at Kanwah.

The Miwat settlement presaged Babur's programme of re-establishing control in and around the Delhi-Agra region by retaking the fortresses and towns he had intimidated or occupied the previous year. Before doing so however, he moved to fulfil a promise he had made to his men, he says, before the 'pagan frontier war'. He had announced, he notes, that after the battle anyone who wished to leave India could do so. Three prominent individuals opted to leave for Afghanistan. These included his brother-in-law Mahdi Khwajah, the third husband of Babur's sister Khan Zada Begim – who had served at Panipat, in Agra, as commandant first at Etawah and then at Bianah, Tardi Beg Khaksar – his host at a midnight *suhbat* near Kabul in ▮▮▮9, his fellow versifier, along with Shaikh Zain, on the Kabul river raft in ▮▮▮▮ber 1525, who evidently served at Panipat and Kanwah and Humayun wit▮ ▮▮▮Badakhshan foot soldiers he had brought when he joined Babur in the Bag▮▮▮▮▮arden on 3 December 1525.

Mahdi Khwaj▮▮ ▮▮not like India and Tardi Beg Khaksar wanted to return to what Ba▮▮▮▮ys was his previous *darvishlik* or Sufi-like life. Babur says he allowed Humayun to leave partly because his Badakhshan troops were not professional soldiers and wanted to return home. He also considered that Kabul was, as he puts it, 'empty' and therefore, but without saying so, considered Humayun would be his vice-regent in a city and region he had designated as *khalisah* or crown dominions. Humayun may well have been eager to leave a situation, where he acted as his father's commander and return to Afghanistan to serve as Timurid sons had commonly done in the past – as a semiautonomous governor. While Babur initially seems to have given Humayun leave to go to Kabul simply to solve two immediate problems, when he wrote a long letter to his son a year and a half later, 26 November 1528, he addresses him as a de facto governor.

To mark his dismay at having more friends abandon him for Afghanistan in the spring of 1527, Babur inserted into this section of the *Vaqayi'* what he describes as a Turki *qit'ah*, or poetic fragment, he had written after others had left him for Kabul after Panipat. It echoes the verse he had sent to Khwajah Kalan the previous year in reply to his friend's denunciation of Hindustan.

O you who, from this country of Hind,
Have gone, having known its pain and torment,
Yearning for Kabul and its delightful climate.
You have gone from Hind in the heat of the moment
At least having gone you have found there
Delight and pleasure, desire and fortune.
God be thanked, we too did not die
Although there was much grief and endless anxiety
Having passed by you by, it passed by us also.[52]

In mid-April, Babur and his men rode slowly back to Agra as he gradually began anew to embed his Timurid Empire in the soil of Hindustan. Taking advantage of the relative security produced by his momentous victory, he toured the country west of Agra after leaving the Bianah area, stopping briefly on 14 April to visit Alur, awarded to the Mongol Tardika. Riding further north to Firuzpur, he met Humayun and his Badakhshan troops before they left for Kabul. In his leisure, he took time to visit a famous spring near the town, where he and his men had *ma'jun* and Babur resumed his earlier efforts to improve Hindustan's landscape.

This spring, he writes, *khali az safa imas*, 'Is not without charm', but, he added, its praise was exaggerated.[53] Nonetheless, he ordered a 10-foot square stone platform erected at its mouth. A few days later, after he resumed the leisurely march back towards Agra, he stopped at another spring, which Tardi Beg Khaksar had praised when the army had passed by the area on its way to Panipat. Alluding once again to Hindustan's lack of 'running waters', he ordered an octagonal stone platform built above the spring. Tardi Beg, who had not yet left for Afghanistan, was there to praise the scene once again as Babur and his men sat and indulged in *ma'jun*. Returning then to the Bianah area, he visited Sikri, spent two days supervising the construction of a garden there, before finally returning to Agra on 15 April.

Even amid these indulgent moments, Babur had begun reclaiming towns and fortresses lost as Rana Sanga' had approached Agra, when, as he puts it, 'Most Hindustanis and Afghans turned away from us and seized all [their] districts and territories'.[54] He sent a number of his reliable men to reoccupy Chandawar, Rapri and Etawah. Others were dispatched to Qanauj and Badaun. Koil/Aligarh had been retaken as early as 18 March.[55] Now Babur also awarded a variety of unnamed districts to his men, a process that had been suspended, he writes, during the *ghaza* against Rana Sanga'. With the monsoons approaching, he then ordered 'everyone' to go to their districts, prepare themselves and return when the rains ceased, ready, he implies, for the new campaigning season.[56]

In the interim, he dispatched an emissary to Shah Tahmasp Safavi in Iran on 17 May and then celebrated Ramadan in the Garden of the Eight Paradises at Agra. The month began on 1 June with religious ablutions and concluded with a return to Sikri for the Ramadan feast of 'Id-ul fitr in the Garden of Victory, which was still under construction. Later in the summer, early August, he fell seriously ill for more than two weeks, the first of many serious illnesses he suffered in India. He now began to experience these episodes more frequently. After recovering, he ritually gave thanks by reciting a passage from the Quran. During the same period in late August, he amused himself by producing 504 variants of a Turki couplet, before falling ill again for nine days in September.

The New Year 934/27 September 1527 began very much as the old year ended – with Babur on tour, first visiting Koil/Aligarh and then riding north to Sambhal, a town abandoned by Babur's commandant earlier in 1527, but now apparently reoccupied. Returning to Agra on 12 October, Babur fell ill again with a fever, which re-occurred for nearly the entire month, prompting him to write a *ruba'i*, two lines of which he includes in the text, while the remainder are found in his *diwan*. These lines echo the prose account of his illness, saying:

> Daily, the fever in my body intensifies,
> Sleep flies from my eyes as night arrives.[57]

It seems likely Babur had contracted dysentery, a common, debilitating illness in India, whose recognisable effects he seems to describe in another *rubai'i*.

> Fever in my heart and water in my eyes
> Pity my sickness, this is my condition.
> Burning during oppressive days and troubled nights
> For me neither rest nor sleep, day or night.[58]

Babur's repeated illnesses in India took an increasingly serious physical and psychological toll on him during the next 2 years, so much so that his long-desired conquest began to seem as much a burden as a triumphant reward.

Otherwise, and perhaps because of his illness, he records little else for more than another month, except for noting the arrival of two of his paternal or Timurid aunts on 23 November – Fakhr-i Jahan Begim and Khadija Sultan Begim. While he simply notes the fact, the arrival of the two women began the trickle of what later becomes almost a flood of Chaghatai Mongol and Timurid kin taking refuge in this new Timurid homeland. On 16 March 1528, a Chaghatai Mongol cousin Tukhta Bugha Sultan, the son of the younger Chaghatai Khan, Ahmad Khan, arrived. Then, six Timurid and Chaghatai women came from Kabul to Agra in mid-October 1528. In her memoir, Babur's daughter Gulbadan Begim revealed how Babur encouraged both his paternal and maternal relatives, Timurids and Chaghatai Mongols, to come to India and 'enjoy prosperity together'.[59] She mentions that a total of ninety-six Timurid and Chaghatai women came and received houses and lands and gifts.

Apart from relatives, the new Timurid state also attracted representatives of Herat high-culture and Naqshbandi Sufis from Mawarannahr. The three Heratis, who arrived in late September 1528 to join Babur's service, were the prominent historian Khwandamir, a poet Maulana Shihab al-Din and Mir Ibrahim, a dulcimer player. Later in December 1528, descendants of Babur's hereditary Naqshbandi Shaikh Khwajah Ahrar also began arriving in Agra, where they were treated like spiritual aristocrats, some of whom married Babur's descendants.[60] His generosity, encouragement and the allure of India's wealth meant that the Timurid society of Mawarannahr and Herat had begun to be reconstituted in Hindustan.

Following yet another visit on 1 December 1527 to the Sikri Victory Garden and a *ma'jun* session on the now finished octagonal platform in the middle of its lake, Babur returned to Agra on 9 December and began planning the next series of cold-season campaigns to pacify the country. As was the case in 1526, his targets were Afghans and Rajputs. Although in December, neither one nor the other immediately threatened his nascent Timurid state. As was the case a year earlier, Afghans initially seemed the lesser threat, so he planned a major assault on Chanderi, about 175 miles south of Agra. Babur does not explain the reason for this new Rajput campaign; he very likely decided to attack Chanderi because its raja, Medini Rao, a feudatory of Rana Sanga', had brought an estimated 12,000 men to the Kanwah battle. His actions and later comments also strongly suggest he had decided to try to destroy Rajput power, beginning with Chanderi and afterwards assaulting Chitor – Rana Sanga's formidable desert fortress.

Still, as he moved south towards Chanderi on 9 December, he also deputed Muhammad 'Ali Jang-jang to confront an Afghan, Shaikh Bayazid Farmuli, a former officer of Ibrahim Ludi, whom Babur had rewarded with revenue from Awadh in June or July 1526. By the fall of 1527, for unexplained reasons, Babur no longer trusted Shaikh Bayazid and sent Muhammad 'Ali Jang-jang to see if he still meant to cooperate with him. His suspicion was confirmed when Shaikh Bayazid and allied Afghans badly mauled Muhammad 'Ali Jang-jang's force sometime in late January 1528. The news reached Babur on 28 January just as he began the siege of Chanderi. He was not able to deal with this resurgent Afghan problem until he finished the Rajput campaign.

After moving by horse or boat to Kali, about 100 miles to the south, Babur and his estimated 7,000 men turned southwest towards Chanderi. By this time, his army had begun to take on some of the traits of an Indian army, most noticeably by employing more Hindustani commanders and by using elephants for transport and in battle. In fact, one Shaikh Guran of Koil or Aligarh was sent ahead to conduct negotiations with Medini Rao, aided by an Afghan, Arayish Khan, who had joined Babur in January 1526 before the Battle of Panipat. When these negotiations failed, Babur and his men began the attack on the fortress on 28 January with three or four ineffective rounds from Ustad 'Ali Khan's mortar.

Much to Babur's own surprise, his men successfully stormed the fortress with relative ease in about 2 hours, prompting many Rajputs within to follow the custom of sacrificial suicide, *jauhar*, stripping naked and fighting to the death, after killing their wives and children. A late sixteenth-century Mughal artist later included scenes of this gruesome spectacle in one of the miniature paintings included in the Persian translation of Babur's *Vaqayi'*. Many Chanderi Rajputs, however, surrendered only to be massacred by Babur's troops, and another 'minaret' of 'infidel' skulls were erected nearby, as Babur composed a chronogram to date his victory.

> For a time this place of Chanderi Was *dar al-harb* and pagan-full.
> I conquered its fortress in battle. Its chronogram
> is Fath dar al-harb [934a.h.].[61]

Following this surprising victory, Babur planned to continue his Rajput campaign with an assault on the territory of another of Rana Sanga's feudatory – a Tomar Rajput convert to Islam known to him as Silhadi or Silah al-Din, who had defected to Babur at Kanwah. He does not explain the reason for this plan, only noting that later he intended to attack Chitor. He abandoned these plans however, when he learned that his troops, which were sent to deal with Shaikh Bayazid Farmuli, had not only suffered defeat and abandoned Lucknow – news he had received just as he began the assault on Chanderi – but afterwards they also retreated from Qanauj. Now marching quickly to the northeast, he dispatched scouts, *qazaq yiğitler*, ahead to find the Afghans who retreated across the Ganges. Later, after Babur's men attacked the Afghans after crossing the river on 13 and 14 March, they fled further down the river without suffering many casualties. Babur pursued them as far as Awadh, but apparently no further, for he went hunting on 1 April, and probably returned to Agra afterwards to wait out the monsoons.[62]

Babur's failure decisively to defeat Shaikh Bayazid Farmuli left the Afghans a major threat lurking down the river, but in fairness, the Afghan question following the Battle of Panipat was bewilderingly complex. The Ludi Sultanate had been a decentralised tribal state composed of distinct and independent Afghan tribes and clans. A few joined Babur after Panipat and served with him at Kanwah, while others deserted him as Rana Sanga' advanced towards Agra.[63] Others, most notably Shir Khan Suri, Humayun's later nemesis, joined him after Kanwah but deserted him shortly afterwards. What is evident from these seemingly inchoate, apparently *ad hoc* and shifting Timurid alliances with Afghans and among Afghans is that, after Panipat and even Kanwah, substantial numbers of Afghans never conceded Timurid sovereignty and in 1527 and 1528, large numbers in the Bihar region allied with Muhammad Ludi in a concerted attempt to resurrect Afghan supremacy in Hindustan.[64] Babur, and after him Humayun and Akbar, returned to the Afghan problem repeatedly, disastrously so for Humayun in 1539 and 1540.

In late September 1528, however, his Rajput campaigns bore fruit. Thus, when in September, he left Agra to visit Gwalior, still held for him by a nephew of Mahdi Khwajah, he received an emissary from Rana Sanga's second son, Bikramajit, who held the important fortress of Ranthambor. He offered his master's 'good will and service', *daulatkhaliq ve kidmatgarliq*, and control of Ranthambor in exchange for 70 *lac*s of revenue. Bikramajit's emissary later asked, instead, for the Bianah fortress in exchange for Ranthambor, but in October when the transfer of Ranthambor was finally being arranged, he was put off with a dubious offer of Chitor itself, in the event Babur might seize it.[65]

Before and after the conclusions of these negotiations, Babur spent time sightseeing or further rearranging the Indian landscape more to his Central Asian and Afghan taste. By repeatedly returning in the narrative to his preoccupation with garden construction and embellishment, he reveals how profoundly important these structures were to him. There is almost a kind of rhythm to his narrative both in the Kabul and in the Hindustan sections, in which he describes garden construction or sightseeing before and after battles or political negotiations. At this moment on 21 and 23 September, while on his way to Gwalior, he stopped at Dhulpur, where he had earlier supervised the removal of part of a hill in order to construct a tank or reservoir, and by a lake he ordered a pillared platform cut out of solid rock and a mosque added nearby. Returning to Dhulpur again on 5 October, he found the work was not so far advanced and so ordered additional stonecutters to be put to work, giving substance to his earlier observation that the availability of vast numbers of workers was one of Hindustan's few charms.[66]

In between his visits to Dhulpur, he visited the palaces of the Gwalior rajas on 27 September. His description of the buildings is a remarkable and instructive passage because of what it says again, of Babur's response to Hindu culture and what it reveals about Babur himself. After taking opium for an earache in the evening of the 27th, and suffering from opium sickness and vomiting the following morning, he toured the palaces of Man Singh and Bikramajit. His account is particularly engaging because, while he found these buildings, *gharib*, strange, both *löpalök* and *bisiyaq*, ponderous and irregular, and described some of the palace rooms as dark and airless, he takes great pains to depict them as an architectural historian might do. That is he writes about them in precise, analytical, attentive and sometimes appreciative detail. He observes, for example, that the elephant sculpture at the eastern or Hati-pul or Elephant Gate, *bir filning suratini mujasam qilib*, 'exactly resembles the image of an elephant'.[67] Thus, while Babur critiques the Gwalior palaces as a Timurid, who prefers the geometrically precise and airy *kushk*s of Samarqand, he examines them with the same inquisitive intelligence and analytical precision that he uses to describe nearly all aspects of his varied human and natural environments.

Babur also mentions that he 'enjoyed seeing' the temples within the palace compounds. He was only offended when, travelling for more sightseeing in the nearby Urwah Valley, he encountered Jain statues carved into the rock. Some of these images, more than 50 feet tall, whose naked genitalia he found offensive and ordered to be destroyed – an act commemorated by a miniature in the Akbar era illustrated text of Babur's *Vaqayi*'. Typically taken with a natural perspective, he writes that the valley itself, which enclosed two lakes, was not such a bad place. The presence of these statues, he remarks, was its only defect. Fortunately, the night before and after the visit, he was able to visit the pleasant flower garden of his resident governor of Gwalior, Rahimdad, the nephew of his brother-in-law Mahdi Khwajah.[68]

Leaving Gwalior on 30 September, they visited a nearby waterfall, where they paused to eat *ma'jun* and listen to musicians and unnamed 'reciters', before riding on that evening to an unnamed *charbagh* located at the birthplace of Silhadi or Salah al-Din, whom he had earlier planned to attack as part of his strategy of conquering Rajasthan.[69] Later, they visited Dhulpur Fort and yet another *charbagh*, which was under construction. Babur critiqued the work of stonecutters, who had failed to make a perfect vertical cut in the rock, and ordered the construction of additional buildings. Then moving on to Sikri and the Garden of Victory, he found that the work on this *charbagh* was not progressing well. He criticised and punished those in charge. Finally on 15 October, he returned to Agra, crossed the Jumna and retired to the Garden of the Eight Paradises.[70]

Timurid Hindustan in 1528

In October 1528, Babur had slightly more than 2 years to live. His narration of events and governance cover the three-month period he remained in Agra and constitutes a 'moment' when he felt that the Timurid empire in Hindustan was beginning to be realised. Within these pages however, readers also find Babur suffering from serious illnesses that afflicted him with ever-increasing frequency. It includes a moving testimony of his ever-darkening moods, mixed with an intense longing to revisit the carefree companionship in the *suhbatlar* of his Kabul days. In these pages, Babur's humanity is manifested anew, but now as a mature and increasingly vulnerable individual.

First, though, he had to deal with financial crises, because the military campaigns and construction projects had left the treasury nearly empty. Despite giving the impression that his rewards and largess after Panipat had exhausted the Ludi coin, some funds must have remained for he writes on 22 October 1528 that the wealth of Iskandar and Ibrahim in Delhi and Agra was only now exhausted. He issued a *farman* that every *wajdar*, every stipendiary, must return 30 per cent of his income to the treasury to pay for new supplies as well as for salaried soldiers – gunners and matchlock men. In these, early days, only one and half years after Panipat, Babur's nascent Timurid-Mughal empire still functioned as a highly personal, pre-bureaucratic conquest enterprise.

Despite financial difficulties, Babur was increasingly optimistic about his embryonic state, and for a time at least pleased with news from Kabul and Herat. In letters apparently sent to Timurid relatives living in Herat on 22 October, he reported that 'hearts were at ease' concerning 'rebels and pagans' of both east and west, Afghans and Rajputs, and in guarded and indirect language, he seems to imply that because the military situation was stabilised, he would be able to return to Kabul the following spring.[71]

Eleven days later on 4 November, he heard that Shah Tahmasp Safavi had won a small engagement against Uzbeks in late August. This was followed by later news in November that the Iranian Shah had destroyed an Uzbek army at Jam in northwestern Afghanistan on 26 September. The same messenger who brought the news of the first Uzbek defeat on 4 November also told Babur that Humayun's wife had given birth to a son, and Kamran was about to marry his cousin – the daughter of Sultan 'Ali Mirza Taghai Begchik, the brother of Babur's wife Gulrukh Begim, probably a Mongol.

Yet, while voicing such optimism and receiving a stream of favourable political and personal news in early November, Babur also suffered another illness, a severe fever. He reports that it left him so weak that he had great difficulty in performing the congregational prayer in the mosque or even the mid-day prayer in his library. He decided that piety might cure him and so decided to versify a Turki translation of the Khwajah 'Ubaidullah Ahrar's text, the *Risala-i Validiya*, using the metre of a work of the famous Naqshbandi devotee and Herat Persian poet Maulana 'Abdur Rahim Jami.[72] Babur began composing couplets of this work of Timurid's hereditary Naqshbandi Sufi 'saint' that very evening, committing himself to complete ten every night. Whereas, in the past year, he writes, it had taken him at least a month to recover from an illness, this time he recovered in six days, 'with God's grace and from his Worship's power', *Tengri 'inayati bileh Hazratning himati*.[73] He had completed fifty-two couplets. Nonetheless, Babur says a sense of melancholia, *afsurdah*, lingered even after his recovery, which was echoed in the preface that he wrote to accompany his verse translation.

> Oh beloved of the Arabian Quraish
> Your grief and suffering are my happiness and joy.
> …
> I am unwell and the road is very distant.
> Life is very short and the road is longer.
> The road's map is unknown to me.
> What should bring me to the goal?
> Not leaving Babur in this despair,
> Cure his ills with Thy means.[74]

This is the first and only time Babur uses the word *afsurdah*. Later, as with this preface to his versification, he only reveals his darkening emotions in verse, the preferred Muslim medium for openly expressing intimate feelings.

Babur had recovered by mid-November and in the latter half of the month, he wrote to Humayun congratulating him for the birth of his son and saying he had done well.[75] Always the censorious father, he questioned the spelling Humayun used for the child's name and criticises his son's earlier letter to Babur for its spelling and more generally for not reviewing what he had written before dispatching it. He also begged him to quit writing in an impossibly opaque style, which was difficult to understand. Humayun had, evidently, adopted the baroque Persianate literary style beloved of so many Iranian writers, such as Shaikh Zain, the author of the Kanwah *Fath Namah*.

Apart from these personal remarks, he filled his letter with political advice, pointedly admonishing Humayun to begin acting like a Timurid warrior. Babur says that Humayun's younger brother Kamran, then governor of Qandahar, had been ordered to join him along with the Kabul *begs* to return north to take Hisar or Samarqand or Herat, or anywhere that seemed promising. (In such ad hoc ways, could empires be enlarged!) He says that this was the time of life when he and his brother ought to 'attack enemies and seize territory', the time 'to risk their lives'.

Then, Babur suggests to him something of a grand Timurid strategy – also apparently, a strategy to stimulate *mulkgirliq* ambitions and activities in his sons. He tells them that if they took Balkh, which had been lost to an Uzbek *Khan* when Humayun left to join Babur in Kabul in December 1525, and then also captured Hisar, Kamran should garrison Balkh and Humayun ought to take control of Hisar, which Babur would then declare as crown domain like Kabul. If Samarqand itself could be won, Babur tells his son emphatically, 'Take Samarqand as your seat!' (*Samarqandta sen olturghıl*).[76] Babur also mentions to Humayun, almost in passing, that if Kamran would regard Balkh as insignificant, he would find him something else after other territories were taken.

During these weeks in November and December, Babur began to plan his next campaigns for the winter season, and he offers additional realistic insights into this formative phase of empire building when he discusses how the campaign was planned. On 11 November, he ordered the army to reassemble and presumably to bring the funds from their lands. On 2 December, he summoned 'Mirzas and Sultans,' Turk and Hind *amir*s for a counsel, saying that the army must move in some direction or other. It evidently went without saying that he needed plunder to sustain the state, as he revealed in his description of a meeting held on 2 January 1529. Then, it was decided that because Nusrat Shah of Bengal had proclaimed his loyalty, it would be improper to campaign against him, and as no other significant source of treasure was available in the east, it would be better to attack in the west, as several places there, presumably meaning Rajasthan, were both close and rich.[77]

During this same period, Babur was also taking the first steps to systematise his empire by measuring the road between Agra and Kabul, obviously in his mind the geographical axis of the state. He ordered that two men, at least one of whom was apparently literate, were to measure this distance and at intervals of 18 miles build distance-marking towers and at 36 miles establish relay stations, where six post horses were to be kept. Royal revenue was to be paid for these stations in *khalisah* or crown lands, whereas local *beg*s were to finance the stations if they were located within their *parganah*s. Concluding this *farman*, Babur quotes at length from his 1521 or 1522 versified Turki text of Hanafi Sunni Islamic law, the *Mubin or Dar fiqh mubaiyan*, 'The Expounded Law', in which he gives the terminology for distances in rhymed couplets.[78] His exact specification of these terms reminds readers yet again of his taste for systematization, which is evident throughout the *Vaqayi'*.

As a preface to his verse, he tells his readers that the Indian measure *kuruh* was to be understood to be equal to what he terms a *mil*, an Indo-European root word. His verse reads:

> Four thousand paces equals a *mil*.
> Know this is what the Indians call a *kuruh*
> They say one pace equals one and a *half qarı*
> Know that each *qarı* in turn equals six *tutam* (hand-widths)
> Each *tutam* equals four *ilik* (finger widths) and further
> Learn this knowledge, each *ilik* equals the space of six grains of barley.[79]

In this Turki verse, the final word of each hemistich or half-line rhymes, making it easier to remember – for his son Kamran as well as for these two men. Thus, the first two hemistichs end in *mil* and *bil* (know), the second in *qadam* (pace) and *tutam* and the third in *ilik* and *bilik* (knowledge).

Just a day after Babur ordered the Agra–Kabul road measured, marked and readied for future communication, he climaxed his *mulkgirliq* ambitions – the dynastic conquest ethos he inherited and embraced as a young Timurid *mirza* in 1494 – by staging a feast in Agra that ceremonially marked the foundation of Timurid Hindustan. This was not one of his common *suhbatarayalıq* pleasure gatherings, but an imperial celebration attended by Iranian, Uzbek, 'Hindu' or Rajput ambassadors and Timurids, Chaghatai Mongols, Naqshbandi Sufi Shaikhs, Samarqand *'ulama'*, his own and his children's retainers and fellow Andijan exiles. It was also attended by villagers from Sukh and Husyar near Isfarah in Ferghanah, who had sheltered Babur during the terrible winter of 1503–04, when he hid from the Uzbeks, before finally fleeing south to Kabul, as well as Afghans, who had helped him during that desperate race to escape Uzbek horsemen. He exchanged gifts and presented ceremonial robes to his elite guests, but even the Andijan and Afghan villagers *in'am buldı* had 'royally conferred on them' *chakmanlar*, jackets or tunics, *qumash khitatlar*, silk robes plus textiles, and gold and silver coins (Illustration 3).

Babur seated the principal guests with the care that Timurids took on ceremonial occasions, a careful arrangement he had experienced when he visited his cousins at the Murghab River and in Herat in the fall of 1506. Thus, he describes the scene:

> Five or six *qarıs* to my right side sat Tukhtah Bughah Sultan [Chaghatai Mongol, son of Ahmad Khan] and 'Askari [Babur's third son (b. 1517)], Khwajah 'Abd al-Shahid and Khwajah Kalan, descendants of his Eminence [the Naqshbandi Shaikh, Khwajah 'Ubaidullah Ahrar], Khwajah Chishti [Chishti Sufi], and Khalifa [Nizam al-Din 'Ali Barlas, Babur's brother-in-law], and coming from Samarqand, the Khwajah's dependents – *hafizes* [Quran reciters] and *mullahs*. Five or six *qarıs* to my left side sat Muhammad Zaman Mirza [Timurid, last surviving male heir of Sultan Husain Baiqara], Tang Atmish Sultan [an Uzbek with probable Timurid marital connections], Sayyid Rafi Safavi [an Iranian who helped

mediate the surrender of Bianah to Babur's men in November 1526] and Sayyid Rumi [a Ottoman Turk who treated Babur for boils in March and April 1529], Shaikh Abu'l Fath [ambassador from Bengal], Shaikh Jamali (?), Shaikh Shihab al-Din 'Arab (?) and Sayyid Dakni [Shirazi, landscape architect].[80]

The Qizilbash or Safavid Iranian ambassadors sat 'seventy or eighty *qaris* off to the right' with one of Babur's companions Yunus 'Ali, the son of Husain's Lord of the Gate. The Uzbek ambassadors were similarly seated to the left accompanied by Babur's long-time drinking companion and fellow writer of off-colour verse Mullah 'Abdullah Kitabdar.

These seating arrangements partly echoed Babur's order, with Timurids and Chingissids to the immediate right and left. Humayun and Kamran were in Afghanistan, so only his 11-year-old son 'Askari sat to his right once removed. Perhaps because of 'Askari's age, Babur's Mongol cousin Tukhta Bugha Sultan – one of the sons of the Chaghatai Mongol Ahmad or Alacha Khan – who had arrived in Ferghanah to join the fight against Shaibani Khan in 1502, sat in the place of honour. Muhammad Zaman Mirza, the last male Baiqara Timurid, sat on the left, along with an Uzbek, Tang Atmish Sultan, who was probably partly a maternal Timurid. Next in precedence were the spiritual aristocrats, the grandson and nephew of Khwajah Yahya, the second son of Khwajah 'Ubaidullah Ahrar. Babur had earlier reiterated his reverence for members of the Ahrari family lineage when in January he honoured another Ahrari Naqshbandi Khwajah 'Abd al-Haqq. *Malazamat qildim*, 'I paid my respects,' he writes, after visiting him.

As these seating arrangements demonstrate in 1528, Babur's state was politically and religiously still predominantly a Central Asian enterprise. It was increasingly an imperial autocratic enterprise, as Babur makes clear when he remarks: 'Between the evening and bedtime prayers I seated five or six *makhsuslar*, special or distinguished people, in my presence'.[81] It is not that Babur had been previously unconcerned with his Timurid status. Prior to this time, he repeatedly demonstrated to readers how acutely sensitive he was to any acts that implicitly or directly challenged his legitimacy, his assumed political superiority as a Timurid *mirza* in a post-Mongol Timurid world. The occasion included repeated expression of impotent anger in his Ferghanah when his erstwhile allies began assuming royal prerogatives, such as Baqi Chaghaniani did later in Kabul. During his visit to Herat, he was also deeply offended when his cousins failed to show him the respect he thought he deserved as the leading Timurid for his occupations of Samarqand and battles with the Timurid dynasty's Uzbek enemies. In 1506, by assuming the Iranian title *padshah*, he claimed an exalted status that raised him above all of his Timurid or even Mongol relatives. Yet, in his account of the camaraderie of innumerable *suhbat*s in Afghanistan, he rarely mentions acting like an elevated *padshah*. But as this evening in December suggests, he had begun the transition from the relatively open fellowship of the campaign to the protocol of an empire. He was now holding court.

Finally, it was sometime at the end of the month when Babur wrote a Turki *ruba'i*, which provides a subtle grace note for these more confident days in the fall and early winter of 1528. The lines celebrate the North Indian winter season, one of the most delightful times of year in Hindustan.

> Winter, although a time of the brazier and the fire,
> Yet this winter in Hind is very amiable.
> A season of pleasure and pure wine,
> If wine is not permissible, then *ma'jun* is also fine.[82]

For a peaceful moment and in this respect at least, Babur enjoyed India, even without alcohol!

Endnotes

1   BN–M, fs. 272a.

2   Ibid, 274b and 291b. Jackson discusses the significance of the term *Hindustan* in the Sultanate period. Jackson, *The Delhi Sultanate*, 86–87.

3   BN–M, f. 293a.

4   Ahmad Gulchin-i-Ma'ânî, *Kârvân-i Hind* (Tehran: Intishârât-i Âstân-i quds-i razavî, Mashhad, Iran: 1990) Volume 1, 71.

5   BN–M, fs. 290a–291b.

6   HN, 95.

7   BN–M, fs. 293b–294a.

8   BN–B, p. 523, n. 2.

9   BN–M, f. 300a.

10   BN–M, fs. 273b, 274a–b and 291a.

11   He does not say he is discussing only Hindus or non-Muslims, but considering his lack of attention to Indo-Muslim society and the nature of his comments, Hindus are the unmistakable target of his critique.

12   BN–M, f. 290b. It may seem curious that Babur includes *madrasah*s, Muslim religious colleges, in his list of things lacking in Hindustan, but he evidently means that Hindus did not have such communal institutions for religious education. There had been, for example, a *madrasah* in Uchch, near Sialkot in the Punjab, since the early-thirteenth century. See Kumar, *The Emergence of the Delhi Sultanate*, 221.

13   See Maria Subtelny, 'Agriculture and the Timurid Chaharbagh: The Evidence from a Medieval Persian Agricultural Manual', in *Gardens in the Time of the Great Muslim Empires*, ed. Attilo Petruccioli (Brill: Leiden 1977), 133–35. Babur mentions a person, who seems to be this man working as a stone-cutter in Dhulpur in 1529. BN–M, f. 358.

14   BN–M, f. 340b.

15   J. W. McCrindle, *Ancient India as Described by Megasthênes and Arrian* (London: Trübner and Co., 1877), 70.

16   Massimo Montanari, 'Food Systems and Models of Civilization,' in *Food: A Culinary History from Antiquity to the Present*, eds. Jean-Louis Flandrin and Massimo Montanari (New York: Columbia University Press, 1999), 69.

17   D. N. Mackenzie, ed., *Poems from the Divan of Khushal Khan Khattak* (London: George Allen and Unwin, 1965), 116.

18   Edward C. Sachau, *Albêrûnî's India* (Delhi: Rupa repr. 2002), Volume 1, 1, 167 and 170.

19   BN–M, f. 294b.

20   BN–M, fs. 295a–b.

21   For this imagery, see Stephen F. Dale, 'A Safavid Poet in the Heart of Darkness: The Indian Poems of Ashraf Mazandarani,' *Iranian Studies*, 36 no. 2 (2003): 197–212.

22 BN–M, f. 296a.

23 BN–B, 526 n. 2, quoting the article of her husband, Henry Beveridge, 'Some Verses by the Emperor Babur,' A. Q. R. January 1911.

24 BN–M, f. 349b. This later phrase offers the sense of Arat's modern Turkish translation. Beveridge, adhering more closely to the phrase: *usta khaneh ikhtilat*, translates it as 'house friend's intimacy'. Both, of course, emphasise these men's deep friendship, repeatedly confirmed by other comments Babur makes about Khwajah Kalan.

25 BN–M, f. 359a. I have translated *ihtimam* in this sentence as nostalgia, believing it most closely represents the feeling Babur describes.

26 BN–M, f. 296b. Whether they had the power to collect these sums is another question.

27 BN–M, f. 294a.

28 BN–M, f. 298a.

29 BN–M, f, 299a.

30 BN–M, fs. 299a–299b.

31 BN–M, fs. 299b–300a.

32 BN–M, f. 300a.

33 H. Blochmann and D. C. Phillott, eds., *The A'in-i Akbari* (Delhi: Crown Publications, repr. 1968), Volume 1, 93.

34 For these gardens, see Ebba Koch, 'The Mughal Waterfront Garden,' in *Gardens in the Time of the Great Muslim Empires: Theory and Design in Islamic Art and Architecture, Supplements to Muqarnas*, ed. Attilio Petruccioli (Leiden: Brill, 1997), 140–60. See also.

35 BN–M, fs. 300a–b–301a.

36 BN–M, fs. 309a, 304a–b and 305a.

37 BN–M, fs. 305a–07a.

38 BN–M, f. 308a.

39 BN–M, fs. 310b–11a, f. 264a and fs. 266b–67a.

40 BN–M, f. 311a–b. This grandson, however, was the son of an Uzbek father and, therefore, he was not a Timurid.

41 He was known later primarily as a poet. For an enthusiastic appreciation of Shaikh Zain's literary abilities with examples of his verse, see Al-Badauni, 'Abdu-l Qâdir Ibn-i-Muluk Shâh, *Muhtakhabu't tawârîkh*, trans. and ed. George S. A. Ranking (Calcutta: Mission Press for the Asiatic Society of Bengal, 1898), Volume 1, 609–11.

42 BN–M, fs. 312b–14a. The *tamgha* was a Mongol and therefore a non-canonical tax, which, as Beveridge notes, was not actually abolished in Timurid India until his great-grandson Jahangir's day. BN–B, p. 553, n. 1.

43 BN–M, f. 314b.

44 BN–M, f. 315a.

45 Ibid.

46 It is not clear from Shaikh Zain's wording whether Babur remained behind the carts, or directly joined the conflict raging in front of him.

47 BN–M, f. 326b.

48 Ibid.

49 BN–M, fs. 324a–b.

50 BN–M, f. 324b–325a.

51 Ibid.

52 BN–M fs. 329b–330a. The fourth line seems to be a play-on-words and may not be rendered here exactly as Babur intended.

53 BN–M, f. 327b.

54 BN–M, f. 328b.

55 BN–M, f. 325b.

56 BN–M, fs. 329a–29b.

57 BN–M, f. 331b and Yücel, *Babur Dîvânı*, no. 319, 263.

58 Yücel, *Babur Dîvânı*, no. 328, 263.

59 HN, 97.

60 For the Naqshbandi connection see Stephen F. Dale and Alam Payind, 'The Ahrâri Waqf of Kabul in the Year 1546 and the Mughul Naqshbandiyyah,' *Journal of the American Oriental Society* 119, no.2 (April–June 1999), 225–26.

61 BN–M, f. 335a. Another chronogram based on the *abjad* numerical values given to letters of the Arabic alphabet. *Dar al-harb* (Abode of War), is the standard Arab-Muslim epithet for non-Muslim territories.

62 A lacuna in the *Vaqayi'* of slightly more than five months makes it impossible to determine what occurred between 2 April and 18 September. See Beveridge's note. BN–B, pp. 602–04.

63 Rita Joshi summarises information about Babur's relations with individual Afghans from 1505, just after he had seized Kabul, until his death in 1530. As she points out, Babur had to deal with each tribe or clan separately – in Afghanistan as well as in Hindustan – and his defeat of Ibrahim Ludi did not result in the surrender of most of the Afghan tribal contingents under Ibrahim Ludi's nominal control, while the Ludi ruler had never controlled substantial numbers of Afghans in the eastern Gangetic Valley. Joshi, 'The Role of Afghan Nobles under Babar and Humayun (AD 1505–1520),' in *The Afghan Nobility and the Mughals 1526-1707*, 32–55.

64 Joshi, *The Afghan Nobility and the Mughals 1526–1707*, 45–47.

65 BN–M, fs. 342b–343a and 345a.

66 BN–M, f. 339b and 344a.

67 BN–M, 340b.

68 BN–M, f. 341b–342b.

69 Beveridge discusses this man, a Rajput convert to Islam, married to Rana Sanga's daughter. BN-B, p. 562.

70 BN–M, f. 344b.

71 BN–M, fs. 345a–b. See also Beveridge's note 2, p. 617.

72 Translated by A. J. E. Bodrogligeti as 'Babur Shâh's Chaghatay Version of the *Risâla-i Vâlidîya*: A Central Asian Turkic Treatise of How to Emulate the Prophet Muhammad,' *Ural-Altaische Jahrbücher*, Volume 54, (1984), 1–61.

73 BN–M, f. 346b.

74 Bilal Yücel, *Bâbür Dîvânı*, no. 2, 97–98.

75 BN–M, fs. 348a–450a.

76 BN–M, f. 348b.

77 BN–M, fs. 350a and 355a–b.

78 BN–B, pp. 437–38.

79 BN–M, fs. 351a–b.

80 BN–M, f. 351b–352a.

81 BN–M, f. 353b.

82 Bilal Yücel, *Bâbür Dîvânı* no. 335, 264.

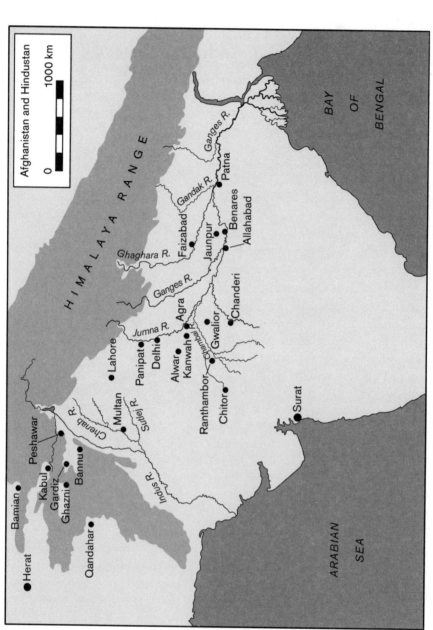

Map 3: A map of Afghanistan and Hindustan

5

Gurbatlıq: An Indian Exile

In December 1528, not only did Babur celebrate the foundation of the Timurid Empire of Hindustan, on 27th of the month, he also completed a second collection of his verse, now known as the Rampur Diwan, named after the Indian town where the manuscript was discovered.[1] The collection includes a copy of his versified translation of Khwajah 'Ubaidullah Ahrar's text, a *masnavi*, a *ghazal*, several *ruba'iyat* and other verse fragments. Babur's *ruba'iyat* contains psychologically revealing lines about his state of mind during the preceding two and half years. They express and magnify the degree of unease or actual depression he sometimes felt during this period of intense activity, and which he hints at in the few long verses he includes in the *Vaqayi'* for 1528.

Having desired Hindustan, as he insists, since taking Kabul in 1504, he increasingly reveals himself to be deeply conflicted by his exile or *ghurbat*, from what he had come to regard as a richer life in a poorer but better place – the Afghan capital. He had already expressed a degree of remorse in his verse reply to Khwajah Kalan's parting poetic shot, which his friend had left on the wall of his house in Agra in 1526. The sense of loss he hints at in that poem and the depression he alludes to after translating and versifying Khwajah Ahrar's verse, Babur expresses poignantly in several of the poems of the Rampur Diwan. He also reiterates his feelings in a letter he sends to Khwajah Kalan on 10 February 1529. Nonetheless, he, quite literally, 'soldiered on' during the next 2 years as he fought to replenish his depleted treasury and expand the perimeter of the Timurid state. All the while he struggled to retain control over his imperfectly subjugated home territories: the Punjab, and the Delhi-Agra Duab and then, there were the illnesses.

A Darkening Mood

In the first Turki *ruba'i* listed in the Rampur collection, written apparently just after Babur had celebrated becoming a *ghazi*, and not a *shahid*, at the Battle of Kanwah, he openly reveals the emotional regret he felt after finally obtaining what he earlier claimed was his long sought goal – Hindustan.

> Since I have neither friends nor districts,
> I have not one moment of repose.
> It was my choice to have come here,
> Yet I am not able to go away.[2]

He amplifies and intensifies the remorseful tone of this verse in the lines of the only *ghazal* he included in this collection. It is an existential poem, invoking the feeling of *ghurbat* or exile. This is a term he invokes three times in the poem he wrote during desperate times in June 1502, when he took refuge with his Mongol uncle in Tashkent before the final collapse of his Ferghanah fortunes. Poets regularly used *ghurbat* in several ways, including in their oft-repeated tales of the separation endured by distraught lovers.[3] In this poem, evidently written sometime between 1527 and 1528, Babur laments his *ghurbat* – or alternatively its synonym *hajran* – from friends, referring almost certainly to Khwajah Kalan and his other compatriots in Kabul – or even in frigid Ghazni. The *ghazal*'s first line must refer to Ramadan, which, in 1528, began in May.

> In exile (*ghurbat*) this month of abstinence ages me.
> Separated from friends exile (*hajran*) has affected me.

After further lines in which he rues his fate, saying he does not know whether he will remain 'on that side', presumably Kabul, or 'this side', certainly Hindustan, Babur speaks movingly in the final four lines of the simultaneous desire and repulsion he felt towards India, alluding again to the separation from his friends.

> I deeply desired the riches of this Indian land.
> What is the profit since this land enslaves me?
> Left so far from you, Babur has not perished.
> Excuse me my friend for this my insufficiency.[4]

Babur's regret for his decision to renounce drinking before the battle of Kanwah contributed to his intensifying sense of loss, expressed in nostalgia for the *suhbat* and *suhbatarayaliq* gatherings during the old days in Kabul. Alluding to that oath he had taken to ensure victory, he writes poignantly:

> I am grief-stricken at abandoning wine.
> Darkening my heart, I am always in a confused state.
> Frozen in grief I am lost.
> With wine I am cheerful and smiling.[5]

The probable dating of these existential poems to 1527 and their almost certain allusion to his old social life is indicated not only by their placement in the Rampur Diwan, but also because they are echoed by a letter he later wrote to Khwajah Kalan in February 1529.

Sometime after this *ruba'i* was written Babur's mood seems to have become even darker, reflecting the depression borne of loneliness, sickness and regret that he hints at, but much less artfully in the *Vaqayi'*. Far more than his relatively unadorned Turki prose narrative, the later Rampur Diwan poems evoke a sense of exhaustion, despair and perhaps even the paranoia of old age. One such *ruba'i*, which judged by its place in the Diwan, was written sometime in 1528, is the darkest of all these verses. It is all the more compelling when read against the positive political situation of that year and the December 1528 imperial celebration.

> Finally neither friends nor companions will be faithful.
> Neither summer nor winter, companions will not remain
> A hundred pities that precious life passes away,
> O, alas that this celebrated time is futile.[6]

The Last Campaign: I

Futile it may have seemed, but following the celebration on 18 December, Babur began planning his next and, as it turned out, his last campaign. Earlier in the month at a meeting he held on 2 December with his commanders, he had begun thinking about his next campaign. He discussed sending off his young son 'Askari to the east with the vague idea of exploiting any military opportunity. On 12 December, as a preface to appointing Askari to command this expedition, he ceremoniously awarded him the insignia and equipment of an adult Timurid prince. 'Askari received a jewelled dagger, a ceremonial coat or *khil'at*, a standard, a horse-tail staff (a Mongol emblem), a kettle drum or *naqarah* (a royal instrument), a string of *tipuchaq* (horses), ten elephants, a string of camels, a string of mules, royal implements and tackling. He was ordered to sit at the head of the *Diwan*.'[7] On 20 December, after taking leave from his father at the *hammam*, he marched for the east.[8]

When 'Askari left Agra, Babur had not decided where he should campaign and did not finally resolve to march eastward for another month. In the meantime, he once again rode to Dhulpur some 34 miles south of Agra to inspect the well and reservoir there. After returning to Agra on 24 December, he received a Safavid envoy on 28 December, who gave him a detailed account of the Safavid victory over the Uzbeks at the Battle of Jam. The envoy's account revealed that the Safavids organised their battle lines according to the Rumi or Ottoman model Babur had used at Panipat.

Two days later with the direction of the next campaign still undecided, Babur received intelligence from a scout. This man had been sent east to contact Sultan Junaid Barlas, who had been appointed to Jaunpur in late 1526, after Humayun had been recalled to Agra to join the confrontation with Rana Sanga'. Junaid

Barlas had evidently remained in Jaunpur region during the following 2 years, and he gave a message to Babur's scout that there was no problem serious enough in the region, which required the *Padshah* to campaign there. He thought that if 'Askari arrived with his '*sultans*, *khans* and *amirs*', all would be fine. Still, Babur hesitated to move west, even after a messenger came from Bengal to report that Nusrat Shah in Bengal was 'submissive and supportive'. He writes that since the road west, where wealthy states might be occupied and their treasuries seized, was so short they ought to wait for more news from the east. He also sent the scout back east towards Jaunpur to urge 'Askari's men to take action against the 'rebels', that is, contingents of Ludi Afghans and Shaikh Bayazid Farmuli.[9]

Finally, on 13 January 1529, Babur's indecision about the next campaign was resolved. At the time, he was once again visiting Dhulpur, where he spent the time in the *Nilufar Bagh*, the Lotus Garden, planning future camping sites for his men and ordering the construction of a *hammam*. While there, he received letters forwarded from Agra that Mahmud Ludi, the son of Iskandar Ludi, had occupied Bihar. This message presumably referred to Bihar Sharif, a Buddhist monastic site in central Bihar province. It had been the easternmost territory of the Ludi State, and theoretically after Panipat, the outer border of Babur's possessions. Thus began the Afghan resurgence that eventually saw Humayun defeated and driven from India in May 1540 by one of Mahmud Ludi's allies, the Afghan Shir Khan Suri.

At this news, Babur hurriedly returned from Dhulpur to Agra, where, at a war council on 15 January 1529, it was decided to march east, but for strategic rather than financial reasons. 'The object of the campaign,' he writes, 'was to suppress the rebel Afghans.'[10] On 20 January 1529, Babur marched out of Agra, stopping first at the Gold-Scattering Garden just 6 miles from the city, the garden where he and his young daughter Gulbadan Begim were to converse meaningfully later in the year.[11] He remained there for a week conducting business and readying his firearms.

On 22 January, he received the envoy of Nusrat Shah of the Husain-Shahi dynasty of Bengal (r. 1518–32), who ritually knelt before Babur for the prescribed three times and handed him a letter and offerings from the Bengali ruler. Babur had earlier rejected the thought of solving his revenue problem by attacking Bengal because Nusrat Shah had pledged his friendship. Nonetheless, the Bengali ruler obviously mistrusted Timurid intentions and sent his envoy to placate Babur, as well as, no doubt, to acquire intelligence. Two days later, still in the garden, Babur took time to welcome a Naqshbandi Shaikh Khwajah, 'Abdul Haqq, whose brother, Hazrat Makhdumi Nura, was a major Naqshbandi figure in this period. By waiting on this man, Babur continued showing reverence for Ahrari Naqshbandis, who later came to represent a type of dynastic Sufi aristocrat both in Kabul, where they possessed a valuable *waqf*, and also in Akbar's India.[12]

After Babur resumed his march on 27 January, he travelled by boat to the town of Anwar about 14 miles from Agra. He remained there for a week, first giving leave on 30 January to the Uzbek envoys who had attended his imperial celebration. The Uzbek party included an Ahrari Naqshbandi, Khwajah Kalan. He was a grandson of Khwajah Yahya, who had encouraged Babur to take Samarqand in 1500. While Uzbeks had subsequently murdered the Khwajah and two of his sons, they later began using Ahraris as political intermediaries, as did Mongols and Timurids. In 1543, the reigning Uzbek Khan, 'Abd al-Latif, restored some previously confiscated lands to one of Ahrar's great-grandsons in 1543, ensuring that the city retained its importance for members of the Ahrari family.[13] The Naqshbandi's Samarqand base was important for the Timurid-Mughuls as Baqi Billah, the *murshid* or Sufi teacher of Shaikh Ahmad Sirhindi, came to India in 1602 from the city. It was Sirhindi, who revived the order in India and sent disciples of his own to establish the Naqshbandi *silsileh* in the Ottoman Empire.

Babur awarded the Uzbek envoys *khilat*s, the ceremonial robes typical of such occasions, as well as thousands of *tankah*s, small silver coins, and special gifts to the servants of his half-sister Mihrbanu Khanim and her son Pulad in Samarqand. The following day on 31 January, Babur turned to family affairs, sending a flurry of messages to Kabul. These included congratulations to Humayun on the birth of his son and for Kamran on his marriage in response to news about his sons he had received earlier. The messengers who took his messages to Afghanistan also carried 10,000 *shahrukhi* coins for each son and presents for Hind-al, the youngest, including a copy of the alphabet written in Babur's invented script, along with *qitah*s written in that script. Humayun and Khwajah Kalan received copies of Babur's Turki translation of Khwajah Ahrar's *Walidiyyah-i risala* and Babur's Indian verse, the *Rampur Diwan*. Kamran also received lines in Babur's invented script.

Slightly more than a week later on 9 February, Babur sent more letters to Kabul, which were primarily concerned with political and administrative affairs. One went to Humayun in response to the news Babur had received more than three weeks earlier that his son had left Kabul with 40,000 men to attack Samarqand. Babur's letter seems to suggest a frontier agreement had been made with the Uzbeks, presumably concluded when their envoys visited Agra. He also strongly reiterated that Kabul had been made crown land and none of his sons ought to seek it for themselves. He told Kamran the same thing, while also referring to Kamran's assignment to Multan and the coming to Hindustan of members of his family. Babur also wrote a separate letter to his old friend and de facto governor of Kabul, Khwajah Kalan, which is the single most revealing letter he includes in the *Vaqayi'*.

The Administration of the Empire

Babur's letter to Khwajah Kalan, a reply to his friend's letter he had received four days earlier, begins with an emotional echo of the sentiments Babur had expressed in the verses of the Rampur *Diwan* and which he had just sent to Kalan.[14] He writes alluding to the message he had just received.

> Shams al-Dîn Muhammad has reached Etawah and the circumstances [of Kabul] have become known. Our desire to go those places,' he writes, 'is immense and boundless. Hindustan affairs are reaching some kind of resolution and, God be exalted, *Tengri ta'alah*, the hope is such that with God's grace things will soon be arranged. After managing this work, if God wills, I shall set out immediately. How can a person forget the pleasures of those lands, especially for such a one who has become repentant and abstinent. How can a person blot from his mind such legally sanctioned pleasures as melons and grapes. After a time a melon was brought. Cutting [and] eating [it] had a strange effect. I was consumed with tears.[15]

In a later part of this letter, Babur returned to the subject of wine and repentance, saying: 'Thus it was written in a letter to 'Abdullah that it had been very unsettling to reside in the vale of repentance. This *ruba'i* partly explains the difficulty.'

> Renouncing wine I am confounded.
> I know not what to do and am bewildered.
> People become penitent and repent.
> I am now penitent for having repented.[16]

Following the poem Babur then continues saying,

> That *ruba'i* was recited last year. During the past two years, the craving and longing for a wine party, a *chaghır-majlisi*, has been so intense and overwhelming that from the longing for wine I was brought to tears. This year, thank God, that inclination has completely left the mind. Probably the good and blessing came from versifying the translation [of Khwajah Ahrar's *Walidiyyah*]. You [Khwajah Kalan] must also repent. Gatherings and wine are delightful with convivial friends and boon companions.

But, Babur pointedly says, alluding dismissively to his old friend's present drinking companions.

> With whom will you hold *suhbat?* - With whom will you drink wine? If your convivial friends and boon companions, *hamsubat* ve *hakasah*, are Shir Ahmad and Haidar Quli, such renunciation should not be difficult.

And he recalls: 'At the time, writing these friendly words of advice, *bu nasihat amiz solar*, affected me profoundly.'[17]

What is particularly compelling about this letter is that Babur blends expressions of personal angst with his deep concern for the governance of Kabul. It raises the larger question of the nature of his rule in this formative period of his Hindustan conquest when he was writing the *Vaqayi'*. Following his heartfelt greeting to Khwajah Kalan, he tells his friend how he wants Kabul to be ruled, and instructs him as to what should be done to improve the city and province. The letter not only raises political issues, but also contains the single extant source that illustrates his engagement with the minutia of rule at this time. While it is confined to the affairs of Kabul, it seems safe to assume that Babur administered his newly acquired Hindustan possessions with the same careful, precise, activist attention he brought to the affairs of the Afghan city. His letter does not include any administrative details of the Kabul city or provincial government, although some inferences of what he may have intended, inherited or even instituted can be made from the administrative section of his 1521 versified Turki text. Babur begins by dealing decisively with the confused political situation in the Afghan capital.

> Kabul's chaotic affairs, *Kabulning namarbutluq*, have been written of [to me]. On this account [after] thinking, it was decided that if there were seven or eight governors in one province how could things be contained and controlled? Given this situation I summoned my elder sister, *ablam*, and wives to Hindustan. I made all Kabul province and its villages crown land, *khalisah*. I also wrote to Humayun and Kamran in this sense. A trusty person must take these letters to these Mirzas. I also wrote in exactly this sense and sent [letters] to the Mirzas. Perhaps it is already known. Now there remains no word or excuse about the safety and prosperity of the province. After this if the fortifications are not strong and the people are not prosperous or if there are no provisions or the treasury is not full it will be charged to the Pillar of the State's [Khwajah Kalan's] ineffectiveness.[18]

Khwajah Kalan, a close friend of Babur's, must have found himself in a difficult situation as governor of Kabul, with two Timurid princes constantly in and around the city and a medley of important Timurid women residents there. Just to reiterate the point about the problems inherent in the women's presence, Babur later adds: 'The minute this letter arrives you must take my elder sister and wives and go as an escort to Nilab [Indus].' This meant at the very least that Khanzadah Begim, his sister, and three of his wives, Maham Begim, Gulrukh Begim and Dildar Begim. 'It is imperative,' he insists, 'that in the same week when this letter arrives you must all definitely leave however much they delay, both because the troops that have gone from Hindustan are suffering in unpleasant quarters and because the province [Kabul] is being ruined.'[19] Many more women than just Babur's sister and wives may have been involved. His daughter, for example, gives a list of women at a celebration hosted by Humayun in 1534, the so-called 'Mystic Feast'. It includes daughters and female relatives of many different Timurids, such as the daughters of Sultan Husain Baiqara and Sultan Ahmad Mirza, who may also have been in Kabul prior to Panipat and Kanwah.[20]

His old friend may have understood the political situation in 1528, but later readers of the *Vaqayi'* might have been perplexed when they tried to reconstruct the state of Babur's Afghan–Hindustan empire in these formative years. First is the question of its territorial extent, which is particularly uncertain following the Battle of Kanwah, when Babur began reconquering those fortresses and provinces he had gained after Panipat and then lost as the battle loomed. Based upon his own account, he controlled or at least dominated the *vilayat* or provinces of Badakhshan, Qunduz, Kabul and Qandahar in Afghanistan. In Hindustan, he controlled or dominated parts of the Punjab, including the trans-Indus districts around Bhirah and Sialkot, but most importantly, Lahore and Multan to the south, Delhi, Agra, Dhulpur, Etawah and Gwalior in the heartland, Bianah with a small fringe of territory in eastern Rajasthan, Chanderi to Gwalior's south, some fortresses or cities in the Duab region such as Koil/Aligarh and, less certainly, the trans-Ganges cities of Qanauj and Sambhal. The Jaunpur situation is less clear, Humayun having briefly occupied the city in early January 1527 – he had earlier been assigned Sambhal – before returning to Agra to join Babur for the Rajput battle.

Babur's actual control of territory was limited to a narrow swath of territory linking fortresses or cities in these regions. He found it difficult to retain authority in the trans-Hindu Kush regions of Balkh and Badakhshan, which were constantly threatened and sometimes occupied by Uzbeks. Timurids seem to have succeeded in pacifying lands bordering the Agra–Kabul road he ordered to be measured. At least small detachments and messengers regularly moved back and forth between these two cities, essentially the then dual capitals of the empire.

Apart from territorial control, there were the issues of political authority. Between 1527 and 1529, Babur governed his Afghan and Timurid lands as two distinct regions. The situation in Kabul city and province was especially complicated because Humayun and Kamran spent so much time there with various relatives, making it difficult for Khwajah Kalan to govern the city. After Panipat, Humayun had returned to Afghanistan with his Badakhshan troops and seemed to be responsible for the north. Kamran, who had held both Kabul and Qandahar during the invasion, was left in charge of Qandahar and then later assigned to Multan, although it is not clear if he went there. In his 1528 letter, Babur pointedly told both sons that he had designated Kabul as *khalisah* or crown land because 'There had been such conquests and victories when he was in the city.'[21]

In terms of his sons' relations with one another, Babur had alluded to this question in his November 1528 letter to Humayun, when he urged Humayun and Kamran to campaign in northern Afghanistan and Mawarannahr and then divide the conquered territory between them. He told his eldest son that he had always given six parts of his conquests to him and five parts to Kamran, thus showing the same preference for his eldest son that he had claimed for himself in Andijan with his bothers Jahangir and Nasir Mirza.

By implication, he did not consider his two youngest sons mature enough to be considered in this theoretical division of territorial spoils. 'Askari and Hind-al, born in 1517 and 1519, respectively, were apparently too young to enjoy effective independent authority during Babur's lifetime. 'Askari was technically placed in charge of Multan at age 11 sometime prior to September 1528, when he was ordered to Agra and then sent on his first campaign to the east in December 1528. Hind-al apparently remained in Kabul until 1529, when at age 10 he was ordered north at short notice to represent the Timurids in Badakhshan, after Humayun had abruptly abandoned his post in the summer of 1529. He had travelled first to Kabul, where he met Kamran, and then hurried to Hindustan when Babur fell ill. It was following Babur's death that the older brothers – half-brothers – began to divide the empire, with Humayun becoming *Padshah*, following which Kamran moved from Kabul and seized independent control of Multan and Lahore in 1531.

In February 1529, however, when Babur wrote to Khwajah Kalan, he was still very much in charge of the empire. After telling him how he wished to stabilise the political situation in Kabul, he turned to the question of administering the city. His instructions represent the only section in the *Vaqayi*', where he offers some insight, however limited, into his actual governance. Following his nostalgic opening greeting to Khwajah Kalan, he mentions finances and then turns to the city and province's infrastructure.

> Some necessary things now will be specified. In some cases an order has already gone out. One of these is that you must add to the treasury. The

necessary things are these: repair of fortifications, provisions, lodging and stipends for arriving and departing ambassadors. You must spend money legally taken from revenue for the congregational mosque building.[22] Then repairs to the caravanserai and the *hammam*, completion of the half-finished brick building done by Ustad Hasan 'Ali in the *ark* [citadel], and consulting about the building with Ustad Sultan Muhammad you must order a suitable design. If the former plan made by Ustad Hasan 'Ali still exists you must complete it exactly in that manner. If not, after consultation, you must erect a nicely designed building so that its floor is level with the floor of the *Diwankhanah* [the audience hall].

Next, Babur mentions other constructions in the province and his perennial concern for pleasant, well-situated garden settings.

Then the Khurd Kabul dam, which is to be built on the Butkhak River, where the gorge opens out toward Khurd Kabul. Then, repair of the Ghazni dam. Then the Bagh-i khiaban [the Avenue of Trees Garden] and the avenue, for which there is too little water. It is necessary to buy and divert a one-mill stream. Then on the southwest of Khwajah Bastah I diverted the Tutumdarah stream atop a small rise, constructed a pool and planted saplings. As it stood opposite the ford and had a nice view it was called the *Nazargah* [the Scenic View]. Here it is also necessary to plant good saplings, well-planned lawns, beautiful and fragrant flowers and sweet smelling herbs.

Babur's letter to Khwajah Kalan offers important insights into his preoccupations as an empire builder. Most obviously, the letter reveals the degree to which the new Timurid-Mughal Empire was still entirely his empire. He personally directed every conceivable aspect of rule, from defusing potentially explosive dynastic political tensions to constructing the infrastructure foundations of the new Timurid state. His earlier order for measuring the Agra–Kabul road, staffed with post horses for swift communication, represented part of this process. He includes no similar evidence in the *Vaqayi'* that illustrates his construction plans for Hindustan, apart from innumerable descriptions of his attempts to repurpose the landscape with Iranian gardens. Nonetheless, it seems reasonable to assume that he was equally concerned to build an imperial infrastructure in Hindustan. His Kabul instructions to Khwajah Kalan demonstrate that he was trying to construct the physical apparatus for an altogether typical late-Timurid Perso-Islamic sultanate.

Heading his concern was the question of revenue. Babur supplies virtually no information about the operation of his financial administration, but it would be a mistake – another of many false common perceptions of early Timurid rule – to imagine that he envisaged sustaining his finances through the kind of 'booty economy' of perpetual conquest that characterised Temür's nomadic empire.[23] As has been mentioned, his initial occupation of eastern Afghanistan required a great deal of 'sword not pen' revenue collection among Afghan tribesmen, and the same was true in Hindustan. Restocking the treasury with plunder was a matter of necessity in the early months and years of the empire, never more obviously so than in December 1528, when he had to decide what states he might overrun to seize funds to sustain his rule.

It is obvious from the order he issued in October 1528 for his assignees to bring 30 per cent of their revenue to the *Diwan* or treasury in Agra that he had not yet achieved sufficient control of even the Delhi–Agra region to establish a functioning land revenue administration – or to resuscitate whatever kind of administration the Ludis had constructed to produce the revenue amounts their records recorded – if they did actually collect these sums. Nonetheless, Babur's knowledge of canonical revenue practice is known, even if his actual revenue administration is not.

In the *Mubin*, he included a section on standard Hanafi Sunni taxation and financial policies, similar to those found in the text known as the *Hidayat*. The author of this well-known text, familiar to Muslims in India as well as in Mawarannahr, was Burhan al-Din 'Ali Qilich al-Marghinani (c. 1135–97) of Ferghanah. Khwajah Maulana Qazi, Babur's tutor and protector in Andijan until murdered by Sultan Ahmad Tambal, was his descendant. Babur was familiar with the *Hidayat* text, which he praises.[24]

Given Babur's *Mubin* text, it is reasonable to assume that his catalogue of Hanafi Sunni taxation policies would have guided his own revenue administration in Kabul and in Hindustan. As was indicated earlier Babur identified three sources of income in Kabul province: land, commerce and domesticated animals or nomadic flocks. He uses Arabic terminology, which he found in al-Marghinani's *Hidayat* text. Land or agricultural taxes were of two kinds: *'ushr* and *kharaj*, the first levied principally from gardens and fruit trees, and second, by implication, from grain-producing fields of various kinds. The *kharaj*, in turn, was divided into two categories: one, a fixed tax on the harvest of one-third to one-half, and the second, based upon actual measurement of the land, the *jarib*.

The second category of taxes, *sava'im*, literally flocks, dealt with domestic animals, including camels and horses, as well as sheep, goats and cattle. Based upon the age of animals and the amount of time in pasture, this tax was collected in kind – often forcibly as tribute from Afghan tribesmen. For example, 1 sheep would be taken from flocks between 40 and 120 in number, 2 from flocks of 120 to 200. The third category of taxes was levied from two types of commerce: commercial activities in the *bazars* taken in cash and external or long-distance trade arriving in and/or passing through the city. *Bazars* merchants were to be taxed at the rate of approximately 5 per cent of gold coins and 2.5 per cent of silver coins of cash-on-hand. Taxes on external trade varied according to whether merchants came from 'friendly', that is, Muslim countries, in which they would be taxed at the rate of five per cent; others could be taxed at double this rate.[25]

Babur may well have implemented such a revenue system in Kabul. He certainly had identified the province's three major sources of revenue in his Kabul gazetteer. Perhaps, the most important long-term aspect of the *Mubin* system is that it describes a land revenue system for agrarian economies based upon field measurement. This method is often associated in the historiography of Hindustan with the interim rule of the Afghan, Shir Shah Suri (r. 1540–45), who displaced Humayun for 5 years, or at the very least with Babur's grandson Akbar. It is also worth recalling in this context that Babur had just earlier began laying out what later became the Grand Trunk Road, using measurements from the same *Mubin* text. Therefore, even if Babur did not have time to establish a financial administration in Hindustan before his death in December 1530, it is likely that he had done so, at least in Afghanistan. It is reasonable to imagine, if not absolutely, to conclude, that Shir Shah and Akbar continued with existing revenue arrangements, rather than assuming an interregnum and a lack of connection between the *Diwan* of Babur's embryonic Timurid Empire and that of his successors.

Apart from revenue, the other instructions Babur included in his letter to Khwajah Kalan were also designed to begin constructing, in these cases literally, a typical pre-modern Perso-Islamic Sultanate. Four of his projects particularly stand out in that respect: the repair of the Kabul fort, building a congregational mosque with state revenues and repairing caravanserais and *hammam*s. Babur is here giving attention to military control, as well as to communal religious observance, repair of revenue-producing commercial structures and renovation of baths, the latter an important social institution. Finally, but predictably, given his attachment to *subatarayalıq* or congenial social life, amid aesthetically pleasing surroundings, his instructions also included diverting streams and improving a garden, which happened to include a particularly lovely *nazargah* or viewpoint. Thus, in Kabul at least, long under Babur's secure control and now governed by his old friend Khwajah Kalan, the Timurid Empire was now manifest in all its essential features.

As for Babur's rule in Hindustan, after Kanwah and still certainly in December 1528, he governed its partly subjugated territories through what may be regarded as a kind of typical post-conquest military feudalism. Babur granted most of the conquered and re-conquered territories Babur granted as military fiefs to his *beg*s – described now in India as *amir*s – to support themselves and their men. In the *Vaqayi'*, he does not cite any technical terms to describe or label these men other than the generic Indo-Muslim term *wajhdar*, the holder *dar* of a *wajh* or territorial assignment. It is a term Firuz Shah Tuqluq used for land assignments in the late-fourteenth century.[26] In the *Vaqayi'*, Babur first uses it when he describes settling the administrative affairs of Andijan, just after his father's death, when he refers to a *wajh istiqamat* assignment, which in Firuz Tuqluq's days meant it could be transferred to a son or other relative.[27] Babur then uses the same phrase again to describe an assignment he gave to Langar Khan at Khushab following the Bhirah campaign in 1519.[28]

When he refers to *wajh*, he apparently means assignments similar to *tiyul*. For example, when he allotted lands in Kabul, he writes that they were given *tiyul-dik*, 'as *tiyul*' – a usage he employs for the last time in the *Vaqayi'* when he mentions Lamghanat, the *tuman* or district to the east of Kabul.[29] He never explains the exact rights and responsibilities of *tiyul* or *wajh* assignments.[30] Nonetheless, his actions suggest that he regarded these grants as temporary or conditional territorial appointments given for the dual purposes of military/political territorial consolidation and military stipends, although he later allotted many to relatives. Babur treated these *wajh* grants differently from the *soyurghal* grants he gave to members of the *'ulama'* in India.[31] Although, in this case too it is difficult to make any firm conclusions as so few of these deeds have survived.[32]

In terms of personnel in Hindustan, Babur continued his earlier practice of appointing Timurids, Chinggisids, in-laws and long-time companions to govern the most recently subjugated and most significant forts and provinces. These men were often intermarried with one another's families. Thus, the ruling circle continued to be composed of a relatively small web of Turco-Mongol aristocrats, now occasionally supplemented by newly-enrolled Hindustan Muslims.

After Panipat, for example, Babur ordered five trusted men to seize the Delhi treasury. These included his brother-in-law Mahdi Khwajah, son-in-law, Baiqara Timurid Muhammad Zaman Mirza, one of Sultan Husain Baiqara's former officials and another of Babur's brothers-in-law Sultan Junaid Barlas. Later in the fall, Mahdi Khwajah was made *shiqdar* of Bianah.[33] When he left Hindustan for Kabul, his son Ja'far Khwajah was given Etawah and his nephew Rahim Dad was assigned to the formidable Gwalior fortress. Muhammad Zaman Mirza served with Babur continuously during these years and in 1529, following the 'eastern campaign', he was given the strategic city of Jaunpur, north of Banaras/Varanasi/

Kashi. Sultan Junaid Barlas, who had been assigned to Dhulpur in August 1526 and then Jaunpur in January 1527, was moved from Jaunpur to Chunar, just upriver from Banaras in May 1529. After Kanwah in 1527, the critically important town of Qanauj was given to the Baiqara Muhammad Sultan Mirza. Koil or Aligarh was given to Kichik 'Ali, a former retainer of Sultan Muhammad Wais, a nephew of Sultan Husain Baiqara. Kichik 'Ali had fought with Babur at Akhsı and Ush in Ferghanah.[34]

The Last Campaign

Following his pause to dispatch correspondence to Kabul, Babur finally resumed his march eastward on 11 February, and on 28 February linked up with 'Askari's forces on opposite sides of the Ganges. After learning on 5 March that the Afghans had fled as his army approached, Babur nonetheless continued marching down the river. He was joined on 6 March by two Chaghatai Mongols, Aisan Temur Sultan and Tukhta Bugha Sultan, sons of his now deceased Mongol cousin, Ahmad Khan (d. 1504). They had joined Babur earlier, but had been serving with 'Askari on the other side of the river. He continues his narrative of the march without explaining the goal, but later events show that initially, at least, he meant to pursue the Afghans fleeing before his troops.

Babur mentions reaching Chunar on 23rd, where a Rumi, an Ottoman Turk, treated him for a boil.[35] A day or two later, while hunting wild elephants in the Chunar jungles, he received reports that Mahmud Khan Ludi was camped near the border with Bihar at the Son River, and Babur ordered a forced march to confront him. On 28 March, Babur now travelling by boat reached the confluence of the Gumti and the Ganges. Meanwhile, he had ordered two of his men, Mughul Beg and Lutfi Beg, to measure both the road and river distance from Chunar to the confluence, one of many indications of his interest in precise measurement. Then on 31 March, the Afghan campaign finally reached a kind of climax near Ghazipur.

There, Mahmud Khan Luhani (Nuhani) visited him, and several other Luhani Afghans, Shir Khan Suri and a number of other Afghan *amir*s sent him letters of submission, *'arza-dasht*.[36] Coincidentally, the same day he learned that the women coming from Kabul had reached the Indus on 18 February. Despite this news and the Afghan's submission Babur continued moving down river, reaching Chausa on 1 April, near where Shir Khan Suri would defeat Humayun in 1539. On 4 April, they reached Buxar, near where his army had camped the previous year, and the site of the critical English India Company victory over a Mughul commander in 1764. He surveyed the site, ate some *ma'jun*, staged a wrestling match and recalled that the previous year he had gone swimming in the Ganges and had also taken opium. Five days later, as Babur continued moving downstream, a scouting detachment of his men frightened Sultan Mahmud Ludi, who was still in the field with as many as 2000 men. He now fled from Babur's advancing army.

Following his success in intimidating, if not destroying, his Afghan foes, Babur turned briefly to consolidating his control of Bihar, first by sending Tardi Muhammad, Muhammad 'Ali Jang-jang's son, with 2000 men and conciliatory *farman*s to the 'Bihar people', presumably to notables of the province. Joining them was Khwajah Murshid 'Iraqi, whom Babur had appointed *Diwan*, or provincial revenue chief. He followed this by appointing the Baiqara Timurid and his son-in-law, Muhammad Zaman Mirza, as governor of Bihar. Babur granted him vice-regal status in a special ceremony, by presenting him with a sword, a belt, a special *tipuchaq* horse and, perhaps most significant, an umbrella – an Indian symbol of royalty. Babur proclaimed the exceptional nature of Muhammad Zaman Mirza's status by having his high-born son-in-law accept the appointment while kneeling before him in what amounted to a sovereign's feudal ritual. Regarding the treasury, a central concern for an impecunious, aspiring emperor, Babur writes that 1 *crore* and 25 *lac*s, of a Ludi-era estimated total of 4 *crore*s and 5 *lac*s, was reserved for the imperial treasury.[37] In theory, therefore, Muhammad Zaman Mirza was entrusted with an enormous income to support himself and his troops, if he could collect the amount listed in the Ludi records.

As Babur was conducting state business, he was awaiting news of the remnants of the Afghan forces that had earlier fled from his army. At this point in his narrative for mid-April 1529, he implies his goal of eliminating Afghan resistance hinged on the attitude of Nusrat Shah – the ruler of Bengal. Two spies, *iki jasus*, returned to Babur's camp on 15 April to report that a Bengali commander, who was fortifying sites along the Gandak River, had brought fleeing Afghans into his force.[38] Such an action, Babur recalls, made a confrontation with the Bengalis increasingly likely, and consequently, he ordered Muhammad Zaman Mirza to remain with him, while he sent a lower ranking officer to Bihar.

The following day, Babur told the Bengali *ilchi* or envoy, Isma'il Mita, to tell Nusrat Shah that the Bengali ruler must shortly deliver his answer to the 'Three Articles' Babur had sent to him earlier. Babur does not summarise these articles, but his comments imply that he demanded Nusrat Shah must continue to observe what Babur realistically characterises as, 'something resembling peaceful relations' and refuse to ally himself with Babur's Afghan enemies.[39] Two days later on 18 April, Babur reports telling Isma'il Mita that while he intended to pursue these enemies, no harm or damage would come to any territory, literally any 'land or water', *yer ve su*, dependent on him.[40] His messages offer additional insight into the process of Timurid *mulkgirliq*, Timurid imperialism, as Babur sought to extend his influence into Bengal by threats and conciliation.

Two days later, he dismissed the Bengali with the 'usual' *khilat* and gifts. A day later, he began trying to draw some prominent Afghans to his side by sending 'conciliatory orders and solicitous words' to Jalal Khan, son of Bihar Khan Nuhani, the former Afghan ruler of Bihar, and to Jalal Khan's mother Dudu. Previously, they had sent letters to Babur and struggled, Babur reports, to escape from the Bengalis. Jalal Khan led one of the three Afghan factions who competed for supremacy in the Gangetic Valley at this time. The other was Sultan Jalal al-Din Sharqi, son of Husain Shah, who had been conquered by Sikandar Ludi and Mahmud Ludi. Therefore, the three Afghan factions were led by the sons, respectively, of the last Ludi ruler of Agra and Delhi, the last ruler of Bihar and the last Sharqi ruler of Jaunpur.

A week later, following the conduct of business, Babur met with Murad Qurchi Qajar, a member of one of the Qizilbash Turkic tribes that brought Shah Isma'il Safavi to power in Iran.[41] He then made an excursion to view nearby lotus flowers, *nilufar,* and visited and circumambulated the tomb of Shaikh Yahya, the former head of the Chishti Sufi order. Babur then met with his Turk and Hind *amir*s. They finally planned to cross the Ganges to confront Nusrat Shah.

Babur takes great care in his narrative of this campaign to explain his use of firearms, now seemingly devoting more attention to their use than he had done even a year earlier. In part, he just seems to have been excited by the operation of these new weapons. He describes how he positioned his firearms' chief Ustad 'Ali Quli, who had developed the new weapons at Panipat, with his mortar and other weapons at a high point between the Saru and Ganges Rivers. The Ottoman Mustafa and his matchlock men, who had also served at Panipat, he stationed opposite part of the Bengali force on the bank of the Ganges. Babur ordered earth ramparts to be thrown up to shelter both groups. When these positions were prepared, four contingents were ordered to cross the river and attack the Bengalis. They were commanded by 'Askari, Sultan Jalal al-Din Sharqi, three Uzbek 'sultans', along with Mahmud Khan Nuhani of Ghazipur and Musa Sultan Farmuli. They were supported by Sultan Junaid Barlas, Babur's brother-in-law, who had brought 20,000 men, Babur writes, from Jaunpur.

On 1 May, Babur and the army crossed the river, and he describes the consequent battle, which occurred over the next four days, in considerable and often confusing detail. Two days later, they camped near Ustad 'Ali's position, where Babur reports that he enjoyed seeing him fire weapons to sink two

Bengali boats with stone projectiles. Afterwards, he sat and took some *ma'jun*, and later that evening, still under the influence of the drug, he slept in one of his boats that had been brought to the shore. The following day, he took a boat to observe more artillery firing. Meanwhile, Bengali forces crossed the river in two places and attacked 'Askari and Muhammad Zaman Mirza's forces, but were beaten off. On 5 May, the battle continued with Bengali cavalry brought up, to be countered by Babur's two Chaghatai Mongol relatives, Aisan Temur and Tukhta Bugha. They crossed the river in boats, with their men swimming their horses across alongside. Then, Babur writes, Lahori and Hindustani troops began crossing by swimming or holding bundles of reeds. At that point, Babur, seeing some Bengalis flee the field, ordered his men, who had crossed, to attack the Bengalis flank. The Bengali commander attacked Babur's forces with foot soldiers and cavalry, but were repulsed and ultimately defeated in a confused melee of combat.[42]

Following this victory, where firearms were used but not evidently to decisive effect – individual initiative, courage and heroism seem to have carried the day – Babur finally was able to enforce a peace upon the Nuhani Afghans and Nusrat Shah of Bengal. Ten days after the battle, he reaped his first political reward as Jalil Khan Nuhani, Darya Khan's grandson, visited Babur with his *amir*s, while Yahya Nuhani, having already sent his younger brother to offer submission, now came in person.

Babur describes how he responded to the submission of 7000 to 8000 Nuhanis, who had arrived 'with expectations', *bileh umidvarlïq*. He gave Mahmud Khan 50 *lac*s from Bihar revenues, after reserving 1 *crore* of these revenues for the royal treasury. He allotted the remainder of the Bihar revenues to Jalal Khan, who agreed to pay 1 crore of tribute or *khidmataneh*.[43] In these arrangements, Babur restored the Nuhanis to their positions in Bihar, but now as his tributaries. Still, they were semi-autonomous tributaries rather than officials of a Timurid state. The Timurid-Mughal bureaucratic state still lay in the future with Babur's grandson Akbar.

Three days later on 19 May, Babur received news from his recently returned emissaries to Nusrat Shah that the Bengali sultan had agreed to his three, but still unspecified, articles and desired peace. Commenting on these developments Babur wrote: 'Because this *yurush* was done to repel rebellious Afghans [and because] some of these rebels had taken themselves off and accepted service [and because] the rest who remained in service with the Bengali, who had received them [and because], the monsoon was imminent, we too, therefore, dispatched peaceful words about the previously stated conditions'.[44]

Four days later, Babur recalls, he felt 'at ease concerning Bihar and Bengal', but he was still determined to destroy two Afghan leaders who had eluded him, Shaikh Bayazid Farmuli and his comrade, Malik Biban Farmuli, whom he had been trying to run to ground the previous year.[45] Babur continued to pursue these two men even though the monsoon rains had begun by 25 May, when a sudden storm, typical of the season, blew through his camp and damaged his papers.

He records a memorable account of the storm, which is all the more meaningful because it apparently occurred when he was writing pages of the *Vaqayi'*.

> That evening after the *taravih* storm, it was the fifth *gari* of the first watch when the monsoon clouds boiled up. Within an instant an intense storm began. A powerful wind arose so that all but a few tents were flattened. I was inside the tent writing. There was no time to gather papers and sections. The tent and its portico fell right on my head. The tent's ventilation flap was shredded. God [Tengri] intervened; there was no injury. Book and sections were completely soaked and collected only with difficulty. Placing them on a wooden coverlet we piled kilims on top. Two *gari*s later it quieted down. Erecting a bedding tent, a candle was lit. Starting a fire after much difficulty we kept busy until dawn drying pages and sections, *auraq u ajza'*.[46]

In mentioning 'pages and sections', Babur seems most likely to be referring to his autobiography, rather than individual letters or orders.

Despite this storm, on 2 June, his serious concern with these two Afghans led him to convene a war council that decided to dispatch a force of elite officers to pursue them. It included two of his Chaghatai Mongol cousins, Muhammad Zaman Mirza and several other important *beg*s and Hindustan *amir*s. Babur persisted in his unsuccessful search for the two Afghans until the third week in June, but finally on 20 June he personally abandoned the pursuit. By then, the monsoon rains had made campaigning too difficult. Besides, as he notes, his horses were worn out, six months to the day after he had ridden east from Agra to attack the Afghans.[47] His men must also have been exhausted by this time. On 21 June, he ordered a return to Agra, and describes how fast he and his men rode to cover the approximately 157 miles in two and a half days.[48]

The Babri Masjid and Timurid Ideology

There is an important architectural footnote to Babur's eastern campaigns. This is the construction of the mosque in Ayodhya or Oudh, later known as the Babri Masjid, Babur's mosque, which Hindus destroyed in 1992. No evidence exists to explain the construction of the mosque, apart from two inscriptions on the building. These inscriptions indicate that Mir Baqi built it at Babur's orders sometime in 935 a.h. (September 1528–September 1529). One inscription reads in part: 'By the order of Babur Shah, whose justice is an edifice touching the heavens very heights. The felicitous Mir Baqi built this abode of angels.'[49] Babur visited the region in March 1529 while on his second eastern campaign, but he does not mention ordering the mosque built. It is impossible positively to identify Mir Baqi, the builder. It seems possible, although completely speculative, that this Mir Baqi was one of Babur's commanders, Baqi Beg Tashkindi, who fought with Babur at Chanderi and in his two eastern campaigns.

He might have constructed or completed the mosque sometime after Babur concluded this second campaign on 20 June 1529. The reason for suggesting this identity is that Baqi Beg retired to lands he had been assigned in and around Lucknow after Babur dismissed him and his commanders on 20 June. He might have had his name ceremonially inscribed as Mir Baqi. Given his position as Babur's officer and access to land revenue resources, he would have possessed the authority and means to finance the mosque. Mir Baqi may also have attributed the order to Babur merely as an action of a respectable officer honouring his sovereign.

Whatever the actual circumstances surrounding the construction of this mosque, Hindu nationalists' decision to make the building a symbol of temple desecration and Muslim oppression forcefully raises a complex question about the relationship between Babur's proudly proclaimed imperialism, his *mulkgirliq* ambitions and his religiosity. Does Babur's presumed order to build this mosque – or patronise its construction – symbolise his intent to establish a Muslim state in Hindustan? Two other mosques had earlier been built in his name: at Sambhal in 1526 and Panipat in 1527. He had earlier told Khwajah Kalan to build congregational mosques in Kabul – the single reference he makes in the *Vaqayi'* to mosque construction.[50]

Babur was a formally observant Muslim. He inherited and consciously embraced the Hanafi Sunni faith of his father 'Umar Shaikh Mirza with its special devotion to the Naqshbandi Sufi order and its Ahrari family representatives. Often he times daily events by reference to one of the five canonical prayers, which he observed when he could, as he illustrates by his account of the difficulties of doing so when he fell ill in Agra. Tutored at a young age by Khwajah Maulana-i Qazi, he religiously abstained from drinking until his early 20s and later invoked the power of Islam to bring him victory at Kanwah by renouncing drinking. While in Kabul, Babur employed an *'alim* to read him the Quran, and in 1521 or 1522, he versified the *Mubin*. Finally, near the end of his life, he allowed himself to be portrayed or instructed Mir Baqi to identify him in the mosque inscription, as a *qalandar*, an itinerant Sufi mystic, 'Celebrated in the world Babur, *qalandar*'. Muslim rulers often made such affirmations late in life to present themselves as worldly beggars, humbled before God and mortality.

Therefore, Babur was both a conspicuously observant and also an intellectually sophisticated Hanafi Sunni Muslim. Yet in the *Vaqayi'* he exhibits an emotional, psychologically-compelling piety only in connection with Sufi *pir*s. He repeatedly alludes to Sufi shrines, protecting one at the mouth of the Sakhi Sarwar Pass in 1505; circumambulating, *tavaf,* the tomb of Khwajah Khwand Said, probably a Naqshbandi Sufi, during a pleasure excursion near Kabul in 1519; circumambulating the important Chishti shrine in Delhi in 1526 and later doing the same at the tomb of the former head of the Chishti order Shaikh Yahya at the Son River in 1529.[51]

Readers of Babur's text cannot fail to notice that he repeatedly expresses an inherited but powerfully-enduring reverence for Khwajah 'Ubaidullah Ahrar (d. 1490) whom his father, and perhaps even the young Babur, had once met in Akhsı. For example, just before taking Samarqand for the second time in 1500, Babur reports recalling that, *Uşbu fursat-tah 'ajab tüş gördüm,* 'At that moment I had a wonderful dream... [that Ahrar spoke to him]' 'saying in Turki: Shaikh Maslahat [of Khujand] has given – and just so within a few days I took Samarqand'.[52] Then in November 1528, Babur, ill with fever, versified Khwajah Ahrar's *Walidiyyah-risala* as a pious act and was relieved of his illness within six days.[53]

In Mawarannahr, Naqshbandi Sufi shaikhs exerted great influence with the Muslim inhabitants, whether Mongols or Turks, as Babur's cousin Haidar Mirza demonstrates in his memoir when he speaks of 'The Eminent Order of the Khwajahs, God Sanctify [Them], *Silsileh-ye Aliyeh-ye Khwajagan Quds Allah*'.[54] An intense, personal belief in the spiritual power of Sufi *pir*s represented the core of Babur's religiosity. As anyone reading the *Vaqayi'* will come to understand that he was not a religious ideologue. When he leaves his predominantly Muslim Central Asian and Afghan lands for Hindustan, he never denounces or even refers to the predominantly Hindu population of India, although Babur does later invoke the rallying cry of *jihad* in desperation at Kanwah. Nor does he indulge in temple desecration or expressions of hostility to Hindus. In the text, it is only when he criticises Mongol barbarism that he asserts the superiority of Islam – not for its core beliefs, but as a faith that inculcates ethical behaviour and values social stability. In India while he refers to Rajput enemies as *kafir*s, or unbelievers, and desecrates Jain statues of naked worshippers, he characteristically criticises Hindus, not for their idol worship or polytheism, but for their social isolation, which he does not try to associate with – and may not have understood – Hindu concepts of pollution and rebirth.

Quite simply, Babur's conquest represents Timurid dynastic imperialism of a conqueror, who happened to be a Muslim. His unwavering ambition was to resurrect Timurid rule with himself as *Padshah*, initially at Samarqand and finally, desperately in Hindustan. He is best seen as the archetypal pragmatic Muslim sultan of the fourteenth-century Arab Muslim philosophical historian Ibn Khaldun – someone who professes Islam, patronises its institutions and respects its scholars, but keeps clerics at a respectful distance while governing according to the imperial, realpolitik traditions of the Sasanian Empire of Iran (224–651 CE).[55]

Babur and his men returned to Agra and dismounted at the *Hasht Bihisht Bagh*, the Eight-Paradises Garden, sometime after nine in the night on 23 June 1529. He may have galloped back so quickly because he had news that his wife Mahim Begim and her adopted daughter Gulbadan Begim were nearing Agra. Two days before they arrived, Babur spent time holding audiences with his paymaster and several unnamed individuals and visiting a Naqshbandi Khwajah, 'Abd al-Haqq, whom he 'attended', *mulazamat qildilar*, as he describes his respectful visit to the Shaikh. 'Abd al-Haqq had arrived in Agra on 24 January 1529, when Babur first 'attended' him. His far more famous brother Khwajah Makdum Nura, who spent most of his career in Mawarannahr, later came to India after Babur's death and met Humayun in Agra.[56] Babur's use of the term *mulazamat* echoes his description of other occasions when he visited either Sufis or female relatives and wished to emphasise a disciple's spiritual deference or his familial respect.

Babur's wife, daughter and servants had left Kabul on 27 January – the day Babur had begun his second eastern campaign. They finally did arrive at midnight on Saturday, 26 June, riding ahead of the other women and servants coming from Kabul. Babur hurried out on foot to meet them as they approached Agra.[57] The young Gulbadan (b. 1523) describes the scene, many years later during Akbar's reign.

> At *namaz-i sham* [the evening prayer] a person came [and] said [to Babur] I passed her Excellency two *kuruh*s [four miles] out. His excellency, my father, could not bear to wait for a horse to be brought but set out on foot and found [her] near the tent, *khanah* of Mahim's *nanachah*. My lady wished to dismount. My father the Padshah did not allow this and walked before my mother before reaching her own *khanah*.[58]

Babur's narrative becomes increasingly sketchy at this point, before it breaks off entirely on 7 September. His eight entries for the period from 26 June to 7 September just briefly mention Mahim's arrival and a formal audience on 7 July, when Babur received gifts from his wife and Humayun. Otherwise, he records audiences with various individuals and political troubles, first in Lahore and second in Gwalior. These only illustrate another dimension of the problems of state building, more prosaic than actual armed conflict with Afghans.

The people of Lahore coming from the city around 10 July reported that one Shaikh Sharaf of Qarabagh had written a letter or possibly a religious judgment accusing Babur of some unnamed oppression, *zulm*, and had distributed the document, which he had sent, to neighbouring towns. Undoubtedly, sensing that such an accusation, which he forcefully denies, could trigger unrest or revolt, he sent one Qambar-i 'Ali Arghun to arrest Shaikh Sharaf, the cleric who had signed his indictment, and another man.

The trouble in Lahore was potentially more serious than an obscure dispute Babur had with his governor of the fortress city of Gwalior, but the latter problem illustrates how much a *padshah* still had to rule through negotiation. The governor was Rahim Dad, the nephew of his long-time officer Mahdi Khwajah, who fought with him at Panipat and Kanwah. On 11 August, Babur was ready to ride south to Gwalior to demand the submission of Rahim Dad, who refused to come to Agra. Babur was dissuaded by his brother-in-law Khalifa/Nizam al-Din 'Ali Barlas, who persuaded Babur to write a conciliatory letter to Rahim Dad. Finally, in the last entry of his autobiography for 7 September, Babur mentions that he forgave the man's faults after the pious Shaikh Muhammad Ghaus interceded for him, but he nonetheless dispatched two other men to take charge of Gwalior.[59]

More meaningful personally and especially at this time in his life is the testimony of his daughter Gulbadan, who offers readers crucial information and moving personal testimony for days and months after Babur's *Vaqayi'* abruptly ends. Near the end of her description of her and her mother's reception in Agra, she writes that following a meal at Khalifa's and his wife's house, she went to pay her respects, *mulazamat*, to 'her father the Padshah', *Padshah-i babam*. After 'falling at his feet', *dar payi uftadam*, she says, 'his highness asked many questions and took me for a time in [his] arms and this insignificant one experienced such happiness that no greater [joy] was possible'.[60] Three months later, Gulbadan reports that she and her mother accompanied Babur when he went to Dhulpur, where she describes the 10-foot square tank he had ordered to be made. Later they went on to Sikri, where she describes a platform in the middle of a tank, where Babur would row, as well as a structure in the Sikri garden, where he would sit and write the book, *nishasteh mushaf minivishtand*. The book could only be the *Vaqayi'*, Babur's autobiography.

Afterwards, he returned to Agra to welcome the arrival of the remaining women who came from Kabul, including his sister Khanzadah Begim – the sister who once offered as a kind of ransom to Shibani Khan Uzbek in 1501 as he escaped from the Uzbek siege of Samarqand. Following a second marriage, she was now the wife of Mahdi Khwajah. When Khanzadah Begim and other women arrived in 1529, they largely completed the migration of Timurid and Chaghatai women that had begun on 23 November 1527 when two Timurid or paternal aunts of Babur, daughters of Abu-Sa'id Mirza – Fakhr Jahan and Khadija – arrived from Kabul, followed in October 1528 by three of their sisters – Gauhar Shad Begim, Badial Jamal Begim and Aq Begim.[61] Gulbadan does not mention the other women who originally left Kabul with her and her mother on 21 January, but they apparently included Shahr Banu, Khanzadah's half-sister and the wife of Khalifa's brother Junaid Barlas. Gulbadan enables readers to understand the full extent of this female migration when she lists the women who attended the famous Mystic Feast, which celebrated the accession of Humayun in 1531.[62]

Thirty-six of these women were Timurids and Chinggisids of one kind or another, including six daughters of Abu Sa'id Mirza, two of Babur's sisters, excluding Khanzadah Begim, a daughter of Husain Baiqara of Herat, and daughters of Sultan Ahmad Mirza of Samarqand, Ulugh Beg Mirza of Kabul, Sultan Mahmud Khan Chaghatai and Sultan Ahmad Khan Chaghatai, a sister of Mirza Haidar and two granddaughters of Sultan Husain Mirza. There were other *begim*s, writes Gulbadan, 'very many' making ninety-six in all, who received 'houses, and lands and gifts'.[63] She adds: 'During the period of four years when he [Babur] was in Agra, every Friday he went to see his paternal aunts', and he also ordered his architect to give priority to every request of theirs, no matter how grand the project.[64]

The Conspicuous Conjunction

By the summer of 1529, with Timurid and Chaghatai Chinggisid women safely arrived in Agra, Babur stood, confidently it seems, at the centre of a newly constituted Timurid-Mongol galaxy. It consisted of Timurid *mirza*s and Chaghatai Chinggisid *khan*s, their wives and relations, loyal Turkic and Mongol *beg*s, Naqshbandi Sufis and scholars, and artists from Husain Baiqara's former court in Herat. If Babur had been more pretentious than he appears, he could have taken the Temür's title for himself – *Sahib-Qiran,* the Lord of the Fortunate Conjunction, the conjunction of Jupiter and Venus. This was a title Jahangir briefly assumed and Shah Jahan openly proclaimed. Yet, just at this moment in 1529 of this memorable imperial conjunction, or because of it, Babur's seemingly inexhaustible energy and resolve weakened and his mood once again grew darker.

After welcoming the last of the *begim*s to Agra, Babur went to the *Bagh-i zarafshan*, the Gold-Scattering Garden, presumably named as a nostalgic reference to Samarqand's Zarafshan River. This was the very garden where he had paused on 20 January 1529 as he began his eastern campaign. According to his daughter Gulbadan, whose foster mother Mahim and other family members accompanied Babur, he told them he was tired, perhaps once again depressed. In the garden, she writes, there was an ablution house, *vozu-khaneh*, and seeing it, Babur reportedly said:

> I despair of governing and kingship. I shall retire to this garden and ask only for Tahir the ewer-bearer as a companion. I shall grant the kingship to Humayun. Upon [hearing] this my esteemed lady [Mahim] and all the children cried and despairing said, 'May God Most High in his mercy keep you in kingship for many years and countless decades and after you may all your children reach a distinguished old age.'[65]

Gulbadan follows her touching recollection of Babur's pensive mood almost immediately by her account of his final and self-sacrificial effort to save his son Humayun – as a son – and also as his chosen heir to the Timurid throne. As Babur's *Vaqayi'* breaks off on 7 September 1529, no other source exists which provides a personally informed account of how Babur performed a ritual that she and others believed saved his seriously ill son and precipitated his own death. What otherwise remains as a kind of preface to her moving narrative is Haidar Mirza's explanation for Humayun's sudden appearance in Agra sometime in the late-summer or early fall of 1529, in which Haidar Mirza also alludes to the last known reference to Babur's governance.

Haidar Mirza reports that sometime in 935 a.h./September 1528–September 1529, Babur ordered Humayun, his representative in Badakhshan since 1520, to return to Hindustan so that he will be present if Babur died.[66] It is commonly believed that Haidar Mirza's account politely masks Humayun's decision to precipitately abandon his critical northern Afghan command because he knew, most probably from his mother Mahim Begim, that Babur had been seriously ill.[67] This idea is corroborated by and perhaps originally based on Abu'l Fazl 'Allami's account in the *Akbar Namah*.[68] However, according to Haidar Mirza, who overlooks Humayun's role in Babur's invasion and the Panipat victory,

> From the year 926 [1520] until 935 [1528–29], Humayun Mirza was in Badakhshan... He [Babur] summoned Humayun Mirza to himself in order that one of his sons might be in the retinue so that in case he died there would be a successor present. For these reasons he summoned

> Humayun [but the people of Badakhshan] said 'Badakhshan is situated within the grasp of the Uzbeks, and they are ancient enemies of Badakhshan. The *amir*s are incapable of protecting Badakhshan'.[69]

Haidar Mirza continued by attributing the rush of events that followed to be a consequence of Humayun's abrupt departure. He writes that unnamed *amir*s of Badakhshan complained that Humayun's deputy, one Faqir 'Ali, was incapable of defending them. Faqir 'Ali was a minor figure, not a distinguished *beg*, who had been assigned to Balkh in 1517 despite being involved in the Mongol rebellion against Babur in March 1506 and very nearly executed at that time.[70] Humayun tried to compensate for his own absence by sending his 10-year-old younger brother Hind-al from Kabul to the Qalah Zafar fort in Badakhshan as a Timurid representative. In the meantime, Badakhshan leaders had sent multiple emissaries to Haidar Mirza's uncle and Babur's Mongol cousin Sa'id Khan Chaghatai to persuade him to come and defend the province. Otherwise, Haidar Mirza reports, the Badakhshan inhabitants were prepared to allow Uzbeks to enter the region.

Sa'id Khan, who had previously taken refuge with Babur in Kabul in 914 AH/ May 1508–June 1509, as a refugee from the Uzbeks, left his base at Kashgar in Xinjiang sometime in the fall of 1529. Accompanying him was Haidar Mirza, who was sent on ahead to Qalah Zafar. He arrived sometime between late December and January only to find that Hind-al had reached the fort eleven days earlier. Haidar Mirza reports that he tried to negotiate the surrender of the Qalah Zafar to Sa'id Khan, but failed. Then lacking food, he opted to raid the country around the fort for supplies and, after Sa'id Khan himself arrived, they besieged the fort unsuccessfully for three months.

According to Haidar Mirza, Sa'id Khan was unwilling to persist in a struggle with Hind-al, given Babur's previous protection of the Khan in Kabul. He told the Badakhshan leaders that he had come to the province to prevent an Uzbek invasion, but given the situation, he could not oppose Babur. The Khan may have told this to Haidar Mirza after he received an angry letter from Babur who learned of his Mongol cousin's entry into Badakhshan, probably sometime later in the winter of 1530, given the time it would have taken for a messenger to reach Hindustan. In what amounts to Babur's last recorded act as Padshah in Hindustan, Haidar Mirza reports that an angry Babur told the Khan that he was sending to Badakhshan the 16-year-old Sulaiman Shah Mirza, son of Wais Khan Mirza and grandson of Mahmud Mirza, the earlier Timurid ruler of the region. On Sulaiman Shah's arrival, Hind-al then turned the fort over to him and travelled south to Kabul, before going much later to Agra, while Sa'id Khan returned to Kashgar.[71]

Gulbadan says nothing about Humayun's abandonment of Badakhshan and his unexpected arrival in India in the fall of 1529, where he is known to have first travelled to Agra. Babur subsequently ordered his son to go to his fief at Sambhal, where he is reported to have stayed for six months. Babur had awarded him Sambhal in July 1526.[72] Instead, following her description of Babur's declaration at the Gold-Scattering Garden, she continues her preoccupation with family affairs. First, she describes the sickness and death of the infant Alwar Mirza, the son of Babur and Dildar Begim, the natural mother of Humayun. She characterises Babur as regretful and sad, *ta'suf u gham*, while Mirza Alwar's mother Dildar Begim was sorrowful and anguished, *gham u ghusseh*, at the death of her child. Gulbadan adds, 'When the grieving exceeded all bounds, the Esteemed Padshah said to my lady [Mahim] and to the Begims, "Come, let us make an excursion to Dhulpur"'. Then, just after they went 'happily and pleasantly by water', a message arrived from Delhi that Humayun had fallen seriously ill.[73]

The news of Humayun's illness so worried Mahim that she left Dhulpur for Delhi, but she met her son in Mathura. Then, writes Gulbadan, '*Har du mader u pesar, manand-i 'Isa u Maryam, mutavajjeh Agra shudand*', 'Both mother and son, like Jesus and Mary, they set out for Agra'.[74] When Babur now returned to Agra, he was shocked at the condition of his son. Mahim told Babur he ought not to be so concerned because he had other sons, but she was sad because she had but one son. Babur replied, Gulbadan writes, 'Mahim, although I have other sons, but I do not love any son as much as your Humayun'. *Mahim, agarcheh farsandan-i digar daram, amma hich farzandi barabar-i Humayun-i tu dust namidaram.* He continued by saying that he wanted his 'beloved son Humayun', the 'rarity of the age' – and not others – to inherit *sultanat and padshahi*, power and kingdom. And while some have theorised that Babur might have preferred another Timurid to succeed him, he unmistakably and publically indicated his choice of Humayun in the letter he had sent to his oldest son, which he includes in the *Vaqayi'*. The idea that he might have preferred Muhammad Zaman Mirza, another Timurid or even a Chinggisid, is purely speculative and perhaps ex-post facto wishful thinking, considering Humayun's loss of India following his defeats by Shir Khan Suri in 1539 and 1540.[75]

In any event, Humayun's condition persisted until one Mir Abu Baqa, in Abu'l Fazl's words 'one of the most distinguished men of the age' and possibly a Naqshbandi shaikh, spoke up. He reported that ancient sages said, in hopeless cases one must sacrifice the single most valuable thing and beseech God for a cure. Babur replied that he himself was Humayun's most valuable thing and added 'I shall be his sacrifice'.[76] Gulbadan reports he said: 'If a life may be sacrificed for a life, I who am Babur, offer my life and soul for Humayun'. *Agar be'ivaz-i jan, jan mubdal shaved, man keh Babaram 'amr u jan hudra be Humayun bakhshidam.* He then circumambulated the sick bed three times and, feeling a strange effect, cried out 'We have borne it away'. Babur then was stricken with a deadly fever, which worsened as Humayun swiftly recovered.

Following Humayun's recovery, he left Agra seemingly unaware of Babur's illness or the seriousness of his condition, but he hurried back after he heard the news. It is Gulbadan who once again supplies the only eyewitness testimony of Babur's last days, reports which she must have learned from Mahim and other women. Her account of his illness persuasively conveys the sense of the irascible self-absorption of a dying man. It begins with her description of Babur repeatedly asking why Hind-al, now age 11, had not yet arrived, which leads him to blame the son of Hind-al's guardian Mir Baqi Beg for delaying him in Lahore, celebrating Mir Baqi's marriage there. He even calls the poor man a *mardak*, his preferred insult for enemies or a term which he simply applies to people he disliked, in this instance just striking out in an emotional outburst. In this passage, Gulbadan seems to be describing the frustration of a semi-delirious man. He repeatedly said, she reports, 'Alas. A thousand times alas that I do not see Hind-al, and asking everyone, when will Hind-al come?'[77]

Yet during his illness Babur turned to dynastic marital questions by commanding Mahim to tell his sister Khanzadah Begim to arrange marriages for Gulrang Begim and Gulchira Begim, Gulbadan's 'Rosecolored' and 'Rosyfaced' sisters. He wanted them married to the two Chaghatai Mongol brothers, Ishan Khan and Tukhta Bugha Khan, the ninth and tenth sons of his deceased Mongol uncle Ahmad Khan. These two men had joined Babur in Hindustan and had been fighting with him during the second eastern campaign. They were brought before Babur and made to kneel before him, thus, formally raising them, as Gulbadan notes, to the status of sons-in-law, '*Har du sultananra zanuzananideh beh damadi sarafraz bekonand.*'[78] By ordering these marriages, Babur replicated his own dual lineage, but on the matrilineal side, yielding Mughul-Timurid offspring and extended it into the next generation.

Babur's health continued to decline. Describing his illness, Gulbadan voices her belief or more probably repeats the stories she heard from her mother and other women that Babur's symptoms resembled those he suffered when he had been poisoned at the order of Sultan Ibrahim's mother in 1525. Yet, she does little more than mention the resemblance, which shifts her narrative from the miracle of spiritual sacrifice to an unexplained sinister possibility. Leaving this idea quickly aside, she continues with her story of Babur's last days during which he reiterated his weariness with what he has termed *sultanat* and *padshahi*, the everyday work of *mulkgirliq*, as well as reconfirming his desire to see Humayun succeed him. Babur repeated his 'earlier wish', *delam dashtam*, when sitting in the Gold-Scattering Garden, to retire to the garden, while giving the *padshahi* to Humayun. He 'commanded', *wasiyat mikonam*, Gulbadan writes, that everyone must acknowledge Humayun in Babur's place, while entrusting Humayun with the care of his bothers, kin and people.

> When the women of the haram and intimate people heard this grievous news they were stunned and bewildered and they cried and lamented. Three days later on December 21st 1530 he passed from the transitory to the eternal world. [79]

Babur was initially buried in the Aram Bagh, appropriately 'The Garden of Rest', across the river from the later site of the Taj Mahal. Gulbadan, seven or eight years old at the time, describes the aftermath of Babur's death in poignant prose recalling her own desolation at his death, as well as the equally devastating loss of Mahim three years later in 1533. Humayun ordered sixty reciters to be appointed to recite the five daily prayers, read the entire *Quran* and pray for *Firdaus-makani*, 'He who dwells in Paradise'. The grave was endowed as a *waqf*, a charitable endowment, supported by the entire revenue of Sikri and 5 *lac*s of revenue from Bianah to support its reciters and *'ulama'*. Mahim financed a twice-daily delivery of food from her own holdings, an ox, two sheep and a goat in the morning and five goats at the afternoon prayer.[80] Babur's body was later carried to Kabul (Illustration 5), sometime between 1533 and 1544, and interred in a simple grave atop a hill offering the type of picturesque view, or *nazargah*, that he had prized throughout his life. His great-grandson Jahangir visited the tomb in 1607 where he read and annotated Babur's *Vaqayi'*.[81] His son Shah Jahan also visited the grave site in 1640 and altered its simple, unadorned construction with his typical architectural élan, adding a white marble enclosure, a mosque and a pool and a house for pilgrims.[82] There it still stands, having survived decades, even centuries of neglect and the post-Soviet Taliban wars.

Endnotes

1   See Beveridge's typically thoughtful note on the Rampur Diwan in Appendix Q of her *Babur-Nama* text, lxi. As she notes, Shah Jahan made a marginal note in the surviving copy identifying the handwriting of the verse as Babur's.

2   Bilal Yücel, *Bâbür Dîvânı*, no. 319: 260.

3   The Ghaznavid poet Mas'ud Sa'd Salmân of Lahore (d. 1121) used *ghurbat* as a principal theme of his verse, and he was far from the first Persian poet to exploit the image. See Sunil Sharma, *Persian Poetry at the Indian Frontier, Mas'ûd sa'd Salmân of Lahore* (Delhi: Permanent black, 2000), 47–56.

4   I. V. Stebleva, *Semantika Gazelï Babura* (Moscow: Nauka, 1982), no. 119: 327; Bilal Yücel, *Bâbür Dîvânı*, no. 124: 190; Azimdzhanova, *Indïskiï Divan Babura* (Tashkent: Fan, 1966), 49–50.

5   Yücel, *Bâbür Dîvânı*, no. 330: 263.

6   Ibid.

7   BN–M, fs. 350b–351a.

8   BN–M, f. 353b.

9   BN–M, fs. 355a–b.

10   BN–M, f. 375b. Babur inserts this comment later in the text, where he describes making peace in May with Nusrat Shah, the ruler of Bengal. He may have done so to explain to readers that despite his suspicion and criticism of the Bengali ruler, he never intended to attack Bengal.

11   BN–M, fs. 356b–357a.

12   See Stephen F. Dale and 'Alam Payind, 'The Ahrârî Waqf in Kabul in the Year 1546 and the Mughûl Naqshbandiyyah,' *Journal of the American Oriental Society*, 119, No. 2 (April–June, 1999), 218–33. This *waqf* served as an economic basis for Ahrari Naqshbandis and a refuge during the Suri interregnum between 1540 and 1555.

13   Dale and Payind, 'The Ahrârî Waqf in Kabul in the Year 1546 and the Mughûl Naqshbandiyyah,' 221.

14   BN–M, fs. 358b–361a.

15   BN–M, f. 359a.

16   BN–M, f. 360b.

17   BN–M, fs. 360b–361a.

18   BN–M, f. 359a–b.

19   Apart from Khanzadah Begim, whom Babur had abandoned in Samarqand in 1501, but who, after being rescued by Shah Isma'il Safavi, was now the wife of Mahdi Khwajah, it would have probably included Shahr Banu Begim, Khanzadah's half-sister, the divorced wife of Husain Baiqara, who was now the wife of Sultan Junaid Barlas, the grandson of Nizam al-Din 'Ali Khalifa. Junaid Barlas served on the left wing at Panipat. There were also family members of

three important Timurids in the city, all relatives of Sultan Husain Baiqara: Muhammad Sultan Mirza, grandson of Mahmud Mirza of Badakhshan and son of Wais Mirza, who ruled later in Badakhshan, fought at Panipat and Kanwah; Qasim Husain Sultan Mirza, son of Husain Baiqara's daughter 'Ayisha Sultan Begim, who was an Uzbek and fought at Kanwah; and Muhammad Zaman Mirza, the grandson and last surviving direct heir of Husain Baiqara and son of Husain's son Badi' al-Zaman Mirza, married to Babur's daughter. He served in Balkh and later in India and contested the throne after Babur's death. See *Humayun Namah* (HN), Introduction, 16–22 for Gulbadan Begim's discussion of relatives in Kabul.

20 HN, 118–123.

21 BN–M, f. 350a.

22 Beveridge, in one of her insightful notes, suggests that the phrase 'legally taken from revenue' may refer to the creation of a *waqf* or endowment in which funds are permanently alienated to support, in this case, a religious institution. BN–B, 646, n. 6.

23 The phrase is Maria Eva Subtelny's apt characterisation of Temür's predatory history in her volume *Timurid's in Transition, Turco-Persian Politics and Acculturation in Medieval Iran*, 14.

24 BN–M, f. 45a.

25 Azimdzhanova, *Gosudarstvo Babura v Kabule i v Indii*. See especially Chapter 12, 'Taxation Policies of Babur.'

26 Jackson, *The Delhi Sultanate*, 316–17.

27 Jackson, *The Delhi Sultanate*, 317.

28 BN–M, fs. 18a and 229b. *Istiqamat* is an Arabic term that connotes integrity, honesty or stability. Babur does not explain the nature of these grants.

29 BN–M, f. 241b. *Tiyul* assignments were land grants usually made to the military. The term's meaning varies greatly from one era and region to another.

30 The term *wajhdar* was still in use during the early years of the reign of his grandson Akbar. For an example, see Saiyid Zaheer Husain Jafri, 'A Farmân of Akbar (1558) from the Period of the Regency,' in *Akbar and His India, ed. Irfan Habib* (Delhi: Oxford University Press, 1997), 266–67.

31 I. P. Petrushevskiĭ describes the *soyurghal* institution in his article 'K Istorii Instituta Soǐurgala,' in *Sovetskoe Vostokovedenie*, ed. V.V. Struve *et al.* (Moscow: Izdael'stvo Akademii Nauk, 1949), 227–46.

32 See Iqbal Husain, 'Akbar's Farmâns – A Study in Diplomatic,' in *Akbar and His India*, ed. Irfan Habib, 66.

33 *Shiqdar*, an important administrative and revenue official in the early Timurid-Mughal era, was later replaced by the term *karori*. Irfan Habib, 'Three Early Farmâns of Akbar in Favour of Ramdas, the Master Dyer,' in *Akbar and His India*, ed. Habib, 275–76.

34 BN–M, f. 113b.

35 BN–M, f. 364a.

36 BN–M, f. 365a–b.

37 BN–M, fs. 367b & 292a–293a.

38 BN–M, f. 368a.

39 BN–M, f. 368b.

40 BN–M, f. 369a.

41 As one of the successor dynasties to the Safavids, the Qajars ruled Iran from 1785 until the early twentieth century.

42 This is the fourth of Babur's battles, Qandahar, Panipat, Kanwah and now Ghogra, which Babur and Shaikh Zain have described in great detail, if not exhaustively, and these accounts collectively represent a unique record of warfare in distinct environments and against markedly different foes.

43 BN–M, f. 375b. Five days later, four more Afghan chiefs and their *amir*s arrived and submitted to Babur.

44 BN–M, fs. 375b–376a.

45 BN–M, f. 376a.

46 BN–M, f. 376b.

47 BN–M, f. 380.

48 Beveridge gives the distance from their last camp to Agra. BN–B, p. 686, n. 1.

49 BN–B, Appendix U. Beveridge analyses the inscriptions and identifies the date using the *abjad* system where each of the twenty-eight letters of the Arabic alphabet is assigned a number.

50 Katherine Blanshard Asher, *Architecture of India*, Part 1, Volume 4 (Cambridge: Cambridge University Press, 1991), 28–29.

51 BN–M, f. 369b. As Beveridge carefully notes, BN–B, 666, n. 3, this man's son, Sharaf al-Din Muniri (d. 1380/81), wrote works that Abu'l Fazl later read to Akbar.

52 BN–M, f. 83b.

53 BN–M, fs. 346a–b.

54 TR, II, 10 and III, 8 n. 3 and see index for Haidar Mirza's multiple references to Naqshbandi lineages.

55 For a discussion of Ibn Khaldun's political analysis, see Dale, *The Orange Trees of Marrakesh: Ibn Khaldun and the Science of Man*, 207–226.

56 According to Haidar Mirza, Khwajah Makhdum Nura was marginalised in Agra by a Hindustani Shaikh Phul, and eventually left Agra for Lahore, where Haidar Mirza met him in 1535/36. Haidar Mirza accounted for his exceptional Timurid rejection of their 'hereditary attachment' to Naqshbandi Khwajahs to Humayun's like of the Arabic sciences and attachment to a man whose 'spells and incantations... suited his 'own temperament,' *muvafeq mizaj-i khud yafteh ast*. TR, III, f. 321, 246. Based on Humayun's own testimony, Haidar Mirza implicitly dismisses Shaikh Phul as something of a fraud.

57　BN–M, f. 380b. Babur notes the coincidence of these dates.

58　HN, f. 14a. Gulbadan Begim, writing so many years later, does not make the scene entirely clear. It seems apparent from the narrative that Mahim's entourage had camped just north of Agra, intending to enter the city the following day. *Nanachah*, 'little mother', as Beveridge notes, is likely an affectionate term for an intimate family servant. HN, p. 101, n. 1.

59　BN–M, fs. 381b–382a.

60　HN, f. 15a.

61　BN–M, fs. 331b & 344b.

62　See Lisa Balabanlilar, 'The Begims of the Mystic Feast: Turco-Mongol Tradition in the Mughal Harem,' *Journal of Asian Studies* 69, no. 1 (February 2010): 123–47.

63　HN, fs. 24a–26b and fs. 11a–b.

64　HN, f. 11b.

65　HN, f. 15b. Ruby Lal discusses the significance of Gulbadan's fascinating memoir in her article 'Rethinking Mughal India, the Challenge of a Princess's Memoir,' *Economic and Political Weekly* 38, 1 (4 January 2003): 53–65.

66　TR, f. 214a. Humayun was technically in charge of the north but he often could be found in Kabul.

67　Beveridge, in her carefully considered attempt to reconstruct Humayun's and Babur's actions in the period not covered by the *Vaqayi'*, indicates Humayun reached Kabul before 26 August 1529. BN–B, 696. This information is based on her husband's note in his translation of *The Akbar Nama* cited above, I, 272, n. 1.

68　See, for example, the opinion of Erskine, *A History of India under the First Two Sovereigns of the House of Taimur, Bâber and Humâyun*, Volume 1, 508–09. Beveridge persuasively argues the same point in her translation of the Turki text. BN–B, pp. 694–98. For Abu'l Fazl's account, partly based on Haidar Mirza's testimony, and his summary of events preceding Babur's death, see H. Beveridge trans., *The Akbar Nama*, Volume 1 (New Delhi: ESS ESS Publications, repr. 1987), 271–77.

69　TR, f. 214a.

70　BN–M, f. 215b.

71　Beveridge, citing Ahmad Yadgar's *Tarikh-i salatin-i Afghanah (History of the Afghan Sultans)* indicates that Babur probably made a trip to Lahore, where Kamran was at that moment, in early 1530, returning to the Delhi region in late March or April, where he spent two months hunting. BN–B, 693–701.

72　BN–B, p. 697. Beveridge, *The Akbar Nama*, Volume 1, 275.

73　HN, f. 16a.

74　HN, f. 16b.

75　Beveridge summarises these theories with her usual care. She supports the possibility that Babur may have preferred Muhammad Zaman Mirza. BN–B, Appendix B, pp. 702–08.

76　Beveridge, *The Akbar Nama*, Volume 1, 275–76 and n. 3.

77 HN, f. 18a.
78 HN, f. 18b.
79 HN, f. 19b.
80 HN, 19b–23b.
81 TJ, I, 108–09.
82 Maria Teresa Shephard Papagliolo lovingly described and photographed the tomb and discussed its later history and 1970 plans for restoration in her study, *Kabul: the Bagh-i Babur: A Project and a Research into the Possibilities of a Complete Reconstruction* (Rome: IsMEO, 1972), 1–33.

Conclusion

Babur's Second Life

In his history of the Mongol Khans, Haidar Mirza Dughlat Kürägän (d. 1551) included what amounted to an obituary of Babur, who, Haidar Mirza gratefully reports, treated him like a son after he took refuge with Babur in Kabul in 1509. Writing in Persian, he says of his older Timurid cousin:

> He is a ruler adorned with accomplishments and praiseworthy characteristics. Of all his qualities, bravery and gallantry are dominant. In Turkish poetry, after Mir Ali Shir, no one has composed so much as he has. He also has a verse composition called *Mubin* on jurisprudence, and it is a very useful treatise and commended by all. He has written a tract on Turkish metrics, and before him no one has ever written on that topic so nicely. He versified His Holiness's ['Ubaidullah Ahrar] treatise the *Walidiyya*. He has also written his 'events' as his history in Turkish is called. It is extremely smooth and flowing, and his pure style is chaste and easy to understand... In music and other things probably no one from his family was ever so accomplished as he. Amazing things and astonishing battles have happened to him, the likes of which have never happened to his peers.[1]

Later in the century Abu'l Fazl 'Allami (1551–1602), Akbar's chronicler, produced a more elaborate memorial to Babur. Using the florid style beloved of literate Persian-speaking intellectuals, such as Shaikh Zain Khwafi, the chronicler of the Battle of Kanwah, Abu'l Fazl, wrote:

> It would be impossible even if volumes were employed to detail the perfections of this Holy One. Among them he possessed the eight essentials of empire, *viz.* (1) high fortune; (2) great designs; (3) conquering power; (4) administrative capacity; (5) civilizing faculty; (6) devotion to the welfare of God's servants; (7) the cherishing of the army; (8) the restraining it from evil.

> And in acquired accomplishments, he was at the head of his Age. He held high rank as a poet and a prose writer, and especially in Turki poetry. The Turki *dîwân* (*dîwân-i-turki*) of his Majesty is of great eloquence and purity, and its contents are charming. His book of *Masnawî* which has

the name *Mubîn* (clear) is a famous composition and is mentioned with great applause by critics. He versified the *Risâla-i-wâldîya* of Khwâja Ahrâr which is a pearl from the ocean of knowledge, and very excellent it was. He also wrote his Acts (*Wâqi'ât*) from the beginning of his reign to the time of departure with fidelity and in a lucid and eloquent style. It is an Institute for all earthly sovereigns and a manual for teaching right thoughts and proper ideas. This Institute of dominion and fortune was, by the world-obeyed king of kings, translated into Persian... in the 34th year of the Divine Era [1580]... so that its exquisite bounties might moisten the lips of all the thirsty and that its hidden treasures might be beheld by those whose hands were empty of learning. His majesty was also eminently skilled in music and composed charming verses in Persian... [and] was also famous for treatises on prosody, and among them is a book called *Mufassal* which is a commentary on the science.[2]

Unlike Haidar Mirza, the soldier and later governor of Kashmir, and Abu'l Fazl, the court functionary and historian, William Erskine, the nineteenth century Edinburgh trained lawyer, East India Company official and Persian scholar praises Babur for his individual qualities and as a writer who reveals the individuality of others. These are the qualities which continued to attract readers in the twentieth and twenty-first centuries, leading scholars, such as Jean-Paul Roux, to justify his biography of Babur with a rhetorical question, 'Why Babur?' to which he answers, 'Because his literary works deliver to us everything, with his qualities and faults, especially his daily inner self, in his most casual moods, in his most profound thoughts, which often could have been our own.'[3] Babur does give readers an deeply engaging sense of himself as a decidedly imperfect person, a driven, egotistical but reflective and often a vulnerable individual trying to survive the literal 'slings and arrows of outrageous fortune' or, in his particular case, an individual trying to find his way through the unchartered minefields of Turco-Mongol politics in the fifteenth and sixteenth centuries, while observing so much and so well.

Muslim authors produced a significant number of retrospective personal narratives before Babur wrote, but most of their works that have been considered to be autobiographies ought to be re-classified as memoirs.[4] These include such works as the spiritual reflections of the Iranian theologian al-Ghazali (1056–1111) and Ibn Khaldun's detailed account of his life in North Africa, Andalusia and Egypt.[5] A few members of the warrior elite produced works that more closely resemble modern autobiographies. Two of these are the *Tibyan*, written by the eleventh-century Berber *amir* of Granada Ibn Buluggin (d. c. 1095) and the *Kitab al-I'tibbar* by the late twelfth-century Arab noble

Usamah ibn Munqidh (d. 1188).[6] Babur belonged to this class of authors as a sultan and a writer, but his work is vastly more ambitious, far more personally compelling and reflective than either of those works, partly due to his inclusion of introspective verse. It is not difficult to argue that Babur's *Vaqayi'* represents the greatest pre-modern autobiography in the Islamic or Central Asian world and that it also constitutes the most compelling royal autobiography ever written in any civilisation.

Babur's appeal as an individual and stature as a writer has remained undimmed since Erskine wrote, but the question of his role as the founder of an empire is more problematic. It is important to reiterate that Babur led a very small force when he entered Hindustan in December 1525. Additionally some of his most trusted commanders, such as the man who seems to have been his closest friend, Khwajah Kalan, returned to Kabul shortly after Panipat, with others following after Kanwah. Even 2 years after Kanwah his total armed force cannot have been very large. Nor did he arrive in India with the acclaim he briefly experienced when he re-entered Samarqand in 1511. Quite the opposite, for as he candidly describes the situation in and around Agra after Panipat, he and his men were surrounded by a hostile local populace. Rulers such as Rana Sanga' and some tens of thousands of well-armed Afghans were even more threatening. His only recourse was to use his small force, composed largely of Turco-Mongol foreigners, to conquer or at least overawe one Indian fortress after another in order to establish the Indian legitimacy that he could gradually accrue from repeated military victories.

He gives the impression that from December 1528 through 1529 he felt confident about the stability of his new Timurid Empire. Yet, when he died in December 1530, his control of Hindustan was decidedly limited. By then he had succeeded in establishing the Timurids as the paramount power in the Punjab, the Duab and the Gangetic Valley. Given his ceaseless activity and attention to every kind of imaginable detail that he demonstrated in the letter sent to an old friend, Khwajah Kalan, in Kabul in February 1529, it seems likely that he would have begun to establish an administration in Agra during this period. Still, he gives no indication that he had been able to move beyond temporary rule through a post-conquest military feudalism of *wajhdar*s to begin creating the administration of a bureaucratic state. His Afghan 'sword not pen' guide to revenue collection held true in Hindustan to a considerable degree at the time of his death. His need to generate revenue through plundering campaigns and partial reliance on funds that his *beg*s – now in his Hindustan section *amir*s – could bring from their *parganah*s indicates that he did not have an effective revenue system in place. He possessed Ludi revenue records, but that does not mean he controlled former Ludi officials, whose own administration is not well understood.

Babur's second campaign against the coalition of Afghan forces in the Gangetic Valley in 1529 highlights the fundamental difficulties of moving beyond military victories to actual governance. While he successfully intimidated Afghans and Nusrat Shah with his army, now endowed with a suddenly effective corps of paid troops wielding firearms, Babur nonetheless left the Afghans intact, even if many Ludis and other chiefs had agreed to accept Babur's authority. With his experience in Kabul he would have known better than anyone else that Afghans, whether Yusufza'is or Hazarahs in Afghanistan, or Ludis, Luhanis or other Afghan tribes in Hindustan, could not be easily controlled, much less effectively subjugated. While riven with conflicting tribal and personal factions, Afghans in India still comprised an ethnic core of fellow Pushtuns in the Punjab, the Duab and the Gangetic Valley. If he had survived, Babur would have had to return again and again to finally subjugate the Indo-Afghan populations. As it was, within six months of Babur's death the Afghan chiefs Bayazid Farmuli and Malik Biban Jilwani or Ludi renewed their challenge to the Timurids.

Babur, based at least on his own record, did everything possible to train his son Humayun to rule, from trying to teach him to write lucid letters to persuading him to exhibit aggressive instincts expected of a young Timurid warrior. Yet, he also bequeathed to him a toxic political legacy, three living brothers and two ambitious Baiqara Timurids. Humayun struggled to rule, while contending with the very same problems that had bedevilled Babur in Ferghanah and to a lesser extent in Kabul – the sovereign ambitions of Timurids.[7]

Yet, while both of Babur's younger brothers had died by 1515, Humayun's brothers, Kamran, Askeri and Hind-al, were active and apparently healthy young *mirza*s in 1530. By their actions, typical of their Turco-Mongol ancestors, they showed that they did not conceive of Timurid Hindustan as a unitary state, but as an opportunity to realise their own sovereign aspirations. They drifted in and out of cooperation with Humayun and competed with one another for precedence. In 1538, Hind-al even briefly proclaimed his sovereignty in Delhi, having the *khutba* read in his name while Humayun was campaigning in the east.[8]

Added to this dangerous political mix were Husain Baiqara's two descendants in India, who, despite being the beneficiaries of Babur's success and generosity, did not display the least bit of gratitude when it came to their benefactor's son. Muhammad Zaman Mirza, Husain Baiqara's grandson, and Muhammad Sultan Mirza, maternal cousin, never offered their loyalty to Humayun, but manoeuvred for political advantage. Gulbadan Begim denounced them for causing what she describes as 'constant disturbance' for Humayun between 1530 and 1540.⁹ Even the Safavid historian Hasan-i Rumlu knew of Muhammad Zaman Mirza's sovereign ambitions and reluctance to accept Humayun's authority.¹⁰

It seems likely that Humayun would have both survived and prospered, had he been able to command the loyalty of these five individuals. He might even have survived without their loyalty but for personal failings. In the course of writing, the *Vaqayi',* Babur suggests that Humayun, among other noticeable character flaws, lacked aggressive instincts and was far too self-indulgent. His son also seems to have spelled badly. Haidar Mirza was far more frank in identifying some of Humayun's serious faults, which he observed after he arrived in India around 1536, joining Humayun sometime later in Agra. While praising the emperor's innately good character, he criticised him for surrounding himself with 'evil, vile and profligate men' and for indulging in opium. Haidar Mirza writes that unnamed people attributed every questionable act of Humayun's to his opium addiction and reports that when he arrived in Agra unidentified, people said that Humayun's 'greatness and magnitude' were nothing compared to what they had been earlier.¹¹ Whatever the precise meaning of this comment, Haidar Mirza's eyewitness reports of Humayun's defeat at the Battle of the Ganges in 1539 suggests that he did not possess the dynamic leadership skills his father exhibited on different occasions.

Still, Humayun campaigned aggressively after he succeeded Babur in December 1530. In 1532, he defeated and killed Sultan Bayazid Farmuli. He later commanded successful campaigns against other Indian rulers, most notably defeating Sultan Bahadur of Gujarat in 1535 before abandoning the campaign. Lacking a personal narrative for Humayun, it is difficult to fairly evaluate his stature as a ruler, commander and individual in these years. Nonetheless, the first-hand account of Haidar Mirza represents the nearest thing to objective reporting at this time.

When it comes to the details of Humayun's loss in 1539, Haidar Mirza, who reports that he himself commanded the Timurid's 13,000 troops, states that the precipitate cause of Humayun's defeat was Kamran Mirza's decision to withdraw from the army and return to his base of Lahore with 1,000 commanders and troops. He states,

> Kamran Mirza's withdrawal was the cause of Shir Khan's good fortune and a reversal in fortune for the Chaghatay [the Timurids]. No matter how much the emperor insisted that most of the commanders and

soldiers be left, Kamran Mirza strove in opposition to take all the Agra
men with them.[12]

Still, the question remains why Haidar Mirza and not Humayun himself
commanded the Timurid forces he later estimates at 40,000, whose leaders
broke ranks and fled as 15,000 Afghans attacked them. Humayun must be
charged with responsibility for allowing such a shocking disintegration of the
Timurid army.

Humayun's subsequent defeat at Qanauj and his abandonment of Hindustan
between 1540 and 1555 meant that Babur's nascent Hindustan empire ceased
to exist. Shir Khan Suri ably governed Hindustan for the next 5 years, before
giving way to less commanding Afghan rulers. The fact of this interregnum has
meant that scholars routinely ignore Babur when discussing the foundation of the
Mughal Empire.[13] Yet, Babur bequeathed the idea of an empire to Humayun and
Akbar and to many Timurids and Chaghatais who fled back to Kabul in 1540. The
idea of a Timurid Empire and its Perso-Islamic culture survived the interregnum.
It was aided no doubt by the many Timurid loyalists, such as Khanzada Begim,
Babur's resilient sister, who cared for the infant Akbar for a brief period in Kabul
just before Humayun retook the city from Kamran.

It was Akbar who ensured that Babur would enjoy a second life within
Timurid-Mughal imperial circles by issuing an order to those who had known
him to write down whatever they recalled of the *Padshah* otherwise known
by his posthumous name *Firdaus-makani*, Dwelling in Paradise. This is the
origin of Gulbadan Begim's book. Noting that she was only 8-years-old when
her father died, Gulbadan writes that she may not recall much, but that she
would record whatever she heard or remembered.[14] She begins by summarising
Babur's history while noting that this was told in his memoirs, which she knew
in one language or another. By the time she wrote or dictated her memoir in
Persian Babur's *Vaqayi'* had been translated into Persian by Mirza Khan, Khan-i
Khanan, the son of Akbar's tutor, Bairam Khan.[15] At that time, the *Vaqayi'* had
also been illustrated in Akbar's atelier, whose artists produced different works
that linked Akbar with the Turco-Mongol past and the broader Perso-Islamic
world.[16]

While Babur has not retained a conspicuous second life in most modern
scholarly or popular literature devoted to the history of the Timurid-Mughal
Empire, events in the last decade of the twentieth century have, in radically
different ways, revived his memory in both India and his Central Asian
homeland. Thus, in 1991 and 1992, Babur's second life suffered from resurgent

political Hindusim, some of whose spokesmen reviled him for constructing the mosque in Ayodhya. At almost exactly the same time, newly minted nationalists in Uzbekistan glorified his memory to bolster the ideology of the suddenly independent Uzbek state.

In India, during the 1980's the Ayodyah mosque that became known as the Babri Masjid symbolised anti-Hindu Timurid Muslim imperialism for groups of organised Hindu activists. The widespread belief that pillars had been taken from a Vaishavite temple to construct the mosque was denounced and Babur was directly blamed for the supposed desecration. It was said that 'Traditions and records of all kinds are unanimous [sic] in holding Bâbar [sic] responsible for the replacement of the Rama temple with the Bâbarî mosque'.[17] In 1992, the issue came to a head when a prayer service was held at the heavily guarded mosque, which led activists to penetrate the police lines and destroy of the building. Subsequently, the site has become an archaeological dig, as politically motivated workers search for physical proof of its Vaishnavite origins.[18] Babur, who was not a well-known figure in India before this event, became even less well understood afterwards among the general population.

Meanwhile, in Mawarannahr, with the collapse of the Soviet Union in 1991, former 'ethnic' Soviet Republics suddenly found themselves transformed into independent states with no fully formed national identities. Uzbeks responded to this challenge by generating an ideology that heralded an Uzbek history of prestigious and widely respected individuals. Among these were the Iranian mathematician al-Khwarizmi (c. 780–850), whose family may possibly have come from Khwarizim, the Herat native Mir 'Ali Shir Nava'i, the founder of classical Turkic verse, and Ulugh Beg, the scientifically inclined Timurid governor of Samarqand, who presided over the astronomical research that made the city famous in the early fifteenth century. With no trace of irony, Uzbek leaders, descendants of the sworn enemy of the Timurids, embraced a cult of Temür, whose enormous statue was placed prominently in the capital Tashkent.

In Andijan, Uzbek members of the devoted Babur Foundation have nearly sanctified Babur. They laid out a lovely park, constructed the 'Babur and the World Culture Museum' and built a lovely hill-side shrine, which enjoys the kind of *maddinazarlıq*, or perspective, which Babur so often praised and enjoyed. Echoing Temür's kiosk in the Sweetheart Garden in Samarqand, where paintings commemorated his conquests, Babur's Timurid-style shrine contains colourful wall paintings illustrating his career. Outside is a marble replica of his Kabul gravestone.[19] In 1994, the President of Uzbekistan Islam Karimov visited the newly erected museum and shrine to Babur and said,

It is worthy to be endlessly proud of our forefather Zahir al-Din
Muhammad Babur. Being one of our great ancestors who shared the
glory of the Uzbek nation with the world, this honorable person taught
us to value our history and look at the future with great confidence.[20]

Historic and contemporary views of Babur aside, how did he imagine his own
second life – as an individual and the founder of an empire in Hindustan. In
the *Vaqayi'* he emotionally, exhaustively, persuasively memorializes himself
as his father's son, by implication and also by objective achievement, more
perfect even then 'Umar Shaikh Mirza. He does so by offering himself
to readers as a cultured Turco-Mongol, Perso-Islamic aristocrat, a brave,
ambitious warrior of the warrior caste, an accomplished poet, an ethically
objective autobiographer, a composer, a formally observant Hanafi Sunni
Muslim and spiritually engaged Naqshbandi Sufi, and a loyal kinsman,
formally and deeply respectful of his female kin. He emerges in his own
telling as a Timurid renaissance man, displaying an enviable and balanced
cache of military, social, religious, literary and artistic virtues. He does so not
only by recounting his own life but also when he identifies the conspicuous
faults of his Timurid and Mongol contemporaries. It is a common human
trait for individuals implicitly to praise themselves by criticizing others. It is
natural to believe that Babur thought himself to be modest, when he criticized
others for their pretension, that he believed he drank companionably, when
he lambasted some *beg*s as uncouth drunkards, that he thought himself to
be an informed art critic, when he writes that the great miniaturist Bihzad
painted beardless chins badly. Most of all it is natural to assume Babur saw
himself as an accomplished poet and scholar of prosody, when he criticizes
his Mongol uncle's Turki verse and critiques the poetry of virtually every
other writer he mentions, including Sultan Husain Baiqara and even Mir 'Ali
Shir Nava'i.

Above and beyond projecting an admirable image of himself in the
autobiographical, *Vaqayi'* as a kind of Turco-Mongol renaissance man, a man of
multiple virtues and historic triumphs, Babur exalts in proclaiming himself as
the founder of a Timurid political renaissance. He accomplished the phoenix-
like rebirth of the seemingly doomed Timurid lineage, which Shaibani Khan
Uzbek had scoured pitilessly from Mawarannahr before occupying Timurid
Herat, whose pathetically corrupt and impotent Timurid rulers Babur recalled
from his visit there in December 1506. During his four years in Hindustan he
strove to create a new Timurid state, a Turco-Mongol dominated state led by a

dynasty whose members had long-embraced the Perso-Islamic culture of Iran and Central Asia as as personal attributes. He conquered and ruled Hindustan largely with a small coterie of Turco-Mongol loyalists, while encouraging his Timurid and Chaghatai Mongol kin and members of Herat high culture to join him, but the Empire inevitably evolved into something distinct from the "pure" Timurid states of Mawarannahr. Like the contemporary Italian Renaissance, which revived classical learning in a distinctly new environment, Babur's resuscitated Timurid fortunes in a geographical, cultural and political setting that radically differed from Mawarannahr and Kabul. It was not possible, after all, for a few thousand Turco-Mongols to create Kabuls throughout Hindustan, as some of Babur's men had done in Agra. Nor was it possible to long ignore society and the great cultural traditions of Hindu India.

It is not surprising, therefore, that historians of the Timurid-Mughal Empire have largely overlooked its Timurid origins. Babur has not been widely known or understood. The Suri Afghan interregnum between 1540 and 1555 made him seem irrelevant and Babur's prestige as a Turco-Mongol conqueror meant little if anything to the Afghan and Hindu population. Yet Babur's Timurid identity had two important long-term consequences in India. First, Babur's descendants long retained their sense of themselves as members of a prestigious and legitimate dynasty, which produced a supremely self-confident and relatively stable state. Their dynastic consciousness and pride was perpetuated by Akbar's artistic reminders of their great ancestor, Timur, and Shah Jahan's embrace of the Timurid idea of the Sahib Qiran, the Lord of the Auspicious (astrological) Conjunction. Within the dynasty these and other reminders of their heritage reinforced the Timurid-Mughals' vision of themselves as legitimate descendants of a great conqueror. They never ceased to consider themselves to be unquestionably authentic rulers, emoting a sense of unchallenged dynastic pride, which Akbar's conquests and Shah Jahan's grandiose architecture reinforced. Timurid-Mughal dynastic assurance produced a dynasty that gave much of the subcontinent a degree of stability and range of governance that had not been seen since Mauryan times (332–187 BCE), if even then. Their confidence, or dynastic arrogance, and administrative prowess produced the wealthy, prosperous and accomplished state that dazzled European travelers – and persuaded thousands of Iranian literati to migrate to Hindustan.

That migration reflected Babur's second legacy, the further and intensified expansion of Perso-Islamic cultural influence in Hindustan beyond what had existed in the Sultanate era and in the years following Temür's 1398 invasion. As an individual who matured in late-Timurid, Perso-Islamic urban civilization exemplified by Husain Baiqara's Herat, Babur initiated a new and cultured dynastic strain of Muslim rule in the subcontinent. He himself set a high standard of cultural awareness, intellectual sophistication and literary accomplishment, and by welcoming representatives of Herat high culture, which he – and the Ottoman historian Mustafa 'Ali, so admired, he initiated the Timurid-Mughal dynastic embrace of the Perso-Islamic civilization. The dynasty's rulers embraced this tradition to a degree and with an enthusiasm that vividly contrasted especially with their immediate Saiyid and Afghan past, and produced a brief moment in historic time that far outshone even Husain Baiqara's acclaimed court. It was funded, of course, with the lavish resources of the South Asian economy where for Iranian literati, gold seemed to be scattered like stars in the evening sky. This wealth also paid the wages of the innumerable craftsmen, who, as Babur recorded, could produce geometrically precise *charbagh* gardens to order in record time. Humayun accentuated the expansive growth of this culture when he returned from exile in Iran and Akbar carried it to new heights, even while patronizing translations of Sanskrit literature and Hindavi musicians.

In that sense Akbar was the Timurid-Mughal renaissance ruler par excellence, an individual who revived the past in a radically different environment. Akbar was a self-conscious Timurid, who carefully preserved and glorified Babur's name and accomplishments, but he was also an Indian, who in response to his South Asian environment expanded the Timurid-Mughal traditions of cultural patronage to India's great indigenous civilization. The sixteenth century was a remarkable period in Hindustan, encompassing as it did the lives of the two greatest – and personally appealing Timurid-Mughal monarchs, Babur and Akbar.

Endnotes

1 TR, II, f. 70b. Translation by William M. Thackston.

2 Beveridge, *The Akbar nâmâ*, I, 277–79.

3 Jean Paul Roux, *Historie des Grands Moghols, Babur* (Paris: Fayard, 1986).

4 For a detailed discussion of autobiographical literature in the Islamic world, see Stephen F. Dale, 'Emperors and Individuals,' *in The Garden of the Eight Paradises, Bâbur and the Culture of Empire in Central Asia Afghanistan and India (1483–1530)* (Leiden and Boston: Brill, 2004).

5 W. Montgomery Watt, *The Faith and Practice of Al-Ghazali* (Oxford: One World Publications, repr. 1994) and Abdesselm Cheddadi, ed., *Ibn Khaldun Autobiographie* (Algiers: CNRPAH, 2008).

6 Amin T. Tibi, ed., *The Tibyan* (Leiden: Brill, 1986) and Phillip K. Hitti, trans., *An Arab-Syrian Gentleman and Warrior in the Period of the Crusades* (New York: Columbia University Press, 2000).

7 See Beveridge, *Akbar nâma*, Volume 1, Chapters 20–29.

8 Ibid., 338–39.

9 HN, fs. 22b–23a.

10 Hasan-i Rumlu, *Ahsan al-tawarikh*, 314.

11 TR, II, f. 182a.

12 TR, II, f. 183a.

13 A recent exception to the short shrift Babur is generally given in histories of the Timurid-Mughals is Michael H. Fisher's *A Short History of the Mughal Empire* (London: I.B. Tauris, 2016) in which Fisher devotes the first two chapters to Babur.

14 HN, f. 2b.

15 AN, I, 278. Bairam Khan, a Qaraquyunlu Turk, whose family had settled in Badakhshan, composed a *diwan* that included Turki verse. See S. Hussamuddin Rashdi and Muhammad Sabir, eds., *Diwan of Bayram Khan* (Karachi: Institute of Central and West Asian Studies, 1971). Mirza Khan would have probably learned Turki from his father. Gulbadan must have spoken Turki as a child. Whether or not she could read it as an adult is not known.

16 For an introduction to Timurid-Mughal painting, see especially Amina Okada, *Indian Miniatures of the Mughal Court*, trans. Deke Dusinberre (New York: Harry Abrams, 1992).

17 Harsh Narain, *The Ayodhya Temple-Mosque Dispute* (Delhi: Penman Publishers, 1993), 61.

18 Regarding Hindu nationalism, see, among many other sources, Thomas Blom Hansen, *The Saffron Wave, Democracy and Hindu Nationalism in Modern India* (Princeton: Princeton University Press, 1999) and Yogendra K. Malik and V. B. Singh, *Hindu Nationalists in India, The Rise of the Bharata Janata Party* (Boulder:

Westview Press, 1994) and for archaeology, see Amy Waldman, 'India's Big Dig: Will it Settle or Inflame a Controversy,' *New York Times*, 3 April 2003, A9.

19 Beatrice Forbes Manz describes the Uzbek cult of Temür in her article 'Tamerlane's Career and Its Uses,' *Journal of World History* 13, 1 (Spring 2002): 16–24. Information about Babur's presence in the Uzbek pantheon is based upon the author's visits to Andijan, at the invitation and with the generous help of representatives of the Babur Foundation. Members of the foundation have worked tirelessly to commemorate the Ferghanah native's memory.

20 Hamid Sulaymon and Saidbek Hasanov, *Babur-Name Miniatory* (Tashkent: Alisher State Museum of State Literature, 2008), 44.

21 TR, II, f. 161.

Glossary

General

Amîr (*A*)	Superior military or political rank, used by Babur when discussing Indian Affairs, in place of *beğ*, which he uses when narrating events in Afghanistan or Mâwarânnahr (western Central Asia).
Ark (*T*)	Interior of a fortress, a citadel or seat of power.
Arıq (*T*)	Irrigation channel or stream.
Aymaq (*T*)	Family, clan or subdivision or a tribe. (Mongol *ayman*).
Beğ (*T*)	Superior military rank (Ottoman *bey*).
Börk (*T-M*)	Felt hat, headgear common to Turco-Mongols.
Caliph/Khalîfah (*A*)	'Sucessor' to the Prophet Muhammad. There were three distinct Caliphal groups: the four original 'Pious' or 'Rightly Guided Caliphs,' (632–661), the Umayyad Caliphs of Damascus (661–750) and the 'Abbasid Caliphs of Baghdad (750–1258).
Chaghatâî (*Chaghatây*) (*T-M*)	1. Chinggis Khan's second son, and his descendants; Babur's matrilineal relatives 2. The nineteenth century European name for the Turkic (Turki) language spoken in Chaghatâî Khân's dominions, which was Babur's native language.
Chahâr Bâgh (*Chârbâgh*) (*P*)	A square or quadrilateral Iranian garden bisected by four water courses and often planted with fruit trees and aromatic plants.
Chapqun (*T*)	A raid by horsemen.
Eshik ikhtiyarı (*T-A*)	'Lord of the Gate,' *Beğ* trusted with superior administrative or political authority. See related phrases: *ulugh ve ikhtiyâr beğ* and *sâhib-i ikhtiyâr*. See especially Arat, *Vekayi Babur'un Hâtıratı*, 606–09.
Farman (*A*)	a government edict or order.

Fatrat (*A*)	Intermission, interval, interregnum.
Ghazi (*A*)	A Muslim frontier warrior, usually associated with early Ottoman Turks fighting on Byzantine frontiers.
Ghulam	A slave soldier; *ghulams* often gained enormous power and sometimes achieved sovereignty, as in the case of the Ghaznavid Sultans, who originated as *ghulams* of the Samanids of Bukhara. Analogous terms are *mamluk* and *janissary*.
Gûnya (*G*)	Rectangularity.
Hamkâsah (*P*)	Boon companion. See also *nadîm* and *musâhib*.
Ichki Beğ (*T*)	Military rank, second to *beğ*.
Il (*T-M*)	Tribe, people. See also *ulus*.
Khân, Qan or Qa'an (*T-M*)	Chief or leader or a Mongol or Turkic tribal confederation.
Kökektash (*T-M*)	Foster brother or sister, 'milk-brother.'
Kürgen (*Gurkan*) (*M*)	Son-in-law, title taken by Temür and Ulugh Beğ and Bâbur on his coins.
Kûshk (*P*)	*Kiosk.* Airy garden buildings Babur admired in Samarqand.
Mâl-i amân (*P*)	Indemnity/protection money levied on conquered territories.
Mâwarânnahr	'The land beyond the river' Amû Daryâ or Oxus. Greek Transoxiana. Western Central Asia.
Mirza	The title taken by all Timurids, from the terms *amir zadeh*, son of an amir.
Mulkgirliq (*A-P-T*)	'The act of kingdom-seizing,' imperialism.
Musâhib (*A*)	Boon companion. See also *hamkasah* and *nadîm*.
Nadîm (*A*)	Boon companion. See also *hamkasah* and *musâhib*.
Nökör, Naukar (*M-T-P*)	Liegeman, follower, dependent, servant.
Parganah (*A*)	District in India, equivalent to a *tuman* in Afghanistan.

Pîr (P)	The head of a Sufi or devotional order, often termed *shaikh*s.
Qauchin (M)	A hewreditary military class and/or Turco-Mongol social group.
Qazaq (T)	Stateless or homeless, a warrior or raider.
Qazaqlıq (T)	State of political brigandage, describing times when Babur or other Timurids or Chingissids lost sovereignty or power.
Rûm (A)	'Rome,' Anatolia, Ottoman Empire.
Sâhib Qirân (A)	Lord of the Fortunate (Astrological) Conjunction. A title Given to Temür after afterwards taken by the Timurid-Mughal emperor Jahângîr and by his successor Shâh Jahân.
Shahid (A)	A Muslim martyr, a witness for the faith.
Shâhrukhî (P)	Timurid silver coin, sometimes known as a *tangah* or *tangah–i misqâlî*.
Suhbat (A)	Conversation, friendly relation, social intercourse.
Suhbatarayalıq (A-T)	Social gathering; for Babur associated with congenial meetings in *chârbâgh*s or Iranian-style gardens.
Sultan (A)	"Power," or an independent ruler, whose authority is based on military force not religious sanctity. exerts political power Term for Muslim rulers who came to power as the 'Abbasid Caliphate declined. Examples were: the Ghaznavids, Delhi Sultans Egyptain Mamluks and Ottomans.
Suyurghal (M)	Fief or semi-permanent land grant. In India generally connected with religious endowments. See also *tiyûl*.
Tagha'î, Taghayı (M-T)	Maternal uncle.
Tiyûl (P)	Land grant of variable size and duration. See also *wajh*.
Tumen, tuman (M-T)	10,000 fighting men; a district theoretically supporting this number of men. The term Babur uses for 'distict" in Mâwarânnahr and Afghanistan.

Tuqqan (*T*)	Relation, children of the same mother.
Tuqqanlıq (*T*)	Blood relationship, uterine relation.
Ulus (*T-M*)	Tribe or people, gathering.
Uruq (*T*)	Family, camp or entourage.
Vilâyat (*A*)	Province, homeland: for Bâbur Mâwannânahr. Term Babur uses for province, a larger area than a *tuman*.
Yiğit (*T*)	Literally 'youth,' an individual warrior with no independent following or means.
Wajh/wajhdâr	Territorial assignment similar to *tiyûl*. *Wajdâr*, a term Babur used when making territorial assignments in India.
Yûrush/yûresh (*T*)	A military assault or attack.

Poetry

Bayt (*A*)	Verse or line of a poem.
Ghazal (*A*)	Lyric or ode, poem of approximately 6–15 lines with rhyme aa, ba, ca etc. for the *misr'a*s or half-lines of each *bayt*.
Masnavî (*A*)	Poem usually longer than a *ghazal* of unrestricted subject and length with Rhyme aa, bb, cc etc. for the *misrâ*'s or half-lines of each *bayt*.
Matla' (*A*)	First *bayt* or line of a poem.
Misra' (*A*)	Half-line of verse.
Qit'ah (*A*)	Short, 'fragmentary' poem, usually of 2–15 lines, often informal with unrestricted topic with thyme ab, ab for the *misra'* of each *bayt* or verse.
Rubâ'î (*A*)	Poem of two *bayt*s or four *misra*'s with rhyme aaba for the *misra'* of each verse.
Takhallus (*A*)	The signature and/or pen name of the author, often fond in the penultimate line in *ghazal*s or in *rubâ'î*s.

Bibliography

Abidin, Farah. 2014. *Suba of Kabul Under the Mughals, 1585–1739*. Delhi: Partridge.

Akhmedov, B.A. 1982. *Istoriia Balkha*. Tashkent: Fan.

Alam, Muzaffar, Françoise 'Nalini,' Delvoye and Marc Gaborieau. eds. 2000. *The Making of Indo-Persian Culture*. Delhi: Manohar for Centre De Sciences Humaines.

Âllami, Abu'l Fazl. Reprinted 1987. *The Akbarnâmâ*. 3 volumes. Translated by H. Beveridge. Delhi: Ess Ess Publications.

_____. Reprinted 1968. *The A'in-i Akbari*, 3 Volumes. edited by D.C. Phillott. Translated by H. Blochmann. Delhi: Crown Publications.

Allen, Terry. 1981. *A Catalogue of the Toponyms and Monuments of Timurid Herat*. Cambridge, Massachusetts: Aga Khan Program for Islamic Architecture.

Aquil, Raziuddin. 2007. *Sufism, Culture and Politics: Afghans and Islam in Medieval North India*. Delhi: Oxford Universty Press.

Arapov, Alexey. 2014. *Historical Monuments of Uzbekistan*. Tashkent: SMI-Asia.

Arrian. 2013. *Alexander the Great: The Anabasis and the Indica*, edited by John Atkinson. Translated by Martin Hammond. Oxford: Oxford University Press.

Asher, Katherine Blanshard. 1991. *Architecture of India*, Part 1, Volume 4. Cambridge: Cambridge University Press.

Azimdjanova, S.A. 1966. *Indiĭskiĭ Divan Babura*. Tashkent: Fan.

_____. 1977. *Gosudarstvo Babura v Kabul i Indii*. Moscow: Nauka.

Babur, Gazi Zahirüddin Muhammed. 1943. *Vekayi Babur'un Hâtiratı*. edited by Y. Hikmet Bayur. Translated by Reşit Rahmeti Arat. Ankara: Türk Tarih Kurumu Basimevi.

Babur, Zahîr al-Dîn Muhammad. 1995a. *Bâbur-Nâma (Vaqâyi')*, Volume 1. edited by Eiji Mano. Kyoto: Syokado.

_____. 1996. *Concordance and Classified Indexes*, Volume II. Kyoto: Syokado.

Al-Badauni, Abd al-Qâdir Ibn-i Mulûk Shâh. Reprinted 1973 *Muntakhabu-T- Tawârîkh*. 3 volumes edited and translated by George S. A. Ranking Patna: Academica Asiatica.

_____. 1898. *Muhtakhabu't tawârîkh*. edited and translated by George S. A. Ranking (Calcutta: Mission Press for the Asiatic Society of Bengal).

Bailey, G.A. 1992. 'The Dynamics of Chinoiserie in Timurid and Early Safavid Ceramics.' In *Timurid Art and Culture*, edited by Lisa Golombek and Maria Subtelny. Leiden: Brill.

Baily, John. 1988. *Music of Afghanistan: Professional Musicians in the City of Herat*. Cambridge: Cambridge University Press.

Bairam Khan, Khan-i Khanan. 1971. *Diwan of Bayram Khan*. edited by S. Hussamuddin Rashi and Muhammad Sabir. Karachi: The Institute of Central and West Asian Studies.

Balabanlilar, Lisa. 2010. 'The Begims of the Mystic Feast: Turco-Mongol Tradition in the Mughal Harem.' *Journal of Asian Studies* 69 (1): 123–47.

Barthold, V. V. Reprinted 1963. 'Ulugh Beg.' *Four Studies on the History of Central Asia*, Volume 2. Leiden: Brill.

Behl, Aditya. 2012. *Love's Subtle Magic: An Indian Islamic Literary Tradition* 1379–1545, edited by Wendy Doniger. New York: Oxford University Press.

Bellew, H.W. Reprinted 1973. *An Enquiry into the Ethnography of Afghanistan*. Graz, Austria: Akademischc Druck –und Verlagsanstalt.

Bertels, Evgenniĭ Eduardovich. 1965. *Izbrannye Trudy, Navoi i Dzhami*. Moscow: Nauka.

Beveridge, Annette S. Reprinted. 1969. *The Bâbur-nâma in English*. London: Luzac.

Bivar, A. D. H. 2014. 'Kushan Dynasty i. Dynastic History.' *Encyclopædia Iranica*. Accessed on 8 December 2014. Available at: http://www.iranicaonline.org/articles/kushan-dynasty-i-history.

Blagova, G.F. 1994. *"Babur-Name" Yazik, Pragmatika, Teksta, Stil*. Moscow: Eastern Literature.

Bodrogligeti, A. J. E. 1984. 'Bâbur Shâh's Chaghatay Version of the *Risâla-i Vâlidîya*: A Central Asian Turkic Treatise on How to Emulate the Prophet Muhammad.' *Ural-Altaische Jahrbücher* 54: 1–61.

Bosworth, C. E. 1977. *The Later Ghaznavids. Splendour and Decay.* Edinburgh: Edinburgh University Press.

_____. 2001. 'The Army of the Ghaznavids.' In *Warfare and Weaponry in South Asia*, edited by Jos J. L. Gommans and Dirk H. A. Kolff, 153–85. Delhi: Oxford University Press.

Burnes, Alexander. Reprinted 2014. *Travels into Bokhara*, Volume 1. Cambridge: Cambridge University Press.

Buriev, A. B. 1937. 'Svedeniya Hafiz-i Abru o Vzaimootnoshinyakh Sredneî Azii S Kitaem v XV v.' In *Iz Istorii Sredneî Azii i Vostochnogo Turkistana XV–XIX vv*, edited by B.A. Litvinskii. Tashkent: Fan.

Courteille, M. Pavet De. 1870. *Dictionanaire Turk-Oriental Des Ovrages De Bâber, D'Aboul-Gâzi et de Mir-Ali-Chir-Nevâi*. Paris: L'Imprimerie Impériale.

Crowe, Yolanda. 1992. 'Some Timurid Designs and Their Far Eastern Connections.' In *Timurid Art and Culture*, edited by Lisa Golombek and Maria Subtelny. Leiden: Brill.

Currie, P. M. 1989. *The Shrine and Cult of Muʻin al-din Chishti of Ajmer*. Delhi: Oxford University Press.

Dale, Stephen Frederic. 2015. *The Orange Trees of Marrakesh, Ibn Khaldun and the Science of Man*. Cambridge, Massachusetts and London: Harvard University Press.

_____. 2003. 'A Safavid Poet in the Heart of Darkness: The Indian Poems of Ashraf Mazandarani.' *Iranian Studies* 36 (2): 197–212.

_____. 2004. *The Garden of the Eight Paradises: Bâbur and the Culture of Empire in Central Asia, Afghanistan and India* (1483–1530). Leiden & Boston: Brill.

Dale, Stephen F., and Alam Payind. 1999. 'The Ahrârî Waqf in Kâbul in the Year 1546 and the Mûghul Naqshbandiyyah.' *Journal of the American Oriental Society* 119 (2): 218–33.

Dankoff, Robert. 1997. 'Baburnama: Chaghatay Turkish Text with Abdul-Rahim Khankhanan's Persian Translation.' *Journal of the America Oriental Society* 117 (4): 744–46.

Dardess, John. 1973. *Conquerors and Confucians: Aspects of Political Change in Late Yuan China.* New York: Columbia University Press.

De la Garza, Andrew. 2016. *The Mughal Empire at War.* London and New York: Routledge.

Dickerman, Edmund H. 1977. 'The Conversion of Henry IV: Paris is Well Worth a Mass in Psychological Perspective.' *The Catholic Historical Review* 63 (1): 1–13.

Di Cosmo, Nicola, Allen J. Frank, and Peter B. Golden. eds. 2009. *The Cambridge History of Inner Asia: The Chinggisid Age.* Cambridge: Cambridge University Press.

Dughlat, Mirza Haydar. 1996. *Tarikh-i Rashidi, 2 Volumes.* Persian Text edited by W. M. Thackston. English text edited and translated by W. M. Thackston. Sources of Oriental Languages and Literatures, 37 and 38. Cambridge, Massachusetts: Department of Near Eastern Languages and Civilizations.

Du Mont, Bernard. 2002. 'Ulugh Beg: Astronom und Herrscher in Samarkand.' *Sterne und Weltraum* 9–10: 38–46.

Eckmann, János. 1996. *Harezm, Kipçak, ve Çağatay, Türkçesi Üzerine Araştırmalar.* Ankara: Sertkaya.

Elphinstone, Mountstuart. 1815. *An Account of the Kingdom of Caubul and its Dependencies in Persia, Tartary and India.* London: Longman et al.

Ernst, Carl W. 1992. *Eternal Garden, Mysticism, History, and Politics at a South Asian Sufi Center.* Albany: Suny Press.

Ershad, Farhang. 1986. *The Historical Migrations of Iranians to India [Muhâjerat-i târîkhî-yi Irâniyân beh Hind].* Tehran: Cultural Studies and Research Institute.

Erskine, William. 1854. *A History of India under The First Two Sovereigns of the House of Taimur, Bâber and Humâyun.* 2 Volumes. London: Longman, Brown, Green and Longmans.

Fleischer, Cornell H. 1986. *Bureaucrat and Intellectual in the Ottoman Empire: The Historian Mustafa Âli* (1541–1600). Princeton: Princeton University Press.

Gibb, H.A.R. ed. and trans. 1971. *The Travels of Ibn Battuta A.D.* 1325–1354. Cambridge: Cambridge University Press for the Hakluyt Society.

Golden, Peter B. 2005. 'The Turkic World in Mahmûd al-Kâshgarî.' In *Complexity of Interaction along the Eurasian Steppe Zone in the First Millenium CE,* edited by Jan Bemmann and Michael Schmauder. Bonn: Rheinische Friedrich-Wilhelms-Universität.

_____. 2006. 'The Türk Imperial Tradition in the Pre-Chingisid Era.' In *Imperial Statecraft Studies on East Asia.* Volume 26. edited by David Sneath, 23–63. Bellingham: Center for Asian Studies, Western Washington University.

_____. 2011. 'Ethnogenesis in the Tribal Zone: The Shaping of the Turks.' In *Studies on the Peoples and Cultures of the Eurasian Steppes*, edited by Peter B. Golden and Cătătlin Hriban, 17–63. Bucharest-Brăila: Editura Academiei Române.

Gommans, Jos J. L. and Dirk H. A. Kolff eds. 2001. *Warfare and Weaponry in South Asia.* Delhi: Oxford University Press.

Grenet, Frantz. 2002. Samarqand, History and Archeology. *Encyclopaedia Iranica*, 20 July (last updated on 20 July 2002). Accessed on 18 April 2017. Available at: http://www.iranicaonline.org/articles/samarqand-i.

Gulbadan Begim. 1902. *The History of Humâyûn (Humâyûn-Nâma).* edited and translated by Annette Beveridge. London: Royal Asistic Society.

Gulchin-i-Ma'ânî, Ahmad. 1990. *Kârvân-i Hind*, 2 Volumes. Tehran: Intisharat-i Âstân-i quds-i razavî.

Habib, Irfan ed. 1997. *Akbar and His India.* New Delhi: Oxford University Press.

_____. Reprinted 2000. 'Three Early Farmâns of Akbar in Favour of Râmdâs: The Master Dyer.' In *Akbar and His India*, edited by I. Habib, 270–88. Delhi: Oxford University Press.

Haidar, Mansura. 2002. *Mirza Haidar Dughlat as Depicted in Persian Sources.* Delhi: Manohar.

Haidar, Navina Najat and Marika Sardar. 2015. *Sultans of the Deccan 1500–1700.* New York: Metropolitan Museum of Art.

Hasan-i Rûmlû. 1978. *'Ahsan al-tawârîkh'*, edited by Abd al-Husain Navâ'î. Tehran: Intishârat-i Bâbik.

Hsiao, Ch'i-ch'ing. 1978. *The Military Establisment of the Yuan Dynasty.* Cambridge, Massachusetts: Council of East Asian Studies, Harvard University.

Ibn Battuta. 1971. *The Travels of Ibn Battuta A.D. 1325–1354.* Translated C. Defrémery and B. R. Sanguinetti, Volume 3. Cambridge: Cambridge University Press for the Hakluyt Society.

Jackson, Peter. 1999. *The Delhi Sultanate.* Cambridge: Cambridge University Press.

Jackson, Peter, and Laurence Lockhart. eds. 1986. *The Cambridge History of Iran: The Timurid and Safavid Periods*, Volume 6. Cambridge: Cambridge University Press.

Jafri, Sayeed Zaheer Husain. 1997. 'A Farmân of Akbar (1558) from the Period of the Regency.' In *Akbar and His India*, edited by Irfan Habib, 266–67. Delhi: Oxford University Press.

Jahangir. Reprinted 1978. *The Tûzuk-i-Jahângîrî*, edited by Henry Beveridge. Translated by Alexander Rogers. Delhi: Munshiram Manoharlal.

Joshi, Rita. 1985. *The Afghan Nobility and the Mughals 1526–1707.* New Delhi: Vikas.

Kaye, G. R. 1918. *The Astronomical Observatories of Jai Singh.* Calcutta: Government Printing Office.

Khan, Iqtidar Alam. 2001. 'Early Use of Canon and Musket in India.' In *Warfare and Weaponry in South Asia* 1000-1800, edited by Jos J. L. Gommans and Dirk H. A. Kolff, 321–37. Delhi: Oxford University Press.

Khansari, Mehdi, M. Reza Moghtader, and Yavari Minouch. eds. 1998. *The Persian Garden: Echoes of Paradise.* Washington, D.C.: Mage.

Koch, Ebba. 1997. 'The Mughal Waterfront Garden.' In *Gardens in the Time of the Great Muslim Empires: Theory and Design in Islamic Art and Architecture, Supplements to Muqarnas,* edited by Attilio Petruccioli,140-60. Leiden: Brill.

———. 2014. *Mughal Architecture* (Revised edition). Delhi: Primus Books.

Köprülü-zâde, M. F. 1915. *Bâbur'in shî'rleri,* 307-27 & 464-80, Istanbul: Millî tetubbu'lar mecmû'ası.

Kumar, Sunil. 2007. *The Emergence of the Delhi Sultanate.* Ranikhet, India: Permanent Black.

Kûnjî-Isfahânî, Fadlullah b. Rûzbihân. 1983. *Sulûk al-mulûk.* Tehran: Intishârat-i Khwârazmî.

Kwândamîr, Ghiyâs al-Dîn b. Humâm al-Dîn al-Husaini. 1954. *Habîb al-siyar fî akhbâr afrâd bashar,* 4 Volumes. Tehran: Intishârat-i Kitabkhânah-i Khayyam.

———. 1979. *The Makarim al-Akhlaq.* T. Gandjei ed. Cambridge: Gibb Memorial Trust.

Lal, Ruby. 2003. 'Rethinking Mughal India, the Challenge of a Princess's Memoir.' *Economic and Political Weekly* 38 (1): 53–65.

Lane-Poole, Stanley. Reprinted 1983. *The Coins of the Moghul Emperors of Hindûstân in the British Museum.* Delhi: Inter-India Publications.

Lawrence, Bruce B. 1992. *Nizam Ad-Din Awliya: Morals for the Heart.* New York: Paulist Press.

Lee, Joo-Yup. 2016a. 'The Historical Meaning of the Term *Turk* and the Nature of the Turkic Identity of the Chinggisid and Timurid Elites in Post-Mongol Central Asia.' *Central Asiatic Journal* 59 (1/2): 101–32.

———. 2016b. *Qazaqlïq, or Ambitious Brigandage, and the Formation of the Qazaqs.* Leiden & Boston: Brill.

Lentz, Thomas W. and Glenn D. Lowry. 1989. *Timur and the Princely Vision: Persian Art and Culture in the Fifteenth Century.* Washington D.C.: Smithsonian Institution Press.

Levy, Reuben. ed. 1951. *The Nasîhat Nâma known as Qâbûs Nâma of Kai Kâ'ûs b. Iskandar b. Qâbûs Washmgîr.* London: Luzac.

Mackenzie, D. N. ed. and trans. 1965. *Poems from the Divan of Khushal Khan Khattak.* London: George Allen and Unwin.

Mano, Eiji. 1993. *The Weeping-willows Passage in the Bâbur-nâmâ*, 28–35. Proceedings of the 27th Meeting of Haneda Memorial Hall. Kyoto: Institute of Inner Asian Studies.

_____. 2005. 'Three Corrections of the Critical Edition of the Bâbur-nâma.' *Şinasi Tekin'in Anısına Uygurladan Osmanliya* 80 (2): 587–92.

_____. 2006a.'On the Persian Original *Vâlidiyya of Khvâja Ahrâr.*' In *History and Historiography of Post-Mongol Central Asia and the Middle East*, edited by Judith Pfeiffer and Sholeh Quinn, 250–56. Wiesbaden: Harrassowitz.

_____. 2006b. 'The Saltanatî manuscript of the Bâbur-Nâma: Its Relationship to the other manuscripts and its value.' *Philological Studies on Old Central Asian Manuscripts*, 31–48 (Contribution to the Studies of Eurasian Languages 10).

_____. 2007. 'Editorial Choices in Preparing the Critical Edition of the *Babur-nama.*' In *Theoretical Approaches to the Transmission and Edition of Oriental Manuscripts*, edited by Judith Pfeiffer and Manfred Kropp, Beirut: Ergon Verlag Würzburg.

Manz, Beatrice Forbes.1989. *The Rise and Rule of Tamerlane.* Cambridge: Cambridge University Press.

_____. 2002. Tamerlane's Career and Its Uses,' *Journal of World History* 13, 1 (Spring), 16–24.

_____. 2007. *Power, Politics and Religion in Timurid Iran.* Cambridge: Cambridge University Press.

Mauhad, Ziya. 1994. 'Qit'ah dar Sh'ir-i Fârsî Sa'dî, Shâ'ir-i Qit'ahsirâ.' *Nashr Danesh* 14 (4): 1373 a.h..

McCrindle, J.W. 1877. *Ancient India as Described by Megasthênes and Arrian.* London: Trübner & Co.

Meisami, Julie Scott. 1987. *Medieval Persian Court Poetry.* Princeton: Princeton University Press.

Minorsky, Vladimir. 1932. 'La domination des Dailamites.' Musée Guimet. Paris: Leroux.

Mîr 'Alî Shîr. 1966. *Muhâkamat al-Lughatain.* edited and translated by Robert Devereux. Leiden: Brill.

Mirza, Muhammad Wâhid. Reprinted 1974. *The Life and Times of Amir Khusrau.* Delhi: Idarah-i Adabiyat-i Delhi.

_____ed. 1981. *The Nuh Sipihr of Amir Khusrau* (in 1318 A.D.). Jaipur, India: Historical Research Documentation Program.

Morgan, David O. and Reid, Anthony. eds. 2010. *The New Cambridge History of Islam, V.3 The Eastern Islamic World Eleventh to Eighteenth Centuries.* Cambridge: Cambridge University Press.

Mukhtarov, A. 1972. 'Inscriptions with Bâbur's Name in the Upper Reaches of the Zarafshan.' *Afghanistan* 25: 49–56.

Mukminova, R. G. 1985. *Sotsial'naya Differentsiatsiya Naseleniya Gorodov Uzbekistana v. XV–XVI.* Tashkent: Fan.

Narain, Harsh. 1993. *The Ayodhya Temple-Mosque Dispute.* Delhi: Penman Publishers.

Nigam, S. B. P. 1968. *Nobility Under the Sultans of Delhi.* Delhi: Munshiram Manoharlal.

N.Y. Metropolitan Museum of Art. 2015. *Bazm and Razm: Feast and Fight in Persian Art.* February 17-May 31.

O'Kane, Bernard. 1987. *Timurid Architecture in Khurasan.* Costa Mesa, CA: Mazda.

Papagiolo, Maria Teresa Shephard. 1972. *Kâbul: The Bagh-i Bâbur, a Project and a Research into the Possibilities of a Complete Reconstruction,* 1–33. Rome: ISMEO.

Papas, Alexandre. 2007. 'Shaykh Succession in the Classical Naqshbandiyya: Spirituality, Heredity and the Question of the Body.' *Asian and African Studies* 7 (1): 36–49.

_____. 2008. 'No Sufism without Sufi Order: Rethinking *Tarîqa and Adab with Ahmad Kâsâni Dahbîdî* (1461-1542).' *Kyoto Bulletin of Islamic Area Studies* 2 (1): 4–22.

Qureshi, Regala Burckhardt. 1986. *Sufi Music of India and Pakistan: Sound, Context and Meaning in Qawwali.* Cambridge: Cambridge University Press.

Râsânen, Martti. 1969–1970. *Versuch Eines Etymologischen Wörterbuchs Der Türksprachen, 2 Volumes.* Helsinki: Suomalais-Ugilainen Seura.

Raverty, Henry George. 1982. *Notes on Afghânistan and Baluchistan* (2nd edition). Quetta: Nisa Traders.

Reynolds, Dwight F. ed. 2001. *Interpreting the Self, Autobiography in the Arabic Literary Tradition.* Berkeley: University of California Press.

Richards, John F. 1965. 'The Economic History of the Lodi Period: 1451-1526.' *JESHO* 8 (1): 47–67.

Rickmers, Willi Rickmer. 1913. *The Duab of Turkestan.* Cambridge: Cambridge University Press.

Robertson, George Scott. 1974. *The Kafirs of the Hindu-Kush.* Karachi: Oxford University Press.

Robinson, J. A. Captain. 1980. *Notes on the Nomad Tribes of Eastern Afghanistan.* Quetta: Nisa Traders.

Roemer, Hans R., 'Husayn Bâyqarâ,' *Encyclopaedia Iranica,* Online 2012 and in print, Vol. XII, Fasc. 5, 508-11.

_____. "Timur in Iran," (1986) in Peter Jackson and Laurence Lockhart eds. *The Cambridge History of Iran 6, the Timurid and Safavid Periods.* Cambridge: Cambridge University Press.

Rogers, Alexander, trans. Reprinted 1978. *The Tûzuk-i Jahângîrî or Memoirs of Jahângîr,* edited by Henry Beveridge. Delhi: Munshiram.

Rosenthal, Erwin I. J. 1968. *Political Thought in Medieval Islam.* Cambridge: Cambridge University Press.

Roux, Jean-Paul, 1986. *Historie des Grands Moghols, Babur*. Paris: Fayard.

Ruy González de Clavijo. 1928. *Embassy to Tamerlane, 1403-1406*, edited by E. Denison Ross and Eileen Power. Translated by Guy Le Strange. New York and London: Harper.

Sachau, Edward C. ed. and trans. 2002. *Albêrûni's India*. New Delhi: Rupa.

Saidov, Abdulkakhor, Anarbaev, Abdulkhamid, Goriyacheva. 2015. 'The Ferghana Valley: The Pre-Colonial Legacy.' In *Ferghana Valley*, edited by Frederick Starr, 3-28. London and New York: Routledge.

Schafer, Edward H. 1963. *The Golden Peaches of Samarkand*. Berkeley: University of California Press.

Serikova, Ludmila, Aziz Kayumov and Temira Saidullaeva. eds. 1963. *Alishir Navou*. Uzbekistana: Izdatelstvo TSK Kampartii.

Sharma, Sunil. 2000. *Persian Poetry at the Indian Frontier: Mas'ûd Sa'd Salmân of Lahore*. Delhi: Permanent Black.

_____. 2005. *Amir Khusraw: The Poet of Sultans and Saints*. Oxford: One World.

Sims, Eleanor. 2002. *Peerless Image: Persian Painting and its Sources*. New Haven and London: Yale University Press.

Simpson, Marianna Shreve and Louise Marlow. 2016. *Princeton's Great Book of Kings: The Peck Shahnama*. Princeton: Princeton University Art Museum.

Stebleva, I.V. 1982. *Semantika Gazeli Babura*. Moscow: Nauka.

Subtelny, Maria Eva. 1977. 'Agriculture and the Timurid Chaharbagh: The Evidence from a Medieval Persian Agricultural Manual.' In *Gardens in the Time of the Great Muslim Empires*, edited by Attilo Petruccioli, 110-28. Leiden: Brill.

_____. 1988. 'Centralizing Reforms and its Opponents in the Late Timurid Period.' *Iranian Studies* 21 (1–2): 123–51.

_____. 2007. *Timurids in Transition, Turco-Persian Politics and Acculturation in Medieval Iran*. Leiden and Boston: Brill.

Sulaymon, Hamid and Saidbek Hasanov (2008). *Babur-Name Miniatory* (Tashkent: Alisher State Museum of State Literature).

Sultan, Izzat. 1985. *Kniga Preznanii Navoi*. Tashkent: Gafura Gulyama.

Szabo, Albert and Thomas J. Barfield. 1991. *Afghânistan: An Atlas of Indigenous Domestic Architecture*. Austin, Texas: University of Texas Press.

Szuppe, Maria. 2003 'Herat iv, Topography and Urbanism.' *Encyclopaedia Iranica*, 15 December (last updated on 22 March 2012). Accessed on 18 April 2017. Available at: http://www.iranicaonline.org/articles/herat-iv.

Tabibi, 'Abdul Hakim. 1368. *Tarikh-i-Mukhtasar-i Harat dar 'ahd-i Taimurian*. Tehran: Hirmand.

Thomas, Edward. Reprinted 1967. *The Chronicles of the Pathan Kings of Delhi*. Delhi: Munshiram Manoharlal.

Tumanovich, N. N. 1989. *Gerat v xvi-xviii vekakh.* Moscow: Nauka.

Vaissière, Étienne de la. 2005. *Soghdian Traders: A History.* Translated by James Ward. Leiden and Boston: Brill.

Vigne, G.T. Reprinted 1982. *A Personal Narrative of a Visit to Ghuzni, Kabul and Afghanistan.* Lahore: Sang-e-Meel.

Watson, Burton. 1993. *Records of the Grand Historian by Sima Qian* (Revised Edition). Han Dynasty II. Translated by Burton Watson. New York: Columbia University Press.

Yücel, Bilâl. 1995. *Bâbür Dîvânı.* Ankara: Atatürk Kültür Merkezi.

Zarcone, Thierry. 2000. 'Central Asian Influence on the Early Development of the Chishtiyya Sufi Order in India.' In *The Making of Indo-Persian Culture*, edited by Muzaffar Alam, Françoise 'Nalini Delvoye and Marc Gaborieau 99–117. Delhi: Manohar for Centre De Sciences Humaines.

Index

Abbasid Caliph (-ate), 10–11, 15, 31
'Abd al-Haqq, Khwajah, 167, 195
'Abd al-Latif, 179
'Abd al-Rahman Afghans, 109
'Abd al-Razzaq (son of Ulugh Beg Kabuli), 87, 90
'Abd al-Shahid, Khwajah, 166
'Abdullah Marwarid, Khwäjah, 81
Abu'l Fazl 'Allami, 6, 39, 148, 198, 200, 209–210
Abu'l Muhsin Mirza (son of Husain Mirza Baiqara), 67
Achaemenids of Iran, 25, 30
Adinapur, 64, 89, 100, 105, 111, 121
Afghanistan, 1–2, 6, 8–11, 13, 15, 18, 21n40, 25–26, 29, 34, 49–50, 59–62, 64–65, 67, 83, 86, 88, 91n11, 100, 102, 109–111, 137–138, 140–141, 143–144, 148, 156–157, 163, 167–168, 171n63, 179, 182–183, 185–186, 212
Agra, 3, 7–8, 14, 32, 60, 73, 106, 116, 120, 122, 129, 137–139, 144–150, 152, 156–163, 165–166, 175, 177–179, 182–183, 185, 190, 192–193, 195–201, 205n56, 211–214, 217
Ajar, 49, 65
Akhsı, 1–2, 23, 27, 30, 33–34, 36, 39–41, 48, 188, 194
al-Biruni, 142–143
Alexander the Great, 25–26, 144
'Ali Masjid, 122
al-Juzjani, Minhaj, 131
Amu Darya, 1, 12, 24, 26, 34, 49, 52n5, 62, 95–96, 99, 118, 119
Anatolia, 24, 60
Andijan, 2, 27, 30, 33, 35–43, 46–48, 61, 64–65, 69–70, 76, 83, 89, 96, 98–99, 107, 123–124, 166, 183, 185, 187, 215

Arat, 88n38, 90n86, 146n91, 165n24
Arat, Resit Rahmeti, 94n86
Armenia, 24
'Askari (son of Babur), 166–167, 177–178, 183, 188, 190–191
Astronomy, 76
Auratipa, 38, 43–46, 66, 84
Awadh, 146, 149, 159–160
'Ayisha Sultan Begim, 23, 42, 203n19
Ayodyah, 215

Babri Masjid, 192–197, 215
Babur/Firdaus-makani, 201, 214
Baburi, 42
Badakhshan, 2, 34, 36, 43, 49, 62, 64, 89, 95, 101, 109–111, 118, 120–121, 123, 127, 131, 140, 156–157, 182–183, 198–200, 203n19, 219n15
Badi' al-Zaman Mirza, 67, 69, 75–76, 85, 203n19
Bahlul Ludi, 119, 124, 153
Bahmanis, 17
Bajaur/Khahr, 100–101, 109, 115, 130, 133n20, 144–145, 149, 151
Balaban, Ghiyas al-Din, 129
Balkh, 30, 60, 67–68, 75, 99, 109–110, 118, 120–121, 124, 165, 182, 199, 203n19
Bamian, 49, 62, 66, 84, 95
Banna'i, 44, 80–81
Barani, Zia al-Din, 16, 139
Baran River, 84
Barlas, Muhammad Baranduq, 74, 85
Barlas Turks, 23, 74, 84–85, 147–148, 151, 177–178, 187–188, 190, 196–197, 203n19
Bayezid I, Sultan, 24
Bazm u Razm, 105–114
Beas River, 123

Begim, Aisan Daulat, 45, 66
Beveridge, Annette Susannah, 85, 133n20, 206n58, 206n67, 206n75
Bhirah, 101–102, 104–106, 113, 118, 130–131, 182, 187
Bianah, Rajasthan, 86, 146–147, 149–150, 155–157, 161, 167, 182, 187, 201
Bihar Khan Nuhani, 190
Bihar Sharif, 178
Bikramajit Raja, 139
Billah, Baqi, 179
Buddhism, 27
Bukhara, 10, 12, 15, 30, 34, 43, 97–99
Burhan al-Din 'Ali Qilich al-Marghinani, 185
Bustan, 7, 46
Buxar, 188

Chaghaniani, Baqi, 49, 63–66, 133n24, 167
Chaghatai language, ix, xi, 3, 37, 89
Chaghatai Mongols, 23–25, 27, 29, 33–35, 40, 43, 45, 50, 53n15, 66, 72, 84, 91n13, 96–97, 127, 131, 137, 158–159, 166–167, 188, 191–192, 197, 214, 217
chahar bagh/charbagh, 8, 14, 32, 113, 124, 148, 162, 218
Chandawar, 152, 157
Chanderi, 159–160, 182, 193
Chang'an/Xian, 29
Chausa, 188
China, 24–29, 32, 34, 47, 60, 141
Chin-ab, 101
Chinese, 2, 24–27, 29, 31–32, 47, 108, 141
Chiniut, 101–102
Chin Temür, Sultan, 125, 127, 153
Chishti, 14, 16, 129, 139, 166, 190, 194
Chitor, 17, 138, 159–161

Damascus, 24
Dayuan/Ferghanah, 1–2, 5–9, 12, 14–15, 23, 25–30, 33–37, 39, 41, 43, 47–51, 64–68, 73, 80, 84, 90, 97, 107, 111, 115, 128–129, 141, 149, 166–167, 176, 185, 188, 212
Delhi, 3, 11, 12, 14, 16, 22, 75, 82, 97, 98, 99, 102, 125, 116, 117, 120, 121-123, 125, 133, 134, 141-143, 146, 152, 159, 169, 175, 178, 180, 183, 187, 193, 202
Delhi Sultanate, 9–14, 17, 21n40, 118, 139
Dhulpur, 146–149, 161–162, 177–178, 182, 188, 196, 200
Dihlavi, Amir Khusrau, 15–16, 28, 81, 139
Dikhat, 46
Dilawar Khan, 120–121, 146
Dildar Begim, 182, 200
Duab, 17, 52n5, 138, 175, 182, 211–212
Dudu (Nuhani), 190
Dughlat, Aba Bakr, 33
Dughlat, Muhammad Husain Kurkan, 38, 66

Egyptian Caliphs, 11
Elphinstone, Mountstuart, 61
Erskine, William, 3–6, 210–211
Etawah, 146–148, 156–157, 180, 182, 187

Fakhr–i Jahan Begim, 158
Farmuli, Malik Biban, 192
Farmuli, Musa Sultan, 190
Farmuli, Shaikh Bayazid, 159–160, 178, 192, 212–213
Ferghanah, 1–2, 5–9, 12, 14–15, 23, 25–30, 33–37, 39, 41, 43, 47–51, 64–68, 73, 80, 84, 90, 97, 107, 111,

115, 128–129, 141, 149, 166–167, 176, 185, 188, 212

Ferishta, 140

Firdausi, 7–8, 15, 28, 152

Firuzpur, 157

Firuz Shah Tughluq, 187

Gandak River, 189

Gardiz, 62, 109–110, 134n50, 144

geometry/geometrical, 14, 32, 107–108, 113, 141, 143, 162, 218

Georgia, 24

Ghaggar/Kakar River, 124

Ghazipur, 146, 149, 188, 190

Ghaznavids, 10, 15

Ghazni, 9, 61–66, 89, 99, 109–110, 124, 131, 143–145, 151, 176

Ghilza'i Afghans, 119

Ghiyas, Mirak-i Sayyid, 141

Ghizhduvan, 99

Ghurids, 10

Greek, 1, 26–27, 31, 141–142

Gulbadan Begim, 3, 126, 140, 159, 178, 195, 203n19, 206n58, 213–214

Gulchira Begim, 201

Gulistan, 7

Gulrang Begim, 201

Gulrukh Begim, 163, 182

Gumal River, 63

Gumti River, 188

Gurkan/Gurkani/Timurid, 23, 31

Gwalior, 139, 141, 146, 149, 152, 161–162, 182, 187, 196

Haidar Mirza Dughlat Kurkan, 197

Hamza Sultan, 95

Hanafi Sunni, 8, 14, 28, 130, 165, 185, 193–194, 216

Han China, 25–26

Hasan-i-Rumlu, 98

Hasan Khan Miwati, 146

Hazarahs, 60, 62, 84, 91n11, 123, 212

Hazrat Makhdumi Nura, 178

Herat, 8, 12–13, 25, 27–30, 32, 44–45, 47, 49–50, 59–60, 66–75, 77–90, 98, 102–103, 105–106, 109, 119–120, 132n6, 139, 141–142, 159, 163–164, 166–167, 197, 215–218

Hidayat, 185

Hind-al (son of Babur), 104, 179, 183, 199, 201, 212

Hindu Beg Qauchin, Jalal al-Din, 104, 106

Hindustan critique, 134-39.

Hindustan Gazetteer, 6, 137, 139–140, 143

Hisar, 49, 65, 72, 75, 95–99, 125, 155, 164–165

Hisar Firuzah, 125

Hujwiri, 15

Husain Baiqara Mirza, Sultan, 5, 8, 12–13

Husain Khan Nuhani, 146, 149

Ibn Battuta, 11–12

Ibn Buluggin, 210

Ibn Khaldun, 10, 12, 15, 24, 195, 210

Ibrahim Ludi, Sultan, 3

Iltutmish, 11, 13–14

Indus/Nilab, 3, 63, 101–102, 104–105, 113, 118, 123, 130, 137, 139, 141, 144, 182, 188

Iran, 9–11, 13 , 15, 24–26, 29–32, 46, 60, 76, 79, 90, 106, 138–139, 149, 158, 190, 195, 217–218

Iraq, 10, 24, 60, 140

Isfarah, 166

Isma'il Mita, 189

Istalif, 106–108, 110, 112, 118, 124, 134n41, 140, 148

Jahangir (son of Akbar), 7, 33, 37, 39, 41, 46, 63, 70, 73, 90, 183, 197, 201

Jahangir (son of 'Umar Shaikh), 35, 48–49, 64–66

Jain statues, 162, 194
Jaipur, 31
Jalalabad/Adinapur, 64, 89, 100, 105, 111, 121
Jalal al-Din Sharqi, Sultan, 190
Jam, battle of, 177
Jami, Maulana Nur al-Din 'Abd al-Rahman, 77
Janab, 102, 104
Jaunpur, 146, 149, 177–178, 182, 187–188, 190
Jhelum River, 101–102, 104
Jumna River, 125–126, 148, 162
Junaid Barlas, Sultan, 147–148, 177, 187–188, 190, 197, 203n19

Kabul, 2–3, 5–7, 9, 14, 18, 29–30, 32, 34, 36, 47, 50–51, 67–68, 70, 72–75, 82–90, 95–96, 99–115, 117–122, 125, 130–131, 137, 139–140, 142, 144–146, 148–152, 156–157, 159, 161, 163–166, 171n63, 175–176, 179–188, 193–195, 197, 199, 202, 209, 211–212, 214, 216–217
Timurid State formation in, 59–66
Kafiristan/Nuristan, 94n90, 133n20
Kahraj Kamran (son of Babur), 7, 61, 120, 124, 140, 150, 163–167, 179, 181, 183, 212–214
Kanwah, Battle of, 86, 104, 126, 138, 146, 150–162, 175–176, 182, 186, 193–194, 196, 203n19, 209, 211
Karnan, 49
Kashgar, 24, 27, 29, 33, 111, 140, 199
Kashmir, 210
Khadijah Sultan Begim, 70
Khalji, Ala al-Din, 16–17, 119, 129
Khaljis, 11, 16–17, 21n40, 129
Khan, Ahmad/Alacha, 29, 167
Khan, 'Alam, 120–121, 123–124, 127, 153
Khan, Arayish, 160
Khan, Chaghatai, 1–3, 5, 111, 199

Khan, Chinggis, 20n29, 23–24, 35, 62
Khan, Ghazi, 123–124
Khan, Hamid, 125
Khan, Ishan, 201
Khan, Islam, 119
Khan, Jalal, 190–191
Khan, Langar, 101, 104, 187
Khan, Nizam, 146–147, 149
Khan Zada Begim, 445, 156
Khidar Khan, 118–119
Khirilchi Afghans, 111
Khitai/China, 28, 47
Khujand, 23, 25, 37–38, 41–42, 46, 194
Khuqand, 49
Khurasan, 10, 12, 25, 30, 35, 49–50, 66–67, 72, 76–77, 85, 106, 131, 140, 149
Khushab, 101–102, 104, 187
Khusrau Shah, 43, 49–51, 61, 63, 90
Khwaf, 149
Khwafi, Majd al-Din Muhammad, 77
Khwafi, Shaikh Zain, 129, 149, 209
Khwajah Kalan, 115, 124, 144–145, 148, 156, 166, 170n24, 175–176, 179–181, 183–184, 186, 193, 211
Khwajaka Khwajah, 46
Khwandamir, 3, 109, 132n6, 159
Khwarizm, 24, 60, 106, 131
Kichik 'Ali, 188
Kish, 23–24
Kitabdar, Mulla Abdullah, 167
Koil/Aligarh, 152, 157–158, 160, 182, 188
Köl-i Malik, Battle of, 98
Kurkan, Haidar Mirza Dughlat, 3, 90, 95–99, 111, 132n4, 194, 198–2, 205n56, 209–210, 213–214, 197
Kushana, 26–27, 29, 53n16

Lahore, 9, 15, 102–103, 119–121, 123, 137, 146, 154, 182–183, 196, 201, 203n3, 206n71, 213

Lamghanat, 64, 89, 187
legitimacy, 7–8, 10–11, 13, 23, 35, 37, 41, 50, 59, 101, 167, 211
Lord of the Auspicious Conjunction, 16, 90
Ludi, Daulat Khan, 16, 102–103, 120–121, 123–124, 146
Ludis, 104, 106, 118, 120, 127–128, 138, 146, 155, 185, 212
Luhani/Nuhani Afghans, 53n18, 146–147, 188, 190–191

Mahdi Khwajah, 129, 147–148, 153, 156, 161–162, 187, 196–197, 203n19
Mahim Begim, 120, 195, 198
Mahmud Khan Luhani/Nuhani, 188
Mahmud Mirza, Sultan, 2
Mahmud of Ghazna, 9
ma'jun, 7, 28, 104, 112–113, 116, 121, 123, 125, 157, 159, 162, 168, 189, 191
Makdum Nura, Khwajah, 195
Mamluks of Egypt, 24
Manicheans, 29
Mano, Eiji, ix, x, xii, 3, 18n1, 88n38
Marghinan, 34, 39
Mas'ud Sa'd Salman, 15, 203n3
Ma'sumah Sultan Begim, 69, 109
Mathura, 200
Maulana Qazi, Khwajah, 34, 70, 185, 193
Mauryas, 142, 217
Mawarannahr, 1–2, 12, 15, 24–26, 28–31, 33–42, 47–49, 51, 52n5, 53n16, 53n18–19, 60–61, 66, 79, 86, 90, 95–96, 98–100, 102, 106, 126–127, 130–131, 137, 141–142, 159, 183, 185, 194–195, 215–217
Mecca, 77, 140
Medina, 140
Medini Rao, 159–160
Megasthenes, 142
Merv, 67, 95–96, 132n4
Mewar, 17, 119, 147

Mihrbannu Khanım, 179
Milwat, 123–124
Ming China, 24
Miran Shah, 1
Mir Najm, 98–99
Mirza, Abu Sa'id, 69–70, 197
Mirza, Alwar (son of Babur), 200
Mirza, Baisunghar (son of Sultan Ahmad Mirza), 36
Mirza, Mahmud, 2, 34, 36, 43, 49, 84, 199, 203n19
Mirza, Muhammad Sultan, 127, 129, 153, 188, 203n19, 212
Mirza, Muzaffar (son of Husain Mirza), 67, 69–70, 85
Mirza, Nasir (son of 'Umar Shaikh Mirza), 49, 55n34, 64, 86, 88–89, 99, 183
Mirza, Sultan Ahmad, 2, 23, 27, 32, 36–37, 69, 182, 197
Mirza, Ulugh Beg Kabuli, 2, 14, 25, 31–32, 34, 51, 60, 66–67, 74, 87, 89, 103, 106–107, 197, 215
Mirza, 'Umar Shaikh, 2, 8, 15, 23, 27–28, 30, 32–34, 36, 73, 78, 193, 216
Miwat, 146, 155–156
Mohammadi Pushtuns, 100
Mongol/Mughul/Mughal, 1–3, 5, 7–8, 11, 16, 23–25, 27–31, 33–43, 45–51, 55n43, 61, 64, 66, 68–70, 72, 74, 76, 82–83, 84, 86–89, 96–97, 99, 104, 106, 108, 111, 122–123, 125, 127–128, 130, 138, 141–143, 151, 153–158, 163, 166–168, 170n42, 176–177, 187–188, 191–192, 194, 197, 199, 201, 209–212, 214, 216–217
Mubin (Dar fiqa mubaiyan), 61, 122, 165, 185–186, 193, 209–210
Mughulistan/Xinjiang, 2, 24–25, 27, 29, 33–34, 43, 47, 53n15, 84, 140, 199
Muhammad 'Ali Jang-jang, 128, 159

Muhammad Amin, Khwajah, 112
Muhammad Ghuri
Muhammad Muzaffar, Sultan, 17
Muhammd b. Tughluq, 11–12, 119
Mulla 'Ali Jan, 122
Multan, 12, 103, 118, 179, 182–183
Muqim Arghun, 51, 64, 66–67, 75, 88
Murghab, 67–69, 72, 75, 85, 166
Murshid 'Iraqi, Khwajah, 189
Mustafa 'Ali, 218
Mustafa Rumi, 151, 153
Mystic Feast, 182, 197

Naqshbandi, 14, 28, 34, 37–38, 42, 46,
    73, 77, 79, 98, 140, 159, 163–164,
    166–167, 178–179, 193–195, 197,
    200, 216
Nava'i, Mir 'Ali Shir, 13, 27, 47, 54n28,
    75, 77, 80, 93n60, 114, 215–216
Nestorians, 29
Nijrau, 111, 113
Ningnahar, 89–90
Nizam al-Din 'Ali Khalifah, 128, 148,
    151, 153, 166, 196, 203n19
Nizam al-Din Auliya, 14, 16, 129
Nuhani, Jalil Khan, 191
Nusrat Shah of Bengal, 17, 165, 178,
    189–191, 203n10, 212

Oghuz Turks, 15
Ottomans, 44, 153–154

Pamghan/Paghman, 64, 66
Pamghan Range, 106–107, 110
Panipat, Battle of, 3, 59, 86, 118–119,
    126, 160
Pashagar, 38
Patna, 142
Persian/Farsi, 3, 7–8, 13–17, 24, 28,
    31, 41–42, 52n4, 73, 77–79, 81–82,
    88, 99, 105, 111, 113, 115, 121–122,
    139, 147, 151–152, 160, 163, 209–
    210, 214

Perso-Islamic, 5, 8–10, 13, 28, 30, 69,
    78, 82–83, 124, 145, 184, 186, 214,
    216–218
Peshawar, 60, 63, 110–111, 123
poetry, 47, 59, 70, 76–78, 81–82, 119,
    151, 209, 216
Pulad Sultan, 112-113, 172
Pul-i Sangin, 96
Punjab, 3, 16–17, 24, 26, 30, 62, 102,
    119–121, 123–124, 138, 144, 146,
    175, 182, 211–212
Pushtun/Afghan, 100–101, 110,
    118–119, 212

Qabadian, 49
Qabus-namah, 6
Qalah Zafar, 199
Qanauj, 146–147, 150, 157, 160, 182,
    188, 214
Qandahar, 60, 66, 83–84, 86, 88–90,
    95, 97, 99–100, 109–110, 112, 118,
    120, 124, 127, 130–131, 150, 155,
    164, 182–183
Qaraquyunlu Turks, 219n15
Qarshi, 95
Qasim Beg Qauchin, 83
Qazaq (liq), 23–51
Qipchaq, 43, 49, 65, 116
Qipchaq steppe, 35
Qizilbash, 97–98, 167, 190
Qunduz, 49, 72, 75, 95–97, 99, 119–
    120, 131, 132n1, 132n4, 182
Qutb al-Din, Khwajah, 129
Qutluq Nigar Khanim, 23, 66

Rahim Dad, 187, 196
Rajputs, 45, 89, 97, 104, 152–155,
    159–160, 163
Rampur Diwan, 117, 175–177, 179–
    180
Rana Sanga', 17, 117, 119, 126, 138,
    146–147, 149–157, 159–161, 177,
    211

Ranthambor, 161
Rapri, 146, 152, 157
revenue, 60, 62, 64, 77, 109, 121, 146,
    153, 159, 161, 165, 178, 184–186,
    189, 191, 193, 202, 211
Roux, Jean-Paul, 210
Rumi, Jalal al-Din Muhammad, 28
Russia, 24
Ruzbihan Kunji, 98–99

Sa'adi, 7, 46
Sa'd al-Din Mas'ud Khurasani
    Taftazani, 78
Safavid Iran, 2, 32
Safavids, 96, 118, 120, 132n6, 177
Safid-Kuh Range, 110
Sa'id Khan, 96, 111, 132n4, 199
Saif al-Din Ahmad, 77
Salman, Mas'ud Salman
Salt Range, 101, 124
Samanid, 10, 15
Samarqand, 2, 5–6, 8, 12, 14, 23–25,
    27, 29–34, 36–38, 41–48, 51,
    53n16–17, 53n19, 55n44, 59–61,
    63, 65, 68–70, 73, 76, 80, 87, 90,
    95–102, 107, 116–117, 131, 139–
    140, 155, 162, 164–167, 179, 194–
    195, 197–198, 203n19, 211, 215
Sambhal, 16, 105, 146–147, 152, 158,
    182, 193, 200
Samu Khail Afghans, 111
Sana'i Ghaznavi, 15
Sanjar Barlas, Sultan, 84
Sar-i-pol, battle of, 98
Sawai Jai Sing II, 31
Sayyid Dynasty of Bengal, 103
Sayyid Dynasty of Punjab and Delhi,
    17
Sayyid Nizam al-Din 'Ali Khalifa, 128,
    148, 151, 153
Sayyid Rafi Safavi, 166
Sayyid Rumi, 167, 177, 188
Seleucid, 26, 142

Shah Beg Arghun, 100
Shah Isma'il Safavi, 77, 90, 96–98,
    127, 190, 203n19
Shah-Nama(h), 7–8, 15
Shah Rukh, 25, 29–31, 34, 44, 77, 103,
    119
Shahrukhi coinage, 60, 91n4, 102, 112,
    121, 140, 179
Shah Shuja' (Beg) Arghun, 109, 120
Shah Sultan Begim, 33
Shah Tahmasp Safavi, 158, 163
Shaibani Khan Uzbek, 2, 34–35, 38,
    42–51, 56n62, 67–68, 70, 74, 76, 78,
    80, 85, 88–90, 95–98, 109, 112, 155,
    167, 216
Shaikh Ahmad Sirhindi, 179
Shaikh Guran, 160
129149209Sherim Taghai Kunji
    Mughul, 87
Shi'ah/Shi'i, 10, 73, 78, 91n11, 96–98
Shihab al-Din Ghuri (Mu'izz al-Din),
    Sultan, 9, 11, 131
Shir Khan Suri, 161, 178, 188, 200,
    214
Sialkot, 119, 123, 169n12, 182
Sih-yaran, Khwajah, 106–107, 110,
    134n46
Sikandar Ludi, 190
Sikri, 150–151, 157–159, 162, 196,
    202
Silhadi/Salah al-Din, 160, 162
Silk, 26–27, 71, 88, 109, 166
Silk Road/Seidenstrasse, 26, 29, 32
Sind, 12, 16, 120, 137, 144
Soghdiana, 29, 53n19
Soghdians, 29
suhbat(-lar)/suhbatarayaliq, 166, 176
Sukh, 49, 166
sultan, 5, 9–11, 15–16, 20n18
Sultan 'Ala al-Din Khalji, 119, 129
Sultanim Begim, 106
Syr Darya, 1, 23–25, 52n5

Tabriz, 31, 127
Tagha'i, Ali Dust, 33, 37, 39, 41
Taj al-Din Arghun, 113
Tajikistan, 49–50, 89
Tajiks, 61, 111
Taj Mahal, 32, 201
Tambal, Sultan Ahmad, 35, 37, 39, 41, 43, 46, 48, 51, 80, 185
Tang Atmish Sultan, 166–167
Tardi Beg Khaksar, 112, 125, 156–157
Tardika, 154, 156–157
Tarkhan, Muhammad, 32
Tarkhans, 43
Tashkent, 2, 33–36, 38–39, 41, 45–46, 48, 53n18, 176, 215
Tashkindi, Baqi Beg, 193
Temür/Timur/Tamerlane, 1
Tibyan, 210
Timurid-Mughal, 1, 3, 12–13, 15–16, 23, 25, 46, 120, 163, 184, 191, 214, 217–218
Timurids, 1–2, 8, 12–13, 17, 23, 27, 29, 31, 34–35, 38, 43–44, 48, 50, 67–68, 70, 85–86, 89, 96, 98, 101, 106–107, 119–120, 127, 129, 141, 144, 150–154, 159, 166–167, 179, 182–183, 187, 197, 203n19, 211–215
Transoxiana, 1, 24, 52n5
Tughluq, 11, 17, 103, 129
Tughluq, Ghiyas al-Din, 129
Tughluqabad, 129
Tukhta Bugha Sultan, 158, 167, 188, 191, 201
tulghamah maneuver, 45, 89, 128, 136n89, 153–155
Tuluva Dynasty, 17
Turki, 13–14, 27–28, 34, 37, 42, 47, 61, 69–71, 79–80, 82, 114–117, 121–122, 130, 135n60, 137–138, 144–145, 151–152, 154, 156, 158, 163, 165, 166, 168, 175, 177, 179, 181, 194, 209, 216
Tusi, Nasir al-Din, 31

'Ubaidullah Ahrar, Khwajah, 28, 38, 43–44, 46, 55n44, 98, 163, 166–167, 175, 194
'Ubaidullah Khan, 98
'ulama, 10–11, 14, 139, 166, 187, 201
Usamah ibn Munqidh, 211
Ush/Osh, 14, 34, 48, 107, 129, 188
Ustad 'Ali Quli, 127, 153, 190
Uzbeks, 1, 2, 25, 34–35, 38, 43–44, 46, 49–50, 60, 64, 66, 68, 75, 84–88, 95–99, 111, 118, 155, 163, 166, 177, 179, 182, 199, 215
Uzgend, 33

Vaqayi', 3, 5–9, 28, 36, 39, 47, 54n20, 65, 78, 83, 94n79, 108, 114, 118, 121, 125, 129–130, 137, 142, 150, 156, 160, 162, 165, 171n62, 175, 177, 180–184, 187, 192–194, 196, 198, 200, 202, 211, 213–214, 216
Varanasi, 149, 187

Wais Mirza, 84, 86, 89–90, 95–97, 109, 118–120, 127, 132n1, 203n19
Waziri Afghans, 111

Xian/Chang'an, 29, 52n9
Xinjiang, 2, 24–25, 27, 29, 33–34, 43, 47, 53n15, 140, 199
Xiongnu, 26

Yahya Ahrari, Khwajah, 43, 167, 179
Yahya Nuhani, 191
Yuezhi/Guishang, 25–26
Yunas Khan, 23, 27, 84
Yusufza'i, Malik Shah Mansur, 108
Yusufza'i Pushtuns, 100–101

Zarafshan River, 30, 44, 198
Zhang Qian, 25–27, 52n9
Zoroastrians, 29, 63
Zu'n-nun Arghun, 67, 75, 85